DRUG USE IN METROPOLITAN AMERICA

DRUG USE IN METROPOLITAN AMERICA

ROBERT M. BRAY
MARY ELLEN MARSDEN
Editors

SAGE Publications
International Educational and Professional Publisher
Thousand Oaks   London   New Delhi

For information:

SAGE Publications, Inc.
2455 Teller Road
Thousand Oaks, California 91320
E-mail: order@sagepub.com

SAGE Publications Ltd.
6 Bonhill Street
London EC2A 4PU
United Kingdom

SAGE Publications India Pvt. Ltd.
M-32 Market
Greater Kailash I
New Delhi 110 048 India

Printed in the United States of America

Library of Congress Cataloging-in-Publication Data

Main entry under title:

Drug use in metropolitan America / Robert M. Bray and Mary Ellen Marsden, editors.
    p. cm.
  Includes bibliographical references and index.
  ISBN 0-7619-0374-7 (cloth: acid-free paper)
  ISBN 0-7619-0375-5 (pbk.: acid-free paper
  1. Drug abuse—United States. I. Bray, Robert M.
II. Marsden, Mary Ellen.
  HV5825.D77ff736 1998
  362.29′12′0973—ddc21   98-19675

99 00 01 02 03 04 10 9 8 7 6 5 4 3 2 1

Acquiring Editor:	Peter Labella
Editorial Assistant:	Renée Piernot
Production Editor:	Diana E. Axelsen
Editorial Assistant:	Denise Santoyo
Typesetter/Designer:	Janelle LeMaster
Cover Designer:	Candice Harman

Contents

4. Drug Use and Homelessness   **79**

Michael L. Dennis, Robert M. Bray,
Ronaldo Iachan, and Jutta Thornberry

8. Drug Use and Pregnancy — 235

Wendy A. Visscher, Robert M. Bray, and Larry A. Kroutil

Appendixes related to the studies do not appear in the book but are available on the Sage Publications world Wide Web site at

      http://www.sagepub.com/bray_druguse.htm

They also appear on the Research Triangle Institute World Wide Web site at

      http://www.rti.org/publications/dcmads/appendix.cfm

Appendixes
  A. Drug Use Among the Household Population
  B. Homeless and Transient Population Study
  C. Institutionalized Population Study
  D. Adult and Juvenile Offender Studies
  E. Current Treatment Client Characteristics Study
  F. Drug Use and Pregnancy Study
  G. Combining Household, Homeless, and
      Institutionalized Data
  H. Members of the DC*MADS Advisory Group
  I.   DC*MADS Technical Reports

List of Tables

List of Figures

Acknowledgments

Many individuals, groups, and organizations made valuable contributions to the conceptualization, design, implementation, and conduct of the Washington, DC, Metropolitan Area Drug Study (DC*MADS). The magnitude of these efforts was much greater than that required for other significant research investigations because of the large number of studies in the project and their many complexities and challenges. We are grateful to all who gave of their time and energy to make the project succeed, but page limitations permit us to cite only some of the major contributors to this effort.

DC*MADS was sponsored by the National Institute on Drug Abuse (NIDA), Division of Epidemiology and Prevention Research (DEPR), and funded under Contract No. 271-89-8340. Elizabeth Y. Lambert, M.Sc., served as the NIDA project officer and provided oversight and guidance to all aspects of the work, including the review and technical editing of the final study reports. Zili Sloboda, Sc.D., and Ann Blanken of DEPR offered administrative support, and Lana Harrison, Ph.D., Arthur Hughes, James Colliver, Ph.D., and Lulu Beatty, Ph.D., provided helpful technical reviews and critiques of the final reports (see "Appendix I: DC*MADS Technical Reports," 1998, available on the Sage Publications World Wide Web site at

http://www.sagepub.com/bray_druguse.htm

and on the Research Triangle Institute World Wide Web site at:

http://www.rti.org/publications/dcmads/appendix.cfm

Although NIDA provided funding for the project, the views, opinions, and findings presented in this book are solely those of the authors and should not be construed as official NIDA position or policy.

The research team for DC*MADS included staff from Research Triangle Institute (RTI), as the prime contractor, and Westat, Inc. (the subcontractor). These two firms conducted most of the research; however, expertise and assistance were provided by other outstanding companies in the DC area, including Birch and Davis, Inc.; Johnson, Bassin, and Shaw, Inc.; and Tiger Research, as well as by independent advisors and consultants. Credit also should be given to all those who contributed to the success of the DC*MADS project by developing questionnaires, constructing sampling frames, coordinating data collection activities, tabulating data, completing various data processing tasks, preparing codebooks, and editing and keying manuscripts for the technical reports and this book.

At RTI, Susan L. Bailey, Ph.D., served as assistant project director and study leader; Judith T. Lessler, Ph.D., provided overall guidance on sampling issues and methods for combining data across populations; Jutta Thornberry coordinated questionnaire development to ensure comparability among the studies as well as leading RTI data collection efforts; Mary Anne Ardini and Tabitha Hendershot managed day-to-day data collection activities; and George H. Dunteman, Ph.D., provided analytical consultation for several of the final reports. Data editing and processing were handled by a dedicated staff of editors, coders, and data entry keyers under the direction of R. Jo Saraphis and Karen S. Woodell. Donald R. Akin, Ronaldo Iachan, Ph.D., and Sara C. Wheeless, Ph.D., constructed weights for the study samples. Lisa E. Packer, Gayle S. Bieler, Emelita de Leon-Wong, Ph.D., Donna D. Medeirus, and the late Teresa D. Crotts provided programming and analytical support. Richard S. Straw provided copyediting and proofreading assistance, and Teresa F. Gurley, Brenda K. Porter, Catherine A. Boykin, and Linda B. Fonville typed the reports. Teresa Gurley and Richard Straw, respectively, also did the typing, copyediting, and proofreading of the manuscript for this book. A positive and supportive working environment for the preparation of this book was provided by the Center for Social Research and Policy Analysis, under the direction of J. Valley Rachal; the Health and Social Policy Division, under the direction of George C. Theologus, Ph.D.; the Statistics, Health, and Social Policy Unit under the direction of Richard A. Kulka, Ph.D.; and RTI's corporate management, under the direction of F. Thomas Wooten, Ph.D., and Alvin M. Cruze, Ph.D.

At Westat, Inc., Veronica Nieva, Ph.D., served as associate study leader and provided corporate liaison; Mary McCall, M.S., worked tirelessly to obtain the cooperation and participation of DC hospitals; Paul Brounstein, Ph.D., provided invaluable assistance in developing the study design, making arrangements with local agencies, and assisting in the data analysis for the studies of criminal and juvenile offenders; James Bethel, Ph.D., and David Marker, Ph.D., developed the sample designs and computed the final weights; and Nadine Rubenstein and Tracy Flaherty coordinated questionnaire development, study procedures, and data collection efforts. Programming at Westat was performed by Sandra Baker, Portia DePhillips, and Camille Clifford. Data editing was supervised by Maura Gost, and the manuscripts and reports were edited by Carol Benson and Barbara Brickman.

Others with key roles in the conduct of DC*MADS include Mitchel S. Ratner, Ph.D., of Tiger Research (initially with Birch and Davis, Inc.), who led the Adverse Effects of Drug Abuse Study, and Gail Bassin of Johnson, Bassin, and Shaw, Inc., who made important contributions to the Area Opinion Leaders Study. George C. McFarland was pivotal as a liaison to the community, and without him, gaining community support and cooperation would have been much more difficult. The DC*MADS 17-person Advisory Group (see "Appendix H: Members of the DC*MADS Advisory Group," 1998, available on the World Wide Web) provided substantive input on the research, including its multifaceted conceptual issues and processes of implementation. Several of the studies relied on special advisory groups (see final reports, Appendix I, 1998) or consultants, who were instrumental in sorting through sensitive issues and procedures.

Finally, we are indebted to those who contributed directly to the preparation of this book. Peter Labella, the Sage acquiring editor, has provided encouragement and guidance throughout the preparation of this book to expedite its publication, and Diana E. Axelsen, the Sage production editor, has directed the task of converting manuscript pages into final finished copy. Professional development awards from RTI were made to Dr. Bray to help support the preparation of the overall manuscript and to Dr. Dennis to help support preparation of Chapter 4. Amy A. Vincus helped draft some of the appendix materials available on the Sage Publications World Wide Web site at www.sagepub.com and prepared tables for several chapters. Richard S. Straw ably coordinated preparation of the manuscript, including copyediting and checking the numerous details necessary to produce the book.

We would be remiss if we neglected to thank the many dedicated professionals and staff of the participating institutions (including shelters, food kitchens, clinics, hospitals, jails, and prisons) for providing support and assistance in reaching the study participants and persons in local, state, and federal government agencies. Most of all, we owe a debt of gratitude to the men, women, and children who participated in the project and were willing to share personal and sensitive information about their lives—without them, this book, and the knowledge and insights it attempts to impart, would not have been possible.

—Robert M. Bray
Research Triangle Institute

—Mary Ellen Marsden
Brandeis University

1 Impact of Drug Use in Metropolitan America

Robert M. Bray
Mary Ellen Marsden
Amy A. Vincus

Drug abuse is exacting an enormous toll on our nation's large cities. The cities are crime ridden, and a substantial amount of the crime is drug related. Laws are violated in the course of manufacturing and selling drugs, and crimes are committed to obtain money to buy drugs. Many residents have fled the inner cities because of the presence of drugs and crime and the lack of employment opportunities. Drug abuse also exacts a huge burden on our health care system in terms of emergency room visits for drug overdoses and medical care for the health care needs of drug abusers. Treatment for drug abusers is costly, and social service agencies are burdened by the multiple problems of drug abusers and their families.

Although the negative effects of drug abuse are harming our major cities, the effects are perhaps more pronounced and certainly more visible in the nation's capital. During the late 1980s, it was apparent that

1

Washington, DC, had one of the most serious drug problems in America. Business and civic leaders began to organize to combat the problem, and a major research effort began to examine the extent of drug abuse and the adequacy of drug abuse treatment and prevention programs to address the problem. A wide variety of indicators, including drug-related homicides, emergency room visits, medical examiners' reports, urinalysis tests of arrestees, and surveys of the local population, demonstrated the severity of the problem. Many key indicators increased dramatically. Drug-related deaths other than homicides, for example, increased by 140%, and arrests for drug violations increased by 70% during the early to mid-1980s (Reuter, Haaga, Murphy, & Praskac, 1988). Indeed, Washington, DC, led the nation in homicides related to drug trafficking (Johnson & Robinson, 1992). Partly because of the magnitude and visibility of the impact of drug abuse in the nation's capital, Washington, DC, was selected as the site for a comprehensive study of drug abuse that would serve as a prototype for related studies in other large metropolitan areas and, by implication, for metropolitan America.

This book describes the findings and implications of a large integrated study, the Washington, DC, Metropolitan Area Drug Study, or DC*MADS, which was designed to examine the magnitude of drug abuse and its effects in an urban area. DC*MADS collected information about the use of alcohol and other drugs and associated negative consequences from all segments of the population in the DC metropolitan statistical area (MSA) to provide a more complete picture of the impact of drug abuse in that area. Interviews were conducted with members of the household population, as well as with homeless and transient persons, institutionalized residents, adult and juvenile offenders, drug treatment clients, and new mothers. Individuals from all segments of an area's total population contribute to the problem of drug abuse in metropolitan America, and an assessment of the magnitude of drug abuse and its effects must examine these household and nonhousehold populations who together compose the total population of a metropolitan area.

Even though the study was conducted in the DC MSA, the situations observed there are typical of those occurring in many cities and surrounding areas across the country. Indeed, as shown in later chapters of this book, drug use in the DC MSA is no greater than in other large metropolitan areas, according to a variety of indicators, and many of the findings reported here are expected to be generalizable to other metropolitan areas.

This chapter sets the stage for examining the methods and findings of DC*MADS in the remaining chapters of this book. It briefly discusses the effects of drug abuse on the nation, trends in use of alcohol and other drugs, and issues surrounding drug use in metropolitan areas. In addition, it introduces the DC*MADS project and provides an overview of the remainder of this book.

1.1 Effects of Drug Abuse

Drug abuse affects all segments of the population, and its effects cannot be understood without examining its impact on the nation's economy, crime rates, health care system, and treatment system. Assessing the magnitude of these effects and the prevalence and distribution of drug use across subgroups of the population in a geographic area is a necessary step in informing resource allocation. Recent estimates conclude that drug abuse costs our nation more than $67 billion per year and alcohol abuse an additional $99 billion per year in terms of expenditures associated with crime, illness and premature death, and the treatment of drug abusers (Institute for Health Policy, 1993). The costs of drug abuse are largely crime related, whereas those of alcohol abuse are driven by productivity loss associated with illness and premature death. The effects of drug and alcohol abuse pose a particularly serious threat to the future of some segments of America, including infants and youth. Indeed, as discussed later in this book, drug and alcohol abuse often is implicated in becoming homeless or institutionalized.

The effects of drug and alcohol abuse can be viewed in terms of its impact on crime, health and health care utilization, youth development and family relationships, the workplace, and other aspects of life. Drug and alcohol abuse affects all segments of the population.

1.1.1 Drug Abuse and Crime

The association between drug abuse and crime is multifaceted. Illicit drug users commit crimes under the influence of drugs or to support their habits; many crimes also are committed in the course of manufacturing, selling, and distributing drugs. In the mid-1990s, more than 1.5 million arrests were made each year for drug offenses, including sales, manufacturing, and possession (Federal Bureau of Investigation [FBI], 1996). Similarly, more than 3.5 million arrests were made for alcohol-related offenses, such as driving under the influence, liquor law violations, drunkenness, and disorderly conduct. Moreover, as many as 83% of those arrested for illicit drug offenses were using illicit drugs around the time of their arrest (National Institute of Justice [NIJ], 1996a). Three fourths of prison inmates reported, in 1991, some illicit drug use in their lifetimes; well over one third had used illicit drugs in the month before their offense, and more than one fourth admitted to being under the influence at the time they committed their offense (Snell, 1993). In addition, America's cities are disproportionately burdened by crime; arrest rates are substantially higher in cities than in suburbs and rural areas (FBI, 1996).

Drug use and violent crime also are linked: Approximately one out of four persons arrested for committing serious violent crimes reported using drugs during the commission of the crime, and more than half of arrestees were found to have used drugs recently (Zawitz, 1992). As discussed in Chapter 6, however, the relationship between drug use and criminal and juvenile offending is complex. Drugs play a significant role in the commission of many offenses, and many offenders have lengthy histories of drug and alcohol use.

1.1.2 Drug Abuse and Health

As the number one health problem in the nation, drug abuse places a major burden on the nation's health care system and contributes to the high cost of health care (Institute for Health Policy, 1993, p. 8). Indeed, about 20,000 deaths each year are directly attributable to use of illicit drugs (Anderson, Kochanek, & Murphy, 1997), and many more deaths are indirectly related. Drug abuse also may contribute to deaths but not be the direct cause, as in the case of motor vehicle crashes. Alcohol abuse accounts for more than 100,000 fatalities each year through direct and indirect causes (Stinson & Nephew, 1996). These deaths result in loss of productivity to the nation as well as immeasurable losses to families and associates.

Major urban hospitals face growing problems in treating newborns of drug-using mothers, victims of drug-related violence, and a large indigent population (Zawitz, 1992). Substance abuse also adds to the burden on health care because of resultant illnesses (some chronic and fatal), injuries (requiring urgent care), or the provision of treatment services (Institute for Health Policy, 1993, p. 38). For example, heavy drinkers spend four times as many days in the hospital as do nondrinkers, and untreated alcoholics incur at least 100% higher health care costs than do nonalcoholics (Holder, 1987). Drug-exposed infants, who are as much as twice as likely to be low birthweight and born prematurely, require greater care than do healthy babies (Chasnoff, 1991). These social and economic costs of drug use and alcohol abuse are borne disproportionately by the nation's larger cities. Abusers of alcohol and drugs are found in the client populations of many health and social service agencies, including not only alcohol and drug treatment agencies but also mental health, criminal justice, and welfare agencies (Weisner & Schmidt, 1993). This suggests that substance abusers place a large burden on health and social service agencies and, furthermore, that these agencies may provide a means for identifying problem users and referring them to treatment.

1.1.3 Drug Abuse and Youth

Many youth experiment with illicit drugs and alcohol, and some develop significant problems with substance use during adolescence. Despite a long-term decline, the rate of past month illicit drug use among youth has increased since the early 1990s. According to the National Household Survey on Drug Abuse (NHSDA), about 9% of youth used illicit drugs in the past month in 1996, up from 5.8% in 1991 (Substance Abuse and Mental Health Services Administration [SAMHSA], 1997a). Moreover, significant increases in past month marijuana/hashish use, cocaine use, and hallucinogen use occurred among youth. Results from the Monitoring the Future study (University of Michigan, 1997) parallel the trends for youth found by the NHSDA and note a steady increase in any illicit drug use since 1991. The proportion of 8th graders using any illicit drug in the 12 months preceding the survey more than doubled between 1991 and 1996 (from 11% to 24%). Similarly, the proportion of 10th graders using drugs nearly doubled during this period. In 1996, more than one third (38%) reported using an illicit drug in the 12 months prior to the survey. Additionally, from 1992 to 1996, the proportion of 12th graders who used illicit drugs in the previous 12 months rose by half and was approximately 40% in 1996.

These increases may stem from a variety of reasons, including perceptions that illicit drug use is less risky in the 1990s than was believed in the 1980s and attitudes and norms indicating greater acceptance of illicit drug use by youth (e.g., Bachman, Wadsworth, O'Malley, Johnston, & Schulenberg, 1997; Harrison & Pottieger, 1996; O'Callaghan, Chant, Callan, & Baglioni, 1997).

Despite increases in illicit drug use among youth, rates of alcohol use among this group have remained fairly stable over the past few years. In 1996, about one in six 8th graders, one in four 10th graders, and nearly one in three 12th graders had been heavy alcohol drinkers, which was defined as having five or more drinks in a row during the 2 weeks preceding the survey (University of Michigan, 1997).

The age of first use of illicit drugs and alcohol appears to be decreasing, and early use of illicit drugs is implicated in problems with drugs and alcohol in young adulthood (Christie et al., 1988). Drug and alcohol use during adolescence also is associated with delays in the developmental functions of young adults (Newcomb & Bentler, 1988). The use of drugs and alcohol during adolescence can lead to later problems.

In addition to the effects of drug and alcohol use on youth, family relationships are negatively affected. Illicit drug use and problem drinking among spouses have been identified as a cause of marital problems and dissolutions, emotional problems of children in those families, and child abuse and neglect (Institute for Health Policy, 1993).

1.1.4 Drug Abuse and the Workplace

Drug and alcohol abuse also brings problems to the workplace. The majority of drug users are workers. About 73% of all current illicit drug users aged 18 or older in 1996 (8.1 million adults) were employed, including 6.2 million full-time workers and 1.9 million part-time workers (SAMHSA, 1997a). Some 15% of illicit drug users and 6% of heavy alcohol users went to work a little high or drunk in the past year (Institute for Health Policy, 1993). These workers exhibit higher employee turnover, higher absenteeism, and lower productivity, and perhaps safety problems for those in the workplace.

Data from both surveys and work site drug testing suggest that some illicit drug use occurs in the workplace and that marijuana/hashish and alcohol are the substances used most commonly. Survey data indicate that substance use at work ranges from a modest to a moderate amount, although much of it may reflect use at a single event, such as an office party. Findings from work site drug testing suggest that the large majority of workers (96% or more) do not use illicit drugs on the job or at times when their use might affect their performance (Normand, Lempert, & O'Brien, 1994). Work site drug use nevertheless is of considerable concern, especially in safety-sensitive occupations (e.g., pilots, truckers, bus drivers, railway engineers). Regular and continual monitoring is required to deter use and to intervene with offenders.

Drug and alcohol abuse thus is bringing about major social and economic problems for the nation and for the nation's cities. Drug and alcohol abuse is widespread, affecting all segments of the population and all aspects of life. This is shown in its negative effects on crime, health, the workforce, and youth. There are many unanswered questions about these issues that point to the need for additional data.

1.2 Drug Use in Metropolitan America

According to the NHSDA, illicit drug use has been declining in the general population since 1979 but continues to affect a considerable proportion of Americans. In 1996, approximately 74 million Americans had ever used illicit drugs, 23 million had used them in the past year, and 13 million had used drugs in the past month (SAMHSA, 1997a). The percentage of the population aged 12 or older using illicit drugs in the past month, however, had decreased from 14% in 1979 to 6% in 1996. Despite this overall decrease, the number of new users of marijuana/ hashish, cocaine, and heroin was increasing. In 1995, there were an estimated 2.4 million new users of marijuana/hashish, 141,000 new users of heroin, and 652,000 new cocaine users (SAMHSA, 1997a).

Although illicit drug use has shown a long-term decline in the household population, it may be stable or on the rise among hard-core users. Gfroerer and Brodsky (1993) showed that the number of weekly users of cocaine did not change significantly from 1985 to 1991, despite a notable downward trend in infrequent cocaine use. More recent data confirm this same pattern through at least 1996 (SAMHSA, 1997a). Furthermore, Gfroerer and Brodsky's (1993) comparisons of frequent cocaine users with nonusers and infrequent users showed that frequent users were more likely to be unmarried, high school dropouts, on welfare, and living in large metropolitan areas. Frequent cocaine users also were more likely than infrequent users to use alcohol and other drugs and to report dependence on cocaine. Approximately 40% of frequent cocaine users reported engaging in some type of property or violent crime in the past year, and frequent cocaine users were more likely than infrequent users to have criminal histories.

Overall, alcohol use also has declined in the U.S. household population, from 63% of the population reporting past month use in 1979 to 51% in 1996. Heavy alcohol use, however—defined in the NHSDA series of surveys as consuming five or more drinks per occasion on at least 5 or more days in the past month—has been more stable, at about 5% to 6% from 1988 to 1996 (SAMHSA, 1997a). Although alcohol is a legal drug and moderate use may have some health benefits, it is one of the most abused drugs and contributes greatly to the social and economic costs of substance abuse to the nation.

Drug and alcohol use is not evenly distributed across the nation or even within cities and towns. Drug use tends to be concentrated in metropolitan areas. In 1991, for example, 7.0% of household residents in large metropolitan areas and 6.2% of residents in small metropolitan areas had used illicit drugs in the past month compared with 5.2% of residents in nonmetropolitan areas (SAMHSA, 1997a). Even though the differences in these percentages are not large, the underlying population counts differ substantially because of varying population bases for the respective areas. These percentages translate to 6.1 million residents in large metropolitan areas who had used illicit drugs in the past month, 4.2 million in small metropolitan areas, and 2.5 million in nonmetropolitan areas. The difference between large metropolitan areas and nonmetropolitan areas was statistically significant. In 1996, past month illicit drug use also was higher in metropolitan than in nonmetropolitan areas: 6.8% in large metropolitan areas, 6.7% in small metropolitan areas, and 3.7% in nonmetropolitan areas.

Within six large metropolitan areas oversampled in 1991 as part of the NHSDA, illicit drug use was generally higher in low socioeconomic areas than in other socioeconomic areas, although the differences were not always statistically significant. For example, in the DC MSA, 6.3% of residents of low socioeconomic areas compared with 5.4% of residents of other socioeconomic areas had used drugs in the past month (SAMHSA, 1993).

1.2.1 Developing Estimates of Drug Use in a Metropolitan Area

Much of what is known about drug use in metropolitan America is based on surveys of drug use in the household population of the nation, the states, or selected metropolitan areas. The NHSDA series of surveys provides much of the data for the nation and for selected metropolitan areas that were oversampled from 1990 to 1993 (e.g., SAMHSA, 1993). Recent statewide telephone surveys have been conducted as part of the Substance Abuse Needs Assessment studies sponsored by the Center for Substance Abuse Treatment (e.g., Bray et al., 1997; Kroutil et al., 1997).

The Community Epidemiology Work Group (CEWG) also tracks drug use trends in 20 major cities across the United States by collecting data from a variety of sources, including treatment programs. These data include drug-related deaths reported by medical examiners' offices, drug-related emergency room episodes, arrests, and arrestee urinalysis results (CEWG, 1996). The Drug Abuse Warning Network (DAWN) provides information about drug-related hospital emergency room episodes and medical examiners' reports in 21 metropolitan areas (SAMHSA, 1997b), and the Drug Use Forecasting (DUF) system provides information on the results of urinalysis testing of arrestees in 23 cities and will soon be expanded to 75 cities as part of the Arrestee Drug Abuse Monitoring (ADAM) system (NIJ, 1996b). In addition, SAMHSA has conducted special analyses of data for 26 states and 25 metropolitan areas from the NHSDA and local area data on drug-related arrests, alcohol-related death rates, and block group characteristics for 1991 to 1993 (SAMHSA, 1996). Selected results from those analyses are presented in Chapter 3 of this book.

Although the NHSDA is the main source for much of our information about the extent of illicit drug use and its distribution across the nation, it has some recognized limitations. Some NHSDA estimates have been criticized because the survey series has excluded or been limited in its ability to cover adequately populations who are potentially at high risk for abusing alcohol or using illicit drugs (U.S. General Accounting Office, 1993; U.S. Senate, 1990). The NHSDA covers residents of household, noninstitutional group quarters (e.g., shelters, rooming houses, dormitories), and civilians who are aged 12 or older and living on military bases; however, it excludes homeless people who never use shelters, active military personnel, treatment clients, and residents of institutional group quarters, such as jails and hospitals.

These nonhousehold populations are small and constitute only about 2% of the total civilian population, but without them household data are likely to underestimate rates of drug and alcohol use for the overall civilian population. In addition, as is shown in later chapters in this book, these nonhousehold populations have relatively high rates of substance use and correspondingly higher needs for services than does the household population. A critical issue in determining the prevalence and trends in drug usage rates among the general population, therefore, is to investigate the prevalence among hard-to-reach segments of the population. Indeed, more complete information about the magnitude of the drug abuse problem among all segments of society in metropolitan areas is needed to design programs to combat drug abuse in our inner cities.

1.2.2 Needed Studies

The prevalence of drug use and the range and complexity of associated problems from its use require both regular and periodic studies to inform policy and to help guide treatment and prevention efforts. Such studies must span the entire population spectrum. As indicated above, household surveys that examine the prevalence of drug use in the general civilian population have the potential of excluding those segments of the population who are difficult to reach and who may include many hard-core users. Thus, estimates of drug use based on household survey data alone may underestimate the extent of drug use in the total population and may not capture large enough numbers of addicts or heavy users to accurately reflect the current nature of drug use.

Examining drug and alcohol abuse among populations generally excluded from household surveys, populations who may have higher rates of drug and alcohol abuse than does the general population, is a first step toward reliable estimation of drug use in the total population. About 2% of the American population currently resides in institutions or is homeless. Surveying people who are inmates, probationers, and parolees is important in the light of their steadily increasing numbers and the correspondence between drug use and crime. This segment of the population has experienced a 5% to 8% annual increase for more than 20 years (Gerstein & Harwood, 1990). Similarly, persons in other types of institutions (e.g., psychiatric, long-term care) also generally are not included in household surveys, and their drug and alcohol use may be greater than that of the household population.

Ballpark estimates of the number of homeless people in need of drug treatment have been made, based solely on the approximate number of homeless people and a median use rate from underrepresented populations. This formulaic approach may provide an approximation of the number of homeless persons in need of drug treatment but falls short of understanding the type and range of problems faced by homeless people. To assess drug use prevalence, drug-related problems, co-occurring problems, and required services, studies are needed that investigate these issues directly among homeless people. Fortunately, as discussed in Chapter 4, a number of studies are under way that begin to address many of these issues.

As the proportion of women in the drug-abusing population grows, identifying substance use patterns among pregnant women also becomes increasingly significant. Pregnant women receive special attention because of the harm that substance use can cause to the fetus. It is difficult, however, to estimate the magnitude of substance use by women during pregnancy and its resulting effects on infants. Such estimation requires representative samples of pregnant women, valid instruments and data collection methods, and study designs that can rule out potential confounding factors related to pregnancy outcomes, such as poor nutrition or the mother's lack of prenatal care.

A 1992 National Pregnancy and Health Survey found that 5.5% of women reported using at least one illicit drug during pregnancy (National Institute on Drug Abuse, 1996). Although useful, these data may not reflect the extent of the problem in metropolitan areas where substance use is more common and in which the need to combat the consequences of substance use during pregnancy may have high priority for public health officials. Pregnant women should be studied further both because the prevalence data are valuable in making policy decisions and because the health of newborns is in jeopardy.

Estimates of the extent of drug and alcohol use among all segments of the population based on studies of those subpopulations will provide more detailed information about the prevalence of use, characteristics of users, and the number of persons who use and are potentially in need of substance abuse treatment or other social services. This more detailed information is needed to design more effective policy and to allocate resources among resulting programs.

Improved data also are needed for local areas to design effective, targeted policies and programs. Much of the information about drug and alcohol use is available only at the national level or for demographic subgroups in the population. More detailed data are needed for metropolitan areas and cities to inform policy and program development.

1.3 The DC*MADS Project

DC*MADS was designed with two broad purposes in mind: (a) to estimate the prevalence, correlates, and consequences of drug abuse among all types of people residing in one metropolitan area of the country during one time period; and (b) to develop a methodology for similar research in other metropolitan areas around the country. DC*MADS focused on hard-to-reach populations such as homeless persons, adult and juvenile offenders, treatment clients, and new mothers. DC*MADS provides a replicable methodological approach for developing estimates of the prevalence of drug abuse among all population subgroups, regardless of their residential setting, in a metropolitan area.

In the DC*MADS set of studies discussed in this book, analyses focus on the capability of household surveys to provide meaningful information on the prevalence, correlates, and impacts of drug use in the total population. Comparing the prevalence of use and numbers of users in the household population with that in selected subpopulations and a total aggregate population suggests whether policy and program development realistically can be based on household survey data alone. Sound policy and program development rest on valid and reliable information about the extent of the problem in a geographic area. Information from household survey data alone may be incomplete and give a distorted view of drug abuse in that area.

In the DC*MADS set of studies, subpopulations were selected for study who either were not included in household populations and therefore were less frequently studied (homeless people, adult and juvenile offenders, and other institutionalized persons) or who posed a significant risk for youth development (new mothers). Treatment clients provided a view of drug use in a hard-core drug-abusing population, enabling observation of the effects of long-term drug abuse, as well as newly emerging drugs of abuse.

All these groups are important from a policy standpoint. They are populations who have high rates of drug and alcohol abuse and are high users of treatment and other social services. They contribute significantly to the problem of drug abuse in metropolitan America. However, more detailed information is needed about the magnitude of their contribution, the role of drug and alcohol abuse in their lives, and the burden they place on the service delivery system.

1.4 Overview of This Book

This book presents the methodology and findings of a comprehensive study of the impact of drug and alcohol abuse in metropolitan America, focusing on the DC MSA. The methodology for DC*MADS is discussed in Chapter 2, including the populations studied, demographic characteristics, questionnaire development and key measures, sampling procedures and data collection methods, and analytic approaches. Chapter 3 presents findings on the household population from the DC oversample included in the 1991 NHSDA. Drug and alcohol use in the DC MSA are discussed, as well as comparisons with other large metropolitan areas. Chapter 3 also offers comparative estimates of drug use prevalence across all the populations studied in DC*MADS.

Studies of DC*MADS subpopulations are discussed in Chapters 4 to 8. The study of drug and alcohol use in the homeless and transient population is described in Chapter 4. The discussion examines changing definitions of homelessness, the relationship between substance use and homelessness, substance use prevalence, co-occurring problems, and service utilization of this population. Drug use among institutionalized populations is presented in Chapter 5, including drug use in different types of institutions and use before and during institutionalization. Drug use among adult and juvenile offender populations is described in Chapter 6, with a focus on the relationships between drug use and offending patterns. Patterns of drug use among a high-use population of drug abuse treatment clients are investigated in Chapter 7. These data provide information about newly emerging drug trends as well as service needs of this population. Substance use among new mothers is examined in Chapter 8, focusing on the prevalence of substance use during pregnancy and the relationships of substance use during pregnancy to low birthweight and complications.

Chapter 9 develops composite estimates of drug use, drawing on household data from the DC oversample of the NHSDA and from surveys of homeless and transient persons and institutionalized persons conducted as part of DC*MADS. Estimates of the prevalence of drug use in the aggregate population in the DC MSA are developed based on a method of aggregating data from the three sources. Finally, Chapter 10 summarizes key findings from the DC*MADS project, describes emerging themes of the book, and discusses implications for policy and research.

Together, the populations and issues that are examined among household and nonhousehold populations in the DC MSA offer key insights into the nature of the multifaceted drug problem confronting metropolitan areas. The studies described in the following chapters document drug use prevalence and related problems, address policy issues, identify needed services, and discuss implications for prevention and interventions for drug-using populations. In addition, the studies suggest a wide range of issues and questions needing further research.

References

Anderson, R. N., Kochanek, K. D., & Murphy, S. L. (1997). Report of final mortality statistics, 1995. *Monthly Vital Statistics Report, 45*(11, Suppl. 2), 1-80.

Bachman, J. G., Wadsworth, K. N., O'Malley, P. M., Johnston, L. D., & Schulenberg, J. E. (1997). *Smoking, drinking, and drug use in young adulthood: The impacts of new freedoms and new responsibilities*. Mahwah, NJ: Erlbaum.

Bray, R. M., Camlin, C. S., Kroutil, L. A., Rounds-Bryant, J. L., Bonito, A. J., & Apao, W. (1997). *Use of alcohol and illicit drugs and need for treatment among the Vermont household population: 1995* (prepared for Vermont Office of Alcohol and Drug Abuse Programs under Contract No. CSAT 270-94-0022). Rockville, MD: Center for Substance Abuse Treatment.

Chasnoff, I. J. (1991). Drugs, alcohol, pregnancy, and the neonate: Pay now or pay later. *Journal of the American Medical Association, 266,* 1567-1568.

Christie, K. A., Burke, J. D., Regier, D. A., Rae, D. S., Boyd, J. H., & Locke, B. Z. (1988). Epidemiologic evidence for early onset of mental disorders and higher risk of drug abuse in young adults. *American Journal of Psychiatry, 145,* 971-975.

Community Epidemiology Work Group. (1996). *Epidemiologic trends in drug abuse: Proceedings* (Vol. 2, NIH Publication No. 96-4127). Rockville, MD: National Institute on Drug Abuse.

Federal Bureau of Investigation. (1996). *Crime in the United States: Uniform crime reports.* Washington, DC: U.S. Department of Justice.

Gerstein, D. R., & Harwood, H. J. (Eds.). (1990). *Treating drug problems: A study of the evolution, effectiveness, and financing of public and private drug treatment systems* (Vol. 1, prepared by Institute of Medicine, Division of Health Care Services, Committee for the Substance Abuse Coverage Study). Washington, DC: National Academy Press.

Gfroerer, J. C., & Brodsky, M. D. (1993). Frequent cocaine users and their use of treatment. *American Journal of Public Health, 83,* 1149-1154.

Harrison, L. D., & Pottieger, A. E. (1996). The epidemiology of drug use among American youth. In C. B. McCoy, L. R. Metsch, & J. A. Inciardi (Eds.), *Intervening with drug-involved youth* (pp. 3-22). Thousand Oaks, CA: Sage.

Holder, H. D. (1987). Alcoholism treatment and potential health care cost saving. *Medical Care, 25,* 52-71.

Institute for Health Policy. (1993, October). *Substance abuse: The nation's number one health problem: Key indicators for policy* (prepared for the Robert Wood Johnson Foundation). Waltham, MA: Brandeis University, Heller Graduate School.

Johnson, C. M., & Robinson, M. T. (1992, April). *Homicide report: Government of the District of Columbia.* Washington, DC: Office of Criminal Justice Plans and Analysis, Statistical Analysis Center.

Kroutil, L. A., Ducharme, L. J., Bonito, A. J., Vincus, A. A., Bray, R. M., Akin, D. R., & Walker, J. A. (1997). *Substance use and need for treatment: Findings from the 1996 South Dakota Household Telephone Survey* (prepared for South Dakota Department of Human Services, Division of Alcohol and Drug Abuse, under Contract No. CSAT 270-95-0028). Rockville, MD: Center for Substance Abuse Treatment.

National Institute of Justice. (1996a). *1995 Drug Use Forecasting: Annual report on adult and juvenile arrestees.* Washington, DC: Author.

National Institute of Justice. (1996b). *1996 Drug Use Forecasting: Annual report on adult and juvenile arrestees.* Washington, DC: Author.

National Institute on Drug Abuse. (1996). *National Pregnancy & Health Survey: Drug use among women delivering livebirths: 1992* (NIH Publication No. 96-3819). Rockville, MD: Author.

Newcomb, M. D., & Bentler, P. M. (1988). *Consequences of adolescent drug use: Impact on the lives of young adults.* Newbury Park, CA: Sage.

Normand, J., Lempert, R. O., & O'Brien, C. P. (Eds.). (1994). *Under the influence? Drugs and the American work force* (prepared by National Research Council/Institute of Medicine, Commission on Behavioral and Social Sciences and Education, Committee on Drug Use in the Workplace). Washington, DC: National Academy Press.

O'Callaghan, F. V., Chant, D. C., Callan, V. J., & Baglioni, A. (1997). Models of alcohol use by young adults: An examination of various attitude-behavior theories. *Journal of Studies on Alcohol, 58,* 502-507.

Reuter, P., Haaga, J. G., Murphy, P. J., & Praskac, A. (1988). *Drug use and drug programs in the Washington metropolitan area: An assessment* (R-3655-GWRC). Santa Monica, CA: Rand Corporation.

Snell, T. (Ed.). (1993). *Correctional populations in the United States, 1991* (NCJ-142729). Washington, DC: U.S. Department of Justice, Office of Justice Programs, Bureau of Justice Statistics.

Stinson, E. S., & Nephew, T. M. (1996). *State trends in alcohol-related mortality, 1979-92: U.S. epidemiological data reference manual* (Vol. 5). Bethesda, MD: National Institutes of Health, National Institute on Alcohol Abuse and Alcoholism.

Substance Abuse and Mental Health Services Administration. (1993). *National Household Survey on Drug Abuse: Main findings 1991* (DHHS Publication No. SMA 93-1980). Rockville, MD: Author.

Substance Abuse and Mental Health Services Administration. (1996, September). *Substance abuse in states and metropolitan areas: Model based estimates from the 1991-1993 National Household Surveys on Drug Abuse: Summary report* (DHHS Publication No. SMA 96-3095). Rockville, MD: Author.

Substance Abuse and Mental Health Services Administration. (1997a). *Preliminary results from the 1996 National Household Survey on Drug Abuse* (DHHS Publication No. SMA 97-3149). Rockville, MD: Author.

Substance Abuse and Mental Health Services Administration. (1997b). *Year-end preliminary estimates from the 1996 Drug Abuse Warning Network* (DHHS Publication No. SMA 98-3175). Rockville, MD: Author.

University of Michigan. (1997, December 18). *Drug use among American teens shows some signs of leveling after a long rise* [Press release]. Ann Arbor: University of Michigan News and Information Services.

U.S. General Accounting Office. (1993). *Drug use measurement: Strengths, limitations, and recommendations for improvement* (prepared for Chairman, Committee on Government Operations, U.S. House of Representatives, GAO/PEMD-93-18). Washington, DC: Author.

U.S. Senate. (1990). *Hard-core cocaine addicts: Measuring and fighting the epidemic* (S. Rep. No. 6, 101st Cong., May 10, Comm. on Judiciary). Washington, DC: Government Printing Office.

Weisner, C., & Schmidt, L. (1993). Alcohol and drug problems among diverse health and social service populations. *American Journal of Public Health, 83,* 824-829.

Zawitz, M. W. (Ed.). (1992). *Drugs, crime, and the justice system: A national report* (NCJ 133652). Washington, DC: U.S. Department of Justice, Office of Justice Programs, Bureau of Justice Statistics.

2

The Washington, DC, Metropolitan Area Drug Study (DC*MADS)

Robert M. Bray

The overriding objectives of the Washington, DC, Metropolitan Area Drug Study (DC*MADS) were (a) to estimate the prevalence, correlates, and consequences of drug abuse among the diverse populations residing in the metropolitan area; and (b) to develop a research model for similar data collection about drug abuse in other major metropolitan areas. To achieve these objectives, a multiyear (1989 to 1995) comprehensive research effort was designed to piece together the many sources of information about drug abuse from a wide range of individuals. This project is the first to focus on all types of people in one metropolitan area—from teenagers to working adults to homeless persons—in order to assess the full extent of the drug abuse problem. A major contribution is the inclusion of populations who have received less research attention, such as homeless people, institutionalized individuals, and juvenile offenders, along with populations who have been studied in more depth and detail, such as persons living in households.

The intent of DC*MADS was (a) to understand the nature and extent of drug use among these various populations individually and collectively; (b) to assess the rates, context, and patterns of use overall and among demographic subgroups of these populations; (c) to examine consequences, correlates, and co-occurring problems related to drug and alcohol use; and (d) to consider the implications of the key findings for policymakers, service providers, and researchers who might undertake similar studies in the future. The project offers insights on these various issues both within and among the subpopulations composing the metropolitan area. In addition, it represents one of the first efforts—and clearly the most comprehensive to date—to combine data across subpopulations—in our case, household, homeless, and institutionalized—to form a composite group that closely approximates the total population for the metropolitan area.

This chapter provides an overview of the DC*MADS project as a whole, followed by a brief description of the individual studies included in this book. It also presents the demographic characteristics of the survey populations for the various studies, discusses the development and content of the questionnaires used in the studies, and offers definitions of key substance use measures that are common across studies. This discussion is followed by an overview of the sampling and data collection methodology and related methodological challenges that were faced in conducting the studies. The chapter next discusses the analytical approach for the studies, including weighted analysis issues and procedures for addressing statistical precision. The chapter concludes with observations about the strengths and limitations of the project. Selected aspects of each study's methods are covered in more detail in appendices prepared along with the studies.[1]

2.1 Overview of DC*MADS and the Issue of Generalizability

DC*MADS was an exploratory attempt to examine drug abuse among all types of people residing in a single metropolitan area during the same period of time, with special focus on populations who were underrepresented or unrepresented in household surveys. Many of these subpopulations represent people who tend to be at substantial risk for drug abuse and its consequences.

DC*MADS consisted of 11 separate, but coordinated, studies that focused on different population subgroups (e.g., homeless people, institutionalized individuals) or different aspects of the drug abuse problem (e.g., adverse consequences of drug abuse) in the Washington, DC, metropolitan statistical area (DC MSA). The studies were the following:

1. Household and Nonhousehold Populations Study,
2. Homeless and Transient Population Study,
3. Institutionalized Study,
4. Adult Criminal Offenders Study,
5. Juvenile Offenders Study,
6. School Dropouts Study,
7. Current Treatment Client Characteristics Study,
8. Area Opinion Leaders Study,
9. Drug Abusing Subgroups Study,
10. Adverse Effects of Drug Abuse Study, and
11. Drug Use and Pregnancy Study.

Data for the household population were drawn from the 1990 National Household Survey on Drug Abuse (NHSDA) and the 1991 NHSDA, both of which oversampled the DC MSA and were analyzed as part of DC*MADS. Analyses and estimation of composite rates focused on the 1991 NHSDA. Data for all other studies were collected as part of DC*MADS.

Initial plans for DC*MADS included additional studies: Young Adults Study, Elementary and Secondary School Pupils Study, Drug Abuser Characteristics Study, Illicit Drug Industry Study, Costs of Drug Abuse Study, and Neighborhood Study. These studies were only partially completed (data were collected but not analyzed for the Young Adults Study) or eventually were discontinued or combined with the 11 completed studies noted above for several reasons. These reasons consisted of resistance from some community leaders and inability to gain their support, the time and potential danger to interviewers required to establish needed rapport with the population (e.g., drug dealers), and

Figure 2.1. District of Columbia Metropolitan Statistical Area (DC MSA)
SOURCE: Washington, DC, Metropolitan Area Drug Study (DC*MADS): 1989-1995.
NOTE: The District of Columbia metropolitan statistical area (DC MSA) includes the District of Columbia; the Maryland counties of Calvert, Charles, Frederick, Montgomery, and Prince Georges; the Virginia counties of Arlington, Fairfax, Loudoun, Prince William, and Stafford; and the Virginia cities of Alexandria, Fairfax, Falls Church, Manassas, and Manassas Park.

lack of sufficient funds to carry out all the studies, largely because of lengthy negotiations (described below) to obtain cooperation and access to the populations.

This book examines 7 of the final 11 studies, each of which focuses on a different subpopulation within the metropolitan area. These seven studies are briefly described in the next section.

DC*MADS took place in the DC MSA (shown in Figure 2.1), which consists of the District of Columbia, five counties in Maryland, and five counties and five cities in Virginia. As shown, the metropolitan area encompasses a reasonably large geographic area and in 1991 had a population of approximately 3.2 million persons aged 12 or older.

Although the study was conducted in the DC MSA, it could just as well have been carried out in any other major metropolitan area across the country and, we believe, with largely similar results. The fact that the study was conducted in a particular large metropolitan area may raise questions about the extent to which its findings are unique to that area or can be generalized to other large metropolitan areas. The question of generalizability is a common one faced by all studies to one degree or another, either because the research design and strategies did not maximize generality or because of biases or other design or procedural limitations (e.g., see Runkel & McGrath, 1972).

For DC*MADS, a very strict and conservative interpretation of generalizability (i.e., a purist viewpoint) would argue that the findings cannot be generalized beyond the DC MSA because its people were the target population for the study and because the findings must be interpreted within the context of the uniqueness and influence of local conditions that are not found elsewhere. A less conservative and more practical perspective, however, would argue that at least some and perhaps many of the findings can be generalized beyond the DC MSA to other metropolitan areas. This latter perspective posits that the purist view is overly narrow and limiting and does not take advantage of the richness of the data or their implications for other areas.

The difference in these viewpoints centers on whether one emphasizes commonalities that exist across metropolitan areas or unique features of particular metropolitan areas. For DC*MADS, it seems plausible that many findings (though clearly not all) can be generalized beyond the DC MSA to other metropolitan areas for several reasons. First, there is evidence, as described in Chapter 3, indicating that substance use rates among the household population in the DC MSA are highly similar to the rates found in other major metropolitan areas throughout the country. Second, there is corroborating information from other studies about the DC*MADS special populations that generally agrees with findings presented here. For example, as discussed in Chapter 4, studies of the homeless and transient population confirm that these people experience a wide range of problems that include relatively high rates of drug use and a variety of other physical, mental, financial, and legal difficulties (e.g., Greene, Ennett, & Ringwalt, 1997; Johnson & Barrett, 1991; Koegel, Burnam, & Farr, 1990; Robertson, Zlotnick, & Westerfelt, 1997; Rossi, 1989). Finally, each of the studies in the DC*MADS project used rigorous and coordinated methodologies (e.g., probabilistic sampling, sensitive interviewing techniques, common core questions across studies) that were designed to minimize bias and increase accuracy of responses.

Even though overall substance use rates in the DC MSA may be comparable to those of other metropolitan areas, rates for specific sub-populations in the DC MSA are likely to vary somewhat from those of other metropolitan areas. Even if that is the case, however, the overall type and range of problems that are observed among the various DC MSA subpopulations are expected to be typical of those in other metropolitan areas.

2.2 Population Studies in This Book

In this book, we focus on seven of the DC*MADS studies, those associated with specific subpopulations: household people, homeless and transient persons, institutionalized individuals, adult offenders, juvenile offenders, treatment clients, and new mothers (i.e., the pregnancy study). The following chapters examine substance use prevalence, correlates, and problems in detail for each population separately and then contrast these findings with those from a composite population formed by combining data from the household, homeless and transient, and institutionalized populations. For convenience and because of their similarity in focus, we discuss the adult and juvenile offender studies together in one chapter.

The sample sizes for each of the studies are shown in Table 2.1 and are arrayed by selected demographic characteristics. For convenience, these sample sizes are presented here in detail as a reference point but are not reported in detail in later substantive chapters. As shown, there was considerable variation in the final sample sizes for the studies. The household population study, drawn from the NHSDA, had the largest sample (n = 2,547), followed by the institutionalized population (n = 1,203), the homeless and transient population (n = 908), and the new mothers population (n = 766). Other than the separate modality populations within the drug treatment client populations, the populations with the smallest sample sizes were the juvenile (n = 198) and adult (n = 158) offenders.

Table 2.1 Unweighted Numbers of Respondents for Each DC*MADS Population, by Demographic Characteristics

Demographic Characteristic	Household	Homeless and Transient	Institutionalized	Adult Offenders	Juvenile Offenders	Long-Term Residential Treatment	Short-Term Residential Treatment	Methadone Treatment	New Mothers[1]
Sex									
Male	1,145	606	1,024	143	194	129	91	115	0
Female	1,402	302	179	15	4	50	44	78	766
Age group (years)									
12-17	651	13	91	2	153	0	0	0	45
18-25	626	146	309	71	45	52	22	8	345
26-34	665	319	408	59	0	87	52	55	285
≥35	605	429	394	26	0	40	61	130	88
Race/ethnicity									
White	1,347	193	212	31	19	47	60	34	53
Black	877	632	861	113	159	114	70	153	655
Hispanic	187	54	60	6	17	15	4	5	45
Other	136	21	64	8	3	3	1	1	13
Marital status									
Single	1,476	502	827	119	188	115	49	101	570
Married	753	88	118	16	1	25	44	30	163
Widowed/divorced/separated	318	297	248	23	0	39	42	62	30

(continued)

Table 2.1 Continued

Demographic Characteristic	Household	Homeless and Transient	Institutionalized	Adult Offenders	Juvenile Offenders	Long-Term Residential Treatment	Short-Term Residential Treatment	Methadone Treatment	New Mothers[1]
Location									
DC	600	556	Not Included[2]	Not Included[2]	Not Included[2]	28	10	165	766
Maryland	1,035	143				70	74	12	0
Virginia	912	209				81	51	16	0
Adult education[3]									
Less than high school	277	361	681	103	43	66	42	79	230
High school graduate	565	352	245	34	2	78	43	66	300
Some college	463	134	144	17	0	30	37	35	101
College graduate or higher	591	38	41	2	0	5	13	13	88
Total	2,547	908	1,203	158	198	179	135	193	766

SOURCE: Washington, DC, Metropolitan Area Drug Study (DC*MADS): 1989-1995.
NOTE: Data entries are unweighted numbers of respondents. Ns within some demographic categories do not sum to the total because of missing data.
1. The new mothers population refers to women in the Drug Use and Pregnancy Study.
2. Location was not included in the questionnaire to protect the respondents' confidentiality.
3. For the homeless and transient and the juvenile offenders populations, persons aged 12 to 17 were excluded from the estimates of adult education.

There was also considerable variation across studies with regard to the mix of demographic characteristics. For example, there was roughly an even number of males and females in the household sample, but considerably more males in the studies of the other populations (excepting the new mothers population, of course). Similarly, racial/ethnic composition showed that the largest number of respondents in the household population was white, whereas for all the other populations, the largest number of respondents was black.

2.2.1 Household Populations Study

The 1991 NHSDA was the 11th in a series of surveys that began in 1971 and whose primary purposes have been to measure the prevalence and correlates of drug use in the United States and to monitor drug use trends over time. The National Commission on Marihuana and Drug Abuse sponsored the first two studies, conducted in 1971 and 1972. From 1974 through 1991, the National Institute on Drug Abuse (NIDA) sponsored the NHSDA. As of October 1, 1992, responsibility for conducting the survey was transferred to the newly created Substance Abuse and Mental Health Services Administration (SAMHSA). A detailed description of the 1991 survey, including information on sampling, data collection, and prevalence estimates and correlates for the nation, is found in the *National Household Survey on Drug Abuse: Main Findings 1991* report (SAMHSA, 1993). In 1990, the NHSDA included a representative oversample of people living in the DC MSA. For the 1991, 1992, and 1993 NHSDAs, this effort was expanded to include oversampling of six MSAs: Chicago, Denver, Los Angeles, Miami, New York, and the District of Columbia. These oversamples were designed to support separate estimates of drug use prevalence for each of these MSAs.

Chapter 3 presents findings about drug use, consequences, and related problems for the household population based on data from the 1991 NHSDA oversample for the DC MSA. Data for the household population were collected as part of the NHSDA, but analyses for DC MSA household members were conducted as part of DC*MADS. In addition to examining data about household members, Chapter 3 also provides a brief overview and capsule summary of key differences among the rates of substance use for all the populations examined in this book.

Appendix A (1998) provides additional information about house-hold sampling and data collection methods for the DC MSA. Further data on the household population are described in two DC*MADS technical reports (NIDA, 1992, 1994b).

2.2.2 Homeless and Transient Population Study

The Homeless and Transient Population Study examined the nature and extent of drug use among people living in nonconventional dwell-ings (e.g., vacant buildings, cars, parks, streets, and emergency shelters) or at risk of becoming homeless in the DC MSA, as indicated by their use of soup kitchens and food banks for homeless people. It also examined the reasons that people move in and out of homelessness, the roles of drug use and crime-related activities, and the problems of mental health, primary care, and economics in this movement. An important strength of the DC*MADS Homeless and Transient Population Study over many other studies of this population was that it sampled homeless persons from four locations (streets, shelters, soup kitchens, and encampments) and across two seasons (winter and spring) using probability methods.

Chapter 4 in this volume summarizes and discusses key findings about drug use and other issues relevant to the homeless and transient population, including physical and mental health problems, illegal ac-tivity, unemployment, and eligibility for entitlements. Appendix B (1998) provides technical information about the sampling and data collection methods. Further substantive and methodological details are provided in the study's final technical report (NIDA, 1993a).

2.2.3 Institutionalized Study

The Institutionalized Study assessed the nature and extent of drug use among people living in correctional institutions, psychiatric institu-tions, group homes, and other selected institutions in the DC MSA in 1991. It is one of the first investigations to examine substance use among residents of a broad range of institutions. It also examined the individual consequences, correlates, and co-occurring problems related to drug use among people in institutions and the social consequences of drug use associated with criminal offending by institutionalized people.

Chapter 5 presents findings about drug use among people in institutions, including patterns of drug use prior to institutionalization, and
findings on other issues relevant to people in institutions, such as physical and mental health problems, arrests and illegal activity, and unemployment. Appendix C (1998) describes the sampling and data collection
methods used in the study. The final technical report provides additional
detailed information about the Institutionalized Study (NIDA, 1994c).

2.2.4 Adult and Juvenile Offender Studies

Two separate studies were conducted of selected offender populations, one for adults and the other for juveniles. The survey of adult
offenders was limited to persons who had been indicted of a felony and
convicted of a crime. This study focused on adults who were sentenced
to incarceration, as well as those sentenced to probation. Results reported
in this book deal only with incarcerated offenders, however, because
probationers had a relatively low response rate—they were difficult to
locate and, when located, often were reluctant to participate in an interview.

The survey of juvenile offenders was limited to juveniles residing
in state-run institutions who had been convicted of a crime. Such facilities are variously referred to as training schools, learning centers, and
correctional centers and are analogous to prisons for adult offenders.
Initially, the study was targeted to include a broader range of offenders
by sampling juveniles at an earlier point in the criminal justice process
(e.g., at time of arrest or at time of conviction); however, statutory
protections associated with juvenile case records precluded this approach. Thus, this study focused on juveniles considered to be the most
serious delinquents.

The focus of the discussion of offender populations addressed in
Chapter 6 is on drug involvement among convicted adult and juvenile
populations. Both surveys examine drug use and offending patterns and
consider the role that drugs play in the commission of predatory and
drug-trafficking offenses. This includes such issues as the levels of drug
use among those who commit crimes, the extent to which predatory and
nonpredatory crime is related to drug use, the relationship of predatory
crime and drug trafficking, and the extent of drug selling among offend-

ers. Appendix D (1998) describes the sampling and data collection methods used in the two studies. The final technical report provides additional detailed information about the Adult and Juvenile Offender Studies (NIDA, 1995b).

2.2.5 Current Treatment Client Characteristics Study

Clients entering drug treatment programs provide important information about the types and range of drug use and associated problems of a known abuser population, and information from them complements information from the other populations examined in this book. Members of the group selected for study were newly admitted to drug treatment programs in the DC MSA during the spring and summer of 1991. Although some treatment clients are classified as institutionalized, persons in treatment programs were not included in the Institutionalized Study to avoid duplication across populations.

Chapter 7 examines the types of drugs being used, patterns and inclinations of use, frequency of use, and general experiences of drug treatment clients with drug usage, including needle use and the context of drug use. It also addresses the consequences and co-occurring problems of drug use and discusses treatment histories, mental health problems, physical illness and primary care history, illegal activities and arrests, and specific problems attributable to the past year use of alcohol or illicit drugs. An important contribution of this study relative to other studies of treatment populations is its use of a probability design to select a statistically representative sample of treatment clients within a defined geographic area. A related advantage is having comparable data for the household population and other important subgroups. Appendix E (1998) describes the sampling and data collection methods used in the study. The DC*MADS final technical report provides additional detailed information about the Current Treatment Client Characteristics Study (NIDA, 1994a).

2.2.6 Drug Use and Pregnancy Study

One of the special population studies in DC*MADS examined drug use among a hospital-based population of new mothers in DC who had just delivered liveborn infants. This particular population was of concern in helping to address some unanswered questions about the extent of drug use during pregnancy and its consequences for both mothers and their babies, including risks of adverse birth outcomes. Using probability sampling methods, we were able to obtain data from all nine nonmilitary hospitals providing obstetric services in DC; eight agreed to participate in the interviewing and abstraction components of the study, and all nine agreed to participate in the urine collection component of the study.

Chapter 8 presents findings about the prevalence of use of illicit drugs, alcohol, and tobacco among the new mother population; relates findings on substance use to infant birthweight with a specific focus on low birthweight; and describes the epidemiological characteristics and health outcomes among drug-using and drug-free mothers and infants. In addition, it addresses several methodological issues surrounding pregnancy-based investigations. Strengths of this study were that the sample included respondents from multiple hospitals and obtained data using a variety of methods, including interviews, record abstractions, and anonymous urine testing from a separate sample of women. Appendix F (1998) describes the sampling and data collection methods used in the study. The final technical report provides additional detailed information about the Drug Use and Pregnancy Study (NIDA, 1995a).

2.2.7 Comparing Findings Across Populations

A key contribution of DC*MADS was to explore empirically the contribution of nonhousehold populations to estimates that approximate the total population. Conceptually, the household, the homeless and transient, and the institutionalized populations collectively define the total population of the MSA. Together, these populations encompass the full range of individuals' possible living situations, and all persons can be characterized as belonging to one of them. This is true for persons within a given MSA, such as was studied here, or at a broader level across several MSAs or across the nation. In that sense, the studies of the household, homeless and transient, and institutionalized populations serve as the foundation pieces of DC*MADS.

Despite their central role, these foundation studies were not able to address numerous issues of concern among other specific subpopulations even though the foundation studies technically included them. This was the case either because large enough numbers of people for these subgroups were not represented in the foundation studies or because additional special issues were too lengthy to ask about along with the main questionnaires. Thus, additional studies within the DC*MADS project were undertaken to provide key information about substance use prevalence and related problems among some of these selected subpopulations, four of which are mentioned above and are addressed in this volume (adult offenders, juvenile offenders, drug treatment clients, and new mothers).

Chapter 9 describes the assumptions, logic, and approach to combining data from the household, homeless and transient, and institutionalized populations into a composite population. It then compares and contrasts data from the household population with those from the composite population to assess the relative importance and contribution of the nonhousehold populations in assessing prevalence estimates of substance use and population counts of the number of illicit drug users. An important contribution of this study is its comprehensive approach to developing a statistical methodology for merging data across populations. The chapter also examines the methodological and practical implications of the findings for future research and for policy issues concerned with planning and addressing substance abusers' treatment needs. Appendix G (1998) describes the methods used to combine data files and adjust the sampling weights for the new composite data set. The final technical report provides additional detailed information about the Household and Nonhousehold Populations Study (NIDA, 1994b).

2.3 Demographic Characteristics

The overview of the DC*MADS population studies presented in Section 2.2 synopsizes the general thrust of these investigations, and the information in Table 2.1 shows the population sample sizes and distribution by demographic factors. To provide a broader perspective for the studies, it is useful to extrapolate beyond the samples and to examine and compare the demographic composition of the study populations. Table 2.2 presents these population estimates and shows notable variation in the demographic characteristics across study populations. The sex distribution shows a striking difference between the household

Table 2.2 Demographic Characteristics of DC*MADS Populations

Demographic Characteristic	Household	Homeless and Transient	Institutionalized	Adult Offenders	Juvenile Offenders	Long-Term Residential Treatment	Short-Term Residential Treatment	Methadone Treatment	New Mothers[1]
Sex									
Male	47.7	75.9	90.7	90.8	97.4	71.9	66.4	63.0	0.0
Female	52.3	24.1	9.3	9.2	2.6	28.1	33.6	37.0	100.0
Age group (years)									
12-17[2]	9.2	15.0[3]	6.9	1.2	77.7	0.0	0.0	0.0	4.0
18-25	14.3	36.8	29.4	45.9	22.3	32.1	17.2	4.7	49.9
26-34	22.9	48.2	36.2	35.9	0.0	47.3	37.1	29.4	35.2
≥35	53.6		27.5	16.9	0.0	20.6	45.7	65.9	10.9
Race/ethnicity									
White	61.9	16.5	20.9	20.1	8.7	35.7	*	20.8	7.3
Black	27.2	75.8	69.3	70.8	79.4	55.8	*	75.4	83.9
Hispanic	5.2	5.9	5.2	4.1	9.8	5.9	2.7	3.1	7.5
Other	5.8	1.8	4.6	5.0	2.1	*	*	*	1.3
Marital status									
Single	33.5	59.7	69.1	75.3	99.6	64.0	37.4	50.3	73.7
Married	50.1	8.3	11.2	10.4	0.4	12.5	33.0	16.5	22.8
Widowed/divorced/ separated	16.3	32.1	19.7	14.3	0.0	23.5	29.6	33.2	3.5

(continued)

Table 2.2 Continued

Demographic Characteristic	Household	Homeless and Transient	Institutionalized	Adult Offenders	Juvenile Offenders	Long-Term Residential Treatment	Short-Term Residential Treatment	Methadone Treatment	New Mothers[1]
Location									
DC	17.5	71.0	Not included[4]	Not included[4]	Not included[4]	12.5	*	82.4	100.0
Maryland	43.1	14.0				47.3	*	5.1	0.0
Virginia	39.4	15.0				40.2	*	12.5	0.0
Adult education[5]									
Less than high school	12.9	40.1	64.8	64.3	94.6	36.6	31.1	41.8	27.7
High school graduate	27.2	39.3	21.7	23.4	5.4	45.8	31.1	34.1	45.2
Some college	22.1	15.2	11.1	11.1	0.0	16.1	28.8	17.6	14.5
College graduate or higher	37.8	5.4	2.4	1.2	0.0	1.5	9.0	6.5	12.6

SOURCE: Washington, DC, Metropolitan Area Drug Study (DC*MADS): 1989-1995.

NOTE: Data entries are percentages weighted to reflect population estimates.

1. The new mothers population refers to women in the Drug Use and Pregnancy Study.
2. For the homeless and transient population, persons aged 12 to 17 were combined with those aged 18 to 25.
3. These respondents ranged in age from 12 to 25.
4. The location was not included in the questionnaire to protect respondents' confidentiality.
5. For the homeless and transient and the juvenile offenders populations, persons aged 12 to 17 were excluded from the estimates of adult education.
*Low precision.

population and the other populations. Whereas the household population was split rather evenly between males and females (48% vs. 52%), the other study populations were predominantly male (at least 60%) except, of course, new mothers.

The age distribution across populations also shows some notable differences among the age categories. The data indicate that more than half of the household population was aged 35 or older. The household and homeless populations were similar in having the largest proportions of their people in the 35 or older category (54% and 48%, respectively) but differed in that the homeless population had a greater proportion of 26- to 34-year-olds than was true in households (37% vs. 23%). Overall, the household and homeless populations were the oldest. The largest age category for the institutionalized population was found in the 26-to-34 age group; for the adult offenders, it was in the 18-to-25 group. The age of the treatment clients varied widely by treatment modality, which reflects, in part, differences in drug use history and experiences. Long-term residential clients were the youngest and methadone clients were the oldest.

Race/ethnicity also shows clear variation among populations. Whereas in the household population, the largest proportion (more than 60%) of respondents were white, in each of the other populations the largest proportion was black. No more than 10% of the study populations were composed of persons of Hispanic or "other" race/ethnicity. Similarly, the household population had the highest percentage of married respondents (about half). In contrast, most of the other populations were composed largely of single people, with the exception of short-term residential treatment clients, who were fairly evenly split among single, married, and widowed/divorced/separated people.

The location of the populations within the DC MSA (Washington, DC, Maryland, and Virginia) showed some variation, but this was not as uniform as for other characteristics. The largest segments of the household population and the long-term residential treatment population were located in Maryland and Virginia. In contrast, the homeless population and methadone clients were more likely to be found in the District of Columbia. The new mothers population was entirely from DC because the final study design included only DC hospitals.

A review of adult education (thus excluding juvenile offenders) shows that from one fourth to about two thirds or more of each of the study populations except the household had no more than a high school diploma. In contrast, only about one third of the household population had no more than a high school education. The highest percentage of college graduates occurred in the household population (38%).

To summarize, comparisons of the demographic characteristics of the DC*MADS populations indicate some notable patterns. Most populations contrasted with the household population, and they tended to be aged 26 or older, black, male, and single, and to have no more than a high school education. The household population was more likely to be 35 or older and white, equally likely to be female or male, and likely to have some college experience. Of course, a number of subgroups did not fit into this nonhousehold pattern (e.g., juveniles, new mothers), but it nevertheless captured the majority of the nonhousehold populations. Comparisons across populations need to take account of their demographic differences to be sure that conclusions are not incorrectly attributed to be population differences when they may simply reflect differences in demographics that place some populations at higher risk for substance abuse.

2.4 Questionnaire Development and Key Substance Use Measures

Having reliable and valid data collection instruments is fundamental to any successful survey because the resulting questionnaire items provide the measures or the building blocks for constructing measures of interest. This section provides an overview of the questionnaire development process and the types of information gathered in the final instruments. It also describes and defines the key substance use measures common to the studies.

2.4.1 Questionnaire Development

Development of the questionnaires for the DC*MADS population surveys was guided by two broad goals: (a) to develop valid survey instruments that would assess substance use and related constructs pertinent to each specific study population, and (b) to develop instruments with a common set of items that would permit and facilitate cross-study comparisons. To this end, a coordinated effort was used across the studies in the DC*MADS project in designing the survey instruments. Questionnaires were constructed using a modular approach in that modules of core items and study-specific items were included. Generally, core modules included questions about drug use, demographics, drug treatment, physical health, legal issues, and employment and finances. Because data collection for the DC MSA household population was conducted as part of the NHSDA, the NHSDA questionnaire served as the foundation for all the DC*MADS survey questionnaires to ensure comparability with the household data.

Study-specific questions focused on additional issues outside the core items that were relevant to a particular population. In some cases, these questions included items that were specific only to one study (e.g., the Homeless and Transient Population Study included a module on history of homelessness; the Drug Use and Pregnancy Study included a module on pregnancy history). In other cases, study-specific items consisted of expanding a core module because of the topic's greater relevance to the population (e.g., the adult offender survey included an expanded module on legal issues that asked about non–drug-related crimes, drug-related crimes, and victimization).

Table 2.3 provides an array of the questionnaire modules that briefly summarizes the common and unique areas included in each of the survey questionnaires. More specifically, the following types of information were included in the respective questionnaire sections noted in the table:

- *Demographic characteristics*, including age, gender, race/ethnicity, marital status, education and training, employment status, and military experience
- *Specific drug use*, including questions about age of initiation, recency of use, and regularity of use for any illicit drug, marijuana/hashish, any cocaine, crack cocaine, inhalants, hallucinogens, heroin, nonmedical use of any psychotherapeutics, any illicit drug except marijuana, any alcohol, heavy alcohol, and cigarettes
- *General drug use* questions about the drugs used in the past 12 months, intravenous drug use, perceived risk of drug use, and symptoms of dependence

Table 2.3 Comparison of Questionnaire Sections for DC*MADS Populations

Questionnaire Section	Household	Homeless and Transient	Institutionalized	Adult Offenders	Juvenile Offenders	Treatment Clients	New Mothers[1]
Demographics	X	X	X	X	X	X	X
Specific Drug Use	X	X	X	X	X	X	X
General Drug Use	X	X	X	X	X	X	X
Drug Treatment Issues	X	X	X	X	X	X[2]	X
Employment and Finances	X	X	X[4]	X[4]	X[4]	X	X[3]
Legal Issues	X	X	X	X	X	X	
Physical Health	X	X	X	X	X	X	
Psychological Status		X	X	X	X	X	X
Life Events History			X	X	X		
Drug Use and Life Events History				X	X		
Norms, Family, and Community				X	X		
Institutionalization			X				
History of Homelessness		X					
Population Movement		X				X	
Pregnancy History							X

SOURCE: Washington, DC, Metropolitan Area Drug Study (DC*MADS): 1989-1995.

NOTE: X = section was included in this study's questionnaire.

1. The new mothers population refers to women in the Drug Use and Pregnancy Study.
2. This study had an expanded section on drug treatment issues.
3. This section was reduced in comparison with employment sections in other questionnaires.
4. The legal issues section was greatly expanded, including offense reporting and drug-related crime coverage.

- *Drug treatment* issues about the number of treatment episodes, age at first treatment, drugs treated for, kind of treatment, reasons for missing treatment appointments, and duration of last treatment episode
- *Employment and finances,* including recency of paid work, kind of work, number of jobs, how often and how much worked, income sources, and expenditures
- *Legal issues,* including questions about the nature of criminal activity and number of resulting arrests
- *Physical health,* including disease prevalence (such as hepatitis or tuberculosis), systemic problems, medication use, pregnancy history (as it relates to cigarette, alcohol, and other drug use), insurance coverage, hospitalizations, emergency room visits, and other sources of medical care
- *Psychological status,* including problems, related hospital admissions, outpatient psychological treatment, and prescribed medicine
- *Life events history* comparing periods of employment, arrests, institutional supervision, treatment and counseling history, and other life events
- *Drug use and life events history* allowing for drug use to be compared with life events
- *Norms, family, and community,* such as items about family time, community activities, judgments, opinions of violence, friends' activities, gang involvement, and opinion of neighborhood
- *Institutionalization,* including information about living arrangements, disciplinary action, acquiring drugs, and services offered at the institution
- *History of homelessness,* including age when first homeless, length of last period of homelessness, and living arrangement before homelessness
- *Population movement,* including type of living arrangement and length at each place
- *Pregnancy history,* including prenatal care; birth control use; medical problems; medications during pregnancy; weight; number of pregnancies; number of miscarriages, stillbirths, and abortions; and a history of livebirths.

As noted in Table 2.3, items on demographics, specific drug use, general drug use, drug treatment issues, and employment and finances were included in all study population surveys. Some type of questions, such as those dealing with institutionalization or pregnancy history, were specific to certain populations. A copy of the instrument for each population is included in that study's final technical report. (DC*MADS technical reports are listed in Appendix I [1998].)

Questionnaires for each study were pretested in their respective populations to ensure that items were clear and readily understood by respondents and that field procedures were functional. They were then circulated to advisory panels (see Appendix H [1998] for a list of the DC*MADS advisory panel) and others with substantive expertise or with expertise in dealing with the respective study populations for comments and recommendations. After the instruments were finalized in English, they were translated into Spanish and given to Spanish-speaking staff to review and critique. Spanish versions of the question-naires were prepared for all seven of the population studies described in this book. Although an effort was made to accommodate persons whose primary language was Spanish, relatively few interviews actually were conducted in Spanish (e.g., 12 for the Homeless and Transient Population Study, 5 for the Institutionalized Population Study, 35 for the Drug Use and Pregnancy Study).

2.4.2 Key Substance Use Measures

Although it is not practical to provide definitions of all variables here, we describe key substance use measures because these variables are fundamental to all the studies discussed in subsequent chapters. The illicit drug use and alcohol use variables are comparable to those used in the 1991 NHSDA (SAMHSA, 1993). Measures of substance use include reports for cigarettes, alcohol, marijuana (including hashish), cocaine (including crack), inhalants, hallucinogens (including phencyclidine [PCP]), heroin, and nonmedical use of each of the prescription-type psychotherapeutic drugs (stimulants, sedatives, tranquilizers, and anal-gesics). Separate estimates were obtained for crack and stimulants. To examine the extent of involvement in illicit drug use, two summary measures were constructed: "any illicit drug use" and "any illicit drug use except marijuana."

The prevalence of use of illicit drugs, alcohol, and tobacco was examined for three time periods: past month, past year, and lifetime. *Past month* use was defined as use of a substance one or more times in the month before the interview and was also referred to as "current use." *Past year* use was defined as use of a substance one or more times in the year before the interview. *Lifetime* use was defined as use of a substance at least once in the individual's lifetime. Analyses presented in this book focus on past year and past month use.

Data on heavy alcohol use in the past month also were collected. Heavy alcohol use was defined as having five or more drinks per occasion on 5 or more days in the past month (i.e., drank heavily at a rate of at least 5 days/30 days). For the Homeless and Transient Population Study, the definition was adjusted to accommodate the period of homelessness if it was less than 30 days. In these situations, a comparable criterion was used based on the number of days of heavy drinking while homeless divided by the number of days homeless. For example, if a person drank heavily (five or more drinks per occasion) on 3 days during a 15-day episode of homelessness, heavy drinking was evaluated on the basis of 3 days/15 days.

2.5 Overview of Sampling and Data Collection Methods

Acquiring permission to conduct the studies in the DC*MADS project and carrying out the studies was both challenging and stimulating. In this section, we provide an overview of our methods and the challenges that we faced in conducting the research.

2.5.1 Sample Design

An important strength of the studies examined in this book is that they used sophisticated sampling methods to define a sampling frame or subpopulation of interest and then to randomly select individuals to be surveyed within specified strata. This sampling approach allows the probability of individuals being selected into the sample to be calculated and permits weights to be computed and attached to the data such that the sample members appropriately represent the population of interest. In most studies, sampling involved at least a two-stage design in which locations (e.g., shelters, census blocks, soup kitchens, treatment facilities, hospitals, prisons, group homes) were randomly selected at the first stage and individuals were randomly selected within locations at the second stage. Some studies stratified locations or institutions at the first stage (e.g., the Institutionalized Study divided institutions into correctional, psychiatric, group homes, and other types), and some studies stratified individuals at the second stage (e.g., the Drug Use and Pregnancy Study sampled new mothers based on infant risk status defined as low birthweight or preterm delivery).

2.5.2 Data Collection

Data collection for the DC*MADS surveys consisted of in-person anonymous interviews in which trained interviewers asked questions of respondents and recorded their answers in a questionnaire booklet. This mode of administration was deemed the most practical to address problems of respondent literacy even though it was recognized that a self-report mode may encourage somewhat greater reporting of sensitive behaviors. For the Drug Use and Pregnancy Study, a mixed mode administration was used in which the interviewer asked questions not considered to be sensitive (e.g., demographics, prenatal care, medical conditions), but respondents answered questions on self-administered answer sheets about sensitive issues concerning their use of illicit drugs, alcohol, and tobacco. This procedure was followed to encourage honest reporting and to ensure confidentiality because many hospital patients had a roommate or other visitors present.

Some individuals who participated in this research were expected to have trouble understanding or completing the interview because of either chronic or acute mental and emotional difficulties or extreme intoxication. When interviewers encountered such persons, they were instructed to administer the short mental status examination known as the Short Blessed Scale Exam (Katzman et al., 1983). If the respondent did not pass the examination, the interview was terminated and the case was classified as ineligible.

Questionnaires for the various studies were designed to last anywhere from 30 minutes to an hour and a half but varied considerably even within studies because of the extent of a particular respondent's drug use history and problems. For example, the median interview length was 35 minutes for the new mothers population and 40 minutes for the homeless and transient population but was 1 hour and 25 minutes for the institutionalized population and the criminal offenders. Respondents either were given $10 at the end of the interviews to compensate them for their time and effort or, in the case of the new mothers population, were given a gift (either a layette or a towel set) with a monetary value of approximately $10. Gifts also were given to the institutions that assisted with the study, where appropriate. For example, shelter and soup kitchen providers were offered packages of toothbrushes, diapers, or coffee and creamer to compensate them for allowing the on-site interviews to be conducted; hospitals were given VCRs or an equivalent alternative of their choosing.

Together, the studies presented situations and problems much different from those encountered in a general household population survey. Interviewers had to exercise good judgment and sensitivity toward respondents and feel comfortable in an unusual data collection environment (e.g., soup kitchen, prison, hospital, drug treatment facility). The ideal interviewers were those who had experience with both survey interviewing and their study population. Because persons with both qualifications often were difficult to find, priority was given to individuals who had experience working with similar populations or on studies that involved sensitive topics on the grounds that their expertise with the population would facilitate entrée, rapport, trust, and credibility in the interviewer-respondent relationship.

Prior to the start of interviewing for each study, data collectors attended a training session on implementation of the sampling and data collection procedures, conduct of the questionnaire, and interviewer-interviewee interactions. These training sessions ranged in length from 3 to 8 days. Lectures, group instructions, and practice sessions were used along with a training manual. Topics and issues addressed during training included (a) overall purpose and goal of the study; (b) procedures used to select facilities (e.g., institutions, shelters) and locations (e.g., census blocks); (c) data collection procedures to be followed, including respondent sampling; (d) techniques of interviewing, including soliciting cooperation, asking questions, recording responses, probing, and maintaining neutrality; (e) techniques for engaging respondents, including issues of sensitivity, security, confidentiality, anonymity, and approaching and interviewing cognitively impaired individuals; (f) question-by-question review of all instruments, including mock role-playing exercises for paired trainees; and (g) administrative procedures, including editing completed instruments, reviewing materials and supplies, supervising others (or being supervised), and reporting production, time, and expenses. Teams were observed in the field by their supervisors and the research staff. Studies had follow-up and refresher training sessions as needed to accommodate staff turnover.

Interviewer safety was a major concern in several field settings, including interviews with incarcerated persons and homeless persons living on streets. For incarcerated persons, arrangements were made individually with each institution for safeguarding interviewers. Institutional staff were always close to the interviewing location, and movement of residents and interviewers within the institution was nearly always by escort. Interviewers were instructed on what to expect and how to behave, and they understood the importance of conservative dress and deportment. No DC*MADS interviewer was injured or physically threatened in an interview setting. For street interviews with the homeless and transient population, data collectors were provided with special supplies to help ensure their safety. These included a white jacket, flashlight, handheld foghorn, and cellular telephone. Furthermore, street supervisors used a rented van to transport interviewers to their assigned blocks, and interviewers were sent out in teams of two to five people as a safety precaution. Despite these precautions, several security problems occurred during the Homeless and Transient Population Study, including threats from drug dealers, gangs, and other criminal elements in the community, but no interviewers were injured and none of the threats originated from a homeless person.

Given the sensitive nature of many of the survey questions, several safeguards were used for all studies in the DC*MADS project to reassure respondents that their answers were strictly confidential. First, respondents were informed that the Privacy Act of 1974 prohibits release of personal identifiers without their explicit permission. In this regard, identifying information was kept separate from data records and maintained in a locked file until after the data had been coded, cleaned, and edited; the identifying information was then destroyed. Second, DC*MADS was authorized by a Federal Certificate of Confidentiality to protect the identity of research subjects by withholding the names and other personal identifying information from anyone not directly connected with the research. This protection included the legal right to refuse to supply information subpoenaed by courts of law. Respondents were informed of this certificate at the time they were asked to take part in a study. Third, an Assurance for the Protection of Human Subjects from Research Risk was issued by the Office for Protection from Research Risks, National Institutes of Health, to ensure that respondents were at minimal research risk. Research activities also were monitored for compliance with the assurance by the institutional review boards (IRBs) at Research Triangle Institute, Westat, and the participating organizations (e.g., hospitals).

2.5.3 Response Rates

Table 2.4 shows, for each of the populations, the counts of the overall sample sizes, the number of persons who were eligible for the study, the number of completed interviews, the eligibility rates (i.e., the number of eligible persons divided by the number sampled), and the response rates among the eligibles (i.e., number of interviews divided by the number eligible). As shown, the eligibility rates were extremely high (more than 95%) for all populations except for the homeless and transient population. The latter rate was somewhat lower because of the problems of screening in the street sample. Many people on the streets were coming from or going to someplace and were unwilling to take the time to talk. The response rates were more than 80% for all populations except juvenile offenders and treatment clients. The rate was lower for juveniles (75%) because of the requirement in one of the states to obtain parental permission prior to conducting the interview; parents were difficult to find and often did not return letters or phone calls. The somewhat lower response rate for drug treatment clients (68.1%) was attributable to clients in outpatient methadone programs; they were either unavailable or terminated treatment almost immediately following admission.

2.5.4 Methodological Challenges

A major strength of DC*MADS is that it was designed to be as comprehensive as possible by addressing the complexities of drug abuse and its consequences across all possible population subgroups residing in a single metropolitan area. Despite this strength, this was the first time such a large-scale study had been undertaken, and it posed numerous methodological challenges. Aside from the Household and Nonhousehold Populations Study (the data of which were collected as part of the

Table 2.4 Survey Response Data and Performance Rates for DC*MADS Populations

Sample Characteristic	Household	Homeless and Transient	Institutionalized	Adult Offenders[1]	Juvenile Offenders	Treatment Clients[2]	New Mothers[3]
Response data							
1. Total sampled (n)	3,117	1,378	1,402	202	264	747	883
2. Total eligible (n)	3,102	1,055	1,346	193	264	744	883
3. Total completed interviews (n)	2,547	908	1,203	158	198	507	766
Performance rates							
4. Eligibility rate (%) = Item 2/Item 1 × 100	99.5	76.6	96.0	95.5	100.0	99.6	100.0[4]
5. Response rate among eligibles (%) = Item 3/Item 2 × 100	82.1	86.1	89.4	81.9	75.0	68.1	86.7

SOURCE: Washington, DC, Metropolitan Area Drug Study (DC*MADS): 1989-1995.

NOTE: Data in this table represent individual respondents. All studies except the household had institutional response components as well as individual response components. Homeless institutions (such as shelters and soup kitchens) participated at a rate of 82.6%. For the Institutionalized Study, 42 of 48 institutions (such as prisons, psychiatric hospitals, and group homes) agreed to participate (87.5%). For the studies of offenders, all 20 correctional facilities in the sample agreed to participate. All nine of the DC hospitals sampled agreed to participate in the Drug Use and Pregnancy Study. Of the selected drug treatment programs, 90% participated in the Current Treatment Client Characteristics Study.

1. The adult offenders population presented in this table encompasses only incarcerated offenders. In comparison to the incarcerated population, the response rate for individuals on probation was notably lower (46.8%).

2. The total includes clients in long-term residential, short-term residential, and methadone treatment. A breakdown by modality is shown in Table 2.2.

3. The new mothers population refers to women in the Drug Use and Pregnancy Study.

4. Eligibility was determined prior to sampling.

NHSDA), all the other studies within the DC*MADS project required permission from local authorities to gain access to the populations of interest. Obtaining this permission required lengthy and sometimes difficult negotiations and often resulted in some accommodations being made in the study design (e.g., the Drug Use and Pregnancy Study had to be changed from a metropolitan area-wide study of 19 hospitals to a DC-based study of 9 hospitals because many of the selected hospitals in Maryland and Virginia declined to participate).

To help in the negotiation process, a 17-person DC*MADS advisory group was formed with persons who had interests and involvement in substance abuse issues or were working with populations that were the target of one or more of the studies in the DC*MADS project (see Appendix H, 1998). In addition to having an overall advisory group, some of the studies convened special advisory panels to assist with study-specific design and access issues. The formal negotiation process included garnering support from relevant local and areawide associations (e.g., DC Metropolitan Area Council of Governments, DC Hospital Association), committees, and key individuals (e.g., DC Commissioner of Public Health), sending letters and materials explaining the study's purpose, making follow-up phone calls, and holding face-to-face meetings with government officials or other key staff.

Even with support from advisory groups and interested local associations, negotiations were still complex. For example, for the Institutionalized Study, most institutions were under the jurisdiction of state or local authorities and thus required permission from governing bodies. The process was complicated by two factors. First, permission was needed from a large number of groups because of the governing structure of the MSA that included multiple local jurisdictions and because various types of institutions (e.g., correctional facilities, psychiatric institutions) were within the purview of separate authorities. Second, it was necessary to coordinate agreement on design features (such as sample frame construction and the location of interviews within a particular facility) across jurisdictions.

All the other studies faced similar kinds of challenges. In all cases, the key initial challenge was to get permission to do the study from gatekeepers who controlled access to the populations. For the homeless population, this included gaining trust and support of shelter and soup kitchen operators; for the juvenile and adult offenders populations, it meant getting the permission of judicial and correctional authorities; for the drug treatment client population, it meant getting support of treatment providers; and for the new mothers population, it meant getting permission from hospital administrators, nurses, and doctors who practiced in the facility. Several groups also required a presentation before *their* IRBs before approving study participation, even though the study already had been reviewed and approved by the IRBs of the research organizations.

Once permission was obtained to proceed with the studies, there were further challenges associated with sampling and data collection. Sampling challenges for various studies included (a) developing accurate and complete source lists for constructing appropriate sampling frames, (b) developing methods for counting homeless people in the street sample because they are mobile and often seek out-of-the-way places where they can safely rest at night, (c) developing procedures to account for the admission and release of facility residents during the field period, and (d) developing overall sampling weights that adjust for known or expected duplication (i.e., multiplicity) for studies with more than one sampling frame.

Some of the data collection challenges involved (a) gaining the confidence and trust of respondents regarding the study purposes and confidentiality of the data; (b) finding and training persons who had prior interviewing experience and who were comfortable working with people in nonhousehold populations and in institutional settings; (c) obtaining parental consent to conduct interviews with juveniles; (d) developing procedures to ensure the safety of interviewers, especially those conducting street interviews with the homeless and transient population; (e) scheduling (and rescheduling) interviews to accommodate the routines of participating institutions and to work around interruptions (e.g., lockdowns and taking "counts" within a correctional facility, the unavailability of birth logs in hospitals because they were in use by hospital staff); and (f) developing procedures to maintain the confidentiality and security of the data.

All these challenges to the DC*MADS project were met satisfactorily, and rigorous methods and approaches were developed that resulted in the successful conduct of these research studies. Additional information and details about study challenges and methods to address them are contained in the final technical reports for the individual studies

(NIDA, 1993a, 1993b, 1994a, 1994b, 1994c, 1995a, 1995b; see also Appendix I, 1998).

2.6 Analytical Approach

Two key issues in conducting data analyses of the studies in the DC*MADS project concern appropriate analysis software to handle complex sampling designs and an understanding of survey errors and procedures for suppressing unreliable estimates. This section briefly discusses both of these issues.

2.6.1 Weighted Analysis Through SUDAAN

As noted by Cohen, Xanthopoulos, and Jones (1986), surveys conducted by government organizations, industry, political organizations, and market research firms need to provide the greatest precision in estimates from sample data for fixed cost and time constraints. Consequently, surveys often are characterized by design components that include stratification, clustering, and disproportionate sampling. Such design features complicate the data analysis while reducing the cost of data collection. Complex survey designs of this type deviate from the assumption of simple random sampling and thus require special consideration with regard to variance estimation and analysis.

All the surveys described in this book used complex survey designs (see Section 2.5) and consequently required specialized software to address these design features. The SUDAAN (SUrvey DAta ANalysis) software package for complex survey designs developed by Research Triangle Institute (1990) was used in DC*MADS analyses. SUDAAN procedures were used to generate statistics, weighted estimates, and standard errors. (For an updated version of SUDAAN, see Shah, Barnwell, and Bieler, 1998.)

2.6.2 Survey Errors and Low Precision Rule

The survey estimates shown in this book are subject to two types of error: nonsampling error and sampling error. Nonsampling error results from such factors as nonresponse, misreporting of data by respondents, and miscoding of responses. Although the extent of nonsampling error cannot be measured precisely, attempts can be made to reduce it through quality control procedures and other means. The final reports for each study describe the quality control procedures that were used to reduce nonsampling error (see Appendix I [1998] for a list of DC*MADS final reports).

Sampling error results from collecting data from a subset rather than from everyone in the population. Also known as sampling variability, sampling error is the variation among a set of estimates that would be observed if repeated samples of the same type were drawn from the same population. The magnitude of sampling error depends on (a) the inherent variability of the measured attribute in the population, (b) the sample size, (c) the extent of homogeneity of the sample on the variable in question (based on such factors as similarity of respondents within sample clusters and dissimilarity between clusters), and (d) the type of sampling and estimation procedures used. Sampling theory provides a basis for calculating the degree of sampling error. Two commonly reported measures are the standard error (*SE*) and the relative standard error (*RSE*; i.e., the *SE* expressed as a percentage of the estimate). *SE*s for the estimates in this book are presented in the final technical reports for the DC*MADS studies (see Appendix I, 1998). *SE*s are used to compute confidence intervals for estimates and also enter into the calculations required to test the statistical significance of the difference between two estimates.

Estimates subject to a high degree of sampling error are considered to have low precision. The precision criterion applied to the estimates in this book was developed for the 1991 NHSDA and is based on the *RSE* of the natural logarithm of the estimate. Specifically, estimates for the household, homeless and transient, and institutionalized populations were suppressed when the $RSE \times [-\ln(p)] > .175$ for $p \le .5$, and the $RSE \times [-\ln(1-p)] > .175$ for $p > .5$. Note that the $RSE \times [-\ln(p)] = RSE(p)/-\ln(p)$.

The studies of the homeless and institutionalized populations used the same suppression rule as the NHSDA to identify low-precision estimates. Because these two studies had considerably smaller sample sizes than did the NHSDA, however, they were likely to have more low-precision estimates. These low-precision estimates are shown and flagged with an asterisk (*) in the tables and figures in Chapters 4 and 5 rather than being suppressed. These flagged low-precision estimates are presented in recognition of their potential utility to investigators involved in related areas of research. Because the expected and overall design effects of these studies were greater than 1.0, the *SE* from a simple random sample design was set as a lower bound for analyses to control for occasional design effects of less than 1.0 in subgroup estimates.

The other studies reported in this book (i.e., treatment clients, adult and criminal offenders, new mothers) also used a suppression rule based on the *RSE* of the natural logarithm of the estimate. Because they had relatively small sample sizes, however, they used a more relaxed cutoff value for suppressing estimates than the household, homeless and transient, and institutionalized studies. Specifically, instead of the .175 cutoff value, they used a .275 cutoff value. That is, estimates for these studies were suppressed when the $RSE \times [-\ln(p)] > .275$ for $p \le .5$, and the $RSE \times [-\ln(1 - p)] > .275$ for $p > .5$. In view of this more relaxed criterion, the low-precision estimates for these studies have been suppressed from the tables and replaced with an asterisk (*) rather than simply being flagged as in the household, homeless and transient, and institutionalized studies.

2.7 Study Strengths and Limitations

All the studies in the DC*MADS project described in this book relied primarily on the veracity of respondents' self-reports of their behavior, which like any methodology has both strengths and limitations. The advantage to self-reports about drug use is that they permit the collection of a rich array of information about the nature and extent of drug use along with information about drug-related consequences and correlates. For example, DC*MADS surveys were used (a) to provide information about prevalence, trends, patterns, and frequency of use; (b) to determine use during selected time periods, such as the past year or the past month; (c) to identify the characteristics of users and nonusers; (d) to determine the relative popularity of specific individual drugs; (e) to identify the route by which drugs are taken (e.g., inhaling, smoking, injecting); (f) to examine the reasons and motivations for taking drugs; and (g) to assess relationships between drug use and other behaviors, such as criminal involvement and activities.

Self-reported data on drug use are limited, however, by the willingness of respondents to reveal their use. In some situations, respondents may have strong motivations not to report drug use behavior honestly (e.g., arrestees may be fearful that honest reporting about their drug use will aid in their conviction). Thus, self-report measures of drug use are suspect when respondents recognize that admitting drug use may result in adverse consequences for them or when they are placed in a situation that encourages them to provide socially desirable responses. Several studies, for example, have found systematic underreporting of drug use among arrestees (e.g., Collins & Marsden, 1990; Harrison, 1995) and other groups, such as pregnant women (see Chapter 8).

There also are potential problems with the validity of survey data, including issues of population coverage and response rates. If the population is not properly represented in the survey or if responses rates are low, biases are introduced that can invalidate the survey results. Nonresponse adjustments, however, are generally made to credible surveys to help compensate for the potential bias of nonsurveyed persons.

Additional information about the validity of self-reports is addressed by Harrison (1995) and in a research monograph by Rouse, Kozel, and Richards (1985). A general conclusion emerging from these various reviews is that most people appear to be reasonably truthful (within the bounds of capability) under the proper conditions. Such conditions include believing that the research has a legitimate purpose, having suitable privacy for providing answers, having assurances that answers will be kept confidential, and believing that those collecting the data can be trusted.

The best protection against all these threats to validity is to be aware of them and to deal with them as forthrightly as possible. The major point is that when the circumstances allow respondents to consider the questions reasonable and justified in terms of purpose, and when respondents can feel reasonably certain that their answers will not be used against them, then self-reports can be sufficiently valid for research and policy purposes. When those conditions are not met, there may well be very substantial underreporting.

The study designs in the DC*MADS project adequately addressed most of these concerns. Pretests were used to identify and eliminate ambiguities in question wording, the respective populations were properly represented in the studies, and the response rates were within an acceptable range. Data collection procedures were used to encourage forthright and honest reporting, and nonresponse adjustments were made to help compensate for the potential bias of nonsurveyed persons. Quality control assessments of the respective studies suggest that these efforts were generally successful (NIDA, 1993a, 1994a, 1994b, 1994c, 1995a, 1995b).

Note

1. Appendixes related to the studies discussed in this book are available on the Sage Publications World Wide Web site at

http://www.sagepub.com/bray_druguse.htm

and on the Research Triangle Institute World Wide Web site at

http://www.rti.org/publications/dcmads/appendix.cfm

See the reference section below for the titles of Appendixes A through I.

References

Appendix A: Drug Use Among the Household Population. (1998).

Appendix B: Homeless and Transient Population Study. (1998).

Appendix C: Institutionalized Population Study. (1998).

Appendix D: Adult and Juvenile Offender Studies. (1998).

Appendix E: Current Treatment Client Characteristics Study. (1998).

Appendix F: Drug Use and Pregnancy Study. (1998).

Appendix G: Combining Household, Homeless, and Institutionalized Data. (1998).

Appendix H: Members of the DC*MADS Advisory Group. (1998).

Appendix I: DC*MADS Technical Reports. (1998).

Cohen, S. B., Xanthopoulos, J. H., & Jones, G. K. (1986). An evaluation of available software for the analysis of complex survey data. In *Proceedings of the Section on Survey Research Methods, American Statistical Association*. Washington, DC: American Statistical Association.

Collins, J., & Marsden, M. E. (1990). *Validity of self reports of drug use among arrestees*. Unpublished manuscript, Research Triangle Institute, Research Triangle Park, NC.

Greene, J. M., Ennett, S. T., & Ringwalt, C. L. (1997). Substance use among runaway and homeless youth in three national samples. *American Journal of Public Health, 87*, 229-235.

Harrison, L. D. (1995). The validity of self-reported data on drug use. *Journal of Drug Issues, 25,* 91-111.

Johnson, T. P., & Barrett, M. E. (1991). *Homelessness and substance use in Cook County* (prepared for Department of Alcoholism and Drug Abuse, State of Illinois). Urbana: Survey Research Laboratory, University of Illinois.

Katzman, R., Brown, T., Fuld, P., Peck, A., Schechter, R., & Schimmel, H. (1983). Validation of short orientation-memory-concentration test of cognitive impairment. *American Journal of Psychiatry, 140,* 734-739.

Koegel, P., Burnam, M. A., & Farr, R. K. (1990). Subsistence adaptation among homeless adults in the inner city of Los Angeles. *Journal of Social Issues, 46,* 83-107.

National Institute on Drug Abuse. (1992). *Prevalence of drug use in the DC metropolitan area household population: 1990* (Technical Report #1 under NIDA Contract No. 271-89-8340, Washington, DC, Metropolitan Area Drug Study, DHHS Publication No. ADM 92-1919, prepared by M. E. Marsden, R. M. Bray, A. C. Theisen, L. E. Packer, & J. M. Greene, Research Triangle Institute). Rockville, MD: Author.

National Institute on Drug Abuse. (1993a). *Prevalence of drug use in the Washington, DC, metropolitan area homeless and transient population: 1991* (Technical Report #2 under NIDA Contract No. 271-89-8340, Washington, DC, Metropolitan Area Drug Study, prepared by M. L. Dennis, R. Iachan, J. P. Thornberry, R. M. Bray, L. E. Packer, & G. S. Bieler, Research Triangle Institute). Rockville, MD: Author.

National Institute on Drug Abuse. (1993b). *Views of area opinion leaders about drug abuse in the Washington, DC, metropolitan area: 1991* (Technical Report #3 under NIDA Contract No. 271-89-8340, Washington, DC, Metropolitan Area Drug Study, prepared by S. L. Bailey, J. H. Cox, R. M. Bray, J. P. Thornberry, & G. Bassin, Research Triangle Institute). Rockville, MD: Author.

National Institute on Drug Abuse. (1994a). *Current treatment client characteristics in the Washington, DC, metropolitan area: 1991* (Technical Report #5 under NIDA Contract No. 271-89-8340, Washington, DC, Metropolitan Area Drug Study, prepared by P. M. Flynn, J. W. Luckey, S. C. Wheeless, J. T. Lynch, L. A. Kroutil, & R. M. Bray, Research Triangle Institute). Rockville, MD: Author.

National Institute on Drug Abuse. (1994b). *Prevalence of drug use in the DC metropolitan area household and nonhousehold populations: 1991* (Technical Report #8 under NIDA Contract No. 271-89-8340, Washington, DC, Metropolitan Area Drug Study, prepared by R. M. Bray, L. A. Kroutil, S. C. Wheeless, M. E. Marsden, & L. E. Packer, Research Triangle Institute). Rockville, MD: Author.

National Institute on Drug Abuse. (1994c). *Prevalence of drug use in the DC metropolitan area institutionalized population: 1991* (Technical Report #4 under NIDA Contract No. 271-89-8340, Washington, DC, Metropolitan Area Drug Study, prepared by D. Cantor, G. H. Gaertner, & L. Keil, Westat, Inc., & R. M. Bray, Research Triangle Institute). Rockville, MD: Author.

National Institute on Drug Abuse. (1995a). *Prevalence of drug use among DC women delivering livebirths in DC hospitals: 1992* (Technical Report #7 under NIDA Contract No. 271-89-8340, Washington, DC, Metropolitan Area Drug Study, prepared by W. A. Visscher, R. M. Bray, L. A. Kroutil, D. A. Akin, M. A. Ardini, J. P. Thornberry, & M. McCall, Research Triangle Institute). Rockville, MD: Author.

National Institute on Drug Abuse. (1995b). *Prevalence of drug use in the DC metropolitan area adult and juvenile offender populations: 1991* (Technical Report #6 under NIDA Contract No. 271-89-8340, Washington, DC, Metropolitan Area Drug Study, prepared by D. Cantor, Westat, Inc.). Rockville, MD: Author.

Research Triangle Institute. (1990). *Software for SUrvey DAta ANalysis (SUDAAN): Version 5.30*. Research Triangle Park, NC: Author.

Robertson, M., Zlotnick, C., & Westerfelt, A. (1997). Drug use disorders and treatment contact among homeless adults in Alameda County, California. *American Journal of Public Health, 87*, 221-228.

Rossi, P. H. (1989). *Down and out in America: The origins of homelessness*. Chicago: The University of Chicago Press.

Rouse, B. A., Kozel, N. J., & Richards, L. G. (Eds.). (1985). *Self-report methods of estimating drug use: Meeting current challenges to validity* (NIDA Research Monograph No. 57, DHHS Publication No. ADM 85-1402). Rockville, MD: National Institute on Drug Abuse.

Runkel, P. J., & McGrath, J. E. (1972). *Research on human behavior*. New York: Holt, Rinehart, & Winston.

Shah, B. V., Barnwell, B. G., & Bieler, G. S. (1998). *SUDAAN user's manual: Version 7.5*. Research Triangle Park, NC: Research Triangle Institute.

Substance Abuse and Mental Health Services Administration. (1993). *National Household Survey on Drug Abuse: Main findings 1991* (DHHS Publication No. SMA 93-1980). Rockville, MD: Author.

3
Drug Use Among Household and Nonhousehold Populations

Mary Ellen Marsden
Robert M. Bray

Epidemiological data on the prevalence, characteristics, and numbers of users of illicit drugs and alcohol among residents of a geographic area can help provide the basis for policy development and program planning for substance abuse services in that area. These data can suggest the size of the population potentially in need of treatment and the type of treatment needed, the groups to which prevention and treatment programs should be targeted, and the areas and neighborhoods with highest need for such programs.

Although information on *all* residents in an area is necessary to guide planning efforts, most studies of substance use prevalence tend to focus on the household population and largely exclude nonhousehold populations among whom drug and alcohol use may be higher. Persons living in nonhousehold settings include homeless and transient persons as well as those who are institutionalized; they generally have shifted from the household population for a variety of reasons, including substance abuse, mental illness, criminal activity, or health problems. Even though rates of alcohol and other drug use may be substantial in nonhousehold populations, few systematic studies of substance use have been conducted across these populations (although research has been conducted on selected populations). Similarly, estimates of drug and alcohol use for the total civilian population are not readily available. In addition, relatively few studies have been conducted of substance use in local areas, such as states, metropolitan areas, or cities and towns. This is somewhat surprising because these smaller areas are responsible for many of the policy decisions regarding substance abuse services and require sound data on which policymakers and planners can base their decisions.

This chapter presents findings from the DC*MADS Household and Nonhousehold Populations Study. It examines and presents data on drug and alcohol use and their correlates in the household population of the DC metropolitan statistical area (MSA) and provides substance use comparisons within segments of the MSA and among large MSAs. In addition, it gives a comparative overview of substance use rates across the range of household and nonhousehold populations that are examined in more detail in this book. The results of integrating information from the household population, the homeless and transient population, and the institutionalized population to develop composite population estimates are discussed in Chapter 9.

3.1 Substance Use Prevalence and Trends in Household and Nonhousehold Populations

To set the stage for examining findings from the DC MSA household and nonhousehold populations, it is useful to examine data from prior studies as a backdrop. Selected findings from household surveys are first considered, followed by results from studies of nonhousehold populations.

3.1.1 Findings From Household Populations

The National Household Survey on Drug Abuse (NHSDA) series has been, since 1971, the primary source of information on the nature and extent of drug use and drug-related problems among household members in the United States. The NHSDA has been criticized, however, because of its failure to adequately cover populations at high risk of abusing drugs or alcohol, including those who are homeless, in prison, or in treatment (U.S. General Accounting Office [US GAO], 1993; U.S. Senate, 1990). Hard-core drug users and use of such drugs as heroin and cocaine are likely to be underestimated with the NHSDA data. Although approximately 98% of the U.S. population lives in households (Substance Abuse and Mental Health Services Administration [SAMHSA], 1993, p. 6), the lack of inclusion of persons living in nonhousehold settings may provide an inaccurate picture of the extent of drug and alcohol use.

Historically, the main focus of the NHSDA has been to provide estimates of substance use for the total United States and broad geographic regions of the nation. In addition, however, in 1991, 1992, and 1993 there were oversamples of six major metropolitan areas: Chicago, Denver, Los Angeles, Miami, New York, and the District of Columbia. Similarly, the DC MSA was oversampled in 1990 (SAMHSA, 1995).

According to the NHSDA, drug use decreased steadily and dramatically in the household population throughout the 1980s to the early 1990s, when DC*MADS began. This long-term decline was evident for most drugs and most age groups. For example, the percentage of the total household population aged 12 or older reporting any illicit drug use in the past month decreased from a peak of 14.1% in 1979 to 6.6% in 1991; past month marijuana/hashish use decreased from 13.2% to 5.1% in the same time period; and past month cocaine use decreased from a peak of 3.0% in 1985 to 1.0% in 1991 (SAMHSA, 1997). Similar trends were observed among young adults aged 18 to 25, the group with the highest rates of use overall. The percentage of young adults aged 18 to 25 reporting any illicit drug use in the past month decreased consistently between each of the surveys in the series, from a peak of 38.0% in 1979 to 15.4% in 1991. Past month marijuana/hashish use among persons aged 18 to 25 decreased from a peak of 35.6% in 1979 to 12.9% in 1991, while cocaine use decreased from 9.9% in 1979 to 2.2% in 1991.

Further declines in drug use for the total household population have been seen since 1991, although the decreases were not statistically significant. Illicit drug use, however, recently has increased for young persons aged 12 to 17. Some 16.3% of youth aged 12 to 17 used drugs in 1979, 5.8% in 1991, and 9.0% in 1996 (SAMHSA, 1997).

At the same time that household surveys were showing a long-term decrease in drug use, other indicators of drug use suggested that trends in drug use were not as consistent. The Drug Abuse Warning Network (DAWN) showed substantial increases in emergency room drug mentions between 1985 and 1988 but decreases in 1990 and 1991 (The White House, 1992, p. 23). The Drug Use Forecasting (DUF) program showed some fluctuation between 1988 and 1991 in the percentage of arrestees testing positive for any drug. Marijuana/hashish use decreased in most sites, and crack cocaine peaked in 1988 and 1989 for most sites but decreased thereafter (Zawitz, 1992). Although epidemiological data from household populations showed long-term decreases in drug use from the late 1970s to the early 1990s, other sources of data were as likely to show increases.

Concerns about the disjuncture between household surveys and other indicators of drug use regarding trends in drug use have resulted in an increasing recognition that household surveys provide only a partial picture of the extent of drug use in the United States. Perhaps most telling was an investigation of the number of hard-core cocaine addicts. According to the NHSDA in 1991, the count was 850,000. This number, however—based on survey data—was less than the number in the criminal justice system and in drug treatment. The true number was likely closer to 2.2 million (U.S. Senate, 1990). Similarly, although the NHSDA estimated the number of current heroin users in 1991 to be 71,000 (SAMHSA, 1997), the true number probably was considerably larger and appeared to be increasing according to a variety of reports from emergency rooms and drug treatment facilities (SAMHSA, 1997, p. 31). Indeed, estimates of heroin use from the NHSDA, although acknowledged to be inadequate, have shown a rapid increase in current heroin users over the past several years, from 71,000 in 1991 to 216,000 in 1996 (SAMHSA, 1997, p. 17).

The NHSDA, although it provides a sound estimate of the number of users in household populations, provides a conservative estimate of the number of users in the total U.S. population because it omits individuals not living in households and is likely to miss those who are at high risk of drug use. These groups include homeless people and those who are living in institutions, many of whom are being treated for drug abuse or who may be incarcerated for drug-related crimes or for crimes in which drug abuse was a contributing factor. Household surveys increasingly have been discussed as good sources of information about casual users but as less appropriate for developing estimates of hard-core users. In our nation's cities, rates of substance use may be substantially greater than estimates for the nation as a whole.

Findings from the NHSDA also indicate that local areas vary in the prevalence of substance use, dependence, and treatment utilization. Using a small-area estimation methodology employing logistic regression models to combine NHSDA survey data with local area indicators—such as drug-related arrests, alcohol-related death rates, and block group level characteristics for 1991 to 1993—estimates were developed for 11 measures of substance use and problems in 26 states and 25 MSAs (SAMHSA, 1996). Findings for the 25 MSAs, including the DC MSA, are reported in Table 3.1.

Data for the DC MSA show that 53.8% of household residents used any alcohol in the past month, and 5.4% used one or more illicit drugs. About 1% met the criteria for dependence on illicit drugs and 3.6% for dependence on alcohol, but not illicit drugs. Fewer than 1% had received treatment for illicit drug use or for alcohol use in the past year. Comparison of these rates with those in the other 24 MSAs shows that the rates were reasonably similar across the MSAs, although there were some notable differences. For example, relative to the DC MSA, rates of alcohol use were higher in the Boston (61.5%), Minneapolis (65.9%), Newark (62.2%), and Oakland (65.0%) MSAs, whereas rates of drug use were somewhat higher in the Anaheim-Santa Ana (8.8%), Denver (8.3%), and Oakland (11.4%) MSAs. The latter finding is consistent with other NHSDA analyses by region that show higher rates of drug use in the West than in the Northeast, North Central, or South regions (SAMHSA, 1993). Rates of dependence and treatment utilization in the DC MSA were similar to those in other MSAs.

Clearly, some variation in substance use rates would be expected across MSAs because of differences in demographic characteristics of the population, local enforcement practices, and availability of and access to substances. The more striking finding from these data is the relative

Table 3.1 Prevalence of Past Month Alcohol and Illicit Drug Use and Past Year Dependence and Treatment for 25 Metropolitan Statistical Areas

Metropolitan Statistical Area (MSA)	Past Month Substance Use		Past Year Dependence		Past Year Treatment	
	Any Alcohol Use	Any Illicit Drug Use	Dependent on Illicit Drugs	Dependent on Alcohol but Not Illicit Drugs	Received Treatment for Illicit Drug Use	Received Treatment for Alcohol Use but Not Illicit Drug Use
Anaheim-Santa Ana, CA	52.3	8.8	2.2	6.0	1.0	0.6
Atlanta, GA	51.0	5.9	1.2	4.5	0.7	0.4
Baltimore, MD	44.8	5.0	0.9	2.2	0.6	0.5
Boston, MA	61.5	6.7	1.7	4.4	1.0	2.2
Chicago, IL	53.8	5.5	0.9	3.5	0.5	0.7
Dallas, TX	50.2	5.7	1.6	3.3	0.7	0.5
Denver, CO	58.4	8.3	1.3	4.6	0.6	1.0
Detroit, MI	54.2	5.5	1.2	3.6	0.8	0.5
El Paso, TX	45.9	3.6	0.8	3.7	0.6	0.5
Houston, TX	50.9	4.1	2.1	2.0	0.8	0.7
Los Angeles, CA	49.3	6.7	1.5	7.1	0.8	0.5

Miami-Hialeah, FL	44.4	3.8	0.7	2.0	0.6	0.5
Minneapolis-St. Paul, MN	65.9	5.2	1.2	3.5	0.9	0.9
Nassau-Suffolk, NY	59.6	6.6	1.0	1.1	0.6	0.5
New York, NY	48.8	6.0	0.9	1.8	0.7	0.3
Newark, NJ	62.2	6.2	1.4	2.5	0.9	0.8
Oakland, CA	65.0	11.4	3.0	3.9	1.4	2.1
Philadelphia, PA-NJ	59.1	5.7	1.0	2.8	0.8	0.6
Phoenix, AZ	53.7	6.8	1.6	3.6	0.7	0.7
San Antonio, TX	54.4	4.4	1.4	2.5	0.5	0.4
San Bernardino, CA	49.1	7.4	2.1	3.9	1.2	1.2
San Diego, CA	49.1	7.1	1.4	3.0	0.7	0.5
St. Louis, MO-IL	55.0	5.2	1.0	2.5	0.7	0.6
Tampa-St. Petersburg, FL	41.2	5.3	1.0	2.1	0.7	0.4
Washington, DC	53.8	5.4	1.1	3.6	0.6	0.9

SOURCE: National Household Survey on Drug Abuse, 1991-1993, model-based estimates (SAMHSA, 1996).
NOTE: All estimates represent prevalence rates (percentages) averaged over the 3-year period from 1991 to 1993 for the household population aged 12 or older.

similarity of the rates across the MSAs. Although Washington, DC, often has been perceived to be a high drug use area, rates within the DC MSA were in fact intermediate to those in many other large MSAs as estimated here. More important, there were few significant differences among the rates across MSAs. These comparisons suggest that the DC MSA, in its rates of alcohol and other drug use, may be representative of other large MSAs and that the findings reported in this book are generalizable to other MSAs.

3.1.2 Findings From Nonhousehold Populations

Data on *trends* in drug use in nonhousehold populations are not as readily available as for household populations. Few studies of such populations as the homeless or institutionalized have been conducted over time; most tend to be one-time studies. Some relevant data are available, however, from the Survey of Inmates in State Correctional Facilities, which has been conducted periodically since 1974. Findings from 1991 showed that about 80% of inmates had ever used illicit drugs and nearly two thirds used them regularly (Beck et al., 1993). About half used them in the month prior to the offense, more than one third used them daily in that month, and about 31% were under the influence of drugs at the time of the offense. These rates were relatively stable between 1986 and 1991.

Regardless of trends in drug use in nonhousehold populations, this survey series on the state prison population and many other studies of nonhousehold populations found substantially higher rates of drug use than those among household populations. Compared with rates of past month drug use in the household population in 1991 of about 7%, about 50% of state prison inmates were users in 1991. Similarly, Harlow (1992) found that more than 40% of all jail inmates in 1989 reported having used at least one illegal drug in the month before their arrest. Consistent with these data, Barton (1982), Anglin and Speckart (1986), and others have documented similar high rates of drug use among criminal offenders.

There also is evidence of high rates of drug use among residents of noncorrectional institutions. The literature on the co-occurrence of psychiatric syndromes and drug use suggests high rates of drug addiction among those with psychiatric disorders. The relationship between depression and alcoholism has been well documented (see O'Sullivan,

1984, for a review), and there is increasing evidence of links between alcoholism and bipolar disorders (Mayfield, 1985). According to evidence cited by Miller and Gold (1991), between 50% and 75% of general psychiatric populations have alcohol or drug disorders.

Weisner, Schmidt, and Tam (1995) estimated prevalence rates for problem drinkers and drug users in the household population and from a nonhousehold sample drawn from persons within alcohol treatment, drug treatment, mental health, criminal justice, and welfare agencies. They found substantially higher rates of problem drinking (48% vs. 11%) and weekly drug use (47% vs. 6%) among the nonhousehold population relative to the household population.

In addition, Fischer's (1989) review of studies of drug use among homeless people found drug use prevalence estimates to vary from 1% to 90%. Despite this variation, in many cases they were substantially higher than comparable rates among household populations. Indeed, a number of studies estimate that one third or more of the people who are homeless have used drugs in the past year (e.g., Davidson, 1991; Interagency Council on the Homeless, 1991; Johnson & Barrett, 1991; Milburn, Booth, & Miles, 1990; Spinner & Leaf, 1992).

3.2 Overview of the Study

This examination of drug use in household and nonhousehold populations is based on the 1991 DC MSA oversample from the NHSDA and surveys of nonhousehold populations conducted specifically as part of DC*MADS, including studies of the homeless and transient population and persons in such institutions as correctional institutions, psychiatric institutions, and group homes. Findings from several other studies within the DC*MADS project also are discussed, including those of adult and juvenile offenders, treatment clients, and new mothers. More detailed discussion of each of these studies is included in the following chapters of this book.

In 1991, the NHSDA oversampled residents of the DC MSA and five other large MSAs across the United States (Chicago, Denver, Los Angeles, Miami, and New York) to enable the development of estimates of drug use in each of these MSAs. The same household survey instrument was administered in these MSAs and other areas across the United States as part of the NHSDA. The 1991 DC MSA oversample included 2,547 in-person interviews for a response rate for this oversample of 76.8%. The survey methodology is described in more detail in Chapter 2 and in Appendix A (1998), as well as in other related reports (National Institute on Drug Abuse [NIDA], 1994; SAMHSA, 1993).

Studies of nonhousehold populations in the DC MSA used instruments patterned after the 1991 NHSDA survey instrument. As described in Chapter 2, all the substudies used a core set of questions on use of alcohol, illicit drugs, and tobacco, as well as adverse consequences for comparison of results across substudies and for comparability with the household survey. This use of a core set of items permitted development of the same measures of substance use and adverse effects across each of the substudies, as well as calculation of composite rates of use in both household and nonhousehold populations, discussed in Chapter 9 of this book.

3.3 Drug Use Among Household Members

This section describes the prevalence of illicit drug and alcohol use among household residents. It also compares the rates of use in the DC MSA as a whole with those in large MSAs and within the DC MSA. Additionally, it contrasts use in low and other socioeconomic status (SES) areas in DC and outlying areas.

3.3.1 Prevalence and Number of Users

Many members of the DC MSA household population had used illicit drugs, alcohol, or cigarettes in their lifetimes, in the past year, or in the past month, as shown in Figure 3.1 and Table 3.2. Almost 40% of the household population had used one or more illicit drugs in their lifetimes, almost 12% in the past year, and nearly 6% in the past month. These percentages translate to 1.3 million persons who had used illicit drugs in their lifetimes, about 370,000 who had used in the past year, and 180,000 who had used in the past month. Marijuana/hashish was the drug most commonly used. Some 36% of the household population used

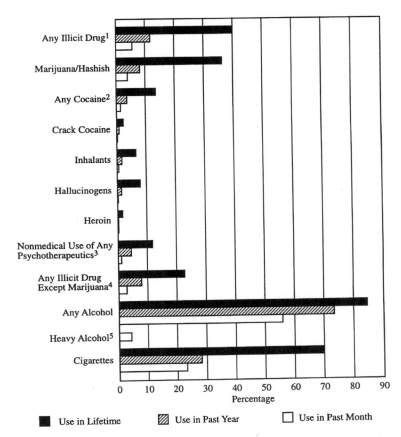

Figure 3.1. Prevalence of Illicit Drug, Alcohol, and Tobacco Use in the DC MSA Household Population

SOURCE: 1991 National Household Survey on Drug Abuse: DC MSA.
NOTE: See Table 3.2 for the data used to prepare this figure.
1. Use of marijuana or hashish, cocaine (including crack), inhalants, hallucinogens (including phencyclidine or PCP), or heroin, or nonmedical use of psychotherapeutics at least once.
2. Includes crack cocaine.
3. Nonmedical use of any prescription-type stimulant (including methamphetamine), sedative, tranquilizer, or analgesic; does not include over-the-counter drugs.
4. Includes cocaine (including crack), inhalants, hallucinogens (including PCP), heroin, or psychotherapeutics for nonmedical reasons.
5. Defined as having five or more drinks per occasion on 5 or more days in the past 30 days.

it in their lifetimes, 8% in the past year, and 4% in the past month, rates that closely mirror the findings for any illicit drug use. Although the rates of use of other illicit drugs were lower, 1.5%—or almost 50,000 of the

Table 3.2 Prevalence of Illicit Drug, Alcohol, and Tobacco Use in the DC MSA Household Population

Substance Used	Lifetime		Past Year		Past Month	
	Percentage	Number	Percentage	Number	Percentage	Number
Any illicit drug[1]	39.9	1,267,405	11.7	370,486	5.7	180,386
Marijuana/hashish	36.2	1,148,121	8.1	256,514	4.1	129,912
Any cocaine[2]	13.5	427,721	3.6	114,538	1.5	47,583
Crack cocaine	2.2	70,251	0.9	29,027	0.3	10,618
Inhalants	6.6	209,853	1.7	52,514	0.7	21,754
Hallucinogens	7.9	251,748	1.5	48,417	0.3	9,105
Heroin	1.7	54,014	0.4	12,314	0.3	8,820
Nonmedical use of any psychotherapeutics[3]	11.7	371,056	4.5	142,118	1.1	35,738
Any illicit drug except marijuana[4]	22.7	721,465	7.8	248,132	3.0	94,910
Any alcohol	84.6	2,684,256	73.5	2,332,210	55.9	1,773,376
Heavy alcohol[5]	—	—	—	—	4.2	131,760
Cigarettes	69.5	2,207,490	28.1	891,575	23.1	732,222

SOURCE: 1991 National Household Survey on Drug Abuse: DC MSA.

NOTE: Unweighted numbers of respondents are given in Table 2.1, and the DC MSA is defined in Chapter 2.

1. Use of marijuana or hashish, cocaine (including crack), inhalants, hallucinogens (including phencyclidine or PCP), heroin, or nonmedical use of psychotherapeutics at least once.

2. Includes crack cocaine.

3. Nonmedical use of any prescription-type stimulant, sedative, tranquilizer, or analgesic; does not include over-the-counter drugs.

4. Use of cocaine (including crack), inhalants, hallucinogens (including PCP), heroin, or nonmedical use of psychotherapeutics at least once.

5. Defined as drinking five or more drinks per occasion on 5 or more days in the past 30 days.

household population—reported any use of cocaine in the past month, and less than 1%—or about 10,000 persons—reported use of crack cocaine. About 3% had used illicit drugs other than marijuana/hashish in the past month.

Alcohol use was widespread among members of the household population, used by about 85% in their lifetimes, 74% in the past year, and 56% in the past month. About 4% of the household population could be classified as heavy drinkers who had drunk five or more drinks per occasion on 5 or more days in the past 30 days.

3.3.2 Comparisons With Large Metropolitan Areas

Overall, there was great similarity in rates of illicit drug use in the lifetime, past year, and past month among members of the household population in the DC MSA compared with household populations of large MSAs and the United States as a whole. Although data presented in Table 3.1 show some differences in substance use among specific MSAs, comparisons of rates for the DC MSA with those for other large MSAs show a close correspondence. As shown in Table 3.3, the percentage of the DC MSA household population who had used any illicit drugs, marijuana/hashish, or cocaine in the lifetime was highly similar to the percentage in large MSAs and slightly higher than that in the total United States. Almost 40% of household residents in the DC MSA and large MSAs had ever used illicit drugs, slightly higher than the 37% in the total United States, which includes small metropolitan and nonmetropolitan (i.e., rural) areas that typically have lower rates of use. Lifetime inhalant use in the DC MSA was slightly higher, and use of hallucinogens and nonmedical use of psychotherapeutic drugs slightly lower, than in large MSAs, as a whole.

Similar to rates of lifetime use, there also was little variation between the DC MSA and large MSAs for estimates of past year and past month use of illicit drugs and alcohol. Almost 12% of DC MSA residents used illicit drugs in the past year, compared with about 14% for large MSAs; comparable figures for past month illicit drug use were 5.7% for the DC MSA and 7.0% for large MSAs.

Like lifetime rates of alcohol use in the DC MSA, large MSAs, and the total United States, rates of past year and past month use also were highly similar, although there was somewhat greater variation than in

Table 3.3 Prevalence of Illicit Drug, Alcohol, and Tobacco Use in the DC MSA Household Population, Large Metropolitan Areas, and the Total U.S. Household Population

Substance Used	Lifetime			Past Year			Past Month		
	DC MSA	Large Metro Areas[1]	Total U.S.	DC MSA	Large Metro Areas	Total U.S.	DC MSA	Large Metro Areas	Total U.S.
Any illicit drug[2]	39.9	39.9	37.0	11.7	13.7	12.7	5.7	7.0	6.3
Marijuana/hashish	36.2	36.3	33.2	8.1	10.2	9.5	4.1	5.4	4.8
Any cocaine[3]	13.5	13.5	11.5	3.6	3.4	3.0	1.5	1.0	0.9
Crack cocaine	2.2	2.3	1.9	0.9	0.6	0.5	0.3	0.2	0.2
Inhalants	6.6	5.6	5.4	1.7	1.3	1.3	0.7	0.6	0.6
Hallucinogens	7.9	8.9	8.1	1.5	1.2	1.2	0.3	0.4	0.3
Heroin	1.7	1.5	1.3	0.4	0.3	0.2	0.3	0.1	*
Nonmedical use of any psychotherapeutics[4]	11.7	13.0	12.5	4.5	4.6	4.5	1.1	1.5	1.6
Any illicit drug except marijuana[5]	22.7	21.2	20.4	7.8	7.5	7.2	3.0	2.9	2.9
Any alcohol	84.6	86.2	84.6	73.5	72.1	68.0	55.9	55.7	50.9
Heavy alcohol[6]	—	—	—	—	—	—	4.2	5.5	5.3
Cigarettes	69.5	70.8	72.7	28.1	30.0	32.1	23.1	25.6	27.0

SOURCE: 1991 National Household Survey on Drug Abuse: DC MSA.

NOTE: Data entries are percentages. Unweighted numbers of respondents are given in Table 2.1, and the DC MSA is defined in Chapter 2.

1. Metropolitan statistical areas (MSAs) with a 1990 population of 1 million or more defined by the U.S. Bureau of Census, and including the DC MSA.

2. Use of marijuana or hashish, cocaine (including crack), inhalants, hallucinogens (including phencyclidine or PCP), heroin, or nonmedical use of psychotherapeutics at least once.

3. Includes crack cocaine.

4. Nonmedical use of any prescription-type stimulant, sedative, tranquilizer, or analgesic; does not include over-the-counter drugs.

5. Use of cocaine (including crack), inhalants, hallucinogens (including PCP), heroin, or nonmedical use of psychotherapeutics at least once.

6. Defined as drinking five or more drinks per occasion on 5 or more days in the past 30 days.

—Not applicable.

*Low precision.

the lifetime estimates. For example, any alcohol use was somewhat higher in the DC MSA and large MSAs than in the total United States for both past year and past month use, whereas heavy alcohol use was slightly lower in the DC MSA compared with large MSAs or the total United States. Cigarette use was slightly lower in the DC MSA than in other large MSAs for the past year and past month; rates were even higher for the total United States. This latter finding reflects the higher rates of cigarette smoking in nonmetropolitan areas.

3.3.3 Comparisons Within the DC MSA

A commonly held belief is that the drug problem is greater in inner cities than in the outlying suburbs, as well as among persons of lower SES relative to higher SES. The household data did not allow us to examine these issues in detail but did permit analyses that begin to approximate these different groups.

Although it was not possible to examine use in the inner city per se, it was possible to compare rates of use in different locations of the MSA. More specifically, rates of use in DC—the center city of the MSA—were compared with rates of use in the Maryland and Virginia suburban portions of the MSA. As shown in Table 3.4, rates of use of illicit drugs and cigarettes generally were higher in DC than in the Maryland or Virginia portions of the DC MSA. Rates of alcohol use were lower in DC than in other areas, whereas heavy alcohol use was highest in Virginia, slightly lower in DC, and lowest in Maryland. Not all the observed differences were statistically significant. Any illicit drug use, crack cocaine use, hallucinogen use, and cigarette use in the *past year* were higher in the District than in the Maryland portion of the MSA, while any alcohol use was higher in Maryland and Virginia than in the District. Fewer differences were found for past month use; crack cocaine use was higher in the District than in Maryland or Virginia, and cigarette use was higher in the District than in Maryland. These findings are consistent with the often found tendency of rates of illicit drug use to be higher in central cities than in outlying areas.

To address the relationship of low income areas to rates of drug use, low SES household members were compared with other SES household members. Low SES was defined as the third of population segments in the urbanized area of the DC MSA with the lowest housing value and

Table 3.4 Prevalence of Illicit Drug, Alcohol, and Tobacco Use in the Past Year and Past Month in the DC MSA Household Population, by Location

Substance Used	Past Year			Past Month		
	DC	Maryland	Virginia	DC	Maryland	Virginia
Any illicit drug[1]	16.9	10.5+	10.7	6.3	5.3	5.8
Marijuana/hashish	12.2	7.2	7.2	4.1	4.3	3.9
Any cocaine[2]	7.4	2.6	3.1	1.8	1.2	1.6
Crack cocaine	2.9	0.3+	0.7	1.2	0.2+	0.1+
Inhalants	2.4	1.4	1.6	1.1	0.3	0.9
Hallucinogens	3.3	0.7+	1.7	0.7	0.2	0.2
Heroin	0.4	*	*	0.1	*	*
Nonmedical use of any psychotherapeutics[3]	5.5	4.3	4.2	1.5	0.9	1.2
Any illicit drug except marijuana[4]	10.8	6.9	7.5	3.9	2.5	3.1
Any alcohol	61.4	73.9++	78.4+++	51.5	55.0	58.7
Heavy alcohol[5]	—	—	—	4.3	3.6	4.7
Cigarettes	32.7	23.3+	31.2	30.0	18.3+	25.1

SOURCE: 1991 National Household Survey on Drug Abuse: DC MSA.

NOTE: Data entries are percentages. Unweighted numbers of respondents are given in Table 2.1, and the DC MSA is defined in Chapter 2.

1. Use of marijuana or hashish, cocaine (including crack), inhalants, hallucinogens (including phencyclidine or PCP), heroin, or nonmedical use of psychotherapeutics at least once.

2. Includes crack cocaine.

3. Nonmedical use of any prescription-type stimulant, sedative, tranquilizer, or analgesic; does not include over-the-counter drugs.

4. Use of cocaine (including crack), inhalants, hallucinogens (including PCP), heroin, or nonmedical use of psychotherapeutics at least once.

5. Defined as drinking five or more drinks per occasion on 5 or more days in the past 30 days.

—Not applicable.

*Low precision.

+Difference between DC and Maryland or Virginia statistically significant at the .05 level.

++Difference between DC and Maryland or Virginia statistically significant at the .01 level.

+++Difference between DC and Maryland or Virginia statistically significant at the .001 level.

Table 3.5 Prevalence of Illicit Drug, Alcohol, and Tobacco Use in the
Past Year and Past Month in the DC MSA Household Population,
by Socioeconomic Status of Area

Substance Used	Past Year		Past Month	
	Low SES[1] Area	Other SES Area	Low SES Area	Other SES Area
Any illicit drug[2]	12.1	11.5	6.3	5.4
Marijuana/hashish	8.4	8.0	4.7	3.9
Any cocaine[3]	3.2	3.8	1.5	1.5
Crack cocaine	1.5	0.7	1.1	0.1++
Inhalants	1.4	1.7	0.6	0.7
Hallucinogens	1.5	1.5	0.4	0.2
Heroin	0.3	0.4	0.1	*
Nonmedical use of any psychotherapeutics[4]	4.1	4.6	1.4	1.0
Any illicit drug except marijuana[5]	7.1	8.1	3.0	3.0
Any alcohol	59.8	78.7+++	45.7	59.7+++
Heavy alcohol[6]	—	—	4.7	4.0
Cigarettes	29.9	27.4	25.1	22.3

SOURCE: 1991 National Household Survey on Drug Abuse: DC MSA.
NOTE: Data entries are percentages. The DC MSA is defined in Chapter 2.
1. Low socioeconomic status (SES) is defined as the third of population segments in the urbanized area of the DC MSA with the lowest housing value and rent. "Other SES" areas are the remaining areas within the DC MSA (including both urbanized and nonurbanized areas).
2. Use of marijuana or hashish, cocaine (including crack), inhalants, hallucinogens (including phencyclidine or PCP), heroin, or nonmedical use of psychotherapeutics at least once.
3. Includes crack cocaine.
4. Nonmedical use of any prescription-type stimulant, sedative, tranquilizer, or analgesic; does not include over-the-counter drugs.
5. Use of cocaine (including crack), inhalants, hallucinogens (including PCP), heroin, or nonmedical use of psychotherapeutics at least once.
6. Defined as drinking five or more drinks per occasion on 5 or more days in the past 30 days.
—Not applicable.
*Low precision.
++Difference between low SES and other SES statistically significant at the .01 level.
+++Difference between low SES and other SES statistically significant at the .001 level.

rent. Other SES comprised the remaining two thirds of the housing units. As shown in Table 3.5, any illicit drug use in the past year and past month tended to be higher in low SES areas, although differences were not statistically significant. Of the specific illicit drugs, however, past month crack cocaine use was significantly higher in the low SES areas than in the remainder of the DC MSA. In contrast, any alcohol use was significantly lower in the low SES area than in other areas within the DC MSA for both past year and past month time periods.

Table 3.6 Prevalence of Illicit Drug Use[1] in the Past Year and Past Month in the DC MSA Household Population, by Demographic Characteristics

Demographic Characteristic	Past Year	Past Month
Total	11.7	5.7
Sex		
Male	15.0	7.9
Female	8.6	3.6
Age (years)		
12-17	8.7	4.1
18-25	23.1	13.3
26-34	19.6	8.7
≥ 35	5.7	2.6
Race/ethnicity[2]		
White	12.7	5.7
Black	11.3	6.8
Hispanic	8.1	2.8
Marital status		
Single	20.3	11.5
Married	6.0	2.4
Widowed/divorced/separated	11.5	3.8
Adult education[3]		
Less than high school	8.5	4.7
High school	10.9	6.4
Some college	14.9	8.5
College graduate or higher	12.2	4.2

SOURCE: 1991 National Household Survey on Drug Abuse: DC MSA.
NOTE: Data entries are percentages.
1. Use of marijuana or hashish, cocaine (including crack), inhalants, hallucinogens (including phencyclidine or PCP), heroin, or nonmedical use of psychotherapeutics at least once.
2. The category "other" for race/ethnicity is not included.
3. Youth aged 12 to 17 ($n = 651$) were excluded from estimates of adult education.

3.3.4 Demographic Correlates of Use

Findings regarding the demographic correlates of illicit drug use in the DC MSA are similar to those of prior analyses of epidemiological data for household populations, as shown in Table 3.6. For both past year and past month use, rates of illicit drug use were about double among males compared with females, and substantially higher rates of use were found among young adults aged 18 to 25 compared with other age groups. Although past year rates of illicit drug use were slightly higher among whites than blacks, past month rates were slightly higher among blacks than whites. Rates of use among Hispanics were substantially lower than among whites or blacks. Single persons had by far the highest rates of use, several times the rates of use of married or widowed/divorced/separated persons. Past year and past month rates of use were highest among those with some college compared with those having other educational status.

3.4 Comparisons of Drug Use Among All Populations

Recall from Chapter 2 that one of the major contributions of the DC*MADS project is the examination of substance use and related problems among all populations in a metropolitan area during a common window of time. As a prelude to findings that will be examined in the following chapters of this book, this section contrasts prevalence rates of drug and alcohol use for each of the DC*MADS populations, both those from households and those not in households.

Table 3.7 presents prevalence data on illicit drug and alcohol use during the past year for each of the DC*MADS populations. As shown, some 11.7% of the household population reported illicit drug use during the past year, compared with more than 50% of the homeless and transient population and about half of the institutionalized, adult offender, and juvenile offender populations. Virtually all long-term residential and methadone treatment clients indicated that they had used illicit drugs in the past year, whereas only about three fourths of short-term residential clients reported such use. The lower levels of reported drug use among short-term residential clients may reflect the fact that many in these settings were alcohol abusers rather than illicit drug abusers. Any illicit drug use was lower among the new mothers (15.5%) than among the other subpopulations but still higher than among the household population as a whole. Findings of relative use of marijuana/hashish were similar to those for any illicit drug use.

Rates of any cocaine use and crack use were markedly higher among the homeless and transient, institutionalized, treatment, and adult offender populations compared with the household population, but rela-

Table 3.7 Prevalence of Illicit Drug and Alcohol Use During the Past Year for DC*MADS Populations

Substance Used	Household	Homeless and Transient	Institutionalized	Adult Offenders	Juvenile Offenders	Long-Term Residential Treatment Clients	Short-Term Residential Treatment Clients	Methadone Treatment Clients	New Mothers
Any illicit drug[1]	11.7	57.7	49.9	53.9	49.5	92.1	77.7	99.0	15.5[2]
Marijuana/hashish	8.1	37.5	31.7	28.0	48.2	51.9	38.4	34.5	7.7
Any cocaine[3]	3.6	48.4	36.9	39.3	6.7	87.0	54.5	84.3	11.5
Crack cocaine	0.9	44.8	30.4	28.3	2.6	80.0	52.8	53.4	—
Inhalants	1.7	2.1	3.4	0.6	4.0	1.7	1.4	0.0	—
Hallucinogens	1.5	6.3	11.1	8.7	9.6	25.5	16.9	5.5	—
Heroin	0.4	9.2	12.7	15.9	0.4	17.1	16.5	97.0	1.4
Nonmedical use of any psychotherapeutics[4]	4.5	11.9	8.6	4.6	4.5	20.4	23.5	37.4	1.5
Any illicit drug except marijuana[5]	7.8	52.3	41.4	43.7	15.4	89.7	72.7	99.0	12.2
Any alcohol	73.5	85.6	67.2	70.0	72.3	90.8	93.9	88.3	37.7

SOURCE: Washington, DC, Metropolitan Area Drug Study (DC*MADS): 1989-1995.
NOTE: Data entries are percentages. Unweighted numbers of respondents are shown in Table 2.1.
1. Use of marijuana or hashish, cocaine (including crack), inhalants, hallucinogens (including phencyclidine or PCP), heroin, or nonmedical use of psychotherapeutics at least once.
2. Use of marijuana or hashish, cocaine (including crack), heroin, or nonmedical use of psychotherapeutics at least once; does not include use of methamphetamine, inhalants, or hallucinogens (including PCP).
3. Includes crack cocaine.
4. Nonmedical use of any prescription-type stimulant, sedative, tranquilizer, or analgesic; does not include over-the-counter drugs.
5. Use of cocaine (including crack), inhalants, hallucinogens (including PCP), heroin, or nonmedical use of psychotherapeutics at least once.
—Not applicable.

74

tively few juvenile offenders used either drug. For example, almost 90% of long-term residential clients, 60% of short-term residential clients, 50% of the homeless and transient population, and about 40% of institutionalized persons used any cocaine in the past year, compared with about 4% of the household population. Only 11.5% of new mothers, however, had used any cocaine in the past year. Inspection of individual drugs for each population indicates that marijuana/hashish was the preferred drug for the household population and juvenile offenders, but cocaine (and crack cocaine) was the drug of choice for all other populations. This suggests that the types of users in these populations may differ on a number of dimensions and that their drug use may vary both quantitatively and qualitatively.

As with cocaine and crack cocaine, use of hallucinogens was notably high among all populations except the household population; it was particularly high among long-term (25.5%) and short-term (16.9%) residential clients. Inhalants, a drug more commonly used by youth, was used more by juvenile offenders (4%) and institutionalized persons (3.4%) than by other groups.

Heroin use appeared to be resurging, after a decline during the 1980s (SAMHSA, 1997). Although heroin use was negligible among the household population and among juvenile offenders, it was not uncommon among the other populations studied here. Virtually all methadone treatment clients reported past year heroin use; those who did not may have underreported use or may have been in treatment during the prior year and were not using at that time. More than 10% of the institutionalized population, adult offenders, and long-term and short-term residential clients used heroin in the past year. Relatively few new mothers reported heroin use, about 1%.

Nonmedical use of psychotherapeutic drugs was highest among methadone clients (37%), followed by short-term (24%) and long-term (20%) residential clients. Adult and juvenile offenders reported rates of about 4.5% that were comparable to that of the household population. Homeless and transient and institutionalized populations showed rates that were roughly double those of the household population.

Alcohol use was common among all groups, with rates of past year use generally ranging from about 70% to about 90%. Rates of use were notably lower among new mothers (38%), but this is to be expected in view of known problems that alcohol can cause during pregnancy.

Comparison of the rates of use across these populations is informative concerning the magnitude of the problem among both household and nonhousehold populations. The notably higher rates of use among the nonhousehold populations relative to the household population suggest that household estimates may be insufficient to describe drug use in the total population of an area. Care must be taken in making comparisons across household and nonhousehold populations because the demographic composition of the populations differs substantially and potentially could explain higher rates of drug and alcohol use among the nonhousehold populations. For example, the homeless and institutionalized populations were largely male, and higher rates of use generally are found among males. Despite this qualification, examination of rates of use in various populations is informative about where rates of use are highest and where treatment services should be targeted.

3.5 Targeting Drug Abuse Treatment and Prevention Services

Although the DC MSA household population constituted the largest proportion of the total population, rates of illicit drug use and alcohol use were found to be much higher among nonhousehold populations. As noted above, for many measures of illicit drug and alcohol use, half or more of nonhousehold populations reported use in the past year. These findings suggest that estimates of use in the household population alone may underestimate the extent of use in the total population. Rates that reflect use in household as well as nonhousehold populations may be more meaningful. As part of the DC*MADS project, composite estimates of use were calculated by merging data from the household population, the homeless and transient population, and the institutionalized population. These combined estimates provide a relatively complete picture of the size of the drug-abusing population in the DC MSA and are described in more detail in Chapter 9.

The substantially higher rates of use in nonhousehold populations compared with the household population suggests that drug abuse intervention, treatment, and prevention services may need to be targeted more heavily to nonhousehold populations. As noted above (see Table

3.7), rates of past year illicit drug use in nonhousehold populations ranged from about 50% to almost 100%. These rates compare with the 11.7% of household residents and the 15.5% of new mothers who reported past year use. As shown in later chapters, these higher rates of use among nonhousehold populations also were indicative of multiple substance use and, for many, comorbid alcohol, mental health, and physical health problems. Furthermore, these problems also were related to patterns of illegal activity, unemployment, income, and service utilization. All of this points to a substantial need for a broad range of services among nonhousehold populations.

As shown in Chapter 1, despite the relatively low overall rate of drug use in the household population, there were some subgroups of household residents who were heavy users of drugs. In addition, as discussed in the following chapters, nonhousehold populations are drawn from the household population, and drug use may be a contributing factor to becoming homeless or institutionalized. Thus, prevention and intervention services also are needed within the household population and should be targeted to high-risk groups to decrease the likelihood of drug use and associated adverse effects.

References

Anglin, M. D., & Speckart, G. (1986). Narcotics use, property crime, and dealing: Structural dynamics across the addiction career. *Journal of Quantitative Criminology, 2*, 355-375.

Appendix A: Drug Use Among the Household Population. (1998). (Available on the World Wide Web at http://www.sagepub.com/bray_druguse.htm)

Barton, W. I. (1982). Drug histories and criminality of inmates of local jails in the United States: Implications for treatment and rehabilitation of the drug abuser in a jail setting. *International Journal of the Addictions, 17*, 414-444.

Beck, A. J., Gilliard, D., Greenfield, L., Harlow, C., Hester, T., Jankowski, L., Snell, T., & Stephan, J. (1993). *Survey of state prison inmates, 1991* (BJS Special Report, NCJ 136949). Washington, DC: Bureau of Justice Statistics.

Davidson, D. (1991). *A snap shot survey of hard to serve homeless clients in Northern Virginia.* Fairfax, VA: Northern Virginia Coalition for the Homeless.

Fischer, P. J. (1989). Estimating the prevalence of alcohol, drug and mental health problems in the contemporary homeless population: A review of the literature. *Contemporary Drug Problems: An Interdisciplinary Quarterly, 16*, 333-390.

Harlow, C. W. (1992). *Drug enforcement and treatment in prisons, 1990* (NCJ 134724). Washington, DC: Bureau of Justice Statistics.

Interagency Council on the Homeless. (1991). *The 1990 annual report of the Interagency Council on the Homeless.* Washington, DC: Author.

Johnson, T. P., & Barrett, M. E. (1991). *Homelessness and substance use in Cook County* (prepared for Department of Alcoholism and Drug Abuse, State of Illinois). Urbana: University of Illinois, Survey Research Laboratory.

Mayfield, D. (1985). Substance abuse in the affective disorders. In A. Alterman (Ed.), *Psychopathology and substance abuse* (pp. 69-90). New York: Plenum.

Milburn, N. G., Booth, J. A., & Miles, S. E. (1990). *Correlates of drug and alcohol abuse among homeless adults in shelters* (final report). Washington, DC: Howard University, Institute for Urban Affairs and Research.

Miller, N. S., & Gold, M. S. (1991). Dual diagnoses: Psychiatric syndromes in alcoholism and drug addiction. *American Family Physician, 43*(6), 51-56.

National Institute on Drug Abuse. (1994). *Prevalence of drug use in the DC metropolitan area household and nonhousehold populations: 1991* (Technical Report #8 under NIDA Contract No. 271-89-8340, Washington, DC, Metropolitan Area Drug Study, prepared by R. M. Bray, L. A. Kroutil, S. C. Wheeless, M. E. Marsden, & L. E. Packer, Research Triangle Institute). Rockville, MD: Author.

O'Sullivan, K. (1984). Depression and its treatment in alcoholics: A review. *Canadian Journal of Psychiatry, 29*, 289-384.

Spinner, G. F., & Leaf, P. J. (1992). Homelessness and drug abuse in New Haven. *Hospital and Community Psychiatry, 43*, 166-168.

Substance Abuse and Mental Health Services Administration. (1993). *National Household Survey on Drug Abuse: Main findings 1991* (DHHS Publication No. SMA 93-1980). Rockville, MD: Author.

Substance Abuse and Mental Health Services Administration. (1995). *National Household Survey on Drug Abuse: Main findings 1993* (DHHS Publication No. SMA 95-3020). Rockville, MD: Author.

Substance Abuse and Mental Health Services Administration. (1996, September). *Substance abuse in states and metropolitan areas: Model based estimates from the 1991-1993 National Household Surveys on Drug Abuse. Summary report.* (DHHS Publication No. SMA 96-3095). Rockville, MD: Author.

Substance Abuse and Mental Health Services Administration. (1997). *Preliminary results from the 1996 National Household Survey on Drug Abuse* (DHHS Publication No. SMA 97-3149). Rockville, MD: Author.

U.S. General Accounting Office. (1993). *Drug use measurement: Strengths, limitations, and recommendations for improvement* (Report prepared for the Chairman, Committee on Government Operations, U.S. House of Representatives, GAO/PEMD-93-18). Washington, DC: Author.

U.S. Senate. (1990). *Hard-core cocaine addicts: Measuring and fighting the epidemic* (S. Rep. No. 6, 101st Cong., May 10, Committee on Judiciary). Washington, DC: Government Printing Office.

Weisner, C., Schmidt, L., & Tam, T. (1995). Assessing bias in community-based prevalence estimates: Towards an unduplicated count of problem drinkers and drug users. *Addiction, 90*, 391-405.

The White House. (1992). *National drug control strategy: A nation responds to drug use.* Washington, DC: Office of National Drug Control Policy, Executive Office of the President.

Zawitz, M. W. (Ed.). (1992). *Drugs, crime, and the justice system: A national report* (NCJ 133652). Washington, DC: U.S. Department of Justice, Office of Justice Programs, Bureau of Justice Statistics.

Drug Use and Homelessness

Michael L. Dennis
Robert M. Bray
Ronaldo Iachan
Jutta Thornberry

D rug use has been identified as one of the antecedents of home-lessness and is common among people who are homeless; moreover, as shown in this chapter and in the authors' final report from which the data have been drawn (National Institute on Drug Abuse [NIDA], 1993), drug use is one of the major risk factors for predicting who will repeatedly experience homelessness. Throughout the 1980s and early 1990s, the problems of homelessness and associated drug use increased dramatically across the nation and were especially visible in major urban areas (Interagency Council on the Homeless, 1991, 1994). Washington, DC, the nation's capital and the center city for DC*MADS, experienced a notably sharp increase in its homeless population during that time period. The 1990 census showed that although Washington, DC, was only the 19th largest city in the United States (1990 population of about 606,900 people), it had the fourth largest shelter population and the highest rate of shelter residents per capita (72.81 per 10,000) (U.S. Bureau of the Census, 1992). The rise in the number of homeless people has presented challenges in Washington, DC, and other large metropolitan areas in understanding the size of the homeless population, the nature and extent of substance abuse and related problems they experience, and the types of services they need.

This chapter presents findings from the DC*MADS Homeless and Transient Population Study addressing three broad issues: (a) the methodological issues important to surveying the homeless population, (b) the prevalence and correlates of substance use among homeless people, and (c) the co-occurrence of substance use and other problems. It also examines the relationship of problems associated with drug and alcohol use and need for services.

4.1 Multiple Faces of Homelessness

To set the stage for the present study, we examine the concept and changing definitions of homelessness that have been used over the past several decades. We also review prior research on substance use among homeless people and identify reasons for noted variation in prevalence rates.

4.1.1 Concept and Definitions of Homelessness

For most of the 20th century, the concept of "homelessness" was largely related to people who were very poor and disassociated from mainstream society (Dennis, 1991; Hopper, 1991; Rossi, 1989). The term "homeless" came into widespread use in the early 1980s in part to avoid the use of derogatory terms such as "alcoholic," "bum," "drunk," "hobo," "transient," and "vagabond" when referring to this subpopulation.

As more data have been gathered about homeless people and as their numbers have increased, it has become apparent that homeless people are a diverse group in terms of demographic characteristics and family circumstances. Homelessness crosses age, gender, and racial/ ethnic lines, although some demographic subgroups are at greater risk of homelessness than others. Homeless people include both single and married individuals; men, women, and children; younger and older persons; and people of black, white, and Hispanic races/ethnicities (Burt & Cohen, 1989). They also are characterized by a variety of family circumstances, including persons living as individuals, couples, male- and female-headed single-parent families, and dual-parent families (Institute of Medicine [IOM], 1988). Indeed, it appears that homelessness has many faces, and those affected by it go well beyond the traditional stereotype of the "skid row bum."

Information about homeless people depends in part on the way they are defined, and over time definitions of homelessness have shifted. Early definitions, prior to 1980, emphasized detachment from traditional family living arrangements as the distinguishing feature of homelessness (Burt, 1992). Persons living alone in so-called skid row hotels, for example, were considered homeless by virtue of their detached family configuration even though they typically had shelter that they paid for and rarely spent nights on the street. The U.S. Bureau of the Census used this definition based on detachment as late as 1960 (Burt, 1992).

Beginning in the mid-1980s, definitions of homelessness shifted to literal ones that emphasized an immediate lack of housing. Only those who slept in nondomiciles (e.g., streets, encampments, vacant buildings) or emergency shelters were considered homeless based on this definition. A methodological advantage of this literal definition was that the universe of homeless persons could be quantified readily by examining where people slept on a given night (Rossi, 1989). Two landmark studies that spurred the use of this literal definition of homelessness were conducted by Rossi, Fischer, and Willis (1986) in Chicago for the Robert Wood Johnson Foundation and by Burt and Cohen (1989) in a national study of soup kitchen and shelter users for the national Food and Nutrition Service.

The literal definition of homelessness also has disadvantages, however. The first is that the line between people who are literally homeless and those who are precariously housed is thin and easily crossed (Bassuk et al., 1996; Rossi, 1989). Consequently, a literal point-in-time definition often excludes people who may be of interest, such as those who reside in low-cost housing, share accommodations designed for one person ("doubled up"), or live in substandard housing. Second, this definition may exclude people who use homeless services and are eligible for assistance under the 1987 Stewart B. McKinney Homeless Assistance Act (Dennis, 1991; James, 1991). Along these lines, it excludes people who are making the transition out of homelessness to single-room occupancy (SRO) hotels and halfway houses even though these people also remain eligible for assistance and once were part of the layperson's concept of homelessness. Third, the episodic nature of homelessness can make broader definitions more useful for clinicians and program planners. In a study of emergency psychiatric admissions, for example, Santiago, Bachrach, Berren, and Hannah (1988) found that changing their definition from "currently homeless" to "homeless in the last three months" increased the number of people identified as homeless by 50% (from 106 to 159). Furthermore, the group added under the expanded definition was at risk of becoming homeless again and may have been in need of aftercare services. They also would have been eligible for assistance under most programs for homeless people.

In the 1990s, therefore, it became increasingly common to expand the definition of homelessness to include people who were making the transition into or out of homelessness (Dennis, 1991; Dennis & Iachan, 1992; Etheridge, Dennis, Lubalin, & Schlenger, 1989; Huebner & Crosse, 1991; James, 1991; Taeuber & Siegel, 1991). This transitional population is marginally or precariously housed and is composed of many who have histories of homelessness. Its members are identified by (a) use of soup kitchens, health care clinics, and outreach programs for homeless people, or (b) pending departure from an institution (e.g., hospital, jail) with no resources or place to go. As discussed later in this chapter, the group of people who cycle in and out of homelessness also appear to cycle in and out of alcohol and drug use.

Although the broader definition of homelessness holds promise for better understanding the service needs of homeless people, it also poses methodological challenges of how to easily identify, locate, and interview members of this population. Field trials being conducted for the homeless and transient component of the 2000 census are currently evaluating ways of reaching this more broadly defined population (Burt, 1996).

4.1.2 Substance Use Among Homeless People

Substance use is recognized as a major problem, by one estimate affecting about one third of the people who are homeless (Interagency Council on the Homeless, 1991). There has, however, been considerable variation in the rates of substance use reported across studies. In an early review of 80 studies, Fischer (1989) found that the estimated rates of drug *use* ranged from 1% to 90%. Studies on homelessness and substance use undertaken since Fischer's review continue to show considerable variability in rates.

Milburn, Booth, and Miles (1990) found that, in a random sample of shelter residents in DC, 60% reported lifetime illicit drug use, 35% past year use, and 24% past month use. Johnson and Barrett (1991) observed similar results. In a sample of shelter, soup kitchen, and SRO hotel users in Illinois, 60% reported lifetime use of illicit drugs, 35% reported past year use, and 20% reported past month use. In contrast, Spinner and Leaf (1992) found higher rates. In a sample of Connecticut shelter residents, 54% reported using drugs in the past month and 7% identified alcoholism or drug use as the major reason they were homeless. Similarly, Davidson (1991) found that the combined rate of substance abuse, mental illness, and mental retardation was 67% among people served by nine shelters in northern Virginia but reached 96% among those who were on the shelters' "do not admit" list on the same day.

Considerable variation was found by the New York City Commission on the Homeless (1992). It found that self-reported drug or alcohol use ranged from 3% among the women in single shelters to 12% among the men in single shelters. Urine tests with a smaller sample of volunteers, however, were 30% to 80% positive for illicit drugs. Drug use was highest in the barracks-style types of shelters and lowest in specialized shelters, such as those designed for women and children. In an earlier study in New York City, Susser, Struening, and Conover (1989) found that 38% of the men entering shelters for the first time had used a drug, other than marijuana, 50 or more times.

Gelberg and Linn (1989) found that, in a purposive sample of shelter and street people in Los Angeles, 50% were current users of illicit drugs. A related study in Los Angeles by Koegel, Burnam, and Farr (1990) found that 66% of homeless people from shelter and soup kitchen samples had problems with mental illness, substance abuse, or both and that they appeared as likely to spend time in the streets as in shelters. Similarly, a California study in Alameda County, home to the city of Oakland, found that more than two thirds of the sample of homeless adults had a lifetime history of substance use (Robertson, Zlotnick, & Westerfelt, 1997) and half of them had a current substance abuse problem.

A study by Greene, Ennett, and Ringwalt (1997) focused on a special subset of the homeless population—runaway and homeless youth. Using a nationally representative shelter sample and a purposive street sample, these investigators found that past month use of marijuana or other illicit drugs was highest among youth living on the street (78%), although youth living in shelters also showed relatively high prevalence rates (57%). The latter group was similar to those with recent runaway or homeless experience (48%). All three groups had substantially higher rates than comparable youth in the household population (29%).

A meta-analysis that focused on six studies with rigorous sampling and diagnostic-level measurement (Lehman & Cordray, 1993) found that the estimated rate of alcohol use *disorders* (i.e., abuse, dependence) ranged from 26% to 67%, and that the rate of other drug disorders ranged from 11% to 48%. Their best estimate of the true 95% confidence intervals using variance weighting, however, was considerably smaller for both alcohol use disorders (46% to 49%) and other substance use disorders (29% to 31%).

As shown in the preceding summary, drug use varies widely across geographic areas, institutions, and homeless population subgroups. It is important to note that this variation is *not* a result of measurement error. Indeed, the reliability of self-reported substance use among homeless people is generally high in terms of test-retest item correlations (e.g., .81 to .99), internal consistency on common scales (e.g., .70 to .96), and interclass correlation of scale scores (.83 to .92) (Calsyn, Allen, Morse, Smith, & Tempelhoff, 1993; Drake, McHugo, & Biesanz, 1995; Weatherby et al., 1994a, 1994b; Zanis, McLellan, Cnaan, & Randall, 1994). Instead, most of the variation in the estimates can be traced to differences across studies in definitions of homelessness (e.g., narrow vs. broad), variations in types of sampling locations (e.g., shelters, streets, soup kitchens), eligibility criteria (e.g., some studies used shelters that tried to exclude drug users), type of assessment (e.g., an emphasis on problems, abuse or dependence), and the time periods and/or range of substances considered.

4.2 Overview of the Study

The DC*MADS Homeless and Transient Population Study was based on and provided a replication of Rossi's classic study of homeless people in Chicago (Rossi, 1989; Rossi et al., 1986). The research was designed to develop estimates of drug use and characteristics of the homeless and transient population in the DC metropolitan statistical area (MSA) on an "average" day between February and June 1991. The initial design included two independent samples of shelters and census street blocks for the winter (February to March) and spring (April to May). Within each seasonal sample, units were randomly assigned to one of the 2-month periods, clustered geographically (half in the center of the MSA and half farther out), then randomly assigned as a cluster to randomly sampled days in the month.

Over the first 3 months of data collection, problems arose with the street component that resulted in a change in the study design. Problems included risks to the safety of interviewers, difficulty in finding eligible respondents, and resulting low numbers of completed interviews. Data collection was suspended in May 1991 to revise and implement an alternative sampling design in June that would address these problems. Design modifications included replacing the street sample with an encampment sample and a soup kitchen sample. These changes also were designed to make the study more compatible with a national study that the Urban Institute and Research Triangle Institute (RTI) conducted for the Food and Nutrition Service (Burt, 1992; Burt & Cohen, 1988, 1989), the Rand Corporation's work in California (Burnam, Koegel, & Duan, 1990; Koegel, Burnam, & Farr, 1990; Vernez, Burnam, McGlynn, & Mittman, 1988), RTI's national study for the Administration on Children, Youth and Families (Ringwalt & Iachan, 1990), and the 1990 Census S-night (Taeuber & Siegel, 1991).

Findings for the Homeless and Transient Population Study are based on 908 in-person interviews conducted anonymously from four overlapping sampling frames. These included (a) 477 interviews with residents in 93 shelters, (b) 224 interviews with patrons of 31 soup kitchens and food banks, (c) 143 interviews with literally homeless people from 18 major clusters of encampments, and (d) 64 interviews with literally homeless people on the street from an area probability sample of census blocks in the DC MSA.

Interview responses were weighted and adjusted for nonresponse and overlap among sample frames. The institutional response rate for shelters and soup kitchens combined was 82.6%. The response rate for eligible individuals across the four frames was 86.1%. More detailed information on the methodology and results are available in the authors' final report (NIDA, 1993), in Appendix B (1998), and in related methodological articles (Dennis & Iachan, 1992; Iachan & Dennis, 1993).

4.3 Population Size and Characteristics

Two key pieces of information that have been the subject of considerable debate and concern to researchers, planners, and service providers are the size and defining characteristics of the homeless population. Other research discussed above (Section 4.1) suggests that these characteristics may vary considerably both among and within metropolitan areas. The data below examine these issues for the DC MSA and identify a number of features that help explain some of the variation across areas and suggest key measures that should be gathered in studies of homeless populations.

4.3.1 Size of the Homeless Population

A national study by Link and colleagues (1994) suggests that 14% of the U.S. population, or about 26 million people, may have experienced homelessness in their lifetime. Despite this estimate, there has been considerable controversy during the 1980s and 1990s about the size of the homeless population, and large discrepancies exist in estimates of its size. Perhaps this should not be surprising given that counting homeless people is extremely difficult; conventional models of enumerating persons are based on counting people where they live, but homeless people often are hard to find (IOM, 1988). As with studies of drug use prevalence discussed above, variation in counts of homeless people in large measure reflects methodological differences in definitions of homelessness, the types of locations included in the samples, and the focus in the studies on counting unique individuals or person-service contacts.

The sampling approach used in the Homeless and Transient Population Study illustrates how the definition of homelessness affects population estimates. Recall that this study included people who were literally homeless (i.e., in shelters, in encampments, or on the street) or who were using emergency food banks and soup kitchens. Of the estimated 10,387 people who met the definition of homeless or transient on an average day, 80% (8,356 people) reported being "literally" homeless during the 24 hours preceding the interview and 20% (2,031 people) did not. Both types of people were counted as homeless, however, because 93% reported a lifetime history of being homeless (including 47% with multiple episodes), 99% had used any homeless/emergency services (including 98% in the past month), and 85% had used emergency housing (including 71% in the past month). This was also consistent from a policy and program planning perspective because these people were presenting for services, eligible for services (because they were at high risk), and using services. If the definition had focused just on those who were literally homeless, the population counts would have been reduced by 20%.

The types of locations included in the sample also can alter estimates of the number of homeless people. Shelters and streets may suffice as sampling locations for identifying people who are literally homeless, but concentrating on only those two sites misses persons who fit a broader definition of homelessness. Indeed, shelters and street samples alone would have missed 28% of the people in the DC*MADS Homeless and Transient Population Study (NIDA, 1993) and half of the people surveyed in Chicago during the mid-1980s (Sossin, Colson, & Grossman, 1988). It is important to note that despite recent advances, the methodology for enumerating people on the street is very limited, and people do actively hide while sleeping on the street—largely from others in their environment who might rob or hurt them or forcibly remove them from private property. In fact, we observed a classic "watering hole" phenomenon in which the estimated number of people sleeping on the street who used shelters or soup kitchens was larger when measured from the service location than when measured directly by trying to find them on the street at night (Iachan & Dennis, 1993).

Finally, a closely related issue that influences estimates of the homeless and transient population is whether the study counts unique individuals or person-service contacts and takes into account the overlap that occurs across sites. In DC*MADS, of the estimated 10,387 homeless people, 56.3% used shelters for at least part of the night, 65.2% visited at least one soup kitchen or food bank mobile unit, 20.5% spent at least part of the early morning hours (4:00 to 5:30 a.m.) on the street or in a non-domicile (e.g., vacant building, under a bridge, in a park), and 1.7% were in an encampment cluster (Iachan & Dennis, 1993). The sum of the population counts from these sites reflects the number of service-provider contacts, but because some people visit more than one location, it overestimates the number of unique individuals. Without adjusting for the overlap, the estimate of the homeless population in the DC MSA would have increased by 42%, from 10,387 unique people to 14,744 person-contacts.

This finding is important for two reasons. First, in contrast to researchers, service providers often use the number of person-contacts when estimating need for services (e.g., someone who needs both a shelter bed and food from a soup kitchen consumes two service slots). Studies, therefore, need to be more specific about whether they are reporting counts of individuals or service contacts and preferably report both. Second, although several studies have tried to use a 1-day survey blitz to minimize duplicated counts of homeless people, DC*MADS data suggest that such an approach yields overestimations of the number of homeless people.

To date, the largest effort to enumerate people who might be homeless was the U.S. Bureau of the Census 1990 effort to count the number of people in emergency housing and on the streets who "looked homeless" (U.S. Bureau of the Census, 1992). Using shelters and a purposively selected set of street locations, the census used a 1-day blitz to cover the entire service system. The 1-day effort was a monumental undertaking and in the DC MSA included 10 times as many street locations as were examined in our study in 4 months. A comparison of census data and DC*MADS data showed that census estimates of DC shelter populations (6,541 residents) were within the 95% confidence interval of the

DC*MADS estimate (i.e., 4,964 to 6,724), but the census estimates of the street population were significantly lower than those estimated in DC*MADS (345 vs. 2,129 people) (Dennis, 1993; U.S. Bureau of the Census, 1992). Special analyses conducted for the 2000 census suggest that, had the census dropped its street component (which consumed most of its resources), added coverage of other emergency services (e.g., soup kitchens, outreach programs), and extended collection from 1 to 30 days, the cost would have been reduced, more people would have been covered, and the census would have located 97.7% of all homeless and transient people (Dennis & Iachan, 1992; Iachan & Dennis, 1993). Attempts to replicate these analyses in other geographic areas, however, met with mixed results (e.g., Koegel, Burnam, & Morton, 1996) and led to a national field trial of this approach (Burt, 1996).

4.3.2 Characteristics of the Homeless and Transient Population

Table 4.1 presents demographic characteristics for each of the four sample frames used in the study. Responses reflect 477 interviews in shelters, 224 in soup kitchens, 143 in encampment clusters, and 64 in the street. As shown, homeless and transient persons in the sample were predominantly male (76%), black (76%), and single (60%); they most often had a high school education or less (79%) and were likely to be unemployed (54%). Table 4.1 also makes it clear that to grasp the full range of homeless people's characteristics, studies must sample from multiple types of locations (e.g., shelters, soup kitchens, streets); studies limited to a single type of location are likely to underrepresent certain subgroups of homeless people and yield biased results for policymakers and program planners (Dennis & Iachan, 1991; Iachan & Dennis, 1991). As shown, men were more likely to be found in encampments, street locations, or soup kitchens than in shelters, whereas women were more likely to be found in shelters than in soup kitchens, in encampments, or on the street. Although about half of the total homeless population was at least 35 years old, nearly two thirds of the people found in encampments were aged 35 or older. Some 60% of the entire homeless population was single, compared with more than 75% among those living on the streets. Although only about 1 in 4 persons in soup kitchens or shelters

Table 4.1 Demographic Characteristics of the DC MSA Homeless and Transient Population, by Sample Location

Demographic Characteristic[1]	Shelter	Soup Kitchen	Encampment Cluster	Street	Total[2]
Sex					
Male	64.8	86.3	87.7	86.5*	75.9
Female	35.2	13.7	12.3	13.5*	24.1
Age group (years)					
12-25	17.0	13.0	6.6	17.2*	15.0
26-34	35.3	36.2	31.8	44.8*	36.8
≥ 35	47.7	50.8	61.6	38.0*	48.2
Race/ethnicity[3]					
White	15.2	16.6	25.3	5.6*	16.5
Black	76.5	77.9	65.4	84.1*	75.8
Hispanic	7.4	4.6	4.0	0.8*	5.9
Marital status					
Single	55.8	57.1	55.0	75.5*	59.7
Married	8.6	8.6	11.8	1.3*	8.3
Divorced/widowed	35.6	34.3	33.2	23.3*	32.1
Location[4]					
DC	74.4	69.6*	91.6	88.7*	71.0
Maryland	8.6	17.1*	2.1	9.4*	14.0
Virginia	17.0	13.3*	6.3	1.8	15.0
Adult education[5,6]					
Less than high school	32.9	45.4	36.0	48.6*	40.1
High school graduate	42.3	36.2	38.2	41.3*	39.3
Any college	24.8	18.4	25.8	10.1*	20.6
Current employment[6]					
Full-time	24.0	24.0	11.5	6.4*	21.5
Part-time	14.5	11.7	14.0	4.9*	12.2
Unemployed	41.1	58.9	53.6	82.5*	54.1
Other[7]	20.4	5.4	20.9	6.2*	12.2
Total population[8]	56.3	65.2	1.7	20.5	100.0
Population estimate[8]	5,844	6,771	174	2,129	10,387

SOURCE: Washington, DC, Metropolitan Area Drug Study (DC*MADS): 1989-1995.
1. Except for population estimates, data entries are percentages.
2. Percentage adjusted for multiplicity between samples.
3. The category "other" for race/ethnicity is not shown because there were too few cases (n = 39).
4. The District of Columbia metropolitan statistical area (DC MSA) includes the District of Columbia; the Maryland counties of Calvert, Charles, Frederick, Montgomery, and Prince Georges; the Virginia counties of Arlington, Fairfax, Loudoun, Prince William, and Stafford; and the Virginia cities of Alexandria, Fairfax, Falls Church, Manassas, and Manassas Park.
5. As with the National Household Survey on Drug Abuse (NHSDA), general equivalency diplomas (GEDs) are not considered in this measure.
6. Persons aged 12 to 17 (n = 13) are excluded from the estimates of adult education and current employment.
7. Retired, disabled, homemaker, student, or "other."
8. Columns are not mutually exclusive for population estimates, which are based on all available data. Encampments are a subset of the street frame. Because of the two- and three-way overlap in the sampling frames, the unadjusted shelter, soup kitchen, and street columns add up to 14,744 person-contacts.
*Low precision.

was likely to be employed full-time, this was true for only about 1 in 16 persons from the street.

Within the DC MSA, there also were some important geographic differences. Most homeless persons were located in DC (71%), with the remainder evenly split between the Maryland and Virginia portions of the MSA. Compared with census estimates for U.S. shelters, homeless people in the DC MSA's shelters were more likely to be male, older, and black, and to have at least a high school education (Barrett, Anolik, & Abramson, 1992).

As shown earlier in Chapter 2 (see Table 2.2), there were also notable differences between the demographic characteristics of the homeless and transient population and the household population. Relative to the household population, homeless and transient people were twice as likely to be divorced or widowed (32% vs. 16%), over 2.5 times as likely to be black (76% vs. 27%) and have less than a high school education (40% vs. 13%), and 4 times as likely to be from DC (71% vs. 18%).

As with demographics, clinical subgroups relevant to program planning also vary by sampling location. Figure 4.1 summarizes the estimated percentage of people in each sampling location who can be classified into the target groups of the two largest relevant federal assistance programs, the 1987 Stewart B. McKinney Homeless Assistance Act and the more recent Shelter Plus Care Program. (Table B.1 in Appendix B [1998] provides the supplementary data used to prepare Figure 4.1.) Overall, 99% of the homeless and transient population fell into one or more of the main target groups, including major physical illness in the past year (70%), heavy alcohol use in the past month (28%), any drug use in the past month (34%), lifetime history of mental illness (28%), currently unemployed (54%), veteran (22%), youth aged 12 to 21 (5%), and/or families of two or more people with one or more minors (23%).

As shown in Figure 4.1, people who were physically ill were more likely to be found in shelters or on the street than in soup kitchens. Heavy drinking was more common among people sampled from street and encampment locations than those from soup kitchens or shelters. Drug use was more common among people sampled from soup kitchens and encampment locations than among those in street or shelter locations. Rates of mental illness varied only slightly by location. Rates of unemployment were twice as high among people on the street as those in

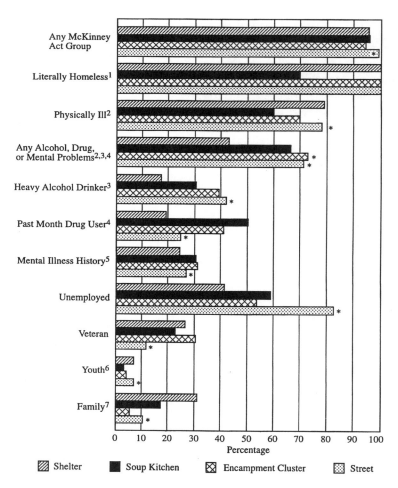

Figure 4.1. Classification of DC MSA Homeless and Transient Population Into McKinney Act Groups, by Location

SOURCE: Washington, DC, Metropolitan Area Drug Study (DC*MADS): 1989-1995.

NOTE: See Table B.1 in Appendix B (1998) for supplementary data used to prepare this figure.

1. Spending the night in an emergency shelter or a nondomicile or having no regular place to stay.

2. One or more major physical problems requiring a doctor's attention in the past year.

3. Having five or more drinks per day on 5 or more days in the past month (or the prorated equivalent while homeless).

4. Use of marijuana or hashish, cocaine (including crack), inhalants, hallucinogens (including phencyclidine or PCP), or heroin, or nonmedical use of psychotherapeutics at least once.

5. Lifetime history of inpatient, outpatient, or pharmacological treatment for psychological or emotional problems.

6. Persons 12 to 21 years old according to the McKinney Act definition.

7. People who regularly live in groups of two or more, provide support for themselves and at least one other person, and who have one or more minor children under age 18.

*Low precision.

shelters. Veterans were three times as common in outdoor encampments than on the street. Youth aged 12 to 21 were more likely to be found on the street or in shelters and least likely to be in soup kitchens. People in family groups were more common in shelters and less common on the street or in outdoor encampments.

These data clearly show that findings and conclusions about homeless people are sensitive to the sampling frames included in the study; failure to include some frames may introduce bias in the results. In judging the impact of potential biases, it is essential to consider both the frame involved and its relative size. A frame that is relatively small typically has less bias potential than does a larger frame. For example, although the *percentage* of veterans was somewhat higher in encampments than in shelters (30.3% vs. 26.5%), the *counts* of veterans were larger in shelters (26.5% × 5,844 = 1,549) than in encampments (30.3% × 174 = 53) because of the larger size of the shelter population (see Table B.1 in Appendix B [1998]).

Another useful way to characterize homeless people is in terms of their stage of homelessness (Dennis, 1991; Farr, Koegel, & Burnam, 1986), which reflects both the number and duration of homeless episodes. This conceptualization recognizes that homelessness is a process that people may cycle through multiple times and that interventions to assist homeless people need to take their specific stage into account. Using length of time homeless and number of homeless episodes, we categorized 18% as newly homeless (first time and fewer than 6 months), 23% as chronically homeless (first time and more than 6 months), 39% as intermittently homeless (more than one episode of homelessness and currently homeless), and 20% as "at risk" of homelessness (using a soup kitchen but not literally homeless).

The newly homeless people were the most common in shelters (30%) and less likely in encampments (12%), soup kitchens (12%), or on the street (7%). In contrast, the chronically homeless were the most common in the street (50%) and less common in shelters (29%), encampments (28%), and soup kitchens (16%). Intermittent patterns of homelessness (which are linked to substance use, as discussed below) were most common in encampments (59%) and less common in the street (44%), soup kitchens (42%), and shelters (41%). By definition, the at-risk segment of homelessness was identified only in soup kitchens (30%).

4.4 Drug Use Prevalence and Correlates

As noted in Section 4.1.2, drug use is common among homeless people. The Homeless and Transient Population Study provides additional data on the prevalence, correlates, and symptoms of dependence to augment those from other studies. These data are particularly informative in that the present study had a broad-based design that covered the full range of homeless and transient people by including four different sampling frames.

4.4.1 Prevalence

The Homeless and Transient Population Study showed that 80% reported lifetime illicit drug use and 93% some alcohol use. Moreover, rates of substance use varied significantly by stage of homelessness, emergency service utilization pattern, and sampling location, as discussed below.

Figure 4.2 presents rates of past year and past month substance use among the DC MSA homeless and transient population. (Supporting percentages for this figure appear in Table B.2 in Appendix B [1998].) As shown in Figure 4.2, more than half (58%) had used an illicit drug in the year prior to the interview. The illicit drug used most frequently in the past year was cocaine (48%), especially crack cocaine (45%). Marijuana/hashish was the next most frequently used drug (38%), followed by nonmedical use of any psychotherapeutics (12%) and heroin (9%). Approximately one out of three people reported using drugs in the past month (i.e., current drug use), with the pattern of individual drug use mirroring the past year pattern. More than 85% reported drinking alcohol in the past year, including 7 out of 10 during the past month, and nearly 3 out of 10 reported drinking five or more drinks on 5 or more days in the past month (or the prorated equivalent while homeless; see Section 2.4.2 for details).

In addition to drug and alcohol use, Figure 4.2 also presents rates of needle use among the homeless population for the past year and past month. One out of every 7 homeless persons had injected illicit drugs in the past year, and about 1 in 20 had done so in the past month. These

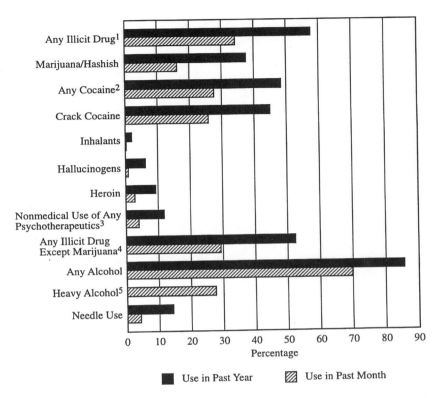

Figure 4.2. Prevalence of Illicit Drug, Alcohol, and Needle Use in the DC MSA Homeless and Transient Population

SOURCE: Washington, DC, Metropolitan Area Drug Study (DC*MADS): 1989-1995.
NOTE: See Table B.2 in Appendix B (1998) for the supplementary data used to prepare this figure.
1. Use of marijuana or hashish, cocaine (including crack), inhalants, hallucinogens (including phencyclidine or PCP), or heroin, or nonmedical use of psychotherapeutics at least once.
2. Includes crack cocaine.
3. Nonmedical use of any prescription-type stimulant (including methamphetamine), sedative, tranquilizer, or analgesic; does not include over-the-counter drugs.
4. Includes cocaine (including crack), inhalants, hallucinogens (including PCP), heroin, or nonmedical use of psychotherapeutics at least once.
5. Having five or more drinks per day on 5 or more days in the past month (or the prorated equivalent while homeless); not asked for lifetime or past year.

rates are of considerable concern because they suggest heavy involvement with drugs, particularly with some of the more addictive drugs, and also place homeless users at high risk for infection from the human immunodeficiency virus (HIV).

4.4.2 Demographic and Homeless Correlates

Table 4.2 examines the relationship between past month illicit drug use and heavy alcohol use with selected demographic subgroups in the Homeless and Transient Population Study. Past month illicit drug use was more common among people who were males, between the ages of 26 and 34, black, single, and living in DC, with either less than a high school education or some college, and who were employed part- or full-time. Similarly, heavy alcohol use was more common among people who were males, black, and living in DC; in contrast, however, it was more common among people over 35 years of age, who were divorced/widowed, with a high school degree (regardless of whether they had some college), and people who were unemployed or working part-time.

Other data indicate that past month illicit drug use was significantly more likely among people sampled in soup kitchens (50%) and encampments (41%) than those on the street (24%) or in shelters (19%). In contrast, heavy alcohol use was more common among people on the street (42%) and in encampments (39%), somewhat less common at soup kitchens (31%), and the least common at shelters (17%). In terms of the stage of homelessness, past month illicit drug use was the most common among people who were intermittently homeless (43%) and at risk of homelessness (37%).

Data on the stages of homelessness are of particular interest for two reasons. First, other longitudinal research suggests that although people who are intermittently homeless make up 39% of the homeless population, they consume more than two thirds of the services during the course of a year (Culhane, Dejowski, Ibanez, Needham, & Macchia, 1994). This happens in part because the vast majority of people who have had a homeless episode experience it only once and for a short period of time. In contrast, those who are intermittently homeless cycle in and out of homelessness and remain homeless for longer periods. Second, soup kitchens and other homeless service providers represent important recruitment points for HIV/health services outreach and research that targets needle and crack cocaine users. The latter finding is important in that it corroborates what has been found during a cooperative agreement funded by NIDA to study the relationship of injection drug and crack cocaine use and the acquired immune deficiency syndrome (AIDS).

Table 4.2 Any Illicit Drug Use and Heavy Alcohol Use in the Past Month, by Demographic Characteristics

Demographic Characteristic[1]	Total Population	Any Illicit Drug Use[2]	Heavy Alcohol Use[3]
Total	100.0	34.3	27.5
Sex			
Male	75.9	38.5	31.6
Female	24.1	21.2	14.7
Age group (years)			
12-25	15.0	21.4	15.2*
26-34	36.8	44.0	26.0
≥ 35	48.2	31.0	32.7
Race/ethnicity[4]			
White	16.5	28.1	16.5
Black	75.8	37.5	30.8
Hispanic	5.9	17.5*	21.3
Marital status			
Single	59.7	35.1	26.4
Married	8.3	32.6*	22.2*
Divorced/widowed	32.1	33.6	29.5
Location[5]			
DC	71.0	39.2	30.0
Maryland	14.0	36.0*	28.3*
Virginia	15.0	9.9	15.4
Adult education[6,7]			
Less than high school	40.1	36.8	23.9
High school graduate	39.3	30.4	30.9
Any college	20.6	37.6*	29.4*
Current employment[7]			
Full-time	21.5	38.0*	24.0
Part-time	12.2	41.6*	30.2*
Unemployed	54.1	35.4	31.0
Other[8]	12.2	17.1	20.1

SOURCE: Washington, DC, Metropolitan Area Drug Study (DC*MADS): 1989-1995.
1. Columns are not mutually exclusive for population estimates, which are based on all available data; data entries are percentages adjusted for multiplicity between samples.
2. Use of marijuana or hashish, cocaine (including crack), inhalants, hallucinogens (including phencyclidine or PCP), or heroin, or nonmedical use of psychotherapeutics at least once.
3. Having five or more drinks per day on 5 or more days in the past month (or the prorated equivalent while homeless).
4. The category "other" for race/ethnicity is not shown because there were too few cases ($n = 39$ for total population and illicit drugs; $n = 21$ for heavy alcohol use).
5. The District of Columbia metropolitan statistical area (DC MSA) includes the District of Columbia; the Maryland counties of Calvert, Charles, Frederick, Montgomery, and Prince Georges; the Virginia counties of Arlington, Fairfax, Loudoun, Prince William, and Stafford; and the Virginia cities of Alexandria, Fairfax, Falls Church, Manassas, and Manassas Park.
6. As with the National Household Survey on Drug Abuse (NHSDA), general equivalency diplomas (GEDs) are not considered in this measure.
7. Persons aged 12 to 17 ($n = 13$) are excluded from the estimates of adult education and current employment.
8. Retired, disabled, homemaker, student, or "other."
*Low precision.

Although almost all the cooperative agreement subjects were recruited via much more expensive street outreach, more than one third of the 22,000+ out-of-treatment injection drug and crack cocaine users being tracked were homeless at the time of intake (Dennis, Wechsberg, Rasch, & Campbell, 1995). Others who were using soup kitchens or other services often used by homeless people were also likely to have been at risk of homelessness.

4.4.3 Symptoms of Dependence

In addition to assessing prevalence of substance use, we investigated the number of homeless respondents who showed symptoms of dependence. Respondents were asked a subset of questions based on the criteria in the *Diagnostic and Statistical Manual of Mental Disorders* (3rd ed., rev.; American Psychiatric Association [APA], 1987): (a) For which drugs, if any, have you needed larger amounts to get the same effect, or, for which drugs could you no longer get high on the same amount you used before? (b) For which drugs, if any, have you had withdrawal symptoms; that is, you felt sick because you stopped or cut down on your use of that drug? (c) For which drugs, if any, have you tried to cut down your use?

During the past year, 58% of the homeless and transient population reported one or more components of dependence related to any drug, 45% related to crack cocaine use, 38% related to marijuana/hashish use, and 30% related to use of one or more other drugs. Moreover, 86% reported one or more components of dependence related to alcohol use, and 48% reported combining their use of alcohol and other drugs. Thus, the dominant substance use disorders in this population appear to be for alcohol and crack cocaine, with marijuana/hashish a distant third.

4.5 Co-Occurring Problems and Service Utilization

Drug and alcohol use often are accompanied by a number of notable problems, such as mental illness, physical illness, illegal activity, and unemployment, as well as different patterns of service utilization that should be taken into account epidemiologically and/or for treatment planning (e.g., Argeriou & McCarty, 1993; Delany, Fletcher, & Lennox, 1994; Devine, Wright, & Brody, 1995; Interagency Council on the Homeless, 1991, 1994; Mowbray, Bybee, & Cohen, 1993; Vazquez, Munoz, & Sanz, 1997). To explore these relationships, we categorized homeless people into one of three groups based on their involvement with drugs: (a) current drug users (any use of one or more illicit drugs in the past month), (b) past drug users (lifetime use with no past month or "current" use), and (c) nonusers of drugs (no lifetime drug use).

Demographically, current users were more likely than past users and nonusers to be male (85% vs. 74% vs. 65%), between the ages of 26 and 34 (47% vs. 38% vs. 17%), black (83% vs. 79% vs. 57%), and living in DC (81% vs. 69% vs. 58%). Both current and past users were more likely than nonusers to be single (61% and 63% vs. 49%) and unemployed (56% and 57% vs. 46%). Past drug users also were more likely to have a high school diploma than were current users or nonusers (47% vs. 35% vs. 31%). Current drug users were most likely to be intermittently homeless (49%), followed by at risk of homelessness (21%), chronically homeless (16%), and newly homeless (14%). Past drug users also were most likely to be intermittently homeless (37%), though less so than were current users, followed by those who were chronically homeless (27%) and newly homeless (21%); they were least likely to be at risk of homelessness (17%). Nonusers were most likely to be chronically homeless (31%), followed by intermittently homeless (29%), at risk of homelessness (22%), and newly homeless (18%).

These three groups are contrasted below in terms of their problems and patterns of service utilization. Relative to the earlier comparison of drug use prevalence by other characteristics, this analysis profiles "characteristics" of current drug users, relative to past users and nonusers of drugs.

4.5.1 Drug- and Alcohol-Related Problems

To examine the immediate consequences of drug use, we asked current and past drug users whether they had experienced any of six common drug-related problems. These problems were becoming depressed or losing interest in things, arguing and fighting with family or friends, getting less work done than usual at school or work, finding it

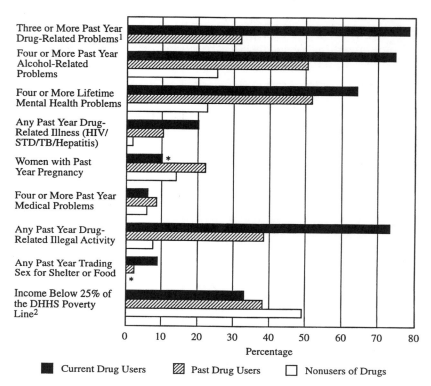

Figure 4.3. Prevalence of Co-Occurring Problems, by Type of Drug User
SOURCE: Washington, DC, Metropolitan Area Drug Study (DC*MADS): 1989-1995.
NOTE: "Current drug users" reported the use of one or more illicit drugs in the past month. "Past drug users" reported illicit drug use in their lifetime, but not in the past month. "Nonusers of drugs" include those who sought treatment for problems with their alcohol use. HIV/STD/TB = human immunodeficiency virus/sexually transmitted disease/tuberculosis. See Table B.3 in Appendix B (1998) for the supplementary data used to prepare this figure.
1. Nonusers of drugs do not fit into the drug-related problem category.
2. Earned income/poverty line income for a given size family, as set forth in the DHHS Poverty Income Guidelines (56 Fed. Reg. 34, 6859-6861 [February 20, 1991]). This poverty line varies according to family size but averaged $7,271/year for an average homeless family of 1.29 people.
*Low precision.

difficult to think clearly, feeling nervous and anxious, and having to get emergency medical help. As shown in Figure 4.3 (and Table B.3 in Appendix B [1998]), current drug users were more than twice as likely as past drug users to experience three or more of the six drug-related problems (78% vs. 32%). Although not shown in Figure 4.3, current drug users also were more likely to have experienced any drug-related problems during the past year (93% vs. 46%).

Respondents also were asked whether they had experienced any of nine alcohol-related problems. The problems were having been aggressive or mad while drinking; been high or a little drunk on the job or at school; been told to cut down on drinking by family members, other relatives, or friends; tossed down drinks fast to get a quicker effect; been afraid one might be or was becoming an alcoholic; awakened unable to remember things done while drinking the day before; had a quick drink when no one was looking; had hands shake a lot after drinking the day before; and had sometimes gotten high or a little drunk while drinking alone. Analyses showed that current drug users were more likely than past users or nonusers to experience alcohol-related problems. This is illustrated in Figure 4.3 for four or more past year alcohol-related problems (75% vs. 50% vs. 25%). The highest rates, however, were among the heavy alcohol users (5 or more drinks weekly), of whom nearly 90% reported four or more alcohol-related problems.

Overall, 48% of the homeless and transient population had received substance abuse treatment, including 23% in the past year and 12% in the past month. As shown in Table 4.3, current users were more likely than past drug users or nonusers of drugs (which included heavy alcohol users) to have been in treatment during their lifetime (61% vs. 47% vs. 29%), past year (35% vs. 19% vs. 11%), and past month (19% vs. 11% vs. 4%); they also were more likely to have been in treatment three or more times (16% vs. 10% vs. 0.5%) (data not shown). Considering these data along with those on prevalence of substance use and stage of homelessness shows a useful characterization of currently homeless people as substance users who have much higher severities of use, repeated failures in treatment, and intermittent homelessness.

Anslyses of people who had been in treatment (data not in table) showed that they were evenly split among those who had last been treated for alcohol abuse (33%), drug abuse (34%), or both (34%); alcohol-only treatment was less common among current drug users and past users than among nonusers (7% vs. 40% vs. 100%). Despite the severity of the substance use problems outlined above, the length of the last treatment episode was fewer than 30 days for 48% of the people; only 17% received more than 6 months of treatment. Current drug users were

Table 4.3 Patterns of Service Utilization, by Type of Drug User

Service Utilized	Current Drug Users	Past Drug Users	Nonusers of Drugs	Total
Any substance abuse treatment	60.9	46.9	29.4	48.2
Past year	34.8	19.3	11.3	23.1
Past month	18.6	10.5	3.5	11.9
Any insurance coverage	22.2	43.0	43.4	36.0
Public	14.4	32.2	35.7	26.9
Covers drug treatment	9.1	10.2	13.4	10.5
Private	5.0*	6.9	3.0	5.5
Covers drug treatment	0.4*	4.7	1.9*	2.7
Any mental health treatment[1]	36.4	25.9	18.7	28.1
Past month	7.8	4.2	2.5	5.1
Any inpatient treatment	21.6	15.5	10.2	16.5
Past month inpatient	0.1*	0.5	0.0*	0.2
Any outpatient treatment	23.0	19.1	12.2	19.1
Past month outpatient	8.0	3.9	2.7	5.1
Any prescribed medication	17.1	18.4	8.0	15.9
Any emergency room use	88.1	81.7	72.3	82.1
Past year	41.7	35.1	32.6	36.9
Past month	8.7	9.3	5.3	8.3
Any hospitalization for primary health care[2]	74.5	87.0	69.0	79.1
Past year	25.4	25.3	21.4	24.6
Past month	4.5	2.9	3.9	3.7
Any outpatient treatment for primary health care[2]	100.0	100.0	100.0	100.0
Past year	56.3	71.7	69.0	65.9
Past month	31.2	35.4	30.4	33.0
Any past year arrests	53.0	27.6	18.5	34.4
Currently on probation/parole	17.3	7.3	1.6	9.6
Aid to Families With Dependent Children and/or food stamps	48.0	58.1	46.6	52.4
Supplemental Security Income	5.5	9.3	11.5	8.5
General assistance	8.8	18.1	20.9	15.5
Any emergency services use in past month[3]	99.3	97.5*	95.0*	97.9
Shelter only	7.9	26.8	32.0	21.3
Soup kitchen only	35.6	24.5	29.4	29.3
Shelter and soup kitchen	55.8	46.3	33.6	47.0

SOURCE: Washington, DC, Metropolitan Area Drug Study (DC*MADS): 1989-1995.
NOTE: Data entries are percentages. "Current drug users" reported the use of one or more illicit drugs in the past month. "Past drug users" reported illicit drug use in their lifetime, but not in the past month. "Nonusers of drugs" include those who sought treatment for problems with their alcohol use.
1. Lifetime use of inpatient, outpatient, or pharmacological treatment for psychological or emotional problems.
2. Hospitalization/outpatient treatment for primary health care covered by insurance.
3. Any use of a shelter, soup kitchen, or both in the past month.
*Low precision.

less likely than past users or nonusers (who were being treated for alcohol only) to have received treatment for 6 or more months (12% vs. 19% vs. 26%). Current drug users also were less likely than past or nonusers to report successfully completing their last treatment episode (48% vs. 55% vs. 63%) and still to be in treatment (12% vs. 26% vs. 7%).

As shown in Table 4.3, a contributing factor to the low rates of utilization among homeless people is that only 13% had insurance that covered either public or private substance abuse treatment. Current drug users were less likely than past users or nonusers to have such coverage (10% vs. 15% vs. 15%).

4.5.2 Mental Health Problems

To investigate the mental health problems of the homeless and transient population, we used a variation of a mental health problem scale from the Addiction Severity Index (ASI) (McLellan et al., 1985). The problems were serious depression, serious anxiety/tension, hallucination, trouble understanding/remembering, trouble controlling self/thoughts, arguing/fighting with others, suspicion/distrust of other people, suicidal thoughts, and suicidal attempts. More than 89% reported one or more of nine problems in their lifetime, including 50% reporting four or more of nine lifetime problems. Figure 4.3 shows that current drug users were more likely than past drug users or nonusers to report four or more of the ASI mental health problems (64% vs. 52% vs. 23%).

As shown in Table 4.3, overall, 28% of the homeless population reported a lifetime mental health treatment history, including 17% inpatient, 19% outpatient, and/or 16% having received prescribed psychotropic medications. In the past month, 5% reported having received any mental health treatment, but this was almost entirely limited to outpatient care. Following the overall pattern of higher comorbid mental health symptoms, current drug users were more likely than past users or nonusers to have a mental health treatment history both in their lifetime (36% vs. 26% vs. 19%) and in the past month (8% vs. 4% vs. 3%). Both overall and in each of the service utilization groups, the most significant finding was that only one fifth as many people were currently in treatment as those who appeared to need it (based on four or more symptoms in the past month).

4.5.3 Physical Health Problems

More than 70% of homeless and transient people reported at least one major medical problem (described further below) in the past year, and 7% had four or more. As noted in Figure 4.3, current drug users were more likely than past users or nonusers to have one or more drug-related illnesses (20% vs. 10% vs. 2%, respectively), which included HIV/AIDS and other sexually transmitted diseases (STDs), tuberculosis, or hepatitis.

A related issue (as a form of disease transmission, risk to mother, and risk to child) is substance use by pregnant women (see also Chapter 8 of this book). Virtually all (93%) of the women in the Homeless and Transient Population Study (24% of homeless and transient population) had ever been pregnant, and 17% had been pregnant in the past year. This was more likely to be the case among past drug users (22%) than among current users (10%) or nonusers (14%), as shown in Figure 4.3. Women indicated that being pregnant was a common reason for stopping drug use.

Substantial numbers of homeless people also experienced other primary care problems. The largest percentages reported problems with their respiratory system (50%), followed by problems with their heart or circulatory system (23%), bones or muscles (17%), digestive system (13%), skin ulcers or rashes (13%), and neurological system (11%). Rates for these conditions did not differ significantly among current drug users, past drug users, or nonusers, as illustrated in Figure 4.3 for those experiencing four or more medical problems.

As shown in Table 4.3, in terms of medical treatment during the past year, current users were more prone to use emergency rooms than were past users or nonusers (42% vs. 35% vs. 33%), about equally likely to be hospitalized for a primary health care problem (25% vs. 25% vs. 21%), and least likely to have outpatient treatment visits for primary health care (56% vs. 72% vs. 69%). Current users also were the least likely to have seen a doctor in any setting (51% vs. 68% vs. 60%). A contributing factor, no doubt, to this pattern of service use is that current drug users were half as likely as past users or nonusers to have any form of health insurance (22% vs. 43% vs. 43%) and/or public insurance (14% vs. 32% vs. 36%).

Private doctors or health clinics were the most common location of the last outpatient visit in the past year (21%), followed by public community health clinics (14%) and shelter or mobile outreach clinics (11%); nonusers were somewhat more likely than others to visit public clinics (20%) and past drug users to visit shelter/mobile clinics (14%).

4.5.4 Illegal Activity

More than 48% of homeless and transient people admitted to having committed a serious crime in their lifetime, and 31% reported one or more lifetime arrests for such crimes. The illegal activities were drug manufacture/sale or distribution; property offense (such as burglary, larceny, or theft); robbery, mugging, or purse snatching with force; or a violent offense, such as assault, kidnapping, rape, manslaughter, or homicide. Current drug users were more likely than past users or nonusers during their lifetime both to have committed serious crimes (64% vs. 52% vs. 14%, respectively) and to have been arrested for them (41% vs. 31% vs. 12%). Examination of individual types of crimes indicated that this pattern held for lifetime illegal activity for drug-related crime, property offenses, and robbery/purse snatching, but not for violent crimes. Similarly, this pattern occurred for lifetime arrests for drug-related crime, property offenses, and robbery/purse snatching, but at lower rates. Notice that, although many studies focus on arrests instead of illegal behavior, these data show notably more people reporting illegal activity than reporting arrests.

Inspection of past year data also indicated that illegal activity was common for homeless people and was related to drug use status. As shown in Table 4.3, past year current users were more likely than past or nonusers to have been arrested for "any" charge, not just the serious charges noted above (53% vs. 28% vs. 19%, respectively), and/or to currently be on probation or parole (17% vs. 7% vs. 2%). Similarly, as shown in Figure 4.3, during the past year, current users (73%) were more likely than past users (38%) or nonusers (8%) to have committed one or more of the following drug- or alcohol-related crimes: driving under the influence of drugs or alcohol, selling drugs, trading sex for drugs, and/or receiving drugs in exchange for making or distributing them. Thus, drug use is closely related to the levels of illegal activity among homeless people.

Additionally, past year current users (9%) were more likely than past users or nonusers (Figure 4.3) to trade sex for shelter or food (2% or less). This has important implications for HIV and other disease prevention efforts.

4.5.5 Employment and Income

Although 99% of the homeless population had been employed at some point in their lifetime, only 62% reported working in the past year and 39% in the past month. Current drug users were more likely than past or nonusers to have worked "any" time in the past month (44% vs. 38% vs. 32%), but somewhat less likely than past users to have worked during the past year (62% vs. 67% vs. 50%) and/or to have had a full-time job during the past year (22% vs. 19% vs. 17%). Despite the latter, current users actually were more likely to have had more than three full-time jobs in the past year (13% vs. 7% vs. 9%). Thus, although current users were working, their employment often was part-time and/or intermittent, and involved multiple employers. In all these contrasts, nonusers of drugs (who were more likely than current users to be female, older, white/Hispanic, married, and housewives or retired, and to have less than a high school education) also were the least likely to be employed part- or full-time.

The average total income for a homeless person was $514 during the past month and came from a variety of sources. The largest single source was earned income ($219/month), followed by other entitlements ($113/month), illegal income ($82/month), other income ($65/month), and earned benefits, such as unemployment insurance ($43/month). The average amount of expenses in the past month was $378, with the largest expenditures going to living expenses ($189), followed by the purchase of illicit drugs ($122). On average, current drug users had higher monthly incomes than past users or nonusers ($626 vs. $503 vs. $345) but also higher expenses ($575 vs. $268 vs. $291); this resulted in their having the lowest net of income minus expenses ($51 vs. $235 vs. $54). On the income side of the ledger, current drug users averaged more income than past or nonusers from both earned ($264 vs. $211 vs. $155) and illegal sources ($178 vs. $46 vs. $0); however, they generally received less income than did past users or nonusers from benefits ($35 vs. $48 vs. $44), other entitlements ($87 vs. $127 vs. $127), or other sources ($69 vs. $79 vs. $25). On the expense side of the ledger, current users reported lower past month living expenses than did past users or nonusers ($140 vs. $212 vs. $223) but higher expenses related to illicit drugs ($346 vs. $5 vs. $0), alcohol ($59 vs. $29 vs. $26), medical care ($15 vs. $8 vs. $17), and other needs ($23 vs. $15 vs. $36). Thus, although current users had a high net legal income less expenses ($214), they also had a negative net illegal income less illegal drug purchases (–$168). In other words, current users were spending more on drugs than they were making on their criminal activities. This suggests that if they reduced their drug use, they would realize an increase in their available income and be less likely to commit crimes.

Overall, homeless and transient people have very low incomes; indeed, only 19.4% of the family incomes were above the poverty line as defined by the U.S. Department of Health and Human Services (U.S. DHHS Poverty Income Guidelines, 1991). This poverty line varies according to family size but averaged $7,271/year for an average homeless family of 1.29 people. Approximately 4 in 10 homeless and transient people were living on less than 25% of the poverty line, and nearly 6 in 10 people were living on income below half of the poverty line. Figure 4.3 shows that current drug users were somewhat less likely than past users or nonusers to be living on incomes below 25% of the DHHS poverty line (33% vs. 38% vs. 49%).

As noted in Table 4.3, during their lifetime, current drug users were generally less likely than past or nonusers to have received assistance from public entitlement programs, such as Supplemental Security Income for low income (6% vs. 9% vs. 12%), Aid to Families With Dependent Children (AFDC) and/or food stamps (48% vs. 58% vs. 47%), or general assistance (9% vs. 18% vs. 21%). Although current drug users were less likely to have these forms of assistance, their rates of losing one or more of these benefits since becoming homeless were identical to past and nonusers (15% vs. 15% vs. 16%). As noted by Rossi (1989), a review of such losses showed that they typically involved technical violations (e.g., not responding to a letter or phone call) and that the vast majority eventually were reversed after a lengthy appeals process. Of particular interest, the 15% loss of benefits reported here was significantly lower than the 70% loss reported by Rossi for Chicago in the mid-1980s. Policy analysts have assumed this improvement is due, at least in part, to initiatives designed to help the homeless and transient population, such as the Food Security Act of 1985, the Stewart B. McKinney Homeless Assistance Act of 1987, and the Hunger Prevention Act of 1988 (Burt, 1992).

4.5.6 Drug User Group Profiles

To help integrate the information presented in the prior sections, the characteristics of homeless people along with problems and patterns of service utilization are summarized briefly for current drug users, past drug users, and nonusers.

Current drug users were the most likely to be male, between the ages of 26 and 34, black, living in DC, single, and unemployed, and to have a high school degree or GED. They were most likely to be intermittently homeless, followed by being at risk of homelessness, chronically homeless, and then newly homeless. Current drug users were the most likely to report drug-related problems, alcohol-related problems, mental health problems, drug-related illnesses (HIV/AIDS, STDs, TB, hepatitis), past year drug-related illegal activity, and illegal income/expenses. They were less likely to have major medical problems and, among the women, to have been pregnant in the past year (but more in the past month). Current drug users were the most likely to have used soup kitchens, to have been in substance abuse or mental health treatment, to have relied on emergency medical services, and to have committed and been arrested for serious crimes. They were least likely to have used shelters, been seen by a doctor in the past year, or received public entitlements.

Past drug users were demographically in between current and nonusers, with most still being male, black, living in DC, single (never married), and unemployed; they were the most likely to have a high school degree or GED. In contrast to current users, past users were less likely to be intermittently homeless, less likely to be at risk of homelessness, and more likely to be chronically or newly homeless. Past drug users generally reported a similar but less severe pattern of problems compared with current drug users, with the major exception that among the women, past drug users were the most likely to have been pregnant during the past year. They also had similar but less frequent patterns of service utilization, with the exceptions that they were the most frequent users of hospital and outpatient medical services for primary care problems and the most likely to have last visited a doctor at a shelter or mobile outreach clinic. We believe this group had been at least partially motivated to stop using drugs because of pregnancy and/or other medical problems.

Nonusers of drugs also were dominated by the above demographic groups but were more likely than current users to be female, older, Hispanic/white, living in Virginia/Maryland, married/divorced/widowed, and homemakers/students/retired, as well as to lack a high school degree or GED. They were most likely to be chronically homeless, followed by intermittently homeless, at risk of homelessness, and then newly homeless. By definition, nonusers experienced no drug-related problems. They were the least likely to experience alcohol-related problems, mental health problems, and drug-related illnesses, and the least likely to be employed. They were the most likely to report major medical problems and to be living at 75% or more below the poverty line. Nonusers of drugs also were the most likely to have used shelters and to be living on Supplemental Security Income or retirement benefits, but they were the least likely to have used soup kitchens, to have been in substance abuse or mental health treatment, to have relied on emergency medical services, or to have committed or been arrested for an illegal activity.

4.6 Discussion and Implications

The findings from this study of homeless and transient people provide key insights about the methodological challenges of studying this population, the characteristics of homeless people, the prevalence and correlates of substance abuse, and the co-occurring problems and service utilization of this small but vulnerable population. Implications of the findings are next discussed for the epidemiology and surveillance of homelessness, the epidemiology and surveillance of substance use, program planning, welfare reform, and local policymakers. We conclude with a brief reprise summarizing the central conclusions of the study.

4.6.1 Epidemiology and Surveillance of Homelessness

Past estimates of the size and characteristics of the homeless population often have varied significantly. Interestingly, this appears to be largely related to differences in sampling methodology and how questions were asked. For the present study, the size of the homeless and transient population for the DC MSA was within the 95% confidence interval of the estimate obtained by the census, which perhaps lends additional confidence to the estimate. It is important nevertheless for future studies to be explicit about their definitions, sampling sites, and measurement approaches, as well as to discuss the generalizability and limits of their findings. Furthermore, in planning future studies of homeless and transient people, it is advantageous to be inclusive where possible in definitions and sampling locations to provide the greatest utility from findings. For example, although a "literal" definition of homelessness may simplify surveillance and program planning, it fails to cover much of the population that is eligible for and receives emergency services. Consequently, such a definition draws an arbitrary line that excludes people who are formerly homeless, at risk of homelessness, or extremely poor.

Implementing surveillance systems for tracking changes in the size and composition of the homeless population is important both for determining appropriate allocations of congressional districts and for apportioning funds from federal, state, and local sources. Having a surveillance system (e.g., survey or other indicator to track problems) that allowed the inclusion of homeless people in the 1990 census would have added about 33 people per 10,000 people in the DC MSA household population; however, it would have varied significantly across the major areas of the MSA from 132.7 per 10,000 in DC to 12.5 per 10,000 people in Virginia and 10.6 per 10,000 in Maryland. These data are consistent with studies by Culhane, Lee, and Wachter (1996) that suggest that homelessness is much less dispersed than general poverty and often is highly concentrated in a few urban areas. Ignoring these geographic differences would mean that some areas would get too little assistance and others may get too much.

Despite the amount of data that has been accumulated about homeless and transient people, many issues require further study. More information is needed, for example, about the movement of people into and out of homelessness to identify the antecedents and structural issues related to the onset of homelessness. Such information should help determine why some people have a single and fairly brief episode of homelessness while others remain homeless for longer periods or experience multiple intermittent episodes of homelessness. Information on these issues will require longitudinal and/or experimental research rather than cross-sectional studies, which generally have been conducted previously. Fortunately, a number of investigations to address these issues are under way (e.g., Culhane et al., 1994; Culhane et al., 1996; Devine et al., 1995; Huebner & Crosse, 1991; Lipton, Nutt, & Sabatini, 1988; Orwin, Sonnefeld, Garrison-Mogren, & Smith, 1994; Sossin, Piliavin, & Westerfelt, 1990).

Cost will remain a significant factor in choosing how to sample and survey homeless people because they are a small and relatively mobile population, which means that even large, stratified probability samples may yield few interviews. In the Homeless and Transient Population Study, finding the 80 eligible people in the street sample and completing interviews with 64 of them cost more than twice as much as going to the shelters, soup kitchens, and encampment clusters to complete the other 844 interviews. Some 71% of the eligible street people and 89% of the respondents were found in DC, and no one who was eligible or even suspected of being eligible was found in a tract or block that had been rated by local experts as having a low probability of having homeless people. Thus, although it may be beneficial to conduct street sampling in such locations as DC or the Los Angeles "skid row" areas (Hamilton, Rabinovitz, & Alschuler, Inc., 1987), sending interviewers to seek homeless people on the street in suburban or rural census blocks is not cost-effective. Use of an encampment or purposely sampled locations (e.g., 1990 census) appears to only minimally increase coverage (we found only 174 of the estimated 2,129 street people that way) and is not representative of the street population.

Data from the present study suggest that it may be possible to locate all but a small percentage of homeless people by sampling and surveying them at locations where they obtain services for homeless people (e.g., shelters, soup kitchens). Although this finding is encouraging, more work is needed to understand its generalizability to other metropolitan areas. Research by Koegel and colleagues (1996) in Los Angeles failed to replicate it; they found only 70% coverage in the city and 50% in suburban areas. The U.S. Bureau of the Census is conducting further studies to evaluate geographic variation in coverage (Burt, 1996).

4.6.2 Epidemiology and
Surveillance of Substance Use

Substance use rates were very high among the homeless and transient population: More than half had used illicit drugs during the past year (58%) and a third during the past month (34%). More than one fourth drank alcohol heavily during the past month (28%). These rates agree with data from prior studies (e.g., Interagency Council on the Homeless, 1991) and further substantiate that homeless and transient people are at high risk of substance use and related problems. They also suggest the need to establish a surveillance system that captures and monitors rates of use among this vulnerable population. Of course, instead of developing a new surveillance system just for homeless and transient people, it would be more efficient to incorporate this population into existing systems.

Of the many surveillance systems used to track substance use in the United States, the two most prominent are the cross-sectional National Household Survey on Drug Abuse (NHSDA; NIDA, 1990) and the National Longitudinal Alcohol Epidemiologic Survey (NLAES; see Grant, 1997). Although neither directly excludes the homeless population (e.g., the NHSDA explicitly includes shelters), their sample selection procedures minimize the presence of people who are homeless and/or in nontraditional or unstable housing situations. A change in their sampling procedures, however, would permit them to oversample homeless people and obtain sufficient data from this population to monitor their substance use and related problems.

Admittedly, the homeless and transient population is extremely small relative to the household population (see Chapters 2 and 3 of this book) and, as is shown in Chapter 9, constitutes less than 0.5% of the composite population made up of household, institutionalized, and homeless people. Accordingly, changes in rates of use among the homeless and transient population will have only a small impact on the overall prevalence estimates from the household population. Still, although small, these differences can become very important to policymakers and program planners as the focus shifts from longer-term rates of any substance use to an emphasis on more recent use, use of needles, use of heroin and other illicit drugs, and dependence criteria.

For the homeless and transient population, the data also suggest that general prevalence rates and cross-tabulations may not tell the whole story. Most of the current users were using multiple substances and had comorbid alcohol, mental, and health problems that were also related to patterns of illegal activity, unemployment, income, and service utilization. Moreover, results appear to be sensitive to the severity and recency of use, not just to the traditional measures that focus on "any use." Further study of the homeless and transient population and/or other more chronic populations is needed to assess how these problems interact and/or to observe people after they have stopped using drugs.

4.6.3 Implications for Program Planning

Findings from surveys of homeless people have been used to help reduce the number of technical violations for general assistance in Chicago (Rossi, 1989), increase food stamp participation rates and allow shelters to accept food stamps (Burt, 1992), increase health care for homeless people (IOM, 1988), and increase the availability of mental health outreach and treatment (Federal Task Force on Homelessness and Severe Mental Illness, 1992). The present study identified a number of additional unmet service needs that can help guide local planners and inform others. For example, although one third of the homeless people were current drug users (and another 46% were past users), only 12% were currently in drug or alcohol treatment and only 13% had public or private insurance to cover it. Of the roughly 60% of current users who had one or more treatment episodes, more than half were in treatment for fewer than 30 days during their most recent treatment episode—a level that would appear insufficient given the severity, post-discharge relapse rates, and co-occurring problems.

In addition, although much of the crime committed by homeless people appears to be drug related, evidence suggests that it is likely to be substantially reduced by treating substance use. Although 37% of current drug users reported four or more symptoms of mental distress in the past month (and 36% had lifetime histories of mental health treatment), only 8% received mental health treatment in the past month. Although an estimated 70% of homeless people had one or more major medical problems and showed a past year pattern of relatively heavy emergency room use (37%) and hospitalization (25%), only 36% were covered by any health insurance. Although funding for shelter or mobile outreach clinics often comes under attack, these clinics provide a major source of health care for a population that would otherwise likely use more expensive care, such as emergency rooms or hospitals; about one of four past year visits to the doctor (other than in an emergency room or hospital) was through public community health clinics, and another one of six was through shelter or mobile outreach clinics.

Clearly, there is a need for more behavioral health treatment for drug, alcohol, and emotional problems. This includes mechanisms to pay for such treatment and shelters that will accept substance users and incorporate these treatment services. Such programs are both feasible and effective (Argeriou & McCarty, 1993; Delany et al., 1994; Devine et al., 1995; Huebner & Crosse, 1991; Miescher & Galanter, 1996; Morse, Calsyn, Allen, & Kenny, 1994; Orwin et al., 1994). Moreover, this is not simply a homeless person's issue but also a drug treatment system and public health issue. For example, across 22 sites in NIDA's cooperative agreement to do AIDS outreach to out-of-treatment drug users, more than one third of the drug users were found to be consistently homeless; this was correlated with such HIV risk behaviors as use of crack cocaine, multiple sexual partners, needle use, and needle sharing (Dennis et al., 1995). In the National Treatment Improvement Evaluation Study (NTIES), among 246 treatment units, an average of 19% (ranging from 7% to 27%) of entering clients had been homeless in the past year (Gerstein et al., 1997). Across modalities, housing assistance was the ancillary service most frequently rated as "very important" (48%) by NTIES's respondents, but it was received by only one third of these people. Despite these findings, homelessness has not received much attention as a mediator of treatment effectiveness nor as an issue for program improvement in the mainstream treatment research literature or practice.

4.6.4 Implications for Welfare Reform

In the mid- to late 1990s, the nation's attention was focused on attempts to move people from welfare to work and/or to seek out new forms of health insurance. The findings from the current study and research on homeless people in general suggest both pros and cons to this "get tough" approach. Virtually all the homeless people in our study had been employed, and one fifth described themselves as "currently working full-time." Thus, it seems likely that the welfare emphasis will spur some of them into further employment, but it also is clear that many homeless people have problems keeping jobs because of drug use, disabilities (mental or physical), and a lack of basic resources (e.g., transportation, housing, food). These situations should allow the use of the waiver protection that is built into the current reform legislation (which can allow up to 20% to avoid the caps). Moreover, because the mainstream welfare system currently is covering only a fraction of the homeless population (e.g., via Supplemental Security Income, Medicaid), many homeless people will continue to rely on charity and/or indigent care from institutions.

Thus, the reforms under way in the mid- to late 1990s are likely to have minimal impact on people who are currently homeless and, if anything, probably will increase their ranks with adults and families who eventually will run out of benefits. This "get tough" approach may have strong societal sanctions and support but is likely to underlie a massive wave of new need that will descend on an emergency shelter and food system that is already largely strained to capacity. This in turn has the potential to increase the number of people begging or living on the street, selling sex for food and shelter, turning to crime for survival, and/or turning to drugs to stop the pain. Whether this de facto social experiment will be judged an overall success or failure, those who work with homeless people and drug users need to start planning how they will cope with the increased demand from the people who inevitably will fail.

4.6.5 Implications for Local Policymakers

Ranging from the inner city to suburban and rural areas, the local policymakers in the DC MSA represent a microcosm of many metropolitan areas. Across municipalities, the two most common issues that policymakers faced were determining who the emergency service system was for and deciding on the kind of system that would work best. In the city, policymakers thought that their services were easier to access and that homeless people came from outlying areas to get them. In the suburbs, policymakers thought that their services were better and that homeless people came from the city to get them. In rural areas, there was denial that homelessness existed. All policymakers were concerned about trade-offs between breadth and depth of services and the potential for clients to become dependent on the emergency system.

One of the most important findings in the current study for local policymakers was that most homeless people were from the same communities where they were found. Indeed, the net rate of nightly movement among municipalities was less than 1%. Approximately 88% of the people became homeless while living within the MSA, generally in the same municipality where they were found, and more than 55% had last attended school within the DC MSA (relatively high in a high-growth MSA). Thus, the overwhelming majority of homeless people became homeless in, and had been longtime residents of, the municipalities in which they were currently residing.

In terms of concentration, more than three fourths of the homeless people in the MSA lived in DC (which is the fourth largest municipality in the MSA but is its urban core). Another 18% were found in six surrounding municipalities, and the remaining 5% were spread out in the remaining (more rural) eight municipalities. Thus, although homelessness was much less common in rural areas, it was still there. Moreover, homeless people in rural areas often needed to go to adjacent communities or into the city to obtain services because their own communities lacked the necessary programs.

Deciding which system to have or build is a complicated issue because most systems are patchworks of private charity, emergency services, and other public services that have grown out of crisis and opportunity rather than the result of urban planning. Fortunately, findings from the current study and related literature offer guidance on key considerations. For instance, it is clear that most people move in and out of homelessness quickly with minimal assistance and never return. Thus, there is a need for a 1- to 7-day emergency service with minimal requirements. Although researchers often have defined homelessness to be chronic when it has lasted for 6 months (Dennis, 1991; Koegel et al., 1990), by the time a person has been homeless 30 days, there are likely to be individual or situational factors complicating a return to independence. This suggests that programs should begin the process of assessment and referral to other appropriate services somewhere between 7 and 30 days (or where the need is self-evident).

When a person is chronically mentally ill, has a disability, or is elderly, a case manager or more extensive assistance program likely will be required. Substance abusers or those with money management problems are at high risk of relapse to homelessness. Ironically, current policies often shun such people from shelters. This suggests a need for specialized services to handle substance abusers and/or teach money management. Providing such services will require programs that also can handle comorbid mental and physical health problems, as well as families, children, and pregnant women. Where such programs already exist, it may be more efficient for local policymakers to buy slots or supplement them rather than start new programs. Where needed programs do not exist, consideration could be given to introducing these additional services in shelters because they have proven to be effective stabilization and treatment sites (Argeriou & McCarty, 1993).

Both chronically and intermittently homeless people are likely to require assistance in obtaining long-term (preferably drug- and alcohol-free) housing for recovery. The DC MSA municipalities varied considerably in the extent to which they embraced and/or encouraged the development of Oxford Homes or other recovery housing with funds made available by individual states after the Anti-Drug Abuse Act of 1988.

Finally, municipalities should avoid becoming entangled in the literal definition of homelessness. Preventing people from becoming homeless is one of the most cost-effective approaches to addressing the problem of homelessness. Rather than exclude "at-risk" persons from using emergency services, communities should identify these people and target them for assistance. Such proactive steps may help these people avoid the far-reaching problems faced by those who become homeless.

4.6.6 Reprise and Conclusions

This chapter has identified 10 key points through reviewing the literature and findings from the Homeless and Transient Population Study.

1. Definitions of homelessness vary considerably and have undergone a series of shifts from a focus on detachment from traditional family living arrangements to literal housing status, to housing status over a period of time, and/or to risk of homelessness that focuses more on the people presenting for emergency services.

2. The estimated size of the homeless and transient population has varied considerably because of differences in definitions, methodology, and measurement of unique people or person-service contacts.

3. Demographic and/or clinical characteristics of the homeless and transient population vary significantly across different sampling and/or geographic locations.

4. Homeless and transient people showed relatively high rates of drug use, alcohol use, needle use, and symptoms of dependence; they varied considerably, however, by the substances and time periods considered, as well as whether the focus is on use, abuse, or dependence.

5. Illicit drug and alcohol use are correlated with the major demographic and homeless variables examined; drug use is lowest in shelters (the focus of much research) and highest in soup kitchens; heavy alcohol use also is lowest in shelters and higher among people on the street, in encampments, and in soup kitchens; and illicit drug use is higher among people who are intermittently homeless and those at risk of homelessness.

6. The majority reported experiencing one or more symptoms of alcohol or drug dependence; moreover, drug symptoms were related to crack cocaine use, marijuana/hashish use, and use of one or more other drugs.

7. Drug use status (i.e., current user, past user, and nonuser of drugs) was highly related to mental health problems, physical health problems, illegal activity, vocational activity/income, and patterns of service utilization.

8. Efforts to monitor the size and characteristics of the homeless population are more important than might be assumed because the homeless population includes people with multiple severe problems and high rates of service utilization.

9. Although homeless people constitute only a small fraction of the general population or of people who use drugs, they represent a significant segment of hard-core drug users, both in and out of treatment, who often are underserved.

10. A graduated service system is needed to assist homeless people because there are multiple pathways both into and out of homelessness and considerable variation in the types and duration of required services.

The problems of homelessness and drug use are interwoven both with each other and with a variety of other co-occurring problems. Variations in definitions, sampling sites, and methodology have hindered the synthesis of early findings and argue for a more comprehensive approach in future research. The persistence of homelessness, the high costs of doing nothing about it, and simple concern for fellow beings dictate the need for further program and policy development in this area. Because much still needs to be learned, the need for growth in services should be closely linked to further program evaluation and research.

References

American Psychiatric Association. (1987). *Diagnostic and statistical manual of mental disorders (DSM-III-R)* (3rd ed., rev.). Washington, DC: Author.

Anti-Drug Abuse Act of 1988, 21 U.S.C., § 1501 *et seq.*, Pub. L. No. 100-690. (1988).

Appendix B: Homeless and Transient Population Study. (1998). (Available on the World Wide Web at http://www.sagepub.com/bray_druguse.htm)

Argeriou, M., & McCarty, D. (1993). The use of shelters as substance abuse stabilization sites. *Journal of Mental Health Administration, 20,* 126-137.

Barrett, D. F., Anolik, I., & Abramson, F. H. (1992, August). *The 1990 census shelter and street night enumeration.* Paper presented at the annual meeting of the American Statistical Association, Boston.

Bassuk, E. L., Weinreb, L. F., Buckner, J. C., Browne, A., Salomon, A., & Bassuk, S. S. (1996). The characteristics and needs of sheltered homeless and low-income housed mothers. *Journal of the American Medical Association, 276,* 640-646.

Burnam, A., Koegel, P., & Duan, T. S. (1990). *LA study of mental illness among homeless people* (1990 National Institute of Mental Health grant application). Santa Monica, CA: Rand Corporation.

Burt, M. R. (1992). *Over the edge: The growth of homelessness in the 1980s.* New York: Russell Sage Foundation.

Burt, M. R. (1996). *National Survey of Homeless Assistance Providers and Clients: Research design.* Washington, DC: Urban Institute and U.S. Bureau of the Census.

Burt, M. R., & Cohen, B. E. (1988). *Feeding the homeless: Does the prepared meals provision help?* (Food and Nutrition Service Report to Congress, October 31, 1988). Washington, DC: The Urban Institute.

Burt, M. R., & Cohen, B. E. (1989). *America's homeless: Numbers, characteristics, and programs that serve them* (Urban Institute Report 89-3). Washington, DC: The Urban Institute.

Calsyn, R. J., Allen, G., Morse, G. A., Smith, R., & Tempelhoff, B. (1993). Can you trust self-report data provided by homeless mentally ill individuals? *Evaluation Review, 17,* 353-366.

Culhane, D. P., Dejowski, E. F., Ibanez, J., Needham, E., & Macchia, I. (1994). Public shelter admission rates in Philadelphia and New York City: The implications of turnover for sheltered population counts. *Housing Policy Debate, 5,* 107-140.

Culhane, D. P., Lee, C. M., & Wachter, S. M. (1996). Where the homeless come from: A study of the prior address distribution of families admitted to public shelters in New York City and Philadelphia. *Housing Policy Debate, 7,* 327-365.

Davidson, D. (1991). *A snap shot survey of hard to serve homeless clients in Northern Virginia.* Fairfax: Northern Virginia Coalition for the Homeless.

Delany, P. J., Fletcher, B. W., & Lennox, R. D. (1994). Analyzing shelter organizations and the services they offer: Testing a structural model using a sample of shelter programs. *Evaluation and Program Planning, 17,* 391-398.

Dennis, M. L. (1991). Changing the conventional rules: Surveying homeless people in nonconventional locations. *Housing Policy Debate, 2,* 701-732.

Dennis, M. L. (1993, September). *Coverage of a service-based methodology: Findings from the DC*MADS homelessness study.* Paper presented at Towards Census 2000: Research Issues for Improving Coverage of the Homeless Population, Arlington, VA.

Dennis, M. L., & Iachan, R. (1991). Sampling issues in estimating the extent of alcohol, drug abuse, and mental illness problems among people who are homeless. In C. M. Taeuber (Ed.), *Enumerating homeless persons: Methods and data needs* (pp. 188-191). Washington, DC: U.S. Bureau of the Census.

Dennis, M. L., & Iachan, R. (1992, August). *Sampling people who are homeless: Implications of multiple definitions and sampling frames.* Paper presented at the 100th annual meeting of the American Psychological Association, Washington, DC, and the joint statistical conference of the American Statistical Association, Boston, MA.

Dennis, M. L., Wechsberg, W. M., Rasch, R., & Campbell, R. S. (1995). *Improving the measurement, power, and analytic models used in cross-site data: Some lessons from the NIDA Cooperative Agreement to Do AIDS Outreach to Drug Users* (NIDA Cooperative Agreement No. U01 DA08007). Research Triangle Park, NC: Research Triangle Institute.

Devine, J. A., Wright, J. D., & Brody, C. J. (1995). An evaluation of an alcohol and drug treatment program for homeless substance abusers. *Evaluation Review, 19,* 620-645.

Drake, R. E., McHugo, G. J., & Biesanz, J. C. (1995). The test-retest reliability of standardized instruments among homeless persons with substance use disorders. *Journal of Studies on Alcohol, 56,* 161-167.

Etheridge, R. M., Dennis, M. L., Lubalin, J. S., & Schlenger, W. E. (1989). *Implementation evaluation design for NIMH McKinney mental health services demonstration projects for homeless mentally ill adults* (4 vols., National Institute of Mental Health Contract No. 282-88-0019). Research Triangle Park, NC: Research Triangle Institute.

Farr, R. K., Koegel, P., & Burnam, A. (1986). *A study of homelessness and mental illness in the skid row area of Los Angeles* (National Institute of Mental Health Grant No. 1NIMH 364809-01). Los Angeles: Los Angeles County Department of Mental Health.

Federal Task Force on Homelessness and Severe Mental Illness. (1992). *Outcasts on main street* (DHHS Publication No. ADM 92-1904). Washington, DC: Interagency Council on the Homeless.

Fischer, P. J. (1989). Estimating the prevalence of alcohol, drug and mental health problems in the contemporary homeless population: A review of the literature. *Contemporary Drug Problems: An Interdisciplinary Quarterly, 16,* 333-390.

Food Security Act of 1985, Pub. L. 99-198, 99 Stat. 1354. (1985, December 23).

Gelberg, L., & Linn, L. S. (1989). Assessing the physical health of homeless adults. *Journal of the American Medical Association, 262,* 1973-1979.

Gerstein, D. R., Datta, A. R., Ingels, J. S., Johnson, R. A., Rasinski, K. A., Schildhaus, S., Talley, K., Jordan, K., Phillips, D. B., Anderson, D. W., Condelli, W., & Collins, J. (1997). *Final report: National Treatment Improvement Evaluation Survey* (Center for Substance Abuse Treatment Contract No. ADM 270-92-0002). Chicago: National Opinion Research Center at the University of Chicago.

Grant, B. F. (1997). Prevalence and correlates of alcohol use and DSM-IV alcohol dependence in the United States: Results of the National Longitudinal Alcohol Epidemiologic Survey. *Journal of Studies on Alcohol, 58,* 464-473.

Greene, J. M., Ennett, S. T., & Ringwalt, C. L. (1997). Substance use among runaway and homeless youth in three national samples. *American Journal of Public Health, 87,* 229-235.

Hamilton, Rabinovitz, & Alschuler, Inc. (1987). *The changing face of misery: Los Angeles' skid row area in transition* (4 vols., Community Redevelopment Agency of Los Angeles). Los Angeles: Author.

Hopper, K. (1991). Who are the homeless? Current knowledge. *Housing Policy Debate, 2,* 757-814.

Huebner, R. B., & Crosse, S. B. (1991). Challenges in evaluating a national demonstration program for homeless persons with alcohol and other drug problems. In D. J. Rog (Ed.), *Evaluating programs for the homeless* (New Directions for Program Evaluation, No. 52, pp. 33-46). San Francisco: Jossey-Bass.

Hunger Prevention Act of 1988, Pub. L. 100-435, 102 Stat. 1645. (1988, September 19).

Iachan, R., & Dennis, M. L. (1991). The design of homeless surveys. In *Proceedings of the Section on Survey Research Methods of the American Statistical Association* (pp. 181-185). Alexandria, VA: American Statistical Association.

Iachan, R., & Dennis, M. L. (1993). A multiple frame approach to sampling the homeless and transient population. *Journal of Official Statistics, 9,* 747-764.

Institute of Medicine, Committee on Health Care for Homeless People. (1988). *Homelessness, health, and human needs.* Washington, DC: National Academy Press.

Interagency Council on the Homeless. (1991). *The 1990 annual report of the Interagency Council on the Homeless.* Washington, DC: Author.

Interagency Council on the Homeless. (1994). *The 1993 annual report of the Interagency Council on the Homeless.* Washington, DC: Author.

James, F. J. (1991). Counting homeless persons with surveys of users of services for the homeless. *Housing Policy Debate, 2,* 733-753.

Johnson, T. P., & Barrett, M. E. (1991). *Homelessness and substance use in Cook County* (prepared for Department of Alcoholism and Drug Abuse, State of Illinois). Urbana: University of Illinois, Survey Research Laboratory.

Koegel, P., Burnam, M. A., & Farr, R. K. (1990). Subsistence adaptation among homeless adults in the inner city of Los Angeles. *Journal of Social Issues, 46,* 83-107.

Koegel, P., Burnam, M. A., & Morton, S. C. (1996). Enumerating homeless people: Alternative strategies and their consequences. *Evaluation Review, 20,* 378-403.

Lehman, A. F., & Cordray, D. S. (1993). Prevalence of alcohol, drug, and mental disorders among the homeless: One more time. *Contemporary Drug Problems, 20*(Fall), 355-383.

Link, B. G., Susser, E., Stueve, A., Phelan, J., Moore, R. E., & Struening, E. (1994). Lifetime and five-year prevalence of homelessness in the United States. *American Journal of Public Health, 84,* 1907-1912.

Lipton, F., Nutt, S., & Sabatini, A. (1988). Housing the homeless mentally ill: A longitudinal study of a treatment approach. *Hospital and Community Psychiatry, 39,* 40-45.

McLellan, A. T., Luborsky, L., Cacciola, J., Griffith, J., McGahan, P., & O'Brien, C. P. (1985). *Guide to the Addiction Severity Index: Background, administration, and field testing results* (DHHS Publication No. ADM 85-1419). Rockville, MD: National Institute on Drug Abuse.

Miescher, A., & Galanter, M. (1996). Shelter-based treatment for the homeless alcoholic. *Journal of Substance Abuse Treatment, 13,* 135-140.

Milburn, N. G., Booth, J. A., & Miles, S. E. (1990). *Correlates of drug and alcohol abuse among homeless adults in shelters* (final report). Washington, DC: Howard University, Institute for Urban Affairs and Research.

Morse, G. A., Calsyn, R. J., Allen, G., & Kenny, D. A. (1994). Helping homeless mentally ill people: What variables mediate and moderate program effects? *American Journal of Community Psychology, 22,* 661-683.

Mowbray, C. T., Bybee, D., & Cohen, E. (1993). Describing the homeless mentally ill: Cluster analysis results. *American Journal of Community Psychology, 21*(1), 67-93.

National Institute on Drug Abuse. (1990). *National Household Survey on Drug Abuse: Main findings 1988* (DHHS Publication No. ADM 91-1789). Rockville, MD: Author.

National Institute on Drug Abuse. (1993). *Prevalence of drug use in the Washington, DC, metropolitan area homeless and transient population: 1991* (Technical Report #2 under NIDA Contract No. 271-89-8340, Washington, DC, Metropolitan Area Drug Study, prepared by M. L. Dennis, R. Iachan, J. P. Thornberry, R. M. Bray, L. E. Packer, & G. S. Bieler, Research Triangle Institute). Rockville, MD: Author.

New York City Commission on the Homeless. (1992). *The way home: A new direction in social policy.* New York: Author.

Orwin, R. G., Sonnefeld, L. J., Garrison-Mogren, R., & Smith, N. G. (1994). Pitfalls in evaluating the effectiveness of case management programs for homeless persons: Lessons from the NIAAA community demonstration program. *Evaluation Review, 18,* 153-207.

Ringwalt, C., & Iachan, R. (1990). *Design summary of proposed study to estimate the characteristics of runaway and homeless youths* (Contract No. 105-90-1703, Administration on Children, Youth and Families). Research Triangle Park, NC: Research Triangle Institute.

Robertson, M., Zlotnick, C., & Westerfelt, A. (1997). Drug use disorders and treatment contact among homeless adults in Alameda County, California. *American Journal of Public Health, 87,* 221-228.

Rossi, P. H. (1989). *Down and out in America: The origins of homelessness.* Chicago: University of Chicago Press.

Rossi, P. H., Fischer, G. A., & Willis, G. (1986). *The condition of the homeless of Chicago.* Amherst, MA, and Chicago: Social and Demographic Research Institute and National Opinion Research Center.

Santiago, J. M., Bachrach, L. L., Berren, M. R., & Hannah, M. T. (1988). Defining the homeless mentally ill: A methodological note. *Hospital and Community Psychiatry, 39,* 1100-1102.

Sossin, M., Colson, P., & Grossman, S. (1988). *Homelessness in Chicago: Poverty and pathology, social institutions and social changes.* Chicago: Chicago Community Trust.

Sossin, M., Piliavin, I., & Westerfelt, H. (1990). Toward a longitudinal analysis of homelessness. *Journal of Social Issues, 46,* 157-174.

Spinner, G. F., & Leaf, P. J. (1992). Homelessness and drug abuse in New Haven. *Hospital and Community Psychiatry, 43,* 166-168.

Stewart B. McKinney Homeless Assistance Act, Pub. L. No. 100-77. (1987, July 22).

Susser, E., Struening, E. L., & Conover, S. (1989). Psychiatric problems in homeless men: Lifetime psychosis, substance use, and current distress in new arrivals at New York City shelters. *Archives of General Psychiatry, 46,* 845-850.

Taeuber, C. M., & Siegel, P. M. (1991). Counting the nation's homeless population in the 1990 census. In C. M. Taeuber (Ed.), *Enumerating homeless persons: Methods and data needs* (pp. 92-122). Washington, DC: Bureau of the Census, U.S. Department of Commerce.

U.S. Bureau of the Census. (1992). [District of Columbia metropolitan statistical area counts for emergency shelters and visible street locations: 1990 Census of Population and Housing]. Unpublished table. Washington, DC: Author.

U.S. DHHS Poverty Income Guidelines, 56 Fed. Reg. 34, 6859-6861. (1991, February 20).

Vazquez, C., Munoz, M., & Sanz, J. (1997). Lifetime and 12-month prevalence of DSM-III-R mental disorders among the homeless in Madrid: A European study using the CIDI. *Acta Psychiatrica Scandinavica, 94,* 1-8.

Vernez, G., Burnam, M. A., McGlynn, T. S., & Mittman, B. S. (1988). *Review of California's program for the homeless mentally disabled* (R-3631-CDMH). Santa Monica, CA: Rand Corporation.

Weatherby, N. L., Needle, R., Cesari, H., Booth, R., McCoy, C., Watters, J., Williams, M., & Chitwood, D. (1994a). Reply to Wish and Mieczkowski. *Evaluation and Program Planning, 17,* 331-342.

Weatherby, N. L., Needle, R., Cesari, H., Booth, R., McCoy, C., Watters, J., Williams, M., & Chitwood, D. (1994b). Validity of self-reported drug use among injection drug users and crack cocaine users recruited through street outreach. *Evaluation and Program Planning, 17,* 347-355.

Zanis, D. A., McLellan, A. T., Cnaan, R. A., & Randall, M. (1994). Reliability and validity of the Addiction Severity Index with a homeless sample. *Journal of Substance Abuse Treatment, 11,* 541-548.

5

Drug Use Among the Institutionalized Population

Gregory H. Gaertner
Linda J. Keil

This chapter examines drug use and related problems among institutionalized persons, including residents of correctional facilities, psychiatric facilities, and homes for dependent and neglected children and adolescents. Although prior research has looked at drug-related issues for selected subgroups of the institutionalized population (e.g., criminal offenders), the DC*MADS Institutionalized Study provides a more comprehensive picture of substance use among persons in a wider range of institutions during a common window of time. Indeed, it provides the most extensive data to date of substance use in this population. Topics included in this chapter are the prevalence and correlates of drug and alcohol use, related problems, and service utilization among the institutionalized population.

5.1 Drug Use and Institutionalization

As a prelude to discussing the findings from the Institutionalized Study, this section reviews prior data on drug use by institutionalized persons and considers contributions to the drug literature offered by studies of the institutionalized population. These studies include discussions of institutional effectiveness in regulating drug use, drug use effects on noninstitutionalized life, the relationship of substance abuse to other physical and psychological problems, and the implications of drug use rates on drug treatment needs.

5.1.1 Rates of Drug Use Before and During Institutionalization

There are good reasons to believe that the institutionalized population has high rates of lifetime drug use and that many of them were involved in drug use at the time of their institutionalization. Barton (1982), Anglin and Speckart (1986), and others have documented the high rates of drug use found among criminal offenders. Harlow (1992) found that 77.7% of all jail inmates in 1989 reported having used at least one illegal drug during their lives and that 43.9% had been using an illegal drug in the month before their arrest. She found this lifetime rate of drug use to be twice that of the household population; the past month rate was seven times that of the household population.

Despite evidence of relatively high rates of drug use before confinement, relatively little is known about *current* drug use by the institutionalized population, that is, drug use while institutionalized. Data that do exist pertain primarily to residents of correctional institutions. Based on data provided by the Census of State and Federal Adult Correctional Facilities, Harlow (1992) reported that about 87% of all state and federal correctional facilities tested inmates for illegal drug use between July 1, 1989, and June 30, 1990. She found that 76% of the institutions checked inmates on the basis of suspicion of use, 42% tested both suspected inmates and random groups, and 14% tested all inmates. Of the institutions testing all inmates or random samples of them, the proportions of positive tests varied by whether the facility was a confinement or community-based facility and by type of drug.[1] Among facilities conducting random testing and testing of all inmates, community-based facilities had higher proportions of positive tests than did state confinement facilities. For example, 8.6% of the 27,050 tests conducted for marijuana and hashish in community-based facilities had positive results. By contrast, 4.7% of the 16,302 tests conducted for marijuana in confinement facilities were positive. These figures are consistent with test results reported by Camp and Camp (1991, p. 64). They reported that among 918,088 tests performed in 35 state corrections agencies that did random testing in 1990, 5.4% were positive for an illicit drug.

Harlow (1992) was careful to point out the limitations of these data for estimating the prevalence of drug use. She noted that urine tests detect the presence of most drugs only 48 to 72 hours after use, and that prisons differed in their testing procedures, procedures for selecting inmates for testing, and the kinds of drugs for which tests were conducted. Furthermore, the test results were not weighted by facility size, so that small facilities that test a large proportion of inmates contributed to the rate of positive tests as much as large facilities that test a small proportion. Thus, the results cannot be considered representative of the correctional population. The same drawbacks apply to the test data reported in Camp and Camp (1991). The data probably are more useful for specifying the characteristics of institutions associated with greater or lesser rates of drug use than for estimating the prevalence of drug use.

Only limited self-report data exist on drug use by alcohol and drug abusers while they are incarcerated. Sobell, Sobell, Maisto, and Fain (1983) summarized the results of one study in which 27 drug abusers reported substance abuse during 24.7% of all days of incarceration (1,772 of 7,179). In a second study (Sobell et al., 1983), 27 of 33 drug abusers reported incarceration in the year prior to treatment, and 70% of them reported some alcohol or drug use while incarcerated.

There also is evidence of drug use among residents of noncorrectional institutions. The literature on the co-occurrence of psychiatric syndromes and drug use suggests high rates of drug addiction among those with psychiatric disorders. The relationship between depression and alcoholism has been well documented (see O'Sullivan, 1984, for a review), and there is increasing evidence of links between alcoholism and bipolar disorders (Mayfield, 1985). According to evidence cited by Miller and Gold (1991), between 50% and 75% of general psychiatric populations have alcohol or drug disorders.

5.1.2 Contributions From Studying Drug Use in the Institutionalized Population

Nearly all surveys of drug use exclude residents of institutions, as well as other nonhousehold populations. Incorporating institutional residents in cross-sectional estimates will provide more accurate rates of drug use in the population; however, how much effect the inclusion of institutional residents would have on cross-sectional estimates depends on two factors: rates of drug use among the institutionalized population and the size of the institutionalized population. Studies of drug use among institutionalized populations may be used not only to improve the accuracy of point-prevalence estimates of drug use but also for several other purposes: (a) to evaluate how effective institutions are in regulating drug use among their residents, (b) to understand how drug use affects the noninstitutional experiences of those committed to institutions and how it may contribute to their becoming institutionalized, (c) to understand how substance abuse interacts with other physical and psychological problems of the institutionalized population, and (d) to assess the needs of institutionalized people for treatment, including the extent to which they are making use of available treatment opportunities and the treatment resources local institutions will need in dealing with drug problems. Each of these issues is considered briefly in the sections that follow.

5.1.2.1 Institutional Effectiveness
in Regulating Drug Use

Information about drug use among the institutionalized population can be used to evaluate how effective institutions are in regulating drug use among residents of institutions. Society, and in particular those who operate institutions, has an obligation to provide safe and therapeutic care and custody for residents of institutions. This obligation includes limits on the use of illicit drugs and associated ills. Understanding the rates of drug use among residents of institutions and the consequences of such use is the first step in understanding whether institutions are exercising appropriate stewardship.

5.1.2.2 Drug Use Effects on Noninstitutionalized Life

Drug use affects the noninstitutionalized lives of those committed to institutions and may contribute to their becoming institutionalized. Rather than being a stable condition, institutionalization in the 1980s and 1990s has been more accurately described as a series of short institutional stays mixed with noninstitutional periods, including household residence and homelessness. In a study of urban mental patients, Lurigio and Lewis (1989, p. 84) noted that 64% of their sample had a history of prior psychiatric admissions, implying considerable movement into and out of psychiatric institutions. Five percent had been admitted and discharged 15 or more times. They also noted that their sample was "quite transient; 42% indicated that they had moved at least once during the six months preceding their hospitalization" (p. 85). A 1-year follow-up of mental patients in nursing homes reported by Bootzin, Shadish, and McSweeny (1989) found that 43% had left the institution. Of those who had moved, 71% had moved only once, 21% had moved twice, 5% had moved three times, and 3% had moved four times. In both samples, there was much mobility both into and out of the institutions and among noninstitutional residences.

Those incarcerated in correctional institutions are also likely to return to prison. In a study of 108,580 prisoners released from 11 state prisons in 1983 (Beck & Shipley, 1989), 18.6% were reincarcerated within 1 year, 14.2% in 1 to 2 years, and 8.6% in 2 to 3 years. In all, 41.4% were rearrested in the 3 years following release. Langan and Cuniff (1992) reported on a more recent survey of 12,370 felons placed on probation in 1986. They found that within 3 years of sentencing, 26% of the felony probationers had been sent to prison, 10% had been sent to jail, and 10% had absconded.

Recent studies also suggest much movement between short-term psychiatric facilities and correctional institutions. Adler (1986) pointed out that because "the mental health social control sector is no longer as available as before to care for this marginal population, the burden to provide such care would fall on police lock-ups and jails" (p. 225). She cited studies showing a pronounced increase in arrest and incarceration of former mental patients. Torrey and colleagues (1992) estimated that 7.2% of inmates of local jails suffer from serious mental illness, which represents a 10-fold increase from 1980. They reported that 29% of jails hold seriously mentally ill individuals without any criminal charges against them.

Analysis of institutional residents in our study confirms a high rate of mobility between institutional and noninstitutional residences. Among institutional residents studied in DC*MADS, if interviews had been conducted in a month selected at random from the previous 4 years, respondents would have been more likely to have been interviewed in the household population than in the institutional population.

5.1.2.3 Relationship of Substance Abuse to Other Problems

Substance abuse among the institutionalized population may interact with the population's other physical and psychological problems. Physical and psychological problems known to be comorbid with drug use include the combined problem of the human immunodeficiency virus, the acquired immune deficiency syndrome, and the AIDS-related complex (HIV/AIDS/ARC), as well as tuberculosis (TB) and depressive and affective disorders.

A survey of prison and jail systems for adults found a rate of 5.2 AIDS cases per 1,000 adult inmates, six times the rate of 0.9 cases per 1,000 in the adult population (Center for Disease Control and Prevention, 1996a). The American College of Physicians, the National Commission on Correctional Health Care, and the American Correctional Health Services Association (1992) reported a similarly disproportionate rate of AIDS infections among prison inmates. Vlahov and colleagues (1991) reported that the rate of HIV seroprevalence among entrants to 10 selected U.S. jails and federal and state prisons ranged from 2.1% to 7.6% for men, and from 2.7% to 14.7% for women. These rates can be compared with seroprevalences among first-time blood donors that were 0.04% for males and 0.02% for females. AIDS and HIV infections among correctional populations also appear to be increasing. A National Institute of Justice (NIJ) survey in 1994 reported 5,279 cases of AIDS among current inmates, representing 5.2 AIDS cases per 1,000 adult inmates—a rate almost six times that of the U.S. adult population (CDC, 1996a).

The Center for Disease Control and Prevention (1996b) also reviewed studies documenting a high rate of TB infection among inmates, ranging from 14% to 25%: "Among inmates of the New York state correctional system, the incidence of TB increased from 15.4 cases per 100,000 inmates during 1976-1978 to 105.5 cases per 100,000 inmates during 1986. By 1993, this incidence was 139.3 cases per 100,000 inmates" (p. 2). The rate of TB infection in New Jersey's state prison system was 109.9 per 100,000, 11 times that of the general population. In a survey of

California Department of Corrections facilities, the rate of TB incidence was 80.3 per 100,000, nearly six times the general population rate for that year (CDC, 1996b).

As of 1989, the prevalence of major psychiatric disorders among correctional populations was between 6% and 14%. More than 13% of jail inmates said that they had taken prescribed medication for an emotional or mental problem, and 8% indicated they had previously been sent to a mental hospital or treatment program by a court (American College of Physicians et al., 1992). Teplin (1990) found significantly higher rates of severe mental disorders among a sample of Cook County Jail inmates than in a comparison sample from the general populations of five large cities participating in the National Institute of Mental Health (NIMH) Epidemiological Catchment Area (ECA) program.

The Council on Scientific Affairs (1990) of the American Medical Association found high rates of substance abuse and sexually transmitted diseases (STDs), as well as significant emotional or physical trauma and depression, among incarcerated juveniles.

5.1.2.4 Drug Treatment Needs
of Institutionalized Residents

Information about drug use among the institutionalized population can help inform their needs for treatment, the extent to which they are making use of available treatment opportunities, and how to assess the treatment resources that local institutions will need in dealing with their drug problems. The recent drug use history of the institutionalized population, and especially those who are incarcerated, presents an opportunity to assess drug abuse treatment and prevention policy. Although institutional residents are never a large fraction of the general population, they do represent an appreciable proportion of people who have very serious drug problems.

Tims and Leukefeld (1992) argued that "jails and prisons offer an opportunity to engage the drug-dependent individual in a rehabilitation process. . . . [F]or many drug abusers, incarceration may be the only contact with treatment providers" (p. 1). Institutionalization provides an opportunity to reach a large group of active drug users and provide them with the tools to reduce their use of drugs when they return to the community.

Unfortunately, many institutions may not be equipped to deal with the needs of substance-abusing residents. Describing the situation in 1978, Barton (1982) showed that the screening and treatment capacities of local jails often were inadequate. More recently, the American College of Physicians et al. (1992) reported that the situation had not improved: "About 5% of jail inmates were receiving treatment for substance abuse . . . [and] 20% of jails reported drug treatment programs involving paid staff" (p. 75). They also cited a recent U.S. General Accounting Office (GAO) study that "found that only about 1% of the estimated 27,000 inmates in federal prisons which have moderate-to-severe substance abuse problems were receiving intensive treatment" (American College of Physicians et al., 1992, p. 75).

5.2 Overview of the Study

The DC*MADS Institutionalized Study was designed to estimate the prevalence and consequences of drug use among the institutionalized population in the Washington, DC, metropolitan statistical area (DC MSA) and to develop a set of methods that would be useful in repeating the study in other metropolitan areas. The study collected such data as types of drugs used, patterns of use, frequency of use, and respondents' general experiences with drug use, drug treatment, and consequences of drug use. It targeted people who were residents of institutions in the DC MSA.

"Institutions" were defined as facilities that provide care and custody for their residents and included prisons and correctional halfway houses, mental and psychiatric hospitals, hospitals for chronically ill people, schools or wards for physically disabled people, juvenile detention centers, and group homes for dependent and neglected children and adolescents. Eligible persons included all current residents aged 12 or older living in sampled institutions that were drawn from a frame consisting of all institutions in the DC MSA as defined by the U.S. Bureau of the Census (1984), with selected exclusions. Some institutions were excluded because they were expected to have minimal drug use (e.g., nursing homes for the aged), were included in another study within the DC*MADS project (college dormitories), were considered transient and not part of the DC MSA (military installations), or posed difficult logistical problems (e.g., developmentally disabled, hearing impaired) (see also Appendix C, 1998).

Face-to-face interviews were conducted in private by specially trained interviewers with 1,203 individuals in 42 participating institutions stratified into four groups: correctional institutions, psychiatric institutions, other institutions, and group homes. A life-events calendar was used to promote recall. Chapter 2 provides an overview of methods used in the DC*MADS set of studies, and Appendix C (1998) and the study's final technical report (National Institute on Drug Abuse [NIDA], 1994) describe in more detail the methods used in this study of the institutionalized population.

5.3 Understanding the Institutionalized Population

Before considering drug use among institutionalized persons, it is important to have a basic understanding of the characteristics of this population and their patterns of institutionalization. We begin with a description of the size and demographics of the institutionalized population and follow this with a brief examination of their patterns of institutionalization.

5.3.1 Size and Demographics of the Institutionalized Population

Table 5.1 shows the distribution of the institutionalized population, by gender, age, race/ethnicity, marital status, adult education, and length of institutionalization. The first four columns present these distributions for each of the main types of institutions: correctional, psychiatric, other institutions, and group homes. The fifth column presents the distribution for all institutionalized persons. As shown in Table 5.1, across all types of institutions in the DC MSA, the large majority of residents of institutions were males (90.7%), about 70% were black, and about 70% were single. Two thirds had not completed high school. Relatively few (6.9%) were under age 18, and the largest age group was

Table 5.1 Characteristics of the Institutionalized Population, by Type of Institution

Demographic Characteristic	Correctional (n = 868)	Psychiatric (n = 207)	Other (n = 55)	Group Home (n = 73)	Total Institutionalized (n = 1,203)
Gender					
Male	94.4	67.6*	46.2*	66.4*	90.7
Female	5.6	32.4*	53.8*	33.6*	9.3
Age (years)					
12-17	4.3*	21.9*	89.1*	0.0*	6.9*
18-25	32.6	7.1*	8.3*	3.2*	29.4
26-34	39.0	13.9	0.8*	26.0*	36.2
≥35	24.1	57.1*	1.8*	70.8*	27.5
Race/ethnicity					
White	18.7	46.0*	5.1*	39.0*	20.9
Black	71.3	45.0*	75.6*	60.2*	69.3
Hispanic	5.3	5.4	9.0*	0.8*	5.2
Other	4.8	3.6	10.4*	0.0*	4.6
Marital status					
Single	70.0	61.9*	98.9*	45.0*	69.1
Married	11.8	10.4	0.3*	2.4*	11.2
Divorced/widowed	18.1	27.6*	0.8*	52.6*	19.7
Adult education[1]					
Less than high school	67.2	34.8*	**	49.5*	64.8
High school graduate	21.8	23.4	**	18.4*	21.7
Some college	9.5	29.4*	**	24.1*	11.1
College graduate	1.6	12.4*	**	8.0	2.4
Length of institutionalization (months)					
≤1	25.8	60.8*	42.5*	15.6*	28.0
More than 1 to 6	39.8	12.7	13.3*	24.9*	37.0
>6	34.4*	26.6*	44.2*	59.5*	35.0
Total sample	88.0	6.4	2.0	3.7	100.0

SOURCE: Washington, DC, Metropolitan Area Drug Study (DC*MADS): 1989-1995.

NOTE: Data entries are percentages.

1. Data on adult education are not applicable for persons aged 12 to 17.

*Low precision.

**Indicates that there were too few cases to report.

26 to 34 years old (36.2%). About 28% were institutionalized 1 month or less, 37% for 1 month to 6 months, and 35% for more than 6 months.

Table 5.1 also shows some differences in the profiles of residents in the four types of facilities. People incarcerated in the DC MSA *correctional facilities* (i.e., prisons, jails, and halfway houses) were largely male, young adults and middle-aged adults (i.e., 18 to 34 years old), black, single, and poorly educated. They were more likely than other institutional residents to stay from 1 to 6 months in a facility. People institutionalized in *psychiatric facilities* (i.e., mental or psychiatric hospitals, hospitals or wards for people with mental retardation) were largely male, single, and older (35 or older). They were more likely than residents of other types of institutions to be white and highly educated and to have a very short stay (1 month or less). People institutionalized in *"other" institutions*, such as homes for dependent and neglected people and emergency shelters, tended to be very young (under age 18), single (because they were so young), and black. Their length of stay was bimodal: either very short (1 month or less) or very long (more than 6 months). People living in *group homes* for people with mental illness(es), mental retardation, or physical disabilities tended to be male, older, black, and divorced or widowed. Their stays were frequently very long (more than 6 months).

It was estimated that the 1991 DC MSA institutionalized population represented in the study sample (which omits nursing homes, residential schools for hearing-impaired people, homes for developmentally disabled people, and religious group quarters) comprised 19,395 persons. As described in more detail in Chapter 9, this number represents roughly 0.6% of the composite population in the DC MSA. Thus, it is clear that the institutionalized population as a group was quite small relative to the total population.

It was further estimated that 88.0% of institutional residents were confined in correctional facilities (jails, prisons, and correctional halfway houses). The remaining 12.0% resided in psychiatric facilities (6.4%), other types of institutions (2.0%), and group homes (3.7%).

5.3.2 Patterns of Institutionalization

Although the previous section describes the institutionalized population on the basis of their residence at the time of the interview, there is much mobility both among institutions and between institutions and household residences or homelessness. Many respondents had been in and out of different types of institutions or household settings or had been homeless for periods of time during the 4 years before the survey.

One of the tasks of this study was to determine the overlaps among the institutionalized population and other populations of interest. To accomplish this, we asked respondents to provide a month-by-month history of their stays in institutional and noninstitutional residences between January 1988 and the interview date. Information was collected for the period between January 1, 1988, and the date of the study interview, which could have been as late as December 31, 1991, yielding a maximum of 48 months of data.

Based on the interview information, we calculated the number of months spent in correctional, psychiatric, group home, other institutional, and household residences, as well as time spent homeless. The proportions of the period that each respondent spent in the various residential statuses were calculated by dividing the number of months in each residential status by the total number of calendar months over the 4-year period for which residential status was available (this varied from 41 to 48 months). These proportions were then averaged over respondents to compute the average amount of time that respondents spent in each status.

Results showed that the average institutionalized respondent had spent most of the 4-year period prior to the study interview in a household (average of 58.5% of the prior 4-year period; NIDA, 1994). By implication, if the month of interview had been picked at random from the 4 preceding years, the respondent would have been more likely to have been interviewed in a household than in an institution. Certainly, the image of permanent institutionalization does not fit the average resident of an institution.

Not surprisingly, where respondents were interviewed during this study was closely associated with how they spent the prior 4 years. Respondents in correctional institutions at the time of the interview had spent 38.1% of the period in correctional facilities and 58.2% of the period in household residences (NIDA, 1994). Respondents in psychiatric institutions had spent 22.6% of the period in a psychiatric facility and 68.0% in a household. These respondents (in psychiatric institutions at the time of the interview) also had spent an average of 3.5% of the prior 4 years in "other" institutions and another 2.7% of these years in group homes.

This finding indicates greater mobility among psychiatric residents than among those from correctional institutions.

Respondents in noncorrectional, nonpsychiatric ("other") institutionalized settings had spent comparatively little time in these institutions during the previous 4 years; only 10.4% of their time was spent in these institutions, whereas 69.7% of their time was spent in household residences and another 18.1% of the time was spent in group homes (NIDA, 1994). This group (i.e., those in other institutions at the time of the interview) therefore was the most mobile over the previous 4 years. The fact that they had spent the greatest length of time in household residences is perhaps explained by the age of these respondents: 89.1% of respondents in other institutions were 17 years of age or younger (see Table 5.1).

Finally, respondents who were in group homes at the time of the interview had spent 41.6% of the prior 4 years in this institutional setting and 42.0% of the period in household residences (NIDA, 1994). They tended to spend more time in other institutional settings than did other respondents. These other settings included psychiatric facilities (9.4% of the time), "other" institutions (4.4% of the time), and correctional facilities (1.7% of the time).

In sum, most institutionalized persons, regardless of the type of institution in which they resided, had spent most of the previous 4 years in household settings. The results suggest that there was comparatively limited overlap among institutions. Correctional residents had spent very little time in noncorrectional institutions, and psychiatric residents had spent little time in nonpsychiatric institutions. Residents of other institutions, however, had spent more of the prior 4 years, on average, in group homes than in these other institutions.

5.4 Drug Use Prevalence and Correlates

This section examines past year and past month use of illicit drugs and alcohol prior to institutionalization and also examines rates during institutionalization, by demographic and institutional characteristics. A typology is constructed to characterize drug use among the institutionalized population prior to their being institutionalized.

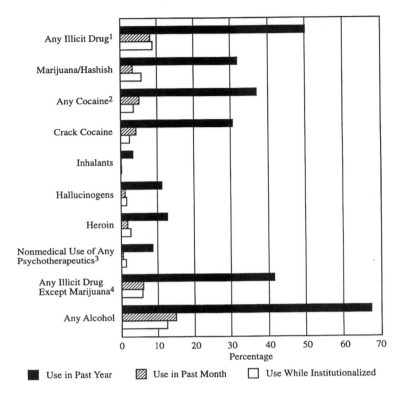

Figure 5.1. Prevalence of Illicit Drug and Alcohol Use in the DC MSA Institutionalized Population

SOURCE: Washington, DC, Metropolitan Area Drug Study (DC*MADS): 1989-1995.
NOTE: See Table C.2 in Appendix C (1998) for the supporting data used to prepare this figure.
1. Use of marijuana or hashish, cocaine (including crack), inhalants, hallucinogens (including phencyclidine or PCP), or heroin, or nonmedical use of psychotherapeutics at least once.
2. Includes crack cocaine.
3. Nonmedical use of any prescription-type stimulant (including methamphetamine), sedative, tranquilizer, or analgesic; does not include over-the-counter drugs.
4. Includes cocaine (including crack), inhalants, hallucinogens (including PCP), heroin, or psychotherapeutics for nonmedical reasons.

5.4.1 Prevalence of Drug Use Among the Institutionalized Population

Rates of past year and past month drug use by residents of institutions are presented in Figure 5.1 (see supporting data in Table C.2 in Appendix C [1998]). The figure also presents rates of drug use while institutionalized. As shown in Figure 5.1, about half (49.9%) of the institutionalized population had used an illicit drug in the year prior to the interview. The illicit drug most frequently reported was cocaine (36.9%), especially crack cocaine (30.4%). Marijuana/hashish was the next most frequently reported (31.7%), followed by heroin (12.7%). The high rate of crack cocaine use in the past year probably reflects the recent growth in popularity of the drug. About two thirds (67.2%) drank alcohol during the past year.

"Current use" of a drug refers to use during the past month. By this definition, comparatively few of the institutionalized population were current users of illicit drugs (8.1%). The largest proportions of current drug users reported using cocaine (5.0%), especially crack cocaine (4.2%), and marijuana/hashish (3.4%). Differences among these rates are not statistically significant. Other drugs were reported as used by fewer than 2% of the respondents. Almost 15% reported using alcohol in the past month, even though alcohol use was not permitted in any of the institutions surveyed.

Past year or past month use can be misleading for the institutionalized population because the period may include days when the respondent was outside the institution and other days while inside.[2] Thus, a more meaningful measure of use may be "use while institutionalized." The proportions of the institutionalized population who used illicit drugs and alcohol at least once while institutionalized also are displayed in Figure 5.1. About 1 in 12 (8.8%) institutionalized persons reported using an illicit drug at some time during their current institutionalization. Note that the prevalence of use of specific drugs is higher in some instances for use while institutionalized than for current use because of differing time periods; the period of institutionalization was longer than 1 month for three fourths of the residents of institutions.

Whether 8.8% represents a high or a low rate of use is a matter of perspective. Certainly, it is a rate well below what we would expect given the high rates of past year use reported by the institutionalized population. In this sense, institutional controls seem effective in limiting access to drugs for this highly drug-prone population. Yet, given the restrictions that the institutionalized population faces in obtaining and using drugs, it is surprising that 1 in 12 were able to acquire an illicit drug during institutionalization.

The illicit drug reported being used most commonly while institutionalized was marijuana/hashish (5.7%). The illicit drug next most frequently used was cocaine (3.5%). Heroin was the next most commonly used (2.6%). These differences are not statistically significant. Other drugs were used by fewer than 2% of the institutionalized population. Alcohol use was reasonably common (12.3%).

For several reasons, these numbers are likely to be underestimates of actual use. First, there is probably some reluctance to report drug use. In addition to the usual criminal sanctions against illicit drug use, in every institution sampled there also were administrative penalties. Second, because it was difficult to define length of institutionalization a priori, there may have been drug use that we classified outside the institution that, in fact, occurred inside the institution. If drug use was reported in the same month as the month of institutionalization and there was no drug use subsequent to the month of institutionalization, use was not classified as occurring within the institution. This approach probably underestimates institutional drug use, but the effect is likely to be small.

5.4.2 Demographic Correlates of Drug Use

Table 5.2 presents rates of any illicit drug use among institutionalized persons in the DC MSA by various demographic characteristics. As shown, gender differences were relatively small across all periods of use (past year, past month, and while institutionalized). Past month drug use rates for males and females were the most similar (8.0% males vs. 8.7% females).

The prevalence of drug use was generally higher among institutionalized persons in the 18- to-25 and 26-to-34 year age ranges than among younger or older persons. More than half (55.2%) of 18- to 25-year-olds and 54.5% of 26- to 34-year-olds reported illicit drug use in the year before the interview, compared with 41.2% of persons aged 35 or older and 37.4% of 12- to 17-year-olds. Past month use was similar among 26- to 34-year-olds (9.8%) and 18- to-25-year-olds (8.1%), but it was marginally higher than drug use rates reported by adults 35 or older (6.8%). Drug use while institutionalized was higher among persons aged 12 to 17 (15.4%) than in other age groups.

There were no significant differences among racial/ethnic groups in reported use of any illicit drug by institutionalized persons, although the use of particular drugs did differ by race/ethnicity. Institutionalized

Table 5.2 Use of Any Illicit Drug During the Past Year, During the Past Month, and While Institutionalized, by Demographic Characteristics

Demographic Characteristics	Past Year	Past Month	While Institutionalized
Gender			
Male	50.5	8.0	9.2
Female	43.4*	8.7	5.2
Age (years)			
12-17	37.4	3.8*	15.4
18-25	55.2	8.1	7.5
26-34	54.5	9.8	8.9
≥ 35	41.2	6.8	8.4
Race/ethnicity			
White	55.1	10.9	7.3
Black	49.2	7.3	9.2
Hispanic	54.0*	4.6*	7.1*
Other	35.7*	11.1*	11.8*
Marital status			
Single	51.7	7.9	9.6
Married	42.2	8.3	8.8
Divorced/widowed	49.1	8.9	6.3
Adult education[1]			
Elementary	54.0	11.6	12.4
Some high school	52.7	6.6	7.2
GED[2]	51.1	10.2	12.8
High school graduate	50.3	7.6	6.5
Some college	44.4	10.0	5.2
Length of institutionalization (months)			
≤ 1	59.7	22.2	2.7
More than 1 to 6	63.4	2.6	6.8
> 6	27.8	2.6	15.8
Total sample	49.9	8.1	8.8

SOURCE: Washington, DC, Metropolitan Area Drug Study (DC*MADS): 1989-1995.
NOTE: Data entries are percentages. $N = 1,203$.
1. Data on adult education are not applicable for persons aged 12 to 17.
2. GED = Graduate Equivalency Diploma.
*Low precision.

blacks and whites had similar rates of drug use in the past year (49.2% blacks vs. 55.1% whites) and past month (7.3% blacks vs. 10.9% whites). Rates of reported drug use by Hispanics were similar to those for blacks and whites, but estimates were of low precision.

Differences in the reported rates of any illicit drug use by marital status and adult educational level were weak and inconsistent. Past year and past month rates of illicit drug use were, however, related to length of institutionalization. Those institutionalized for more than 1 month had much lower rates of past month drug use than did those institutionalized for less than 1 month (2.6% vs. 22.2%, respectively). This difference would be expected because persons institutionalized less than 1 month spent some part of the month outside the institution, where access to and use of drugs were less constrained. Similarly, past year use was lower among those institutionalized for more than 6 months (27.8%) than among those institutionalized for more than 1 month but fewer than 6 months (63.4%) or for 1 month or less (59.7%).

The last column of Table 5.2 presents percentages of each demographic group who reported having used any illicit drug while institutionalized. Few of these differences are significant. Men were more likely than women to have used an illicit drug while institutionalized (9.2% men vs. 5.2% women). Those who were 12 to 17 years old at the time of the interview were nearly twice as likely as those in any other age group to report having used an illicit drug during the current institutionalization (15.4% for 12- to 17-year-olds vs. 7.5% for 18- to 25-year-olds, 8.9% for 26- to 34-year-olds, and 8.4% for those 35 or older). This finding may reflect the lower levels of security used for this age group. Those who were 12 to 17 years old tended to be located in group homes and institutions classified as noncorrectional and nonpsychiatric (e.g., homes for dependent and neglected children). Use during institutionalization also was higher among those institutionalized more than 6 months (15.8%) than among those institutionalized for 1 month or less (2.7%) or 1 month to 6 months (6.8%). This finding suggests that residents may "learn" ways of accessing drugs the longer they are institutionalized.

5.4.3 Drug Use by Type of Institution

Rates of illicit drug use varied by type of institution, as illustrated in Table 5.3 for past year prevalence. Inmates of correctional facilities had the highest rates of any illicit drug use in the past year among the institutionalized population. A majority (52.2%) of those incarcerated in correctional facilities reported using an illicit drug in the past year, with the most common drugs being cocaine (39.2%), marijuana/hashish (33.5%), heroin (13.5%), and hallucinogens (11.9%).

Table 5.3 Past Year Use of Illicit Drugs and Alcohol, by Type of Institution

Substance Used	Correctional (n = 868)	Psychiatric (n = 207)	Other (n = 55)	Group Home (n = 73)	Total Institutionalized (n = 1,203)
Any illicit drug[1]	52.2	44.4*	8.7*	24.9*	49.9
Marijuana/hashish	33.5	26.9*	4.1*	12.3*	31.7
Any cocaine	39.2	24.1*	0.5*	24.5*	36.9
Crack cocaine	32.2	19.1*	0.5*	22.3*	30.4
Inhalants	3.1	8.9*	4.1*	0.8*	3.4
Hallucinogens	11.9	7.3*	0.0*	6.1*	11.1
Heroin	13.5	8.3*	0.5*	8.2*	12.7
Nonmedical use of any psychotherapeutics[2]	8.5	12.7*	0.3*	8.6*	8.6
Any illicit drug except marijuana[3]	43.0	40.0*	4.6*	24.5*	41.4
Any alcohol	69.0	64.9*	42.1*	39.8*	67.2

SOURCE: Washington, DC, Metropolitan Area Drug Study (DC*MADS): 1989-1995.
NOTE: Data entries are percentages.
1. Use of marijuana or hashish, cocaine (including crack), inhalants, hallucinogens (including phencyclidine or PCP), heroin, or nonmedical use of psychotherapeutics at least once.
2. Nonmedical use of any prescription-type stimulant (including methamphetamine), sedative, tranquilizer, or analgesic; does not include over-the-counter drugs.
3. Use of cocaine (including crack), inhalants, hallucinogens (including PCP), heroin, or nonmedical use of psychotherapeutics at least once.
*Low precision.

More than 40% of residents in psychiatric institutions used illicit drugs in the past year, and the drugs most frequently used were marijuana/hashish (26.9%), cocaine (24.1%), and psychotherapeutics (12.7%). A very low rate of past year use of illicit drugs was reported by residents of "other" institutions (8.7%). Marijuana/hashish and inhalants were the most frequently reported drugs used by this group in the past year (4.1% for each). Past year use of other illicit drugs was reported by fewer than 1% of respondents. In contrast, alcohol use was frequently reported in the past year (42.1%).

Past year rates of use of illicit drugs for residents of group homes were generally similar to rates of use among residents of psychiatric facilities and were not significantly different, because of large variability in the rates for the two types of institutions. Keep in mind that much of the use reported during the past year reflected at least some periods of time when residents were outside the institutions. Overall, about one fourth of residents of group homes had used drugs in the past year.

5.4.4 Characterizing Drug Use
Prior to Institutionalization

Analyses in the prior sections illuminate the key problem in understanding drug use among the institutionalized population. Institutional residents constitute a population exhibiting a much lower rate of illicit drug use while institutionalized than when not institutionalized. These persons migrate among institutions, households, and homelessness. When institutionalized, their drug use decreases dramatically, but when residing in a household or when living as homeless, their drug use increases.

A typology was developed for this study in order to characterize the institutionalized population in terms of their patterns of drug use in the period prior to the interview. This typology classifies respondents in terms of the drugs they were using in the 6 months prior to their current institutionalization and the frequency with which they used them. The purpose of the typology is to describe the drug use and treatment needs of the institutionalized population and to isolate where these problems and needs are greatest.

This typology was developed using a two-step process. First, a priori, separate classes were created for (a) all respondents who reported no use of illicit drugs or alcohol during the preinstitutional period (unweighted $n = 207$) and (b) all respondents who used only alcohol during the preinstitutional period (unweighted $n = 260$).

Second, a cluster analysis (e.g., see Everitt, 1980, 1993) was conducted on the remaining cases. Conceptually, cluster analysis is similar to factor analysis, except that instead of grouping common variables or test items, the procedure seeks to group respondents in terms of their similarity in scores on a set of criterion variables (in this case, average frequency of use of the set of illicit drugs and alcohol).

The number of clusters to emerge is, within limits, arbitrary, and the adequacy of the solution depends largely on its ease of interpretation. A three-cluster solution seemed to produce the most substantively reasonable classification. Figure 5.2 is a graphical representation of the five-group typology consisting of the three drug user groups, as well as those who used neither illicit drugs nor alcohol and those who used alcohol only. We can describe each of the groups based on their patterns of drug use. Additional details are provided in NIDA (1994). Some 11% of the population (unweighted $n = 172$) could not be classified because they were institutionalized from January 1988 to the date of the interview.

No Use (unweighted $n = 207$). This group, 17.1% of the total, reported no use of any of the illicit drugs or alcohol during the 6 months prior to institutionalization.

Alcohol Only (unweighted $n = 260$). This group, 28.2% of the total, used no illicit drugs during the preinstitutionalized period. More than a quarter of this group drank daily or almost daily for 1 or more months during the period. The remainder drank in lesser amounts, and, by definition, none abstained throughout the period.

Alcohol/Marijuana Users (unweighted $n = 271$). This group constituted 27.8% of the total. More than a third of this group (37.6%) drank alcoholic beverages daily or almost daily a month or more, and about half (50.5%) drank less regularly. Almost 12% (11.9%) did not drink at all during the 6 months before institutionalization. Nearly 3 in 10 of this group used marijuana/hashish daily or almost daily for 1 or more months during the period, and about a third used it at lesser rates. Some 38.5% did not use the drug at all. A majority (63.9%) of the group of alcohol/marijuana

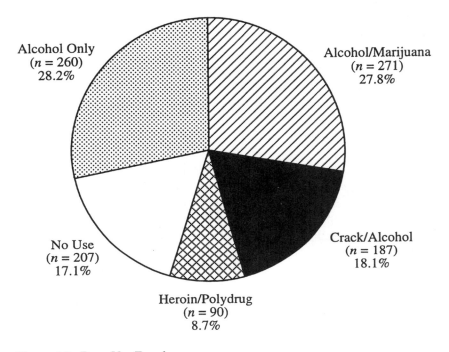

Figure 5.2. Drug Use Typology
SOURCE: Washington, DC, Metropolitan Area Drug Study (DC*MADS): 1989-1995.
NOTE: Percentages are based on weighted data. Ns are unweighted.

users never used crack cocaine during the preinstitutional period. About 10% (9.9%) of this group used crack cocaine daily or almost daily for a month or more of the preinstitutionalization period, and more than a quarter used it at lesser rates. Few of the alcohol/marijuana user group reported using any of the other illicit drugs regularly during the preinstitutional period.

Crack/Alcohol Users (unweighted n = 187). This group, 18.1% of the total, used crack cocaine quite heavily: 72.2% used it daily or almost daily 1 or more months in the 6 months before institutionalization. More than half also drank heavily (54.1% drank daily or almost daily 1 or more months during the period). Marijuana/hashish use was also present, although less than in the other drug-using groups. Use of other drugs was quite infrequent.

Heroin/Polydrug Users (unweighted n = 90). This group, 8.7% of the total, included heavy users of heroin, cocaine other than crack, and other drugs. More than three fifths (60.9%) used heroin daily or almost daily for some month(s) before institutionalization, and 63.9% used types of cocaine other than crack as frequently. Nearly half (48.8%) used crack cocaine daily or almost daily, and more than a quarter (28.9%) used marijuana/hashish daily or almost daily. About two fifths (41.1%) drank daily or almost daily 1 or more months during the period.

This typology reveals that the majority of residents of institutions were drug users in the 6-month period prior to institutionalization, and many used multiple drugs. Only 17% used neither alcohol nor drugs prior to institutionalization. This finding suggests that substance abuse treatment needs to be provided in many types of institutions not specifically serving substance abuse populations; moreover, because many institutionalized persons have abused both alcohol and drugs, combined alcohol and drug abuse treatment should be offered.

5.5 Substance Abuse Problems, Treatment, and Primary Care Utilization Among Institutionalized People

Not only are the majority of institutionalized persons users of alcohol and other drugs, but many also have experienced problems related to use, have been in substance abuse treatment, or have used primary care services. The DC*MADS Institutionalized Study provides a look at the social and medical consequences and comorbid conditions of drug use by the institutionalized population.

5.5.1 Alcohol- and Drug-Related Problems

Those who had used alcohol in the 12 months before the interview were asked a series of questions on alcohol-related problems they might have experienced in the prior year. Similarly, those who had used any illicit drug in the past year were asked a series of questions on drug-related problems that they might have experienced. Those institutionalized persons who reported past year use of drugs or alcohol were also very likely to have reported problems with that use, as shown in Table 5.4. Nearly half (49.7%) of institutionalized persons reported use of an illicit drug in the past year. Among these users, four of five (79.8%) reported one or more problems with drug use. Nearly one third (30.2%) reported having had five or six problems. Some two thirds (67.1%) of the institutionalized population had used alcohol in the past year. Of these, four out of five (82.9%) reported problems relating to their drinking. Nearly one in seven (14.5%) of the institutionalized population reported seven to nine problems.

Crack/alcohol use seems associated with as many drug-related problems as heroin/polydrug use. Crack/alcohol and heroin/polydrug users were equally likely to report a wide variety of problems relating to drug use (90.2% of crack/alcohol users and 95.1% of heroin/polydrug users reported one or more drug-related problems). Three quarters (77.1%) of alcohol/marijuana users reported one or more problems relating to drug use. More than 40% of crack/alcohol and heroin/polydrug users reported five or six problems from their use in the past year.

Among alcohol users, the majority reported alcohol-related problems, and alcohol problems tended to be greater among those who also used drugs. For example, although only 9.3% of the alcohol-only group reported seven to nine problems, 22.9% of crack/alcohol users and 18.3% of heroin/polydrug users reported the same number of problems.

5.5.2 Substance Abuse Treatment

Earlier in this chapter, it was noted that the institutionalized population exhibited relatively high rates of substance abuse. This finding raises a number of questions concerning the likelihood that institutionalized persons will seek treatment and the availability and efficacy of such treatment. This section describes findings relevant to these questions. Table 5.5 shows percentages of the types of drug users prior to institutionalization who had received treatment. The table also depicts several aspects of the most recent treatment program, including type

Table 5.4 Drug- and Alcohol-Related Problems During the Past Year, by Preinstitutionalized Drug Use Typology

Type of Problem	Alcohol Only (n = 260)	Alcohol/Marijuana (n = 271)	Crack/Alcohol (n = 187)	Heroin/Polydrug (n = 90)	Total Institutionalized[1] (n = 1,188)
Drug-related problem					
Used any illicit drug during past year	—	82.1	80.8	79.7*	49.7
Number of drug problems					
0	—	23.0	9.8	4.9*	20.1
1-2	—	32.0	17.9	20.8*	23.3
3-4	—	24.5	29.3	27.8	26.3
5-6	—	20.6	43.0	46.5	30.2
Alcohol-related problem					
Used alcohol during past year	90.8	79.5	73.2	69.5*	67.1
Number of alcohol problems					
0	29.0	10.2	7.7	11.8	17.2
1-3	43.0	40.2	39.7	44.3*	41.2
4-6	18.7	37.3	29.7	25.7*	27.2
7-9	9.3	12.3	22.9	18.3	14.5

SOURCE: Washington, DC, Metropolitan Area Drug Study (DC*MADS): 1989-1995.

NOTE: Data entries are percentages.

1. Includes problems reported by nomusers, alcohol-only group, and those who were unclassified (n = 172 respondents who were institutionalized longer than 4 years).

*Low precision.

Table 5.5 Substance Abuse Treatment Among Institutionalized Drug and Alcohol Users, by Drug Use Typology

Treatment Characteristics	Alcohol Only (n = 260)	Alcohol/Marijuana (n = 271)	Crack/Alcohol (n = 187)	Heroin/Polydrug (n = 90)	Total[1] (n = 1,188)
Treatment history					
Never	62.6	45.0	37.5	22.6	45.2
1-2 times	31.0	42.1	55.0	55.7*	43.2
3 or more times	6.3	12.9	7.5	21.8	11.6
Most recent type of treatment					
Alcohol use only	44.3*	21.4	8.8*	2.9*	20.1
Drug use only	23.1	47.7*	48.0	50.8*	41.0
Both	32.6*	30.9	43.1	46.3*	38.9
Recency					
> 1 year ago	40.0*	43.2	54.1	39.5	44.3
Within past year	42.1	42.2	32.1	37.5*	38.8
In treatment	17.8*	14.6	13.8	23.0*	16.9
Length (days)					
0-30	53.3*	50.5	52.9	43.8*	50.9
31-182	33.3	35.7	36.0	41.3*	35.3
≥183	13.4	13.9	11.1	15.0*	13.8

SOURCE: Washington, DC, Metropolitan Area Drug Study (DC*MADS): 1989-1995.
NOTE: Data entries are percentages.
1. Includes nonusers and unclassified (n = 172 respondents who were institutionalized more than 4 years).
*Low precision.

(alcohol only, drugs only, both alcohol and drugs), recency, and length of treatment.

Respondents who had ever used any illicit drug or alcohol were asked a series of questions about each time they received substance abuse treatment during the period from January 1988 until the date of the interview. If the most recent treatment occurred prior to 1988, respondents were asked the same series of questions about their most recent treatment exclusively. Table 5.5 summarizes the findings for the most recent treatment with regard to drug and alcohol abuse treatment received by the institutionalized population.

Just over half (54.8%) of the institutionalized population who had ever used alcohol or any illicit drug had received substance abuse treatment at least once. The heroin/polydrug users were most likely to have received substance abuse treatment at some time during their lives (77.5%). The crack/alcohol group appeared to be an underserved population in terms of substance abuse treatment (62.5% had ever received treatment). Although nearly three quarters (72.2%) of this group said they used crack cocaine daily or almost daily, 37.5% had never received substance abuse treatment of any kind. Among those who had received treatment, the crack/alcohol group was least likely to have been treated recently (within the past year). Those who had received treatment were very likely to have been treated for 30 days or less, which is likely an insufficient amount of time for treatment of cocaine-related problems.

Although many of those who had received substance abuse treatment had most recently been treated for both drug and alcohol abuse (38.9%), this study suggests more could benefit from such a dual emphasis. This is especially true among the crack/alcohol group, the majority of whom used both crack and alcohol on a daily or almost daily basis, and 90% of whom reported one or more problems related to drugs *and* one or more problems related to alcohol within the past year (see Table 5.4).

Respondents who had received substance abuse treatment at some time during their lives and those who had never received treatment, but had tried to get help, were asked whether they had ever tried unsuccessfully to get into treatment. Among the institutionalized population, 45.2% had never received substance abuse treatment. Of these, approximately one third (30.1%) had tried unsuccessfully to obtain treatment at some time during their lives (see NIDA, 1994). Heroin/polydrug users and the crack/alcohol group were most likely to have been unsuccessful in an attempt to obtain treatment. The most frequent reason given for failure to obtain desired treatment was "too long a waiting list." Financial reasons (no money, no insurance) also were frequently cited as reasons for not being able to obtain treatment.

5.5.3 Primary Care Utilization and Insurance Coverage

Table 5.6 presents percentages of residents of institutions who had been hospitalized or treated in an emergency room during their lifetimes or during the year before they were interviewed. The table also indicates whether they reported coverage by insurance plans and, if so, whether such plans were public or private.

The drug use groups differed in their rates of self-reported hospitalization. Overall, 67.7% of the institutionalized population had been hospitalized overnight at some time in their lives. The alcohol/marijuana, crack/alcohol, and heroin/polydrug groups were more likely to have been hospitalized than were the alcohol only or nonuser groups. More than three quarters (76.7%) of the heroin/polydrug group had been hospitalized overnight at some time, as had 74.0% of the crack/alcohol group and 69.7% of the alcohol/marijuana group. By contrast, only 61.0% of alcohol-only users and 61.9% of nonusers had ever been hospitalized overnight. Similarly, the three drug use groups were more likely than the alcohol-only and nonuser groups to have reported ever receiving treatment in an emergency room. For example, 87.5% of heroin/polydrug users and 83.3% of the crack/alcohol group had been treated in an emergency room, compared with 64.8% of nonusers.

These differences are less apparent when only past year hospitalizations and emergency room visits are considered. More recent rates of hospitalization were lower, and the differences between drug use groups were inconsistent. Overall, in the past year, 15.1% of the institutionalized population had been hospitalized, and the rates did not differ significantly by substance use group.

Less than a quarter of the institutionalized population had received emergency room treatment in the year prior to the interview, and the

Table 5.6 Lifetime and Past Year Services for Primary Care Problems and Insurance Coverage, by Preinstitutionalized Drug Use Typology

Service/Insurance	Nonusers (n = 208)	Alcohol Only (n = 260)	Alcohol/Marijuana (n = 271)	Crack/Alcohol (n = 187)	Heroin/Polydrug (n = 90)	Total[1] (n = 1,188)
Service utilization						
Lifetime hospitalization	61.9	61.0	69.7	74.0	76.7	67.7
Past year hospitalization	17.8	12.7	16.7	18.9	13.9	15.1
Lifetime ER[2] use	64.8*	77.7	88.8	83.3	87.5	79.3*
Past year ER use	25.3	21.3	19.9	31.2	20.2	21.5
Past year outpatient treatment	80.8	79.4	82.4	85.4	81.5*	81.4
Any insurance coverage	46.2	37.8	41.6	30.7	26.3	37.8
Type of insurance[3]						
Public	36.3*	21.3	15.5	26.1*	21.9*	25.3
Private	61.3	78.4	83.2	73.9*	75.3*	73.6
Both	2.4*	0.3*	1.3*	0.0*	2.8*	1.1

SOURCE: Washington, DC, Metropolitan Area Drug Study (DC*MADS): 1989-1995.
NOTE: Data entries are percentages.
1. Includes 172 respondents who were institutionalized longer than 4 years.
2. Emergency room.
3. Estimates are of those who reported having past year insurance coverage.
*Low precision.

153

proportion receiving emergency room treatment usually did not vary significantly by substance use group. The only exception is that the crack/alcohol group visited emergency rooms significantly more frequently (31.2%) than did the other groups. When the institutionalized population used emergency room facilities in the year prior to the interview, heavy drug-using groups were far more likely to report drug involvement in the visit (data not shown). For example, of the heroin/polydrug group reporting past year use of emergency room facilities, 47.9% reported that the visit was related to drug use. Similarly, of the crack/alcohol group using emergency room facilities in the year prior to the interview, 23.4% said the visit was related to drug use. These rates are significantly higher than for the other substance use groups.

The data in Table 5.6 also indicate a high rate of utilization of outpatient services. More than four fifths (81.4%) of the institutionalized population had been treated as an outpatient in the year prior to the interview. This rate did not differ significantly by substance use group.

In general, the institutionalized population was unlikely to have current insurance or health plan coverage. Just over a third (37.8%) reported that they had coverage. Of those who did have coverage, about one fourth (25.3%) reported publicly funded coverage (e.g., Medicaid). Thus, in spite of relatively high rates of past year medical care utilization, the institutionalized population frequently lacked insurance to pay for these services.

There are significant differences among the drug use groups with regard to insurance coverage. The heaviest drug-using groups were least likely to be insured. Just 26.3% of the heroin/polydrug group and 30.7% of the crack/alcohol group reported coverage, even though their rate of service utilization was high. Thus, the heavier drug-using groups—the groups most likely to require services—were least likely to be able to afford them.

The facts that the heavier drug users tended to utilize health care and treatment resources at high rates but also tended not to have insurance coverage combine to present a large and unfunded social cost of the institutionalized population that was even greater among those who abused drugs heavily. Indeed, insurance coverage for three fourths of those covered was drawn from public sources, such as Medicaid and Veterans' Administration (VA) benefits.

5.6 Discussion and Implications

The implications of our findings are now considered in several areas: the prevalence of alcohol and other drug use among the institutionalized population, the effectiveness of institutions in regulating drug use among their residents, the effects of drug use on becoming institutionalized, interactions between substance abuse and other physical and psychological problems, and treatment needs and resources.

5.6.1 Prevalence of Drug and Alcohol Use Among the Institutionalized Population

Drug and alcohol use were common among the institutionalized population prior to institutionalization but also continued after admission for many residents. Almost half of the institutionalized population had used an illicit drug in the past year, 8.1% in the past month, and 8.8% while institutionalized. About two thirds drank alcohol in the past year, about 15% in the past month, and 12.3% while institutionalized. Although the past year and past month time periods may include use during a time in which current residents were not institutionalized, clearly many residents were using drugs and alcohol during their institutionalization. The prevalence of use was lower for those institutionalized longer periods of time but was particularly high among those in correctional institutions.

5.6.2 Effectiveness of Institutions in Regulating Drug Use Among Residents

A major contribution of the DC*MADS Institutionalized Study was to obtain information about drug and alcohol use among institutionalized persons prior to and during the time they were residents of institutions. Although findings showed that 8.8% used illicit drugs and 12.3% used alcohol while institutionalized, these are likely to be underestimates. These percentages should be viewed, however, in the context of institutionalized people as a group being very likely to use illicit drugs and alcohol. The rates of use while institutionalized were far below the rates of use the institutionalized population experienced prior to institutionalization, in noninstitutional settings, where they spent most of their time.

Thus, although institutions have, and should have, a goal of *no* illicit drug or alcohol use while residents are under their care and custody, it is unclear how attainable this goal is. An equally important goal must be to give residents the tools and opportunities to curtail their use in noninstitutional settings; that is where most of their time is spent and where most use occurs. Giving the institutionalized population the tools to cope with drug and alcohol abuse outside the institution ultimately may make their return to institutionalization less likely because many residents are committed to institutions for crimes related to substance use or for substance abuse treatment.

5.6.3 Effects of Drug Use on Becoming Institutionalized

This chapter gives ample evidence that institutionalized substance abusers experience substantial behavioral, health, and psychological problems. Indeed, many members of the institutionalized population were incarcerated or committed because of their drug use.

A typology of preinstitutionalization drug and alcohol use was developed that may have value for practitioners. It includes five categories of drug and alcohol use prior to institutionalization: no use, alcohol use only, alcohol/marijuana use, crack/alcohol use, and heroin/polydrug use. This typology is useful in isolating particular problems of social, psychological, and physical functioning.

The typology classifies more than 25% of the institutionalized population as having had very serious drug involvements prior to institutionalization: 18.1% were classified in the crack/alcohol drug use group, and 8.7% were in the heroin/polydrug use group. These groups were very likely to report daily use of crack cocaine and heroin, respectively, during the period prior to their institutionalization. The fact that both of the latter drug-using groups also used alcohol heavily is an empirical finding, not a definitional convenience. In this sense, the typology gives the practitioner information about the kinds of treatment that are needed for these groups and suggests that a combined drug *and* alcohol treatment regimen is likely to be required. Only about one third of the institutionalized population who had received recent substance abuse treatment, however, received it for both alcohol and drug abuse.

5.6.4 Interactions Between Substance Abuse and Other Physical and Psychological Problems

The Institutionalized Study documented high rates of problems with the use of illicit drugs and alcohol, and these problems appeared to be more serious among the groups using drugs more heavily. The majority of the institutionalized population who had used drugs or alcohol in the past year reported problems with their use. The institutionalized population, however, and especially the heavy drug-using groups, were unlikely to have resources, in the form of insurance, to get the care they would need outside the institution.

5.6.5 Treatment Needs and Resources

Just over half of the institutionalized population had received substance abuse treatment at some time during their lives. Given the level of reported problems related to drugs and alcohol, however, it appeared that substantially more could have benefited from treatment. This was particularly true among the crack/alcohol users. Three quarters of this group used crack cocaine on a daily or almost daily basis prior to institutionalization. Nearly 40% of heavy crack cocaine and alcohol users had never received treatment, and those who had received treatment were less likely than those from other groups to have been treated recently. Furthermore, more than half of those who had been treated received short-term treatment of fewer than 30 days, a term of treatment unlikely to result in a lasting reduction of crack cocaine use.

Institutionalized individuals who used illicit drugs also were highly likely to have used alcohol extensively, in addition to a variety of drugs. Although a substantial minority of those who had received treatment were in programs that focused on both drugs and alcohol, the findings reported here suggest that more could have benefited from a polydrug treatment focus. Treatment focusing on multiple drugs and alcohol abuse would match observed drug use patterns better than treatment that focuses on any single drug problem alone.

Examination of resources available to the institutionalized population showed that nearly one third of those who had never received treatment had tried unsuccessfully at some time to obtain it. The reasons most frequently given for failure to obtain desired help were long waiting lists and financial difficulties, such as no health insurance. By themselves, these findings are not likely to be surprising to anyone in the service community; however, the proportion of the institutionalized population who had tried unsuccessfully to obtain treatment may be new information. Although providing substance abuse education and treatment to residents of institutions will not guarantee that their substance use will diminish when they are released, results presented here suggest that when offered, these services are utilized by institutional residents, particularly those whose drug and alcohol use is highest.

In sum, the institutionalized population showed high rates of drug and alcohol use, even in institutions not specifically oriented toward substance abuse treatment. Although many residents had used drugs and alcohol prior to institutionalization, about 1 in 10 used drugs or alcohol during the time in which they were institutionalized. This finding suggests the need for greater supervision of this population during institutionalization, although it is recognized that not all use could be eliminated.

The role that drug and alcohol use plays in a person becoming institutionalized is unclear, but the relatively high rates of use among this population suggest that many residents may need substance abuse treatment while institutionalized. Clearly, many need treatment prior to institutionalization, when their rates of drug and alcohol use are high, but they often are unable to pay for it and consequently may not receive it.

The institutionalized population is an example of a multiple-problem, high-service-using population. Even though most residents of institutions eventually return to the household population, they have substantial service needs prior to and during institutionalization. Some of these service needs are related to drug and alcohol use, and improved prevention and treatment programs could help decrease the numbers of people in institutions. Although residents of correctional institutions were particularly likely to have used alcohol and other drugs, rates of use also were high in psychiatric and other types of institutions.

Notes

1. "All inmates" is defined as choosing the questionnaire response "systematic tests of all inmates." It is unclear whether facilities interpreted this question correctly. Community-based facilities are those in which a majority of inmates leave the facility each day, unaccompanied (Harlow, personal communication, November 15, 1992).

2. Although this also is true of past year use, a much larger proportion of the institutionalized population spent at least some time outside the institution in the prior year than in the prior month. For this reason, past year use by the institutionalized population more closely resembles noninstitutional use.

References

Adler, F. (1986). Jails as a repository for former mental patients. *International Journal of Offender Therapy and Comparative Criminology, 30*, 225-236.

American College of Physicians, National Commission on Correctional Health Care, & American Correctional Health Services Association. (1992). The crisis in correctional health care: The impact of the national drug control strategy on correctional health services. *Annals of Internal Medicine, 117*, 71-77.

Anglin, M. D., & Speckart, G. (1986). Narcotics use, property crime, and dealing: Structural dynamics across the addiction career. *Journal of Quantitative Criminology, 2*, 355-375.

Appendix C: Institutionalized Study. (1998). (Available on the World Wide Web at http://www.sagepub.com/bray_druguse.htm)

Barton, W. I. (1982). Drug histories and criminality of inmates of local jails in the United States: Implications for treatment and rehabilitation of the drug abuser in a jail setting. *International Journal of the Addictions, 17*, 414-444.

Beck, A. J., & Shipley, B. E. (1989). *Recidivism of prisoners released in 1983* (NCJ 116261). Washington, DC: Bureau of Justice Statistics.

Bootzin, R. R., Shadish, W. R., & McSweeny, A. J. (1989). Longitudinal outcomes of nursing home care for severely mentally ill patients. *Journal of Social Issues, 45*, 31-48.

Camp, G. M., & Camp, C. G. (1991). *Corrections yearbook, 1991*. South Salem, NY: Criminal Justice Institute.

Center for Disease Control and Prevention. (1996a). HIV AIDS education and prevention programs for adults in prisons and jails and juveniles in confinement facilities, 1994. *Morbidity and Mortality Weekly Report, 45*, 268-271.

Center for Disease Control and Prevention. (1996b). Prevention and control of tuberculosis in correctional facilities. *Morbidity and Mortality Weekly Report, 45*, RR-8.

Council on Scientific Affairs. (1990). Health status of detained and incarcerated youths. *Journal of the American Medical Association, 263*, 987-991.

Everitt, B. (1980). *Cluster analysis*. London: Heinemann Educational Books.

Everitt, B. S. (1993). *Cluster analysis* (3rd ed.). London: Edward Arnold.

Harlow, C. W. (1992). *Drug enforcement and treatment in prisons, 1990* (NCJ 134724). Washington, DC: Bureau of Justice Statistics.

Langan, P. A., & Cuniff, M. A. (1992). *Recidivism of felons on probation, 1986-89* (NCJ 134177). Washington, DC: Bureau of Justice Statistics.

Lurigio, A. J., & Lewis, D. A. (1989). Worlds that fail: A longitudinal study of urban mental patients. *Journal of Social Issues, 45,* 79-91.

Mayfield, D. (1985). Substance abuse in the affective disorders. In A. Alterman (Ed.), *Psychopathology and substance abuse* (pp. 69-90). New York: Plenum.

Miller, N. S., & Gold, M. S. (1991). Dual diagnoses: Psychiatric syndromes in alcoholism and drug addiction. *American Family Physician, 43*(6), 51-56.

National Institute on Drug Abuse. (1994). *Prevalence of drug use in the DC metropolitan area institutionalized population: 1991* (Technical Report #4 under NIDA Contract No. 271-89-8340, Washington, DC, Metropolitan Area Drug Study, prepared by D. Cantor, G. H. Gaertner, & L. Keil, Westat, Inc., & R. M. Bray, Research Triangle Institute). Rockville, MD: Author.

O'Sullivan, K. (1984). Depression and its treatment in alcoholics: A review. *Canadian Journal of Psychiatry, 29,* 289-384.

Sobell, L. C., Sobell, M. B., Maisto, S. A., & Fain, W. (1983). Alcohol and drug use by alcohol and drug abusers when incarcerated: Clinical and research implications. *Addictive Behaviors, 8,* 89-92.

Teplin, L. A. (1990). The prevalence of severe mental disorder among male urban jail detainees. *American Journal of Public Health, 80,* 663-669.

Tims, F. M., & Leukefeld, C. G. (1992). The challenge of drug abuse treatment in prisons and jails. In C. G. Leukefeld & F. M. Tims (Eds.), *Drug abuse treatment in prisons and jails* (NIDA Research Monograph No. 118, DHHS Publication No. ADM 92-1884, pp. 1-7). Rockville, MD: National Institute on Drug Abuse.

Torrey, E. G., Stieber, J., Ezekiel, J., Wolfe, S. M., Sharfstein, J., Noble, J. H., & Flynn, L. M. (1992). *Criminalizing the seriously mentally ill: The abuse of jails as mental hospitals.* Washington, DC: Public Citizen's Health Research Group and National Alliance for the Mentally Ill.

U.S. Bureau of the Census. (1984). *Persons in institutions and other group quarters* (PC80-2-40). Washington, DC: Government Printing Office.

Vlahov, D., Brewer, T. F., Castro, K. G., Narkunas, J. P., Salive, M. E., Ullrich, J., & Muñoz, A. (1991). Prevalence of antibody to HIV-1 among entrants to US correctional facilities. *Journal of the American Medical Association, 265,* 1129-1132.

6 Drug Involvement Among Offender Populations

David Cantor

This chapter provides information on the connection between drug use and offending. Although the nature of the relationship between drug use and crime is much debated, the existence of the relationship is not. Using data from the Adult Criminal Offenders Study and the Juvenile Offenders Study within the DC*MADS project, this chapter reports estimates of the proportion of offenders using drugs and how this drug use is related to their recent offending patterns. The goal is to approximate how much crime is directly or indirectly linked to involvement with drug trafficking or drug use. Using such an approximation, one can then begin to place the importance of drugs within a larger perspective of overall crime control.

6.1 Relationship of Drug Use and Offending

To set the stage for the data from the offender studies, it is important to examine evidence showing the relationship between drug use and offending behavior. To do that, this section considers the nature of the

161

relationship between drug use and crime, data on the drug-crime link, and other associated issues.

6.1.1 Nature of the Relationship

The correlation between drug use and criminal offending is well established. Numerous studies have provided evidence that many people who use drugs also commit crimes and vice versa (Chaiken & Chaiken, 1982; Tonry & Wilson, 1990; Zawitz, 1992). The etiological explanations that link these two behaviors also have been the object of a large body of research, although the exact causal links are subject to some debate (e.g., Center for Substance Abuse Prevention [CSAP], 1993; Chaiken & Chaiken, 1982; Collins, Hubbard, & Rachal, 1985; Elliott, Huizinga, & Menard, 1989; Johnston, O'Malley, & Eveland, 1978; Osgood, Johnston, O'Malley, & Bachman, 1988; White, 1991; Zawitz, 1992). This debate is reflected in explanations for changes in the crime rates in Washington, DC. From 1985 to 1991, the homicide rate exploded by more than 220% (24 per 100,000 to 79 per 100,000; National Council on Crime and Delinquency [NCCD], 1996) and was largely attributed to systemic violence (Goldstein, 1989) associated with the distribution of crack. More recently, the rate of homicide has been slowly decreasing (79 per 100,000 in 1991 to 69 per 100,000 in 1994; NCCD, 1996), but this decrease is not fully understood. One explanation is that the markets for the distribution of drugs in DC may have become more stable, with a subsequent decrease in the number of violent encounters. At the same time, the number of cocaine-using offenders has gone down. For adults, use of cocaine dropped from 51% testing positive at time of arrest in 1991 to 41% in 1994 (NCCD, 1996).

These explanations for changes in the homicide rate are not entirely consistent with the changes in other types of crimes over this period. Although homicide was increasing, other crimes of violence were not increasing at nearly the rate one might expect from the increase in drug use (increases of approximately 50% between 1985 and 1991; Criminal Justice Research Center [CJRC], 1992). The rate of change for the major property crimes (e.g., burglary, motor vehicle theft) was increasing, but the increase was not as great as that for violent crimes (e.g., burglary increased 33% between 1985 and 1991). Along with these trends, indicators of drug use also were rising.

This differential rate of change among these crimes is somewhat counter to what one would expect when reviewing the literature that links drug use and criminal offending. Studies on the violence associated with crack use have found both lethal violence and nonlethal violence, such as robberies and assaults, to be associated with this drug (e.g., Fagan & Chin, 1990). This research generally has found that the strongest link between drug use and offending is in the commission of property crimes (Anglin & Speckart, 1986; Ball, Rosen, Flueck, & Nurco, 1982); however, despite indications from several data sources that crack use was on the rise in DC during the period from 1985 to 1991, the crime rates for property crimes were not increasing at nearly the same rate as for violent crimes.

These seeming "contradictions" are related to three issues associated with previous research and social indicators of drugs and crime. The first issue is that the link between drug involvement and predatory offending (i.e., illegal acts, such as violent offenses or property offenses in which "someone definitely and intentionally takes or damages the person or property of another" [Glaser, 1971, p. 4]) may not be as direct as implied by previous studies. Research that has found a link between drug use and other criminal activity has focused on relatively specialized populations who have been recruited either through purposive sampling methods or from drug treatment programs. Generalizing from these individuals to wider offender populations may exaggerate the direct effects that drug use has on the total volume of predatory crime. Other research involving more general populations, especially juveniles, generally has concluded that indirect relationships exist between the two deviant behaviors of drug involvement and offending (Chaiken & Chaiken, 1982; Elliott et al., 1989; Osgood et al., 1988).

The second issue is that indicators of drug use among criminal justice populations do not generally distinguish among different types of drug users. For example, one of the primary sources of information on drug use among those who are inclined to commit crimes are urine tests administered at arrest (Wish & O'Neil, 1989). This method of measuring drug use, however, does not measure the intensity of use over a particular time period; it measures only the drugs that the individual ingested just prior to the time of arrest. Consequently, these data do not indicate whether use is higher at the time of committing a crime or if the use directly contributed to the reason the crime was committed.

The third issue is that indicators of drug use among those committing crimes pertain to events that come to the attention of the criminal justice system. This set of crimes constitutes a small subset of the total number of crimes that actually occur in the population. Most crimes committed do not result in an arrest (e.g., Chaiken & Chaiken, 1982), and there very well may be a relationship between the type of offenders who are most likely to be caught by the police and important personal characteristics (e.g., levels of drug involvement [see Harrison, 1992, p. 207]). For example, the small increase in the early 1990s in reported robberies and assaults relative to homicides in Washington, DC, may have been the result of victims associated with systemic violence (i.e., rival drug dealers or dealer-customer dyads) not reporting the offense to the police. Unreported robberies and assaults would depress statistics on police-reported crime because police attention is tied directly to someone (usually the victim) reporting the event to the police. Homicides, however, generally come to the attention of the police regardless of whether citizens report them.

6.1.2 Data on the Drug-Crime Link

Estimates of drug involvement in violent criminal events have been provided in a number of studies by Goldstein and colleagues. These studies have used police records (Goldstein, 1989) and ethnographic interviews (Goldstein, Bellocci, Spunt, & Miller, 1991) to classify offender motivations associated with violent events according to a tripartite scheme: (a) economic-compulsive, (b) psychopharmacological, and (c) systemic. Economic-compulsive motives refer to the need to obtain money or other material wealth to buy drugs or to support a drug habit. Psychopharmacological motives refer to the direct impact of drug use on violent behaviors (i.e., violence is motivated either by the "high" associated with drug use or by withdrawal symptoms). Systemic motives refer to violence associated with the drug trade, such as market competition, interdealer rivalries, and trafficking patterns and routes.

Police departments have begun to gather supplementary information that provides more details about the link between drug involvement and a particular incident (Ryan, Goldstein, Brownstein, & Bellucci, 1990). At the local level, many police departments have begun classifying particular offenses as to whether they are related to involvement with drugs. For example, in many big cities (e.g., New York), homicide is now classified by whether the incident is related to drugs. At a national level, the National Incident Based Reporting System (NIBRS) being implemented to replace the present Uniform Crime Reporting (UCR) system used by the Federal Bureau of Investigation (FBI) asks the police to describe different aspects of the criminal event with respect to drug-related characteristics. The National Crime Victimization Survey (NCVS) also includes a question about the victim's perceptions of whether the offender was high on drugs at the time the event occurred.

Ryan and colleagues (1990) discussed several issues associated with the use of information from police-based recordkeeping systems. The most general observation is that the police may not be fully informed of the exact purpose or definitions needed to fill out incident forms that ask for information on the drug-related characteristics of an event. As a result, there may be substantial differences in the information provided by police as part of their routine paperwork and the information that is needed to classify cases by different drug-related characteristics. For example, when comparing police- and researcher-based classification of the same set of homicides, Ryan and colleagues (1990) found substantial differences not only in the percentage of events that were considered "drug related" but also in the distribution of drug-related events within Goldstein's (1989) tripartite framework of economic, pharmacological, and systemic events.

An alternative to police indicators of the drug-crime link are surveys of offenders. The advantage of survey methods is that the domain of events that can be described is not restricted to those that come to the attention of the police. Additionally, offenders are in a position to describe the event using details that may be known only to them. Survey methods, however, also have limitations. One problem is potential measurement error resulting from the use of self-reports. These errors may range from not remembering the event to intentional deception by the respondent. The scope and magnitude of measurement error are not well documented for self-reports of offenses and motives associated with committing crimes. Despite these problems, self-report methods have provided a valuable resource in providing critical information on drug abuse and criminal offending (Chaiken & Chaiken, 1982; Elliott et al., 1989).

Most surveys of offenders have been with special populations recruited using purposive methods or with drug treatment populations. Although very useful in investigating the etiology of the drug-crime relationship, these types of surveys do not provide much perspective on the magnitude of the problem among a more general population of persons who commit crime. The exceptions are surveys sponsored by the Bureau of Justice Statistics (BJS) that periodically interview incarcerated adults and juveniles; these BJS surveys collect information on the respondents' offense history and whether the respondents were under the influence of drugs at the time of committing the offense for which they were arrested (e.g., Beck et al., 1993; Beck, Kline, & Greenfeld, 1988; Innes, 1988). For example, according to the most recent BJS survey with a sample of adult state prisoners in 1991, 31% of state inmates committed their offense while under the influence of drugs and 17% committed the offense to obtain money to buy drugs (Beck et al., 1993, p. 22).

These data are useful as a national indicator of the link between drugs and crime, especially as the series continues in the future. These surveys may be less useful, however, in understanding issues and problems for metropolitan areas, such as the DC Metropolitan Statistical Area (DC MSA), where the drug and crime problems can be unique (e.g., Inciardi, Horowitz, & Pottieger, 1993, pp. 112-116). They also are fairly limited in the details they provide on the drug-crime link.

6.1.3 Remaining Issues

Policymakers and researchers have only relatively crude indicators linking drug use and crime in a particular locality. Several issues remain to be fully enumerated.

First, what are the levels of drug use among those who commit crimes? As shown by a number of indicators, drug use among those who are criminally active is very high. Very little data exist, however, on the drug use patterns of these individuals over extended periods of time. This issue is important when determining the resources needed to treat and/or sanction drug users based on the severity of the offender's drug problem. As noted above, data have been collected on drug use patterns among special populations, many of whom were recruited because of their drug problems. Very little is known about these patterns for more general populations of active adult offenders. (See Hser, Longshore, and Anglin [1994] for a discussion of methods to estimate the prevalence of drug use among offenders in the "criminal" population.)

Second, how much predatory and nonpredatory crime is related to drug use? Current indicators of crime do not break down the proportion of events that result from economic (e.g., stealing money or selling drugs to support a habit) and/or pharmacological motivations (e.g., release of inhibitions) associated with drug use. Data on such motivations are important when one is trying to better understand how much crime is attributable to drug use and/or how trends in crime are affected by changing drug use patterns.

Third, what proportion of predatory crime is a result of drug trafficking? A large proportion of crime associated with drugs is related to trafficking. The primary indicator of these crimes is the number of arrests made by the police. This, however, is partly an indicator of police activity associated with enforcing laws against selling drugs. Perhaps more important, there is very little data on predatory offenses associated with the drug trade. Unlike their reporting of predatory crimes, citizens do not generally report instances of drug selling to the police. Consequently, the primary way this type of crime comes to the attention of the police is through some type of police action (e.g., arrest).

Fourth, what is the prevalence and frequency of drug selling among offenders? Drug trafficking brings a number of problems to the community, through disruption of social order as well as associated violence and property crime (see the third issue discussed above). There is very little information on how often these activities occur in a cross section of criminal offenders. As with drug use, more complete knowledge of how often different types of trafficking activities occur and the motivation behind committing them would provide some perspective on the magnitude and scope of this type of illegal behavior.

This chapter builds on prior research and describes new data from two surveys of adult and juvenile offenders to provide estimates of the connection between drugs and offending. Although these data do not offer any clear etiological picture of the connection, or exact estimates of the amount of crime associated with drugs, they offer some perspective on the influence that drugs may have on the overall level of crime.

6.2 Overview of the Studies

The discussion below is based on data from two DC*MADS surveys: the Adult Criminal Offenders Study and the Juvenile Offenders Study. The first was of adults who had been indicted of a felony, convicted of a crime, and sentenced to incarceration within the DC MSA. The second was with juveniles who were convicted of crimes and who were resident in a state-run facility targeted for the most serious offenders. There are two important differences between these two studies: (a) the adults were an incoming cohort of convicted offenders, whereas the juveniles were residents in the facilities at the time of the survey, and (b) the juvenile sample represents a more restrictive population. Of those arrested, relatively fewer juveniles end up in a state-run correctional facility than do adults. Furthermore, although there is some overlap in the ages included in the two studies, the adult offender sample was incarcerated in adult institutions, and the juvenile offender sample was incarcerated in juvenile institutions.

For both surveys, a lengthy (1.5 hours) in-person interview was conducted on previous offending patterns (including the most recent crime committed) and involvement with drugs. The drug and offending data represent the 3-year period prior to incarceration. In some cases, it is additionally restricted to the periods prior to or after the arrest that led to the current incarceration. The analyses are based on a total of 158 adult and 198 juvenile interviews, representing response rates of 81.9% and 75.0%, respectively (see Chapter 2 and Appendix D [1998] for a more detailed discussion of the methodology used and populations covered).

6.3 Drug Use and Offending Patterns

As one might expect, the rates of drug use and offending in the convicted incarcerated adult and juvenile populations indicate serious involvement with both activities. The surveys paint a broad picture of the extent to which these convicted adult and juvenile offenders used drugs prior to and after arrest and incarceration.

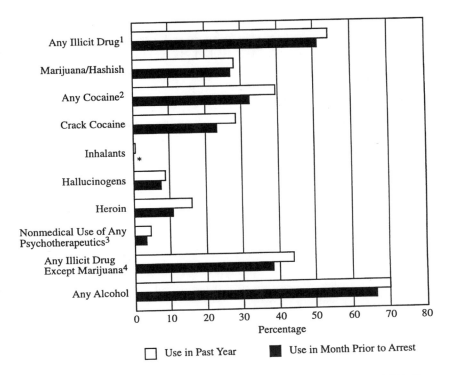

Figure 6.1. Prevalence of Illicit Drug and Alcohol Use Among DC MSA Convicted Adult Offenders Sentenced to Incarceration

SOURCE: Washington, DC, Metropolitan Area Drug Study (DC*MADS): 1989-1995.
NOTE: "Adult" refers to convicted adult offenders indicted of felonies and sentenced to incarceration. See Table D.1 in Appendix D (1998) for the supporting data used to prepare this figure.
1. Use of marijuana or hashish, cocaine (including crack), inhalants, hallucinogens (including phencyclidine [PCP]), or heroin, or nonmedical use of psychotherapeutics at least once.
2. Includes crack cocaine.
3. Nonmedical use of any prescription-type stimulant (including methamphetamine), sedative, tranquilizer, or analgesic; does not include over-the-counter drugs.
4. Includes cocaine (including crack), inhalants, hallucinogens (including PCP), heroin, or psychotherapeutics for nonmedical reasons.
*Estimate is less than 0.5% or is based on a rate of less than 0.5%.

6.3.1 Patterns Among Adults

Most of the adults reported using a wide range of drugs, as shown in Figure 6.1 (see supporting data in Table D.1, Appendix D [1998]). For example, approximately 54% reported using some type of illicit drug in the past year, with approximately the same proportion reporting use of an illicit drug during the month prior to the arrest that led to the conviction for which they were serving time. These rates did not change dramatically when marijuana was excluded from the illicit drug use mix. An estimated 44% reported using an illicit drug other than marijuana in the past year, and about 38% reported using this type of drug in the month prior to arrest.

Table 6.1 shows the prevalence of drug use among adult offenders in the past year and in the month prior to arrest by their demographic characteristics (age, race, marital status, and adult education). There were significant differences in the rate of use across age and educational attainment categories. Those aged 26 to 34 had the highest rate of use, followed by those aged 35 or older, then the youngest group, aged 18 to 25. This pattern is similar to the one for incarcerated institutionalized populations (see Chapter 5 in this book; Beck et al., 1993; National Institute on Drug Abuse [NIDA], 1994). It differs from the rate for the general population (NIDA, 1992), in which the 18-to-25 age group had the highest rates of drug use. One interpretation of this pattern is that the high rate of use among middle-aged criminal populations is a "period effect." Individuals in their mid- to late 20s have been found to have initiation and maintenance patterns different from those in the oldest and youngest age groups, especially for the use of crack cocaine (Johnson, Natarajan, Dunlap, & Elmoghazy, 1994).

Frequency of drug use also was quite high and was closely related to the level of supervision for the adult offender. As shown in Table 6.2, among adult offenders incarcerated after their arrest, 37.3% were using an illicit drug daily or almost daily just prior to arrest, 17.5% were using crack cocaine at this rate, and 10.6% were using heroin at this same rate. As one might expect, drug use frequencies for all the drugs were dramatically lower after arrest once the individual was incarcerated (all differences between before and after arrest are statistically significant). For example, daily/almost daily illicit drug use was 37.3% in the month before arrest and 8.0% in the month after arrest. Although this is a notable difference, 8% is still relatively high considering that these individuals were incarcerated after arrest (e.g., NIDA, 1994). This finding may result, in part, from the imprecision of the method. Respondents had to remember both when they were incarcerated and when they were using particular drugs. Although the interviewer was trained to draw a link between incarceration status and drug use, this may not have worked in

Table 6.1 Percentage of Convicted Adult Offenders Sentenced to Incarceration in the DC MSA and Reporting Illicit Drug Use, by Personal Characteristics and Time Period

Characteristic	Past Year	Month Prior to Arrest
Age (years)		
18-25	38.7	36.4
26-34	72.3	67.3
≥35	56.8	56.8
Race/ethnicity		
White	38.4	51.8
Black	56.8	51.5
Hispanic	*	*
Other	*	*
Marital status		
Never married	54.2	54.2
Married/divorced/widowed	57.0	43.5
Adult education		
Elementary	*	*
Some high school	50.5	40.0
GED[1]	76.8	74.4
High school graduate/some college	51.5	51.5

SOURCE: Washington, DC, Metropolitan Area Drug Study (DC*MADS): 1989-1995.
NOTE: Data entries are percentages and represent convicted adult offenders indicted of felonies and sentenced to incarceration (n = 156). Any illicit drug use is defined as any use of marijuana or hashish, cocaine (including crack), heroin, or nonmedical use of psychotherapeutics at least once; it does not include use of methamphetamine, inhalants, or hallucinogens (including phencyclidine or PCP).
1. GED = Graduate Equivalency Diploma.
*Low precision (see Appendix D, 1998).

Table 6.2 Frequency of Use of Illicit Drugs and Alcohol by Convicted Adults Sentenced to Incarceration in the DC MSA Before and After Arrest, by Incarceration Status 1 Month After Arrest and Type of Drug

Substance Used/ Frequency of Use	Incarcerated		Not Incarcerated	
	Use Month Before Arrest (n = 158)	Use Month After Arrest (n = 153)	Use Month Before Arrest (n = 153)	Use Month After Arrest (n = 153)
Any illicit drug[1]				
Daily/almost daily[2]	37.3	8.0	29.6	27.7
Weekly/monthly	16.5	1.0	17.3	9.2
Never	46.2	91.0+	53.0	63.1
Marijuana/hashish				
Daily/almost daily	11.6	3.4	17.2	15.3
Weekly/monthly	17.4	2.2	7.1	4.6
Never	71.0	94.5+	75.7	80.1
Crack cocaine				
Daily/almost daily	17.5	4.6	7.8	6.9
Weekly/monthly	10.1	**	9.2	10.1
Never	72.4	95.4+	83.1	82.9
Other cocaine				
Daily/almost daily	9.1	1.2	4.6	6.2
Weekly/monthly	7.0	1.1	10.2	7.5
Never	83.9	97.7+	85.1	86.3
Heroin				
Daily/almost daily	10.6	1.2	6.2	6.2
Weekly/monthly	**	**	4.7	9.3
Never	89.4	98.8	89.2	84.5
Any alcohol				
Daily/almost daily	30.9	5.6	30.3	33.2
Weekly/monthly	36.9	6.8	33.7	20.0
Never	32.2	87.6+	36.0	46.8

SOURCE: Washington, DC, Metropolitan Area Drug Study (DC*MADS): 1989-1995.

NOTE: Data entries are percentages and represent convicted adult offenders indicted of felonies and sentenced to incarceration.

1. Any illicit drug use is defined as any use of marijuana or hashish, cocaine (including crack), heroin, or nonmedical use of psychotherapeutics at least once; it does not include use of methamphetamine, inhalants, or hallucinogens (including phencyclidine or PCP).

2. Maximum frequency across all drugs used during period.

***Estimate is less than 0.5%. +Difference between before and after arrest is statistically significant at the .05 level.

every case. Consequently, offenders may have misdated, to some extent, their drug use relative to incarceration.

For individuals not incarcerated after arrest, the frequency of drug use before arrest was comparable to the rate for those who were incarcerated. For this group of adult offenders, about 30% used an illicit drug daily or almost daily in the month prior to the arrest. In contrast to the above results, however, none of the drug use frequencies were dramatically lower among those who had been arrested. For example, 24.3% of the adult offender population had used marijuana/hashish in the month prior to arrest, which compares to 19.9% in the month after arrest. Similarly, for crack cocaine, approximately equal proportions used the drug before and after arrest.

6.3.2 Patterns Among Juveniles

As shown in Figure 6.2, drug use was lower among the juvenile offender sample than among the adult offender sample, and the drugs used differed (see also supporting data in Table D.1, Appendix D [1998]). About half of the youth reported using an illicit drug (49.5%), with only about a third (34.3%) reporting drug use in the month prior to the conviction. Much of the drug use reported was for marijuana/hashish, with much lower rates of drug use being reported for other types of drugs. Approximately 48% of the juveniles reported use in the past year, compared to 15% for illicit drugs other than marijuana/hashish.

Table 6.3 provides rates of drug use among juvenile offenders by age, race/ethnicity, and gang membership. For use in both the past year and the past month prior to arrest, the younger age group (ages 12 to 15) had lower rates of drug use than the older group (ages 16 to 19); however, these differences are not statistically significant. The largest differences are by gang membership, especially for the past year. In this case, 61.2% of the youth who self-reported as being in gangs used a drug in the past year, which compares to 36.4% of those not in a gang.

The frequency of drug use by juvenile offenders followed a pattern similar to the one for adult offenders (see Table 6.4). The frequency was high in the month prior to arrest, and it was dramatically lower after incarceration. Of those youth incarcerated after arrest, 22.4% used illicit drugs (primarily marijuana/hashish) before arrest on a daily/almost

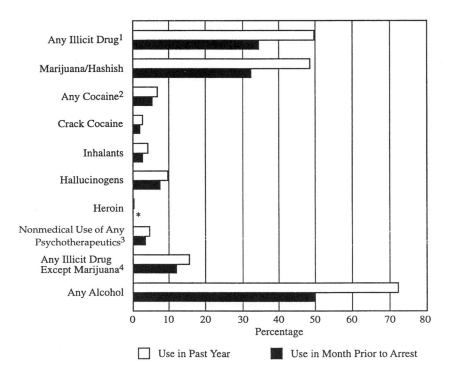

Figure 6.2. Prevalence of Illicit Drug and Alcohol Use Among DC MSA Convicted Incarcerated Juvenile Offenders

SOURCE: Washington, DC, Metropolitan Area Drug Study (DC*MADS): 1989-1995.
NOTE: "Juvenile" refers to juvenile residents in a secure state-run juvenile correctional facility. See Table D.1 in Appendix D (1998) for the supporting data used to prepare this figure.
1. Use of marijuana or hashish, cocaine (including crack), inhalants, hallucinogens (including phencyclidine or PCP), or heroin, or nonmedical use of psychotherapeutics at least once.
2. Includes crack cocaine.
3. Nonmedical use of any prescription-type stimulant (including methamphetamine), sedative, tranquilizer, or analgesic; does not include over-the-counter drugs.
4. Includes cocaine (including crack), inhalants, hallucinogens (including PCP), heroin, or psychotherapeutics for nonmedical reasons.
*Estimate is less than 0.5% or is based on a rate of less than 0.5%.

daily rate, whereas only 3.6% reported using it at this rate after arrest. For those youth not incarcerated after arrest, 18.6% reported using illicit drugs prior to arrest on a daily/almost daily basis, and 21.6% reported using them at this rate after arrest.

Table 6.3 Percentage of Convicted Incarcerated Juvenile Offenders From the DC MSA Reporting Illicit Drug Use, by Characteristics and Time Period

Characteristic	Past Year	Month Prior to Arrest
Age (years)		
12-15	42.4	23.1
16-19	51.8	37.8
Race/ethnicity		
White	49.0	31.6
Black	51.6	45.2
Gang membership		
Yes	61.2+	39.9
No	36.4	28.1

SOURCE: Washington, DC, Metropolitan Area Drug Study (DC*MADS): 1989-1995.
NOTE: Data entries are percentages and represent juvenile offenders who were juvenile residents in a secure state-run juvenile correctional facility ($n = 198$). Illicit drug use is defined as any use of marijuana or hashish, cocaine (including crack), heroin, or nonmedical use of psychotherapeutics at least once; it does not include use of methamphetamine, inhalants, or hallucinogens (including phencyclidine or PCP).
+Chi-square test for differences between subgroups is significant at $p < .05$.

Table 6.4 Frequency of Use by Convicted Incarcerated Juvenile Offenders From the DC MSA of Illicit Drugs and Alcohol Before and After Arrest, by Incarceration Status 1 Month After Arrest and Type of Drug

Substance Used/ Frequency of Use	Incarcerated		Not Incarcerated	
	Use Month Before Arrest (n = 135)	Use Month After Arrest (n = 135)	Use Month Before Arrest (n = 60)	Use Month After Arrest (n = 60)
Any illicit drug[1]				
Daily/almost daily[2]	22.4	3.6	18.6	21.6
Weekly/monthly	12.1	3.0	15.4	6.4
Never	65.5	93.5+	66.0	72.0
Marijuana/hashish				
Daily/almost daily	22.4	3.6	14.8	21.9
Weekly/monthly	11.4	3.0	14.0	6.5
Never	66.3	93.5+	71.1	71.6
Crack cocaine				
Daily/almost daily	1.3	**	**	**
Weekly/monthly	**	**	3.2	3.2
Never	98.7	100.0	96.9	96.9
Other cocaine				
Daily/almost daily	1.3	**	1.3	**
Weekly/monthly	3.6	**	2.9	2.9
Never	95.1	100.0	95.8	97.1
Heroin				
Daily/almost daily	**	**	**	**
Weekly/monthly	**	**	**	**
Never	100.0	100.0	100.0	100.0
Any alcohol				
Daily/almost daily	12.6	1.8	29.5	23.9
Weekly/monthly	35.0	3.0	25.5	25.2
Never	52.4	95.2+	45.1	50.9

SOURCE: Washington, DC, Metropolitan Area Drug Study (DC*MADS): 1989-1995.
NOTE: Data entries are percentages and represent juvenile offenders who were juvenile residents in a secure state-run juvenile correctional facility.
1. Any illicit drug use is defined as any use of marijuana or hashish, cocaine (including crack), heroin, or nonmedical use of psychotherapeutics at least once; it does not include use of methamphetamine, inhalants, or hallucinogens (including phencyclidine or PCP).
2. Maximum frequency across all drugs used during period.

6.3.3 Types of Crime Committed by
Adult and Juvenile Offenders

In terms of offending, the vast majority of adults reported committing drug-trafficking offenses, with substantial numbers also reporting both property and violent crimes. As shown in Table 6.5, the high rate of drug offending was, in part, a function of the arrest and incarceration policies associated with the criminal justice system. In the early 1990s, police and prosecutors in the DC MSA devoted much of their effort to arresting and convicting individuals involved in drug-trafficking activities. Almost three fourths of the adult sample had been indicted of some type of drug offense in the previous 3 years.

The data for juvenile and adult offenders are quite different when the types of offenses that had been committed are examined. In general, the adults reported less offending (particularly violent crimes) than did the juveniles. A large majority (71%) of adult offenders reported involvement in drug-trafficking activities in the 3 years prior to the interview. Most of this activity involved selling drugs directly to buyers, with the second most common activity being the production of drugs. An estimated 62% of adults reported committing a property crime, and 43% reported a violent crime. A similar proportion of the juveniles reported drug-trafficking offenses (80%) and property offenses (67%). Compared with the estimates for adults (43%), a much larger percentage of juvenile offenders reported a violent crime (72%). The violent crimes included a number of very serious acts, including homicide and rape. What is most striking in these comparisons is that when asked if they had "shot, stabbed, killed" or "raped" someone in the past 3 years, 21% of the adults and 49% of the juveniles reported a crime.

These differences may result, in part, from differences in the two subpopulations. One of the primary reasons that juveniles are sent to secure, state-run facilities is that they are violent. Consequently, a sample of incarcerated juveniles would be expected to contain proportionately more violent individuals than would be found in the adult population. The adult offender population nevertheless contained relatively serious offenders who were at least indicted of a felony and had been sentenced to prison. About 25% of adult offenders were indicted of a violent felony offense.

178

Table 6.5 Percentage of Offenders Committing a Crime at Least Once in the Previous 3 Years, by Type of Offender and Type of Crime

Type of Crime	Adults (n = 152)	Juveniles (n = 198)
Property crime	62.0	66.5
Steal motor vehicle	12.3	32.2
Buy, hold, sell goods	41.7	37.3
Steal < $50	15.1	22.6
Steal > $50	19.8	22.6
Break in to steal	17.7	18.2
Forgery/fraud	18.2	6.9
Prostitution	13.8	7.3
Violent crime	42.5	71.8
Attack to seriously hurt	23.6	51.6
Use force to get money	21.2	42.5
Threaten with weapon	26.2	59.6
Shoot, stab or kill; forced sex	20.5	48.6
Drug-trafficking offenses	70.5	79.7
Sell directly to buyers	59.2	77.2
Find buyers	29.6	21.8
Cut, package, or cook drugs	47.7	43.9
Trade drugs for sex	29.4	36.2
Trade drugs for something other than sex	43.6	48.4
Buy in wholesale lots	30.6	26.8
Other crime	68.6	87.9
Driving under the influence	50.1	30.4
Carry hidden weapon	41.6	76.8
Damage property	17.7	51.8

SOURCE: Washington, DC, Metropolitan Area Drug Study (DC*MADS): 1989-1995.
NOTE: Data entries are percentages and represent convicted adult offenders indicted of felonies and sentenced to incarceration and convicted incarcerated juveniles. Specifically, the data entries represent the percentage of offenders committing a crime at least once since 1988.

6.4 Links Between Drug Involvement and Predatory Crime

Although data on the prevalence of drug use among criminal and juvenile offenders help to elucidate the link between drug involvement and offending, the data do not directly link the two activities. In this section, data from the adult and juvenile offender surveys are presented on direct links between drug involvement and offending, including (a) the percentage of crimes committed by offenders using drugs, (b) the number of criminal events reported to be motivated by involvement with drugs, and (c) the frequency and nature of drug-trafficking activities.

To obtain data that could link drug involvement and predatory offending, both adult and juvenile respondents were asked to provide detailed information about the last predatory crime they had committed. The information was collected using (a) an open-ended question asking "what happened," (b) follow-up probes that asked respondents to attribute specific motives for the crime, (c) a specific question about drug use at the time of the event, and (d) specific questions on the possible facilitative role of drug use in the occurrence of the crime. This information was then used to classify the criminal event by whether it was drug related and to estimate the percentage of offenders who were taking drugs when they committed a crime. In addition, those reporting any type of drug-trafficking activity were asked about what role they played in the activity and the frequency with which they performed each role.

6.4.1 Drug Use at the Time of a Violent or Property Crime

One indicator of the role of drugs in criminal and juvenile offending is the prevalence of drug use among those who commit a particular crime. The extent to which offenders are using drugs shortly before or at the time of an offense has been thought to play at least a facilitative role, if not a directly causal role, in the commission of predatory crimes. The prevalence of use at the time of a criminal event provides one indicator of this. Such data are available at a national level for state prisoners residing in facilities at the time of data collection (Beck et al., 1993). To estimate a prevalence rate, the adult and juvenile surveys contained questions about whether drugs had been used before the last predatory offense was committed. Table 6.6 presents these prevalence data for both adult and juvenile offenders.

For adults, approximately half (48.1%) of the offenses were committed while the offender was using alcohol or illicit drugs. Alcohol (29.8%) was the drug used most often, followed by crack cocaine (18.2%) and marijuana/hashish (11.6%). There were no major differences across violent and property crimes in the percentage using alcohol or drugs. For juveniles, there was a prevalence rate of 12.7% for alcohol, 15.1% for illicit drugs, and 21.4% for either alcohol or illicit drugs. There were no statistically significant differences between violent and property crimes for juvenile offenders.

Interestingly, these data indicate that alcohol played at least as great a role, if not greater, as did illicit drugs in the commission of crime. For adults, significantly more offenders used alcohol than specific types of drugs. After all the illicit drugs were combined into a single category, alcohol and (any) illicit drugs were about equal. A similar result occurred for juveniles, except the level of use just prior to or during the event was significantly lower. This lower rate may be accounted for in part by the significant underreporting of drug use by juvenile respondents.

Although half the events reported by adults were committed by an offender using some type of drug, it is unclear what role this may have played in the actual commission of the crime. For example, drug use may be related indirectly to offending by facilitating illegal behavior, primarily through eliminating inhibitions, or it may have no effect at all. Data collected on the survey provide information from the respondent's perspective on the extent to which drug use, intentionally or unintentionally, may have played a role in the event. One set of questions asked whether respondents, who reported using drugs prior to the offense, had intentionally done so to "make the crime easier." A second set of questions asked whether the offender "would have committed the crime without taking drugs." The former tries to pinpoint whether drugs were used intentionally to commit the crime, and the latter attempts to estimate the facilitative role that drugs may have played in the commission of the crime. These data are discussed for adult offenders because too few juvenile offenders reported drug use for reliable comparisons of estimated rates.

Table 6.6 Percentage of Most Recent Predatory Crimes Committed by Offenders in the DC MSA and That Were Preceded by Drug Use, by Type of Drug, Type of Offender, and Type of Predatory Crime

Substance Used Before Crime[2]	Adults			Juveniles		
	Violent (n = 33)	Property (n = 66)	Total (n = 99)	Violent (n = 103)	Property (n = 40)	Total (n = 143)
Alcohol or any illicit drug	43.2	50.3	48.1	23.2	16.2	21.4
Alcohol	31.1	29.3	29.8	13.2	11.3	12.7
Any illicit drug	27.8	35.8	33.3	17.0	9.7	15.1
Marijuana/hashish	12.2	11.4	11.6	16.1	9.7	14.4
Crack cocaine	12.5	20.8	18.2	NA	NA	NA
Other illicit drugs	6.4	8.0	7.5	NA	NA	NA
Any illicit drug except marijuana	*	NA	NA	2.4	**	1.8
More than two drugs	NA	8.7	7.0	NA	NA	NA
At least two illicit drugs	NA	NA	NA	1.5	**	1.1

SOURCE: Washington, DC, Metropolitan Area Drug Study (DC*MADS): 1989-1995.

NOTE: Data entries are percentages and represent either (a) convicted adult offenders indicted of felonies and sentenced to incarceration or (b) juvenile residents in a secure state-run juvenile correctional facility. Illicit drug use is defined as any use of marijuana or hashish, cocaine (including crack), heroin, or nonmedical use of psychotherapeutics at least once; it does not include use of methamphetamine, inhalants, or hallucinogens (including phencyclidine or PCP).

1. Based on self-reports of last predatory crime committed since 1988. Predatory crime includes *property crime* (steal a motor vehicle; buy, hold, or sell stolen goods; steal something worth less than $50; steal something worth more than $50; break into building to steal; fraud; prostitution) and *violent crime* (attack to seriously hurt; force someone to have sex; threaten with a weapon; shoot, stab, or kill). Columns do not add to 100% because the denominators include cases that were missing on the variable for motivation to commit the crime.

2. Respondents could provide more than one answer.

NA = not applicable. Adults and juveniles were asked different sets of questions.

*Low precision.

**Estimate is less than 0.5%.

Of those adults who used drugs prior to committing any type of predatory crime, 22.9% reported intentionally doing so to make it easier to commit the crime (data not shown). Combined with the fact that 48.1% reported using a drug before the crime (see Table 6.6), these data imply that 11.0% (48.1% × 22.9%) of the offenders had used a drug intentionally to assist in committing their last predatory crime. In contrast, 58.7% reported a facilitative role of the drug use by saying that they would not have committed the crime without first taking drugs. After we accounted for the number of offenders who reported drug use at the time of the event, approximately 28.2% of all offenders (48.1% × 58.7%) reported a facilitative role of drugs in their last predatory crime. These data suggest that although a relatively small percentage of offenders had used drugs intentionally to assist them in committing a crime (11.0%), more than twice as many attributed a relatively strong role in the commission of the crime (28.2%).

6.4.2 Linking Drug Involvement
to Violent and Property Offending

The adult and juvenile surveys provide one way to begin disentangling the drug-crime nexus, by developing estimates of the basic roles that drug activity may play in the commission of both predatory and nonpredatory crimes. Table 6.7 classifies the most recent crime committed by adult and juvenile offenders according to Goldstein's tripartite scheme discussed earlier. The patterns are quite different between the adult and juvenile offender populations. For the adults, a total of 40.4% (18.6% + 7.9% + 13.9%) of the predatory crimes were classified as drug related, and 57.3% were classified as nondrug-related. Adult offenders reported about the same percentage of violent and property crimes as being drug related (42.6% of violent and 39.4% of property; data not shown). There are clear differences, however, among the particular drug-related reasons across these two types of crimes. A large percentage of the property crimes by adults were related to drug use, either for an economic motive or for psychopharmacological reasons (32.5%). This is in contrast to violent crime, for which drug trafficking (i.e., systemic violence) accounted for the largest proportion of drug-related violent crimes (28.8%).

Table 6.7 Self-Reported Motivation Associated With Most Recent Predatory Crime Committed Since 1988 Among Offenders in the DC MSA, by Type of Offender and Type of Predatory Crime

	Type of Offender and Type of Predatory Crime[1]					
	Adults			Juveniles		
Motivation[2]	Violent (n = 35)	Property (n = 68)	Total (n = 103)	Violent (n = 119)	Property (n = 44)	Total (n = 163)
Drug-related						
Economic (obtain money to support drug habit)	10.7	22.3	18.6	4.2	4.3	4.2
Psychopharmacological (physiological effects)	*	10.2	7.9	0.8	**	0.6
Systemic (associated with the drug trade)	28.8	6.9	13.9	16.9	5.8	14.2
Nondrug-related						
Economic (obtain money)	*	27.1	19.4	20.6	40.6	25.6
Protection, payback, revenge (fights, ongoing disputes)	37.9	**	12.2	50.2	2.4	38.2
Good opportunity (easy target)	6.0	23.5	17.9	2.0	15.4	5.3
Excitement	*	5.5	4.7	1.4	22.0	6.6
Other (peer pressure, help friend, etc.)	*	4.6	3.1	1.3	5.8	2.4

SOURCE: Washington, DC, Metropolitan Area Drug Study (DC*MADS): 1989-1995.

NOTE: Data entries are percentages and represent either (a) convicted adult offenders indicted of felonies and sentenced to incarceration or (b) juveniles resident in a secure state-run juvenile correctional facility.

1. Based on self-reports of last predatory crime committed since 1988. Predatory crime includes *property crime* (steal a motor vehicle; buy, hold, or sell stolen goods; steal something worth less than $50; steal something worth more than $50; break into building to steal; fraud; prostitution) and *violent crime* (attack to seriously hurt; force someone to have sex; threaten with a weapon; shoot; stab, or kill). Columns do not add to 100% because the denominators include cases that were missing on the variable for motivation to commit the crime.

2. Data entries are based on the most important reason given by the respondent for committing a crime.

*Low precision.

**Estimate is less than 0.5%.

183

These data on adult offenders reveal several interesting patterns. First, although a large percentage of the crimes was related to drug involvement, a substantial number of crimes were not related to drugs, at least as reported by adult criminal offenders. This finding might explain the somewhat inconsistent correlation of aggregate crime trends and drug use indicators (e.g., see Section 6.1). Second, a relatively small percentage of adult crimes were linked directly to psychopharmacological reasons. Of those attributable to this motive, virtually all were reported as property offenses. This estimate contrasts with data provided in Section 6.4.1, which attributed 28.2% of the offenses reported by adult offenders as being committed, in part, because of taking drugs just prior to the crime.

The differences could reflect the degree to which drug use may have led to the crime. The lower estimate was taken from questions in which adult respondents were asked an open-ended question about "what happened." Respondents were likely to report those things that stuck out the most about the criminal event. The upper estimate resulted from data obtained by a closed-ended question that asked directly if he or she "would have done it without using drugs." Responses to this question, then, encompass a wider range of roles that drug use may have played, from a facilitative role of reducing inhibitions to a very strong psychopharmacological effect in which the adult offender may not even have remembered what happened at a later point in time.

The pattern is quite different for juvenile offenders: 19.0% of the most recent predatory crimes reported by the youth were classified as being drug related (4.2% + 0.6% + 14.2%). This proportion is surprisingly low, given that the juvenile offender sample was largely composed of youth reporting a high level of drug-trafficking activity. Among the specific reasons, systemic violence associated with drug selling was the most common (14.2%), followed by economic (4.2%) and psychopharmacological (0.6%) reasons. This overall distribution is due, in part, to the relatively high percentage of violent crimes reported by the juvenile respondents. Approximately two thirds of the most recent predatory crimes committed by the juveniles were classified as violent crimes. For violent crimes, 21.9% were drug related, compared with 10.1% of the property crimes. The primary reason for drug-related violence is systemic in that systemic motivations accounted for more than one sixth (16.9%) of the motivations for all violent crime. Systemic motivations were not often cited as important for the commission of property crimes (5.8%).

For violent juvenile crime, a large percentage of the events were classified as protection, payback, and revenge (50.2% of violent crimes), which is a nondrug-related reason. Some portion of this activity could be related to membership in a gang and any drug involvement within the gang. More than half the sample reported being in a gang in the year before the survey (61.2%), with drug use being reported at a much higher rate for those in a gang (Table 6.3). Many other dynamics, however, were related to gang-related crime but unrelated to drug trafficking. Furthermore, Washington, DC, is not known as a city with a large number of street gangs (Klein & Maxson, 1994).

About one fifth of the drug-related violent crimes were attributable to drug use, either as economic motives or as psychopharmacological (4.2% + 0.8% = 5.0% out of 21.9%). This estimate is significantly lower than the one for adults, and the difference is partly the result of the types of crimes reported across the two populations. A higher percentage of adult crime was violent and was largely attributed to drug trafficking (i.e., systemic violence). For violent crimes, the percentage of the drug-related crime attributable to drug use was about the same for both adults and juveniles (between one fifth and one quarter). In contrast, when focusing on property crime, four fifths of the events were attributable to drug use among the adults compared with two fifths for juveniles.

6.5 Frequency of Drug Trafficking and Reasons for Involvement

Reiss and Roth (1993, pp. 200-205) distinguished among the different roles that individuals play within the drug-trafficking market. These roles range from activities involving interactions with drug buyers to those involving work with other drug sellers. To distinguish among these different roles, respondents were asked about six types of activities associated with drug trafficking (Fagan & Chin, 1990): (a) selling drugs directly to buyers; (b) finding buyers, holding drugs, or performing street security; (c) cutting, packaging, or cooking drugs; (d) trading drugs for sex; (e) trading drugs for something other than sex; and (f) buying wholesale, organizing sellers, or laundering money.

The data presented in Table 6.5 provide indicators of the prevalence of these activities for adult and juvenile offenders. The extent to which each role was reported is very similar across the two populations. For both, the most common activity was selling directly to buyers; however, juveniles showed a significantly higher prevalence than adults (59.2% for adults vs. 77.2% for juveniles). The frequency with which the offenders engaged in these activities varied by type (see Table 6.8). The most frequent activity was selling directly to buyers: 36.0% and 53.3% of adults and juveniles, respectively, did so at least once a day. The other activities were not engaged in as nearly as often. For example, only 10.9% and 6.8% of adults and juveniles, respectively, bought wholesale, organized sellers, or laundered money this often.

The primary reason given for first starting to sell drugs was economic. More than 6 of 10 adult drug traffickers reported that wanting to purchase things other than drugs was the primary reason for first starting to traffic in drugs (data not shown). Other reasons were cited by adults at a much lower rate. For example, the second highest was that of family or peer influence, which was mentioned by 15.1% of the respondents. Another 5.9% said their initial involvement stemmed from an appreciation or aspiration to the drug seller's lifestyle. Only 6.8% of the adult drug sellers noted that they initially got involved in drug sales to purchase drugs for themselves. This pattern is similar for the juvenile offenders. The most common reason stated for initial initiation was economic. None of the juveniles reported first getting into trafficking because of a need to purchase drugs.

The economic importance of first involvement in drug sales is consistent with the way offenders reported using the money from these activities. Some 69% of adults reported that trafficking provided all (40.8%) or most (28.8%) of their income. This pattern is similar for juveniles, with 88.0% of youth reporting that all or most of their income came from this activity. When asked how they spent most of the money that was earned from trafficking, large majorities of both age groups reported spending it on consumer goods (73.8% adults and 96.8% juveniles). In contrast to the reasons for initial involvement, however, a substantial number of both adults (44.5%) and juveniles (42.7%) reported spending significant amounts of money to buy drugs. This finding is

Table 6.8 Frequency of Drug-Trafficking Activities, by Type of Offender and Type of Activity

Frequency/Type of Drug	Sell Directly to Buyers	Find Buyers	Cut, Package, or Cook Drugs	Trade Drugs for Sex	Trade Drugs for Something Other Than Sex	Buy in Wholesale Lots
Adults[1] (n = 158)						
Never	37.3	68.7	46.3	68.0	54.3	65.5
Once a month or less	12.2	5.9	17.2	18.0	19.1	9.2
Once every 2-3 weeks	2.5	1.8	4.9	1.9	3.1	3.2
Once a week	12.0	7.5	12.2	9.0	15.0	11.3
At least once a day	36.0	16.1	19.4	3.1	8.6	10.9
Juveniles[2] (n = 197)						
Never	22.7	75.9	54.4	62.1	51.6	71.5
Once a month or less	13.7	5.2	10.5	18.3	21.3	7.3
Once every 2-3 weeks	2.4	1.2	4.0	6.9	4.1	2.4
Once a week	7.9	2.9	18.9	8.5	18.5	12.0
At least once a day	53.3	14.8	12.2	4.1	4.5	6.8

SOURCE: Washington, DC, Metropolitan Area Drug Study (DC*MADS): 1989-1995.
NOTE: Data entries are percentages and represent either (a) convicted adult offenders of felonies and sentenced to incarceration or (b) juveniles resident in a secure state-run juvenile correctional facility.

some indication of the number of persons who move from getting into the business for economic reasons but transition to becoming users themselves.

6.6 Discussion and Implications

Data from the DC*MADS Adult Criminal Offenders Study and Juvenile Offenders Study provide important findings that help elucidate our understanding of the relationship between drug use and offending behavior. These findings, of course, apply to a subset of offenders who have been convicted and subsequently incarcerated. They also must be interpreted within the context of the limitations of the current studies.

6.6.1 Drugs and Crime

Convicted offenders are heavy drug users, even shortly after they have been arrested for a crime, as long as they are not in jail. Drugs also play a significant role in the commission of property and violent crimes, although to different degrees for adult and juvenile offenders. For adult offenders, 39.4% and 39.5% committed their last property and violent crimes, respectively, for some type of drug-related reason. A smaller percentage of crimes was reported as being related to involvement with drugs by the juvenile offenders, and the percentages differed by whether it was a violent (21.9%) or property crime (10.1%).

These findings shed some light on the complicated psychopharmacological relationship between drug use and predatory offending. For example, 43.2% of the violent crimes and 50.3% of the property crimes committed by adults were preceded by use of a drug. Alcohol was the most commonly used drug by adults for both types of crimes, with crack cocaine making up a substantial portion of the illicit drug use. Fully half of those adults who used drugs reported that they would not have committed the crime if they had not taken the drug (i.e., approximately 20% of the convicted incarcerated population). These figures contrast with the 7.9% of adult offenders who cited drug use as the major reason for committing a crime. Taken at face value, these findings indicate that although a relatively small percentage of the crimes committed by this adult population can be attributed directly to drug use, a significantly larger number of crimes were at least facilitated by drug use.

An alternative way to view these numbers, however, is that a relatively large number of the most recent crimes were not directly linked to reported involvement with drugs. For juveniles, this may be in part a function of the high underreporting of drug use.

Analyses not reported here provide strong indications that for the juvenile offenders there was substantial underreporting of drug use that varied by type of drug (NIDA, 1995). Marijuana/hashish was the least underreported, with cocaine being the most underreported. Although some underreporting is expected simply from memory or other cognitive processing errors (Cantor, Gaertner, & Keil, 1994), the extent of this problem with the juvenile offender data suggests a deliberate attempt by the youth to conceal information from the interviewer.

Even for the adult offenders, the majority of the predatory crimes were not linked to involvement with drugs. These motives accounted for a relatively small percentage of the violent crimes. It is likely that these percentages will vary greatly by more specific types of crimes within these two broad categories of offenses. It is also likely the case, for example, that a much larger percentage of the homicides committed by these individuals were linked to drug trafficking. The sample sizes were not big enough to develop estimates at this level of detail; however, when looking at more prevalent violent crimes, which make up the vast majority of crimes reported by the offenders in this study, these data indicate that many of the events were not associated with drugs. It would seem that much more than reducing drug use has to be done if social policy is to significantly reduce the high levels of crime in the United States.

6.6.2 Limitations of Findings

Several limitations surround these general conclusions and focus on two methodological issues related to using survey data to generalize to the general population of offenders. First, the sample frames missed a significant number of persons who commit crimes. Both frames were restricted to offenders who not only were caught by the police but also were convicted and incarcerated for a crime. The research was thus limited to a relatively small proportion of offenders who deeply penetrated the criminal justice system. This limitation is especially relevant for the estimates for juvenile offenders because a very small number of youth were ever resident in state-run facilities (NIDA, 1995).

To the extent that the sample was shaped by varying criminal justice policies, caution is required in generalizations or inferences to larger populations. Relatively small changes in the sample frame can have significant effects on the results. For example, the incarcerated population in the DC MSA (NIDA, 1994) reported fewer drug-related predatory crimes than did the entering cohort of offenders discussed above. This finding may have occurred because, at the time the sample was drawn, convictions were being weighted toward drug offenders. Similarly, among those who had been recently convicted, a substantial difference was found in the amount of drug-related crime between those sentenced to incarceration and those on probation (NIDA, 1995).

A second limitation relates to measurement error resulting from the interviewing process itself. Measurement error can result from the methods used to contact the respondents, the mode in which the interview was conducted (i.e., in-person, interviewer-administered), and the types of questions asked. The contact procedures were developed to remove, as much as possible, the appearance of any association between the project staff and criminal justice employees. Interviews in prisons nevertheless still require prison guards to escort sampled persons to and from the interview room; moreover, the interview itself is conducted in a prison setting. The interview mode also has been shown to be important in the reporting of sensitive information. Self-administered questionnaires have been shown to yield higher estimates of such activities as drug use in general population samples (Tourangeau & Smith, 1996). This study was based on in-person interviews, and the results might have varied if a self-administered questionnaire had been used.

The form and content of the questions also affect the estimates discussed above. For example, very little is known about the accuracy of classifying crimes into drug-related and nondrug-related events. These items are important for providing insights about drug use and offending; however, little is known about the types of errors associated with these items. Their validity depends on how a respondent interprets the question and reconstructs the details of the criminal event, including his or her motivations for committing the crime. These details are shaped by the objective experience as well as subjective motivations and intentions.

Retrospective reports like these often are difficult for respondents and are influenced by a number of factors, such as the respondent's mood at the time of the interview (e.g., Banaji & Hardin, 1994; Clark, Collins, & Henry, 1994; Salovey, Sieer, Jobe, & Willis, 1994).

Despite these limitations, the analyses discussed in this chapter provide an important anchor on the role drugs play in the commission of both predatory and drug-trafficking offenses. The use of probability-based methods, if interpreted within the constraints of the sample frame and other measurement problems, begins to quantify the importance of the drug-crime nexus. This needs to be considered when developing intelligent policies related to both drug abuse and crime.

References

Anglin, M. D., & Speckart, G. (1986). Narcotics use, property crime, and dealing: Structural dynamics across the addiction career. *Journal of Quantitative Criminology, 2,* 355-375.

Appendix D: Adult and Juvenile Offender Studies. (1998). (Available on the World Wide Web at http://www.sagepub.com/bray_druguse.htm)

Ball, J. C., Rosen, L., Flueck, J. A., & Nurco, D. N. (1982). Lifetime criminality of heroin addicts across the United States. *Journal of Drug Issues, 3,* 225-239.

Banaji, M. R., & Hardin, C. (1994). Affect and memory in retrospective reports. In N. Schwarz & S. Sudman (Eds.), *Autobiographical memory and the validity of retrospective reports* (pp. 71-88). New York: Springer-Verlag.

Beck, A. J., Gilliard, D., Greenfield, L., Harlow, C., Hester, T., Jankowski, L., Snell, T., & Stephan, J. (1993). *Survey of state prison inmates, 1991* (BJS Special Report, NCJ 136949). Washington, DC: Bureau of Justice Statistics.

Beck, A. J., Kline, S. A., & Greenfeld, L. A. (1988). *Survey of youth in custody, 1987* (BJS Special Report, NCJ 113365). Washington, DC: Bureau of Justice Statistics.

Bureau of Justice Statistics. (1991). *Criminal victimization in the United States, 1989* (National Crime Survey Report, NCJ 129391). Washington, DC: Author.

Cantor, D., Gaertner, G., & Keil, L. (1994). The validity of self-reported drug use among the incarcerated. In *Proceedings of the Survey Research Section of the American Statistical Association* (pp. 104-116). Washington, DC: American Statistical Association.

Center for Substance Abuse Prevention. (1993). *Prevention strategies based on individual risk factors for alcohol and other drug abuse* (DHHS Publication No. ADM 1996-93). Rockville, MD: Author.

Chaiken, J. M., & Chaiken, M. R. (1982). *Varieties of criminal behavior.* Santa Monica, CA: Rand.

Clark, L. F., Collins, J. E., & Henry, S. M. (1994). Biasing effects of retrospective reports on current self-assessments. In N. Schwarz & S. Sudman (Eds.), *Autobiographical memory and the validity of retrospective reports* (pp. 291-304). New York: Springer-Verlag.

Collins, J. J., Hubbard, R. L., & Rachal, J. V. (1985). Expensive drug use and illegal income: A test of explanatory hypotheses. *Criminology: An Interdisciplinary Journal, 23,* 743-764.

Criminal Justice Research Center. (1992). *1991 crime and justice report*. Washington, DC: Government of the District of Columbia, Office of Grants Management and Development.

Elliott, D. S., Huizinga, D., & Menard, S. (1989). *Multiple problem youth: Delinquency, drugs and mental health problems*. New York: Springer-Verlag.

Fagan, J., & Chin, K. (1990). Violence as regulation and social control in the distribution of crack. In M. De La Rosa, E. Y. Lambert, & B. Gropper (Eds.), *Drugs and violence: Causes, correlates, and consequences* (NIDA Research Monograph 103, DHHS Publication No. ADM 90-1721, pp. 8-43). Rockville, MD: National Institute on Drug Abuse.

Glaser, D. (1971). *Social deviance*. Chicago: Markham.

Goldstein, P. J. (1989). Drugs and violent crime. In N. A. Weiner & M. E. Wolfgang (Eds.), *Pathways to criminal violence* (pp. 16-48). Beverly Hills, CA: Sage.

Goldstein, P. J., Bellocci, P. A., Spunt, B. J., & Miller, T. (1991). Volume of cocaine use and violence: A comparison between men and women. *Journal of Drug Issues, 21*, 345-368.

Harrison, L. D. (1992). The drug-crime nexus in the USA. *Contemporary Drug Problems, 19*, 203-245.

Hser, Y., Longshore, D., & Anglin, D. (1994). Prevalence of drug use among criminal offender populations: Implications for control, treatment and policy. In D. L. Mackenzie & C. D. Uchida (Eds.), *Drugs and crime: Evaluating public policy initiatives* (pp. 18-41). Thousands Oaks, CA: Sage.

Inciardi, J. A., Horowitz, R., & Pottieger, A. E. (1993). *Street kids, street drugs, street crime: An examination of drug use and serious delinquency in Miami*. Belmont, CA: Wadsworth.

Innes, C. A. (1988). *Profile of state prison inmates, 1986* (Special Report, NCJ 109926). Washington, DC: Bureau of Justice Statistics.

Johnson, B. D., Natarajan, A. M., Dunlap, E., & Elmoghazy, E. (1994). Crack abusers and noncrack abusers: Profiles of drug use, drug sales and nondrug criminality. *Journal of Drug Issues, 24*, 117-141.

Johnston, L. D., O'Malley, P. M., & Eveland, L. K. (1978). Drugs and delinquency: A search for causal connections. In D. B. Kandel (Ed)., *Longitudinal research on drug use* (pp. 137-156). Washington, DC: Hemisphere.

Klein, M. W., & Maxson, C. L. (1994). Gangs and crack cocaine trafficking. In D. L. Mackenzie & C. D. Uchida (Eds.), *Drugs and crime: Evaluating public policy initiatives* (pp. 42-60). Thousands Oaks, CA: Sage.

National Council on Crime and Delinquency. (1996). *Crime and justice trends in the District of Columbia*. Washington, DC: Author.

National Institute on Drug Abuse. (1992). *Prevalence of drug use in the DC metropolitan area household population: 1990* (Technical Report #1 under NIDA Contract No. 271-89-8340, Washington, DC, Metropolitan Area Drug Study, DHHS Publication No. ADM 92-1919, prepared by M. E. Marsden, R. M. Bray, A. C. Theisen, L. E. Packer, & J. M. Greene, Research Triangle Institute). Rockville, MD: Author.

National Institute on Drug Abuse. (1994). *Prevalence of drug use in the DC metropolitan area institutionalized population: 1991* (Technical Report #4 under NIDA Contract No. 271-89-8340, Washington, DC, Metropolitan Area Drug Study, prepared by D. Cantor, G. H. Gaertner, & L. Keil, Westat, Inc., & R. M. Bray, Research Triangle Institute). Rockville, MD: Author.

National Institute on Drug Abuse. (1995). *Prevalence of drug use in the DC metropolitan area adult and juvenile offender populations: 1991* (Technical Report #6 under NIDA Contract No. 271-89-8340, Washington, DC, Metropolitan Area Drug Study, prepared by D. Cantor, Westat, Inc.). Rockville, MD: Author.

Osgood, D. W., Johnston, L. D., O'Malley, P. M., & Bachman, J. G. (1988). The generality of deviance in late adolescence and early adulthood. *American Sociological Review, 53,* 81-93.

Reiss, A. J., & Roth, J. (Eds.). (1993). *Understanding and preventing violence: Panel on the understanding and control of violent behavior.* Washington, DC: National Academy of Sciences.

Ryan, P. J., Goldstein, P. J., Brownstein, H. H., & Bellucci, P. A. (1990). Who's right: Different outcomes when police and scientists view the same set of homicide events, New York City, 1988. In M. De La Rosa, E. Y. Lambert, & B. Gropper (Eds.), *Drugs and violence: Causes, correlates, and consequences* (NIDA Research Monograph 103, DHHS Publication No. ADM 90-1721, pp. 239-264). Rockville, MD: National Institute on Drug Abuse.

Salovey, P., Sieer, W. J., Jobe, J. B., & Willis, G. B. (1994). The recall of physical pain. In N. Schwarz & S. Sudman (Eds.), *Autobiographical memory and the validity of retrospective reports* (pp. 89-106). New York: Springer-Verlag.

Tonry, M., & Wilson, J. Q. (Eds.). (1990). *Drugs and crime.* Chicago: University of Chicago Press.

Tourangeau, R., & Smith, T. W. (1996). Asking sensitive questions. *Public Opinion Quarterly, 60,* 275-304.

White, H. R. (1991). Marijuana use and delinquency: A test of the "independent cause" hypothesis. *Journal of Drug Issues, 21,* 231-256.

Wish, E. D., & O'Neil, J. (1989). *Cocaine use in arrestees: Refining measures of national trends by sampling the criminal population.* Paper presented at the National Institute on Drug Abuse Technical Review Session on Cocaine Use.

Zawitz, M. W. (Ed.). (1992). *Drugs, crime, and the justice system: A national report* (NCJ-133652). Washington, DC: U.S. Department of Justice, Office of Justice Programs, Bureau of Justice Statistics.

7 Patterns of Use Among Drug Treatment Clients

Patrick M. Flynn
James W. Luckey
Sara C. Wheeless

The Current Treatment Client Characteristics Study was de-signed to examine the extent and consequences of drug use among a group of known abusers—clients entering drug abuse treatment. Studies of clients in drug treatment provide important information about patterns and consequences of drug use that are relatively rare among the general population but are fairly common among treatment clients (Rounsaville & Carroll, 1991). For example, only 1% of the 1994 U.S. household population aged 12 or older had ever used heroin, and the highest rate of lifetime heroin use among any age group (26- to 34-year-olds) was less than 2% (Substance Abuse and Mental Health Services Administration [SAMHSA], 1993). In contrast, more than one third of those in two of the treatment modalities studied here had used heroin in their lifetime, and nearly all (97%) of those entering metha-done treatment had done so. Such studies also can provide information on newly emerging drugs of abuse. This chapter examines the prevalence of drug use among treatment clients, the consequences and correlates of use, and special issues, such as access to treatment.

7.1 Value of Epidemiological Studies of Drug Treatment Populations

Epidemiological studies of clients entering drug abuse treatment can provide important information on known abusers to complement evidence from studies of both household populations and other nonhousehold groups. A study of those in treatment yields a sufficient number of drug abusers to examine in some detail the patterns of drug use, the negative effects of drug use, associated behaviors and co-occurring conditions, the need for specific types of treatment services, and access to treatment among heavy and frequent drug users. Although treatment clients are not representative of all heavy drug users or those in need of treatment, they can inform us about the problems and needs of this population. Indeed, only a small portion of those who need treatment actually receive it, perhaps about one in four (Regier et al., 1993). The majority of drug abusers in treatment are receiving care in outpatient settings, and about one in nine receive care in hospital inpatient or other residential settings (Office of Applied Studies [OAS], 1993). Comparing abusers who are and are not in treatment also can yield information on which abusers do seek treatment.

7.1.1 Multiple Problems of Drug Abusers

Previous studies have found that drug abusers are subject to significant medical, psychological, employment, legal, and other problems associated with their use. They are a multiple-problem population requiring multiple services both to aid in recovery and to retain them in treatment a sufficient length of time to foster change. Drug abusers, particularly injection drug users, are characterized by a number of serious medical problems related to their use. These range from human immunodeficiency virus (HIV) and tuberculosis to various cardiac conditions (Haverkos & Lange, 1990; Schlenger, Kroutil, Roland, & Dennis,

1992; Selwyn et al., 1989). Not only are they more likely to experience these serious medical conditions, but they also are likely to have poor health related to their limited access to health care and to the long-term debilitating effects of drug use. Drug abusers also are likely to have co-morbid psychiatric conditions associated with their use that require special-ized services and that can impede the progress of treatment (Flynn, Craddock, Luckey, Hubbard, & Dunteman, 1996; Hubbard et al., 1989; Rounsaville & Carroll, 1991; Rounsaville, Weissman, Crits-Cristoph, Wilber, & Kleber, 1982; Woody, McLellan, Luborsky, & O'Brien, 1985).

Many drug abusers also are involved in illegal activities in addition to their drug use. In fact, the link between drugs and crime (see discus-sion in Chapter 6) is a major justification for public expenditures on drug abuse treatment, and many treatment clients are referred to treatment by the criminal justice system on either a formal or an informal basis. According to the Treatment Outcome Prospective Study (TOPS) of cli-ents entering treatment during the early 1980s, about one third of clients in outpatient treatment and about 60% in residential treatment had committed offenses in the year before entering treatment; moreover, about one third of outpatient drug-free and residential clients and few outpatient methadone clients had been referred to treatment by the criminal justice system (Collins, Hubbard, Cavanaugh, & Rachal, 1983; Hubbard et al., 1989). These proportions are substantiated by the 1990 Drug Services Research Survey (DSRS), which found that 48% of drug abuse treatment clients were receiving treatment as a condition of pro-bation or parole (Batten et al., 1992). Drug abusers also experience many employment and family problems. They may need vocational training or education to assist with securing employment (Dennis, Karuntzos, McDougal, French, & Hubbard, 1993; French, Dennis, McDougal, Karun-tzos, & Hubbard, 1992).

7.1.2 Characteristics of the Treatment Population

Data from several nationally based studies provide evidence on the characteristics of the treatment population. According to the 1991 Na-tional Drug and Alcoholism Treatment Unit Survey (NDATUS), the survey in the series conducted close in time to this study of treatment clients, more than 800,000 clients were in substance abuse treatment programs on the point prevalence date of September 30, 1991 (OAS, 1993). (NDATUS has been replaced by the Uniform Facility Data Set [UFDS] and is part of the Drug and Alcohol Services Information System [DASIS].) Almost three fourths of the clients in treatment on that date were male; the majority (61.5%) were white, about 20% were black, and 14.1% were Hispanic. More than 60% of the clients were aged 25 or older, with about one third aged 25 to 34 years and one fourth aged 35 to 44 years. Almost half (45%) were being treated for alcoholism, 29% for the abuse of other drugs, and about one fourth for the abuse of alcohol and other drugs. The Drug Abuse Treatment Outcome Study (DATOS), a study of clients entering treatment between 1991 and 1993 in 11 cities nationwide, found an upsurge in the use of cocaine relative to the TOPS treatment population of the 1980s (Craddock, Rounds-Bryant, Flynn, & Hubbard, 1997).

Despite the wide variety of research that has been done among drug treatment clients, most of the studies have been limited to a single treatment program or a single treatment modality. National-level studies of treatment clients, such as TOPS and DATOS, have used nonprobability sampling designs. Although these studies have involved the largest number of treatment programs ever studied and the greatest number of clients ever interviewed since the Drug Abuse Reporting Program (Simpson & Sells, 1990), they do not provide probability-based national estimates. NDATUS, now the UFDS, is designed to capture information annually from all treatment programs nationwide; however, NDATUS captures only limited data on client characteristics and does not provide estimates adjusted for nonresponse. A SAMHSA-funded study in progress, the Alcohol and Drug Services Survey (ADSS), uses a nationally representative sample of alcohol and drug treatment facilities to examine treatment programs, treatment clients, and treatment outcomes across the nation.

The present study of drug abuse clients in the Washington, DC, metropolitan statistical area (DC MSA) expands the knowledge base of drug abuse by selecting a statistically representative sample of treatment clients within a defined geographical area. The study allows development of population estimates for those who were in treatment at the time the data were collected. A related advantage of this study over previous research is having comparable data for the household population and other important subgroups. This allows examination of the nature of abuse patterns in a drug treatment population and the consequences associated with these patterns of use, as well as comparison of the treated population with abusers not in treatment. Studying drug treatment clients also permits consideration of special issues, such as access to treatment and drug use during pregnancy among a group of known female drug abusers.

7.2 Overview of the Study

The participants in the study consisted of clients admitted to drug treatment programs in the DC MSA during the spring and summer of 1991. The study examined the types of drugs used, patterns and trends of use, frequency of use, and general experiences of drug treatment clients. More specifically, the study was designed to provide estimates of the prevalence of use of illicit drugs and alcohol for the DC MSA drug treatment population. It described the demographic correlates of illicit drug and alcohol use, including gender, age, race/ethnicity, marital status, geographic location, education, and employment. Demographic characteristics, drug use patterns, and problems associated with drug use were compared among the clientele admitted to three treatment modalities. The patterns, current context, and histories of drug use were identified, and the relationships between current and past illicit drug use, symptoms, treatment, and key areas of functioning were examined. In addition to these substantive topics, methodological implications were examined and recommendations from our experiences are provided for future investigations.

Treatment programs in the DC MSA were selected to represent current approaches to drug treatment. These included four common and traditional types of modalities: long-term residential, short-term residential, outpatient methadone, and outpatient drug-free. Briefly, long-term residential programs include therapeutic communities and other residential programs with durations of 6 months or longer. Short-term residential programs primarily were inpatient chemical dependency programs with a usual duration of 20 to 60 days. Methadone programs are designed to treat opiate dependence through a daily dose of methadone, as well as group and individual counseling and other ancillary services. Outpatient drug-free programs do not prescribe methadone and are not tied to another modality in a continuum of care; they constitute a varied type of program that may prescribe medications other than methadone to aid recovery. Programs that were targeted primarily at alcohol abuse or serving adolescents were outside the scope of the study. Adjustments were made throughout the study to allow for the real-world requirements of conducting research in community-based programs. Upon completion of field data collection, 640 interviews were completed with clients admitted to 28 treatment programs in the DC MSA during the 6-month period from March through August, 1991.

Because of treatment practices and design factors, as well as client self-selection, treatment modalities tend to serve different clientele (Gerstein & Harwood, 1990). For example, methadone programs are designed to treat opioid abusers and dispense methadone even though their patients may be abusing other substances concomitantly. Thus, methadone programs selectively serve opioid-abusing populations, and the treatment of choice for many opioid abusers is often methadone. Recognizing these program and client selection factors, we expected different drug use patterns to emerge among admissions to the different treatment modalities and therefore report findings for clients from each modality separately. Data in this chapter cover findings from 507 interviews with long- and short-term residential and methadone clients. Low response rates in the outpatient drug-free stratum (21.1%) precluded the development of acceptable estimates for outpatient drug-free treatment clients in the DC MSA.

Additional details on the study methodology can be found in Chapter 2 and in Appendix E (1998) as well as in the final technical report for the study (National Institute on Drug Abuse [NIDA], 1994). That report also provides additional tables and findings not included here.

7.3 Prevalence of Drug Use
Among Treatment Clients

This section presents findings on the past year and past month prevalence of use of illicit drugs and alcohol among clients entering drug abuse treatment in the DC MSA in 1991. The drugs examined include marijuana or hashish, cocaine, crack cocaine, cocaine other than crack, inhalants, hallucinogens (including phencyclidine [PCP]), and heroin, as well as nonmedical use of prescription psychotherapeutic drugs (stimulants, sedatives, tranquilizers, and analgesics).

7.3.1 Drug Use During the Past Year and Past Month

Figure 7.1 presents data on the use of illicit drugs and alcohol in the past year by DC MSA drug treatment clients who were admitted to long-term residential, short-term residential, and methadone treatment (see also supporting data in Table E.1, Appendix E [1998]). The interviews were conducted at admission, and the questions covered the time period immediately preceding treatment. Methadone clients were the most different from those in the other two modalities regarding past year drug use.

The prevalence of any illicit drug use in the *past year* prior to entering treatment was lower among short-term residential clients than among long-term residential or methadone clients. Crack cocaine was the most commonly used specific illicit drug among both long-term and short-term residential clients. The prevalence of any cocaine use in the past year was comparable for long-term residential and methadone clients, but crack cocaine appeared to be the preferred form of cocaine among long-term residential clients. The situation was reversed with methadone clients, for whom cocaine other than crack was more common than crack use. A little more than seven out of eight clients in all three modalities had used alcohol in the past year. As expected, heroin use in the past year was much more prevalent among methadone clients, with an estimated 97.0% reporting use in the past year.

Figure 7.2 presents percentages of use of illicit drugs and alcohol in the *past month* prior to entering treatment, which is also referred to as "current" use (see also supporting data in Table E.1, Appendix E [1998]). As was the case with drug use in the past year, findings on drug use in the past month indicate important differences among the modalities. About half the residential clients used some illicit drugs in the past month, but a much higher percentage of methadone clients (93.3%) were

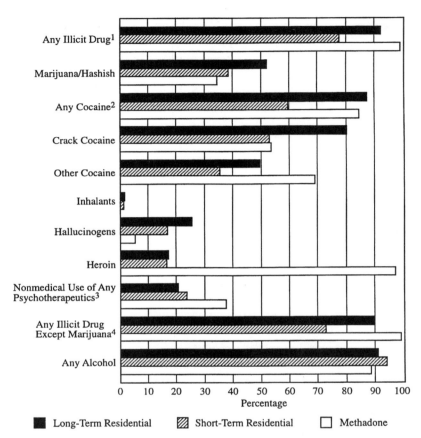

Figure 7.1. Prevalence of Past Year Illicit Drug and Alcohol Use Among DC MSA Drug Treatment Clients

SOURCE: Washington, DC, Metropolitan Area Drug Study (DC*MADS): 1989-1995.
NOTE: See Table E.1 in Appendix E (1998) for the supporting data used to prepare this figure.
1. Use of marijuana or hashish, cocaine (including crack), inhalants, hallucinogens (including phencyclidine or PCP), or heroin, or nonmedical use of psychotherapeutics at least once.
2. Includes crack cocaine.
3. Nonmedical use of any prescription-type stimulant (including methamphetamine), sedative, tranquilizer, or analgesic; does not include over-the-counter drugs.
4. Includes cocaine (including crack), inhalants, hallucinogens (including PCP), heroin, or psychotherapeutics for nonmedical reasons.

current drug users. Short-term residential clients reported a higher prevalence of heavy alcohol use (five or more drinks on 5 or more days in the past 30 days) than use of any specific illicit drugs. Crack cocaine was the most commonly used illicit drug in the past month among residential

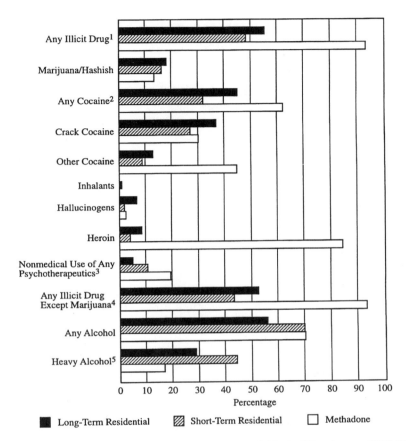

Figure 7.2. Prevalence of Past Month Illicit Drug and Alcohol Use Among DC MSA Drug Treatment Clients

SOURCE: Washington, DC, Metropolitan Area Drug Study (DC*MADS): 1989-1995.
NOTE: See Table E.1 in Appendix E (1998) for the supporting data used to prepare this figure.
1. Use of marijuana or hashish, cocaine (including crack), inhalants, hallucinogens (including phencyclidine or PCP), or heroin, or nonmedical use of psychotherapeutics at least once.
2. Includes crack cocaine.
3. Nonmedical use of any prescription-type stimulant (including methamphetamine), sedative, tranquilizer, or analgesic; does not include over-the-counter drugs.
4. Includes cocaine (including crack), inhalants, hallucinogens (including PCP), heroin, or psychotherapeutics for nonmedical reasons.
5. Defined as having five or more drinks on 5 or more days in the past 30 days.

clients. Although a sizable percentage of methadone clients used crack cocaine in the past month, use of cocaine other than crack was more prevalent among this group. As expected, heroin was the most commonly used illicit drug in the past month among methadone clients. A majority of long-term residential clients and more than two thirds of short-term residential and methadone clients consumed alcohol in the past month.

Taken together, the findings from past month and past year drug and alcohol use patterns indicate that those entering drug treatment used a wide range of drugs, but with quite different patterns across the three treatment modalities. Long- and short-term residential clients were most likely to be current users of cocaine, with a preference toward crack cocaine. This finding is consistent with DATOS findings, which showed an increase in cocaine use relative to heroin use in the treatment population of the 1990s (Craddock et al., 1997). Although heroin use predominated among methadone clients, use of forms of cocaine other than crack and use of psychotherapeutics were much more common in this modality than in the other two. Heavy alcohol use also was quite common across all treatment modalities, indicating a need to address both alcohol use and illicit drug use during the course of treatment. Although the study population was entering treatment for drug problems, nearly half of the long-term residential clients and less than half of the short-term residential clients reported *no* illicit drug use in the past month. In contrast, virtually all methadone clients (93.3%) reported some illicit drug use in the past month. Several explanations are possible for these findings.

One possible explanation for the relatively low rates of current (i.e., past month) drug use reported by residential clients is that recent circumstances may have influenced clients' access to drugs. Specifically, clients may not have used drugs in the past month if they were incarcerated or were already in treatment and transferred to a new program. In particular, 35.1% of long-term residential clients were in treatment as a formal or informal condition of probation or parole, and more than half (53.2%) were currently on probation or parole. Similar results have been found in other studies. For example, in another study in which data were collected around 1992 to 1993 in the DC MSA, one third of the clients in the methadone, long-term residential, and outpatient drug-free programs studied were court referred (Hoffman, Eckert, Koman, & Mayo, 1996). These data suggest that a sizable proportion of long-term residential clients in the DC MSA may have been incarcerated for at least some, if not most, of the month prior to the current treatment admission and as a result may have had limited access to drugs. In addition, data indicated that 70.8% of long-term residential and 60.8% of short-term residential clients previously had been in treatment at least once. Furthermore, 36.6% of long-term residential clients and 21.0% of short-term residential clients with previous treatment episodes had been in treatment within the week or month prior to their current admission. These data from Hoffman and colleagues (1996) suggest that the lower rates of reported past month illicit drug use in these two modalities in our study may be accounted for in part by clients who were incarcerated or in treatment elsewhere at least part of the time before their treatment admission.

Another explanation involves the fact that in our study, 44.3% of the newly admitted short-term residential clients were heavy alcohol users in the past month, compared with only 28.8% in long-term residential treatment and 16.9% in methadone programs. Thus, the finding that less than half of the clients entering short-term residential treatment reported using illicit drugs in the past month may be due in part to a portion of the clients entering this modality for alcohol abuse or dependence, without their having recently used other drugs.

A further explanation for these findings concerns the possible effects that admission requirements might have on the willingness of newly admitted clients to report drug use. Specifically, evidence of opiate use is a requirement for admission to methadone treatment. Thus, if individuals want to be admitted to a methadone program, it clearly would be in their interest to report recent use of heroin or other opiates. Although individuals seeking entry to the two residential modalities would still need to establish that they have a problem with drugs, the need for them to demonstrate recent use as a condition for enrollment is not as important as with methadone treatment. Furthermore, some potential clients seeking admission to these modalities may believe that reports of no recent drug use may actually *improve* their chances of gaining admission if treatment providers perceive this as evidence of the applicants' desire to quit completely (i.e., they have begun the process of quitting drug use on their own but recognize their need for help; see Flynn et al., 1995).

Similarly, some of the newly admitted clients in these two residential modalities might be underreporting their drug use out of denial of their drug abuse problem or out of a desire to "put the best foot forward" in the interview. For example, Hubbard and colleagues (1989, p. 32) noted that urinalysis results, which provide a biological measure of use in the previous 3 to 7 days, indicated a tendency of clients to underreport drug use. Underreporting was particularly pronounced for recent drug use. Indeed, when DC*MADS was being designed, study advisers with backgrounds in the drug treatment field cautioned that there might be considerable denial of drug use by new treatment admissions, particularly denial of more recent drug use. In contrast, however, Chiauzzi and Liljegren (1993) suggested that "denial" of drug use among clients entering treatment may be more of an expectation of treatment professionals than what actually occurs. They also noted that inaccuracies in client self-reports may result from cognitive impairments rather than denial; therefore, changes in self-reports with increased time in treatment may reflect recovery of previously impaired memory, rather than an acceptance of the addiction.

Potential concerns about the quality of clients' self-reports on admission to treatment may outweigh methodological problems associated with sampling and interviewing clients after they have been in treatment for a while. Just as clients entering drug treatment represent a special group of drug abusers (Regier et al., 1993; Rounsaville & Carroll, 1991), clients who remain in treatment are likely to differ in important respects from clients who enter treatment but drop out shortly thereafter. For example, TOPS data indicate that 9.6% of residential clients dropped out of treatment within a week or less, and an additional 22.5% dropped out between 2 to 4 weeks after entry (Hubbard et al., 1989, p. 95). Clients who remain in treatment for a week or more, or a month or more, may differ from clients who are entering treatment.

In summary, differences were observed across the three treatment modalities in the types of drugs used, with heroin use most common among those entering methadone treatment and cocaine use among those entering residential programs. Cocaine was used widely by clients in all modalities, even surpassing the use of marijuana, which in household studies is the most commonly used drug (SAMHSA, 1993). Indeed, fewer than 20% of clients in all modalities had used marijuana in the past month. Heavy alcohol use also was relatively common, indicating the need to treat alcohol abuse and the health risks of using alcohol in combination with other drugs.

Table 7.1 Past Month Use of Any Illicit Drug, by Demographic Characteristics and Treatment Modality

Demographic Characteristic	Long-Term Residential (n = 179)	Short-Term Residential (n = 135)	Methadone (n = 193)
Total	55.3	48.2	93.3
Sex			
Male	51.4	52.4	90.8
Female	65.2	40.0	97.5
Age group (years)			
18-25	59.1	*	*
26-34	50.7	*	95.5
≥35	59.6	45.6	92.4
Race/ethnicity[1]			
White	62.5	44.7	*
Black	54.6	*	94.1
Hispanic	*	*	100.0
Marital status			
Single	50.5	44.4	93.4
Married	65.8	54.4	*
Divorced/widowed	62.6	46.2	96.8
Location[2]			
DC	*	*	92.5
Maryland	63.2	54.2	100.0
Virginia	49.4	54.1	*
Adult education			
Less than high school	41.6	44.8	92.6
High school graduate	63.1	46.9	93.7
Some college/college graduate	63.4	52.1	93.9
Current employment			
Full-time	59.4	57.5	96.0
Unemployed	53.8	*	93.0
Other[3]	55.3	*	*

SOURCE: Washington, DC, Metropolitan Area Drug Study (DC*MADS): 1989-1995.
NOTE: Data entries are percentages. Unweighted numbers of respondents are given in Table 2.1.
1. The category "other" for race/ethnicity is not included.
2. The District of Columbia Metropolitan Statistical Area (DC MSA) is defined in Chapter 1.
3. Retired, disabled, homemaker, student, or "other."
*Low precision.

7.3.2 Demographic Correlates of Users

Table 7.1 presents estimates of past month illicit drug use prevalence among demographic subgroups of treatment clients. As shown, in long-term residential programs, past month illicit drug use was more prevalent among females than males. In contrast, illicit drug use was more prevalent among males than females in short-term residential treatment. In both types of residential programs, clients who were currently married were more likely to report illicit drug use than were clients who were single. In long-term residential treatment, about 42% of clients with less than a high school education used illicit drugs in the past month, compared with 63% of clients who were high school graduates or who had at least some college. Drug use prevalence was more similar among demographic subgroups of methadone clients.

In each modality, marijuana use in the past month was more prevalent among males than among females, and the prevalence of marijuana use tended to be higher among whites than among blacks (data not presented for types of drugs). In the residential modalities, marijuana use was also more prevalent among clients who were employed full-time. Among long-term residential and methadone programs, crack cocaine use in the past month was more prevalent among females than among males and was less prevalent among people who were employed full-time.

Residential clients aged 35 or older had a lower prevalence of crack cocaine use in the past month than did clients in younger age groups. Among methadone clients, the pattern was reversed, with clients in this oldest age group having a higher prevalence of crack use than did clients aged 26 to 34. In each modality, crack cocaine use in the past month was more prevalent among blacks than among whites. The situation was reversed with heavy alcohol use, which was more prevalent among whites than among blacks.

In summary, there were notable differences across demographic groups in the types of drugs used in the past month. In a few instances, these differences were consistent across all three treatment modalities. Those who were employed full-time were more likely to use marijuana or be heavy alcohol users than those employed part-time or not at all. Blacks were more likely to be current users of crack cocaine, whereas whites were more likely to be heavy users of alcohol.

7.3.3 Patterns of Drug Use

Developing a meaningful scheme for summarizing drug use patterns, one that considers combinations of drugs used, is a difficult and complex task because of the varying quantities and types of substances used. The frequent and often concurrent use of multiple substances among large proportions of this population further confounds the task. The likelihood of use and patterns of use vary with user preferences, drug availability, and effects experienced from the drugs. For example, clients may have one or more preferred drugs that are frequently used, other drugs that are used as a substitute when the drug of choice is not available, drugs used to enhance or moderate the effects of a primary drug, and drugs used simply because of their availability. In addition, there are different routes of administration as well as different styles of use, such as chronic or daily use, periodic bingeing, and intermittent use.

Because of these complexities, there is no easy way to describe drug use patterns that is simple enough to be easily understood but comprehensive enough to capture all the variations. The approach we chose is one used by Hubbard and colleagues (1989), drawing on the work of Bray, Schlenger, Craddock, Hubbard, and Rachal (1982), that uses seven mutually exclusive hierarchical patterns to categorize drug use. This general approach to classification was developed and first used in TOPS with a sample of clients entering treatment from 1979 to 1981 across metropolitan America. The hierarchical groups were derived empirically based on the most common use patterns. In TOPS, patterns were defined based on at least weekly use of each type of drug. Recently, the patterns were updated and modified based on clients entering metropolitan treatment programs from 1991 to 1993 (Craddock et al., 1993). The update was necessary to reflect the increase in cocaine use in the time between the two studies.

The more contemporary patterns were used in this study to describe the drug use patterns in the DC metropolitan area. Because data were not collected on the frequency of illicit drug use, however, the categories used were based on any drug use in the past year. Respondents were classified into a single pattern by comparing their use with an ordered listing of the patterns. Once respondents fit a pattern, they did not qualify for any of the succeeding patterns (hence, the hierarchical nature of the categorization scheme). The seven general patterns in their hierarchical order are

1. heroin with no cocaine use,
2. heroin with cocaine use (regardless of other illicit drugs used),

Table 7.2 Past Year Patterns of Drug Use, by Treatment Modality

Patterns of Drug Use	Long-Term Residential (n = 179)	Short-Term Residential (n = 135)	Methadone (n = 193)
Heroin/no cocaine	0.8	3.9	14.7
Heroin with cocaine	16.3	12.5	82.3
Any cocaine alone	24.4	17.4	0.7
Cocaine with other drugs	46.3	29.6	1.3
Heavy alcohol use only[1]	3.6	17.5	0.0
Minimal use	4.4	14.2	0.0
No illicit drug use or heavy alcohol use	4.3	4.9	1.0

SOURCE: Washington, DC, Metropolitan Area Drug Study (DC*MADS): 1989-1995.
NOTE: Data entries are percentages. Patterns are defined hierarchically in their table order. Thus, a client appears in a pattern only if he or she did not qualify for one of the preceding patterns.
1. Defined as having five or more drinks on 5 or more days in the past 30 days.

    3. any use of cocaine alone,
    4. cocaine used in combination with at least one other illicit drug other than heroin,
    5. heavy alcohol use (without use of any illicit drugs),
    6. minimal use (which includes use of any other illicit drugs), and
    7. no illicit drug use or heavy alcohol use.

Patterns of drug use in the past year by treatment modality are shown in Table 7.2. When examining patterns of use in the past year in the DC metropolitan area, the most striking finding is the pervasiveness of cocaine use. Clients in methadone programs almost exclusively (97.0%) fit into the two patterns involving heroin use. (This finding was expected given that methadone is designed for the medical treatment of heroin addiction. The 3% who did not report use fitting into the two heroin patterns may have been in treatment or other restrictive environments that precluded use, or they may have incorrectly reported their heroin use.) What was striking was the extent of cocaine use even among methadone clients, with 82.3% of the clients in the heroin with cocaine pattern and only 14.7% in the heroin/no cocaine pattern. The cocaine epidemic had even infiltrated a population addicted to heroin, requiring methadone programs to address this drug as well as heroin.

Approximately one in six clients in the residential modalities were also users of heroin in the past year (17.1% for long-term residential,

16.4% for short-term residential). Heroin use also was typically coupled with cocaine use. The cocaine patterns, which included cocaine used alone or in combination with other drugs, were highly prevalent among clients in the two residential modalities. Among long-term residential clients, 87.0% used cocaine in the past year as did 59.5% of the short-term residential clients.

These findings are similar to the findings from DATOS (Craddock et al., 1993), with most long-term residential clients using cocaine, either alone or in combination with other drugs. There is a somewhat similar pattern with short-term residential clients, but with a larger proportion abusing alcohol, and methadone clients using heroin, either alone or in combination with cocaine. These findings are in contrast to the earlier TOPS findings that show a greater percentage of clients using heroin alone.

The DC findings are consistent with patterns of abuse that are appearing elsewhere across metropolitan America. Cocaine has grown in popularity and multiple drug use is common; moreover, cocaine and heroin are often used with other drugs (Craddock et al., 1997). The nature of the change in drug use trends can be explained in part by such factors as cost, availability, preference, and substitution.

7.3.4 Frequency of Use and Components of Dependence

When considering frequency of use in the past month of the various drugs, the dominance of cocaine is again apparent. Marijuana use in the past month by clients in each treatment modality was likely to be relatively infrequent, if clients used marijuana at all. Among users, the most commonly occurring frequency of use was 1 to 2 days per month. Use of crack cocaine however, was relatively frequent. A large proportion of clients in all three modalities used it on 5 or more days in the past 30 days. Approximately one quarter of methadone clients, a group who typically used heroin almost daily, also were frequent users of other forms of cocaine (data not shown).

Clients either tended not to use alcohol at all in the past month or else to use it on 5 or more days. An estimated 30.6% of short-term residential, 30.4% of methadone, and 44.2% of long-term residential clients had not used alcohol in the past month; however, 37.7% of all long-term residential, 38.9% of methadone, and 54.3% of short-term residential clients used alcohol on 5 or more days. Approximately half to three quarters of those using alcohol on 5 or more days were classed as heavy drinkers, having five or more drinks on at least 5 days in the past 30 days.

A subset of the National Household Survey on Drug Abuse (NHSDA) symptoms of dependence associated with alcohol or other drug use was used to examine the prevalence of combined alcohol and drug use in the past year. The symptoms of dependence were derived from criteria used in the *Diagnostic and Statistical Manual of Mental Disorders*, Version III, Revised (DSM-III-R; American Psychiatric Association [APA], 1987). Combined use was defined as using other drugs at the same time or within a couple of hours of using alcohol. The symptoms of dependence included needing larger amounts of alcohol or other drugs to get the same effect, having withdrawal symptoms as a result of reducing or stopping consumption, or trying to cut down on use.

Large majorities of clients in each treatment modality used illicit drugs in combination with alcohol in the past year (81.9% of long-term residential clients, 68.8% of short-term residential clients, and 73.5% of methadone clients). Approximately three quarters of the clients in the residential modalities who used crack cocaine in the past year reported that they needed to use crack in larger amounts. In addition, slightly less than half of the clients in these two modalities who used crack experienced withdrawal symptoms because of their use of crack, and a majority of the users tried to cut down on their use of crack. Similar percentages of short-term residential and methadone clients used crack cocaine in the past year, but the latter were less likely to have used crack in combination with alcohol and were less likely to attribute components of dependence to their use of crack. Methadone clients were much more likely than clients in the residential modalities to attribute symptoms of dependence to heroin use in the past year than to use of any other substances. Similar percentages of clients in each modality used alcohol in the past year; however, methadone clients were less likely than clients in the other two modalities to attribute symptoms of dependence to their use of alcohol. Short-term residential clients also were more likely than long-term residential clients to report withdrawal symptoms associated with alcohol use.

7.3.5 Needle Use

With the risk of human immunodeficiency virus (HIV) infection and acquired immune deficiency syndrome (AIDS) from use of contaminated needles, injection drug use became a topic of increased concern during the decade before the DC study. We examined data on needle use behaviors and found that heroin and cocaine were the drugs most likely to be injected, with methadone clients most likely to inject heroin and long-term residential clients slightly favoring cocaine. The vast majority of methadone clients (89.5%) had used needles to inject drugs during their lifetimes, a fact that would be expected because injection is the most common route of administration for heroin. More than one fourth of the residential clients, however, also had injected drugs in their lifetimes, placing them at significant risk of having HIV infection. Approximately half of all methadone clients had used needles that had been used by others or had given their needles to someone else to use, indicating a high risk of transmission of HIV among this group. Although sharing of needles was less common among residential clients, more than 10% from each of these modalities had used someone else's needle and had given their needles to others.

Because the majority of methadone clients reported injecting drugs in the past month, they are clear targets for efforts aimed at reducing the risk of needle use. With more than one fourth of residential clients having injected drugs during their lifetimes, a large proportion of DC MSA residential treatment clients were at risk of having HIV in 1991. We suspect similar trends across other major metropolitan areas throughout the United States.

7.3.6 Context of Drug Use

Across all three modalities, the usual place for using drugs was at home, either the drug abuser's or someone else's. Methadone clients differed from the other two groups in that they were much more likely to report using drugs in their own home (83.7%) compared with someone else's home (52.7%). With clients entering the long-term residential treatment, the situation was reversed; these clients were more likely to use drugs in someone else's home (79.6%) than their own home (65.8%). Short-term residential clients were almost equally as likely to use drugs in the two settings. Methadone clients also were more likely to use a shooting gallery than those from residential programs, a difference that would be expected given that they were the most likely to inject drugs. Drug use in public places (i.e., parks, vacant buildings, cars, bars, rest rooms, and concerts) was relatively common among clients from all three modalities. Clients reported using drugs both alone and with a variety of other persons present. Methadone clients were somewhat more likely to use drugs alone compared with those from the other two modalities and were somewhat less likely to report use with others (e.g., sexual partner, friends) than residential clients. Between 19.3% and 32.5% of clients from the three modalities used drugs with family members.

In summary, a sizable majority of clients reported drug use in a home, either their own or someone else's. There also was a large percentage from each modality who reported use in public places, which indicates that, at least in some locations, drug use is either a visible problem or an accepted or tolerated behavior. Reports on other people present while drugs were being used suggest the social context of use. The majority of clients reported using drugs with others (with friends and sexual partner the two most frequently cited groups). Many cited using drugs with family members. Drug use being so closely woven into the social network presents an enormous challenge for treatment professionals across America to assist clients to develop alternative, drug-free networks.

7.4 Consequences and Correlates of Drug and Alcohol Use

This section presents findings related to consequences and comorbid problems among drug treatment clients associated with their drug use. Comorbidity refers to problems that occur together but may or may not be directly or causally related. Information is presented here on treatment histories, mental health problems, physical illness and primary care history, illegal activities and arrests, and specific problems attributable to the past year use of alcohol or illicit drugs.

7.4.1 Substance Abuse Treatment History

Drug abuse treatment histories were examined with a focus on the current treatment episode, including waiting list findings, whether clients entered treatment as a condition of parole or probation, reason(s) for enrolling in treatment, and information about who persuaded the client to enroll. More than half of the clients entering long-term residential and methadone treatment were wait listed prior to entering treatment. This was in contrast to about one fifth of the short-term residential clients who were placed on a waiting list. Approximately one third of the long-term residential clients entered treatment as a formal or informal condition of parole or probation. About 20% of methadone and 10% of short-term residential clients entered treatment as a legal condition.

Clients typically gave multiple reasons for entering treatment, with the most commonly cited being a desire to get off drugs and disgust with their lifestyle. Approximately half of the clients across the modalities said that it was their own idea to enter treatment. Among the short-term residential clients, friends, family, members, and coworkers were the next most frequently cited group who persuaded them to enter treatment; a few said they were there because of the courts. In contrast, for the clients in the long-term residential and methadone modalities, the courts were more influential than family members in getting people into treatment.

A majority of clients from each of the three modalities previously had received treatment for drug or alcohol abuse, with methadone clients having the largest number of previous treatment episodes and short-term residential clients the fewest. Only 14.7% of methadone clients were entering treatment for the first time, compared with 39.2% of the short-term residential clients. When considering the most recent previous admission, illicit drug use was the primary target of treatment for methadone clients, whereas alcohol abuse, either alone or in conjunction with other substances, was a common problem for residential clients. With the long-term residential group, alcohol abuse was the most frequently treated problem, followed by crack cocaine use and use of cocaine other than crack. Among short-term residential clients, treatment of alcohol abuse also predominated, followed by crack cocaine use, use of heroin, and use of cocaine other than crack. Across all three modalities, the most commonly cited reason for terminating previous treatment was successful completion of the program, followed by transfer to a different program or relapse.

In summary, the majority of clients in all three modalities previously had been treated for drug or alcohol problems. Even though the study excluded programs that treated only alcohol problems, alcohol abuse was the most frequently cited reason for previous treatment among residential clients.

7.4.2 Physical Illness and Treatment

Similar percentages of clients in each of the three modalities were told in the past year that they had one or more potentially drug-related illnesses (see Table 7.3). An estimated 5.8% of the methadone clients indicated that they were told in the past year that they had AIDS or the AIDS-related complex (ARC), or that they were infected with HIV. Approximately 10% of residential clients and 5.1% of methadone clients reported that they were told they had other sexually transmitted diseases (STDs), such as syphilis or gonorrhea, in the past year. Relatively small percentages of clients in each modality were told in the past year that they had tuberculosis. More than half of the clients across modalities reported the occurrence of one or more other primary care problems in the past year. Among all three groups, respiratory problems, such as bronchitis, asthma, pneumonia, flu, or colds, were most common. Nearly three fourths of short-term residential clients had insurance coverage in the past year, compared with only about a third or less of the long-term residential and methadone clients. Large majorities of clients in each of the modalities used a hospital emergency room in their lifetimes, and approximately 30% to 37% used an emergency room in the past year. Short-term residential clients showed the highest prevalence of emergency room use in the past month, followed by methadone and long-term residential clients.

Caution should be used when interpreting the data on drug-related illnesses and primary care problems. The data probably are conservative estimates of the true prevalence of medical conditions among clients entering drug treatment. Prevalence data on drug-related illness were based on whether respondents were told that they had the particular condition in the past 12 months and reported it here. Thus, the percent-

Table 7.3 Primary Care Problems, Insurance Coverage, and Medical Treatment, by Treatment Modality

Condition/Treatment	Long-Term Residential (n = 179)	Short-Term Residential (n = 135)	Methadone (n = 193)
Any drug-related illness, past year	12.8	17.0	13.1
AIDS/ARC/HIV[1]	1.1	0.0	5.8
Other STDs[2]	10.4	10.7	5.1
Tuberculosis	0.6	1.9	2.4
Hepatitis/yellow jaundice	1.3	4.5	1.8
Any other primary care problems, past year	76.3	83.8	55.6
Respiratory[3]	57.4	63.6	42.9
Heart/circulatory	15.6	29.9	25.7
Digestive	17.6	15.2	9.6
Bone/muscle	19.0	19.8	11.7
Neurological	14.8	15.7	7.8
Skin ulcers/rashes	11.2	12.7	12.7
Number of medical conditions, listed above, past year			
None	22.1	13.6	40.7
1-3	70.5	78.7	50.0
4 or more	7.4	7.7	9.3
Past year insurance coverage	34.7	73.3	30.9
Past year medical use			
Hospitalization	17.5	35.6	22.4
ER use[4]	29.0	36.2	36.5
Alcohol-related ER use	3.6	10.2	0.0
Drug-related ER use	4.4	8.3	12.6
Both alcohol- and drug-related ER use	4.5	3.7	5.0
Outpatient treatment	86.8	79.5	86.1

SOURCE: Washington, DC, Metropolitan Area Drug Study (DC*MADS): 1989-1995.
NOTE: Data entries are percentages.
1. Acquired immune deficiency syndrome (AIDS), AIDS-related complex (ARC), and human immunodeficiency virus (HIV).
2. STDs are sexually transmitted diseases (e.g., syphilis, gonorrhea).
3. Such as bronchitis, asthma, pneumonia, flu, or colds.
4. Any use of an emergency room (ER).
*Low precision.

ages shown in Table 7.3 for the drug-related illnesses may more closely reflect the *incidence* (i.e., occurrence of new cases) of these different problems in the past year rather than the *prevalence* (i.e., total of new and previously existing cases) of these problems, if clients still had these problems in the past year but answered "no," based on whether they had been "told" they had the problem. In addition, treatment clients who had never been screened for a problem in the past year (e.g., HIV) may have had the problem (e.g., HIV infection), even though they had not been told about it in the past year.

7.4.3 Mental Health Treatment

Most clients entering residential drug treatment or methadone treatment in the DC MSA had past histories of mental health problems. In general, however, methadone clients were somewhat less likely than clients in the other two modalities to indicate past mental health problems. An estimated 95.5% of long-term residential clients, 89.3% of short-term residential clients, and 76.9% of methadone clients indicated one or more mental health problems in their lifetimes. Mental health problems were more common among residential clients. An estimated 70.3% of long-term residential clients and 60.4% of short-term residential clients indicated a lifetime history of four or more mental health problems. In contrast, 36.3% of methadone clients indicated a lifetime history of four or more problems, and 40.6% had one to three lifetime problems. Approximately 70% of long-term residential and more than 60% of short-term residential clients experienced mental health problems in their lifetimes of serious depression, serious anxiety or tension, arguing or fighting, and/or feeling suspicious or distrustful of others. Fewer than half of all methadone clients indicated lifetime histories of serious depression or anxiety. In only one instance, that of arguing or fighting, did more than half of methadone clients indicate that they had experienced a specific problem. An estimated 40.5% of short-term residential clients received some form of treatment for mental health problems in their lifetimes, as did 27.9% of the long-term residential and 22.0% of the methadone clients.

Approximately 85% of residential clients and 68.1% of methadone clients indicated at least one mental health problem in the past month. Approximately 45% of residential clients had four or more problems. Across all three modalities, the most commonly occurring mental health problems in the past month were serious anxiety or tension and suspicion or distrust of other people. Although serious depression in the past month was less prevalent among methadone clients than among clients in the other two modalities, it was the third most common mental health problem for this group (25.3%). With the other two modalities, depression was the sixth most common problem.

In general, comorbidity of heavy alcohol use and treatment for mental health problems was more prevalent among short-term residential clients than among clients in the other two modalities. Approximately two thirds of the short-term residential clients were either heavy alcohol users in the past month or had a lifetime history of mental health treatment. In contrast, only one third of the methadone clients and less than half of the long-term residential clients (46.9%) were either heavy alcohol users or had a history of mental health treatment. Nearly one in five short-term residential clients were *both* heavy alcohol users in the past month *and* had a lifetime history of mental health treatment, compared with 9.4% of long-term residential clients and 3.4% of methadone clients.

In summary, many of the clients entering drug abuse treatment had a history of both lifetime and past month mental health problems, although a relatively small proportion had received mental health treatment. Heavy alcohol use was common among drug treatment clients, indicating the importance of incorporating alcohol treatment strategies into drug treatment programs.

7.4.4 Illegal Activities and Arrests

Table 7.4 presents findings on the percentages of clients in each treatment modality who reported having been engaged in different criminal activities in their lifetimes and who had been arrested for various crimes in their lifetimes. Only those respondents who reported that they ever engaged in a particular criminal activity were asked whether they ever had been arrested for that crime; however, the percentages of clients who were arrested refer to the entire client population in each modality, not just those clients who had engaged in the criminal activity.

The lifetime prevalence of criminal involvement was relatively high in all three modalities, with the percentages of short-term residential clients committing offenses or being arrested tending to be lower than the corresponding percentages of clients in the other two modalities. An estimated 81.4% of long-term residential and 77.5% of methadone clients

Table 7.4 Illegal Activities and Arrests for Criminal Offenses in the Lifetime, by Treatment Modality

Illegal Activities/Arrests	Long-Term Residential (n = 179)	Short-Term Residential (n = 135)	Methadone (n = 193)
Drug manufacture/sale or distribution			
Committed	72.5	44.0	63.9
Arrested	41.4	18.2	49.1
Property offense, such as burglary, larceny, or theft			
Committed	40.4	29.4	42.2
Arrested	24.9	14.9	34.5
Robbery, mugging, or purse snatching with force			
Committed	14.2	17.5	20.1
Arrested	8.3	5.8	13.6
Violent offense, such as assault, kidnapping, rape, manslaughter, or homicide			
Committed	25.3	17.2	13.9
Arrested	16.4	9.6	8.5
Any of the above			
Committed	81.4	53.3	77.5
Arrested	59.8	31.0	65.8

SOURCE: Washington, DC, Metropolitan Area Drug Study (DC*MADS): 1989-1995.
NOTE: Data entries are percentages. Only those respondents who indicated that they had engaged in illegal activities were asked about arrests, but percentages are for the entire population of each modality (see accompanying text).

had engaged in at least one of the four kinds of criminal activity queried in their lifetimes, and 59.8% and 65.8% of the clients in these two modalities, respectively, had been arrested. In contrast, only slightly more than half of the short-term residential clients had been involved in a criminal activity, and fewer than a third ever had been arrested. Among all three modalities, lifetime involvement in the manufacture, sale, or distribution of drugs was the most commonly occurring criminal activity, and involvement in property offenses (e.g., burglary, larceny) was the second most prevalent activity. Methadone clients who engaged in crimes related to drug manufacture, sale, or distribution or who engaged in property offenses were more likely to be arrested for these crimes than were long-term residential clients who engaged in a similar activity. Approximately three fourths of methadone clients who were involved in drug manufacture, sale, or distribution had been arrested for those crimes, compared with fewer than 60% of long-term residential clients who engaged in similar crimes. Approximately four fifths of methadone clients who committed property offenses were arrested, compared with approximately three fifths of long-term residential clients who committed property offenses.

Selected illegal activities and arrests in the past year for clients in each of the three treatment modalities also were examined. With the exception of driving under the influence of alcohol or other drugs, long-term residential clients were more likely than clients in the other two modalities to have engaged in a variety of drug-related criminal activities in the past year and to be on probation or parole. An estimated 57.9% of methadone clients and approximately two thirds of the clients in the residential modalities drove a car in the past year while under the influence of alcohol or other substances. More than half of all long-term residential clients sold illicit drugs in the past year, compared with approximately 30% of clients in the other two modalities. The prevalence of trading sex for drugs or money in the past year among long-term residential clients was twice that of the prevalence among methadone clients.

7.4.5 Problems Directly Attributed to Drug and Alcohol Use

An estimated 96.4% of methadone clients, 90.6% of long-term residential clients, and 86.1% of short-term residential clients experienced one or more specific problems in the past year that they directly attributed to their use of illicit drugs. More than four fifths of long-term residential and methadone clients became depressed or lost interest in things in the past year as a result of their use of illicit drugs. An estimated 70.1% of short-term residential clients experienced the same problem in the past year because of their use of illicit drugs. More than four fifths of long-term residential clients, more than three fourths of methadone clients, and more than two thirds of short-term residential clients had arguments or fights with family or friends, found it difficult to think clearly, or felt nervous or anxious in the past year because of their drug use. Drug use is a problem not only for an individual and those in his or her immediate proximity; it also places a burden on institutions. Approximately one in three methadone clients, one in four short-term residential clients, and one in five long-term residential clients had to get emergency medical help in the past year because of their drug use.

More than four fifths of the residential clients experienced one or more specific problems in the past year because of their use of alcohol, compared with three fifths of methadone clients. Methadone clients were less likely than clients in the other two modalities to indicate that they experienced problems in the past year because of their alcohol use. Approximately half or more of residential clients indicated that they had been aggressive or mad while drinking, were afraid they might be or become an alcoholic, had experienced memory loss as a result of their drinking, and/or had a quick drink when no one was looking. In particular, nearly two thirds of the short-term residential clients indicated that they were afraid they might be an alcoholic or become one.

In summary, a large majority of clients in each modality reported the occurrence of problems in the past year that were attributed specifically to their use of illicit drugs. A sizable proportion of those entering drug treatment also reported problems associated with their use of alcohol. Clients in the two residential modalities were more likely than methadone clients to report the occurrence of alcohol-related problems in the past year.

7.5 Special Topics

This section covers three special topics related to drug use among clients entering residential and methadone treatment in the DC MSA and other metropolitan areas across America. The first section covers age at first use, examining differences across age cohorts. Next, drug and alcohol abuse during pregnancy is examined. The last section examines clients' accessibility to treatment, including ease of admission and, among methadone clients, factors relating to attending the program.

7.5.1 Age at First Use

Our findings on age at first use of five major substances (alcohol, marijuana, heroin, other cocaine, and crack cocaine) among those who have used the substance in their lifetimes were examined. These ages of first use imply a sequencing or ordering of use of the five drugs. When considering all age groups combined, alcohol was the first substance used, and the general pattern was observed within each of the age groups. With illicit drugs, the average age at first use for all clients was lowest for marijuana. This was the typical pattern across each of the three age groups as well. An age cohort effect was observed for age at first use of illicit drugs, with older clients starting use of illicit drugs at a later age. This age cohort effect was not evident for alcohol. Average age of first use of crack cocaine was uniformly higher than for use of forms of cocaine other than crack, with the number of years between the two increasing with the older clients. For example, with the oldest of the short-term residential clients, the average age at first use was 25.2 for cocaine and 33.8 for crack, a difference of 8.6 years. With the 26- to 34-year-olds, this difference was 5.2 years, and among the 18- to 25-year-olds, it was 2.0 years. Differences observed in age at first use of crack cocaine versus other forms of cocaine likely reflect the fact that crack is a relatively recent form of cocaine, a form that was not readily available until the mid-1980s (Inciardi, 1991). Particularly with clients in the oldest group, crack cocaine was not available when they were in their teens or early 20s.

In summary, the average age at first use was lowest for alcohol among clients of all age groups and across all three modalities. The average age at first use for marijuana was the lowest for all illicit drugs. Although consistent with the literature on sequencing of drug use (Kandel & Logan, 1984; Newcomb & Bentler, 1986), these data present only the average age at first use.

7.5.2 Drug Use During Pregnancy

Although Chapter 8 is devoted exclusively to drug use among pregnant women, this study provided an opportunity to inquire retrospectively about drug use during pregnancy among a group of known abusers. Moreover, although constraints were posed by small sample sizes and limited data, there is clear evidence that drug use during pregnancy is a serious problem among women in treatment. A large majority (more than 88%) of female clients in each of the three modalities had been pregnant during their lifetime. Those who had been pregnant ($n = 157$) were asked about their use of illicit drugs and alcohol during their most recent pregnancy. Because of the small number of women in short-term residential programs who recently had been pregnant, there are few reportable findings for this modality.

Female treatment clients who did not use some type of drug, including alcohol, during their most recent pregnancy were in the minority. Women in long-term residential programs were most likely to have used alcohol (64.4%), followed by illicit drugs (38.9%), during their last pregnancy. In contrast, women in methadone programs were most likely to have used illicit drugs (46.7%), followed by alcohol (27.3%). Heroin was the most frequently cited illicit drug used by methadone clients (38.5%). Very few of the women reported use of crack or other forms of cocaine during their most recent pregnancy.

Although the small number of respondents, particularly from the short-term residential programs, resulted in many low-precision estimates, it appeared that among this population of drug abusers, use of alcohol and other drugs was relatively common during pregnancy. Preliminary findings, however, suggested that the pattern of illicit drug use did change during pregnancy in several ways. Comparing drug use in the past year with use while pregnant suggests that these women reduced their illicit drug use, especially that of cocaine, after becoming pregnant. Even methadone clients reported that they had used less heroin during pregnancy than in the past year. An exception to this finding was the relatively high level of use of "other" drugs (which included inhalants and hallucinogens as well as nonmedical use of stimulants, sedatives, tranquilizers, or analgesics) among the long-term residential clients. The reduction in substance use after becoming pregnant also was observed with alcohol.

A limitation of these data is that they did not provide information about the amounts of drugs that were used or the timing of their use during pregnancy. It is also possible that these estimates of use during pregnancy were conservative because of underreporting, particularly because respondents could have feared that reporting use would have resulted in legal action against them.

7.5.3 Access to Treatment

Clients also were asked about the ease of admission to treatment. Methadone clients, all of whom had to travel daily to a program site to obtain their dosage, were queried about how difficult it was to attend the program after admission. For the majority of clients, obtaining admission to treatment was "not very hard." The largest percentage of short-term residential clients (85.3%) indicated this, followed by long-term residential clients (70.9%); however, 42.6% of the methadone clients reported that gaining admission to treatment was "somewhat" or "very" hard. Among those methadone clients who found it somewhat or very hard to attend the program, the most frequently cited barriers were obtaining transportation (42.6%) and the long distance of the program from their home (35.5%).

These findings, which indicate that clients other than those in methadone treatment do not encounter major difficulties in accessing treatment, should be interpreted with caution. No information is available on those who did not enter treatment. There may or may not be a significant number of drug abusers who did not enter treatment because of problems with accessibility. More than half of those entering long-term residential and methadone treatment were placed on a waiting list, which can serve as a barrier. No information was available on those wait listed who opted not to enter treatment when a slot became available.

7.6 Discussion and Implications

The findings from this study of treatment clients provide important information about the prevalence of drug abuse and its consequences and co-occurring problems. The findings, however, must be viewed in the context of the study's primary goal, which was to examine drug use characteristics among a population of known drug abusers. Those newly admitted to drug treatment programs were selected as an identifiable and accessible group of drug abusers. Thus, the findings from this study should not be generalized to populations of abusers who do not seek treatment.

7.6.1 Prevalence and Correlates of Drug Use

Those entering drug treatment in the DC MSA in 1991 used many types of drugs and typically had a long history of use. Findings from this and related studies demonstrate that trends of abuse have changed over the past decade. Cocaine (including crack) had become the most widely used drug among newly admitted treatment clients in the DC MSA. National data indicate that from 1979 to 1981, opiates were the predominant drug of abuse among those entering treatment (Hubbard et al., 1989). DC data for 1982 and 1983 indicate a similar situation, with heroin as the most abused drug (NIDA, 1983) during that period.

Studying a treatment population permits examination of issues related to heroin and heavy cocaine use, both relatively uncommon behaviors. Obtaining a sufficient sample size of either of these groups with a household survey has proven to be problematic. For example, Gfroerer and Brodsky's (1993) analysis of frequent cocaine users was based on 169 respondents identified from the 32,594 completed interviews in the 1991 NHSDA. Similarly, only 127 of the 1991 NHSDA respondents indicated they had used heroin in the past year and 33 in the past month (U.S. General Accounting Office, 1993).

Being able to access groups of heavy cocaine and heroin users provides an opportunity to improve understanding of the characteristics of these users, patterns and context of drug use, consequences, and comorbid conditions. For example, methadone clients, almost all of whom use heroin, have patterns of primary care problems different from clients entering the other two modalities, where cocaine use predominates. Methadone clients were much more likely to have an HIV-related illness (5.8%) than long-term (1.1%) or short-term residential clients (0.0%). Monitoring the prevalence of HIV and related illness among methadone clients provides sentinel information on the extent of infection among a high-risk population.

Drug treatment clients constitute a population who have, along with problems of drug abuse, a wide range of health and human service needs. Drug abuse does not occur in isolation but is associated with a wide range of problems, which points to the need for broad-based treatment that addresses not only the individual's addiction but also the problems commonly occurring with abuse. Addressing these problems may require treatment programs that provide psychological, vocational, educational, medical, and social services or effective linkages with other multifaceted programs. For example, the majority have had a mental health problem at some point in their lifetimes, but across the three modalities reported here, only between 22.0% and 40.5% had received mental health treatment. Similarly, between 55.6% and 83.8% had a primary care problem in the past year.

Changes in patterns of drug use during the decade before the study among those entering treatment, most notably the pervasiveness of cocaine use, highlight the importance of developing and implementing treatment strategies that focus on this drug. Cocaine use was prevalent even among those entering methadone treatment, a modality traditionally associated with heroin use. Thus, methadone treatment programs, which are designed to address the use of heroin and other opiates, must adapt their approaches to treat cocaine abuse among their clientele.

Finally, when combined with a study of the drug treatment system that provides relatively complete information on capacity and utilization, a study of clients entering treatment and their experiences in accessing treatment can provide a method for assessing the current system and ways for enhancing access. Between 20.5% and 51.5% of clients in this study were placed on a waiting list before being admitted, and between 9.4% and 14.7% reported it was "very hard" to gain admission to treatment, with the greatest difficulty reported by persons in methadone treatment. These findings suggest that the drug treatment system in the DC MSA was operating at or near capacity in 1991. Although this study was not designed to address the issue of the adequacy of the treatment system, assessing who could not access services may provide valuable information for doing so.

7.6.2 Limitations of the Findings

This study has several important methodological limitations that affect the conclusions that can be drawn. Foremost of the limitations is that the results were based on clients entering three treatment modalities (i.e., long- and short-term residential and methadone programs). Outpatient drug-free programs were included in the original sample design, but the low response rate precluded the development of acceptable estimates for clients from this modality. The outpatient drug-free modality typically treats the largest number of clients, and those served in this modality generally are quite different from the population described in this chapter. With the advent of managed care, the outpatient drug-free modality requires additional attention, as it is often viewed as the least costly and least restrictive treatment modality. Future patterns of access and utilization, because of managed care's emphasis on cost, may change significantly, and the outpatient drug-free modality will require more careful consideration. Thus, the study covers only three of the four major modalities in the formal drug treatment system. Because of the lack of acceptable estimates for outpatient drug-free clients and because of the distinctiveness of clients in different modalities, no combined estimates for all drug treatment clients are available.

A second limitation is that drug treatment currently is undergoing many changes. Such factors as managed care, which has become more prominent in the drug treatment system since 1991, might result in changes in populations being served in metropolitan areas or in the services provided.

A third potential limitation is the lack of external validation for the interviews. Past studies suggest that drug use often is underreported. Hubbard and colleagues (1989) found that among clients entering treatment, underreporting is more of a problem with more recent use. Consistent with that, a sizable proportion of the clients in this study reported no use in the past month. Several explanations are possible for lower rates of past month use, such as underreporting, denial, memory limitations, or lack of access to drugs during this period.

7.6.3 Methodological Challenges

This study faced a number of challenges similar to those encountered in other surveys of community-based treatment populations. The key challenges included developing a suitable sample frame, obtaining accurate interview responses, obtaining a representative subject pool from the four major treatment modalities, and acquiring support and access from treatment programs and providers.

The first challenge was to obtain a comprehensive list of all drug treatment programs in the MSA for the sampling frame. The mailing list from the 1989 NDATUS was used as a starting point to construct the sampling frame, but because the list was not complete and did not provide information about type of care and client flow necessary to establish sampling rates, other steps were needed. These included (a) augmenting the NDATUS list by cross-checking it with other sources (e.g., directories of programs, listings in telephone directories) and (b) conducting a brief telephone screener with all eligible facilities to verify and adjust the NDATUS information and obtain information on type of care and client flow.

The second challenge in conducting this research was setting the timing of research interviews for clients admitted to treatment for drug problems. Many treatment professionals expect denial of drug use from individuals entering treatment (Chiauzzi & Liljegren, 1993), and many clients may be suffering from the acute phases of drug intoxication, which might impair their ability to recall and relate information accurately during an interview. Although there are advantages in delaying interviews for several weeks, early attrition could bias study findings. The advantages and disadvantages of delaying interviews 2 to 3 weeks were considered, and a decision was made to interview clients at admission, recognizing that underreporting of drug use might occur. This decision also allowed questions to be asked about drug and alcohol use upon entering treatment rather than during the early part of treatment.

The third challenge was to obtain a representative sample from the four treatment modalities. Because of self-selection and program selection factors, the major treatment modalities tend to serve and treat different clientele (Gerstein & Harwood, 1990). They also present different logistical problems in accessing clients for research purposes. Clients admitted to long-term residential, short-term residential, and methadone treatment programs are more readily accessible than those entering outpatient drug-free treatment modalities. Residential treatment clients are in one place, and methadone clients present themselves at the clinic each day to be medicated. Outpatient drug-free clients are the least available and often are available only once per week at or around a scheduled clinic appointment. Clients from this latter treatment modality present the biggest challenge to obtaining sufficient response rates in probability samples needed to estimate prevalence rates. Although various strategies were tried to obtain an acceptable response rate for this group, none could be devised within the resource constraints of this particular study. Extra resources and efforts are needed for interviewing outpatient drug-free treatment clients if the intent is to obtain a statistically representative sample.

Finally, the fourth challenge was acquiring access to treatment programs. Recruiting programs to participate in research studies was difficult and time-consuming. Some programs had insufficient local or in-house authority to grant authorization to participate, and others had to seek authorization and approval from regulatory and funding agencies or parent corporations to participate. Allowances also were needed for agency and program institutional review boards (IRBs) to meet and approve human subject research protocols.

7.6.4 Recommendations for Future Research
With Clients Entering Drug Treatment

Although probability samples can be used to develop population estimates for drug treatment clients, these types of studies offer certain challenges. One is the lack of a single, comprehensive list of drug treatment providers. The first recommendation is to begin with the most complete listing available (e.g., the National Facility Register developed for the UFDS) but supplement it with other sources (e.g., state regulatory and licensing bodies, funding sources, treatment provider organizations, telephone directories, treatment directories). At the individual level, clients should be sampled with a liberal plan, and field activities should be monitored closely to ensure an adequate number of respondents.

To assess the accuracy of responses, overlapping and logically consistent interview items can be woven throughout the questionnaire to provide an internal consistency check on response accuracy. The advantages and disadvantages of possible interview points or time frames (e.g., at admission, 1 week or 2 weeks after admission) should be considered in the design, with selection of a point-prevalence period consistent with plans for analyses and population estimation. If resources permit, one or more biological markers (urine, hair, etc.) should be used to establish the validity of responses. Analytic plans should be developed to adjust substance use estimators based on both self-reports of use and results from biological measures (cf. Poole, Flynn, Rao, & Cooley, 1996).

Finally, sufficient lead time should be allowed prior to the start of data collection to recruit programs to participate in the research, and field data collection plans should be tailored to the modalities of interest. Resources then can be allocated differentially according to the difficulty of obtaining interviews, allocating additional support for outpatient drug-free settings, where clients are the least accessible.

In summary, rigorous scientific studies of treatment populations can be conducted, but they require sufficient resources and ample planning to successfully develop population estimates, whether these are for local, regional, state, or national populations. Final research results will be only as good as the sum of the parts (instrumentation, sample frame, fieldwork, analyses, etc.), and each part is as critical as all others. Attention therefore should be given to every detail, no matter how paltry it may seem, during the process of the research.

References

American Psychiatric Association. (1987). *Diagnostic and statistical manual of mental disorders (DSM-III-R)* (3rd ed., rev.). Washington, DC: Author.

Appendix E: Current Treatment Client Characteristics Study. (1998). (Available on the World Wide Web at http://www.sagepub.com/bray_druguse.htm)

Batten, H. J., Prottas, J. M., Horgan, C. M., Simon, L. J., Larson, M. J., Elliott, E. A., & Marsden, M. E. (1992). *Drug Services Research Survey: Final report phase II*. Waltham, MA: Brandeis University, Institute for Health Policy.

Bray, R. M., Schlenger, W. E., Craddock, S. G., Hubbard, R. L., & Rachal, J. V. (1982). *Approaches to the assessment of drug use in the Treatment Outcome Prospective Study*. Research Triangle Park, NC: Research Triangle Institute.

Chiauzzi, E. J., & Liljegren, S. (1993). Taboo topics in addiction treatment: An empirical review of clinical folklore. *Journal of Substance Abuse Treatment, 10*, 303-316.

Collins, J. J., Hubbard, R. L., Cavanaugh, E. R., & Rachal, J. V. (1983). *Criminal behavior before and during drug treatment: 1979-1981 admission cohorts* (RTI/1901/01-03S). Research Triangle Park, NC: Research Triangle Institute.

Craddock, S. G., Hubbard, R. L., Rounds, J. L., Fletcher, B., Tims, F. M., Flynn, P. M., & Luckey, J. W. (1993). *Alcohol and drug use patterns in four modalities of drug abuse treatment: Initial findings from DATOS*. Unpublished manuscript, Research Triangle Institute, Research Triangle Park, NC.

Craddock, S. G., Rounds-Bryant, J. L., Flynn, P. M., & Hubbard, R. L. (1997). Characteristics and pretreatment behaviors of clients entering drug abuse treatment: 1969 to 1993. *American Journal of Drug and Alcohol Abuse, 23*(1), 43-59.

Dennis, M. L., Karuntzos, G. T., McDougal, G. L., French, M. T., & Hubbard, R. L. (1993). Developing training and employment programs to meet the needs of methadone treatment clients. *Evaluation and Program Planning, 16*, 73-86.

Flynn, P. M., Craddock, S. G., Luckey, J. W., Hubbard, R. L., & Dunteman, G. H. (1996). Comorbidity of antisocial personality and mood disorders among psychoactive substance-dependent treatment clients. *Journal of Personality Disorders, 10*(1), 56-67.

Flynn, P. M., Hubbard, R. L., Luckey, J. W., Forsyth, B. H., Smith, T. K., Phillips, C. D., Fountain, D. L., Hoffman, J. A., & Koman, J. J., III. (1995). Individual Assessment Profile (IAP): Standardizing the assessment of substance abusers. *Journal of Substance Abuse Treatment, 12*, 213-221.

French, M. T., Dennis, M. L., McDougal, G. L., Karuntzos, G. T., & Hubbard, R. L. (1992). Training and employment programs in methadone treatment: Client needs and desires. *Journal of Substance Abuse Treatment, 9*, 293-303.

Gerstein, D. R., & Harwood, H. J. (Eds.). (1990). *Treating drug problems*. (Vol. 1). Washington, DC: National Academy Press.

Gfroerer, J. C., & Brodsky, M. D. (1993). Frequent cocaine users and their use of treatment. *American Journal of Public Health, 83,* 1149-1154.

Haverkos, H. W., & Lange, W. R. (1990). Serious infections other than human immunodeficiency virus among intravenous drug abusers. *Journal of Infectious Diseases, 161,* 894-902.

Hoffman, J. A., Eckert, M. A., Koman, J. J., III, & Mayo, D. W. (1996). Profiles of clients in government-funded drug user treatment settings. *Substance Use & Misuse, 31,* 453-461.

Hubbard, R. L., Marsden, M. E., Rachal, J. V., Harwood, H. J., Cavanaugh, E. R., & Ginzburg, H. M. (1989). *Drug abuse treatment: A national study of effectiveness.* Chapel Hill: University of North Carolina Press.

Inciardi, J. A. (1991). Crack-cocaine in Miami. In S. Schober & C. Schade (Eds.), *The epidemiology of cocaine use and abuse* (NIDA Research Monograph No. 110, DHHS Publication No. ADM 91-1787, pp. 263-274). Rockville, MD: National Institute on Drug Abuse.

Kandel, D. B., & Logan, J. A. (1984). Patterns of drug use from adolescence to young adulthood: I. Periods of risk for initiation, continued use, and discontinuation. *American Journal of Public Health, 74,* 660-666.

National Institute on Drug Abuse. (1983). *Community Epidemiology Work Group proceedings: Vol. I. Drug abuse patterns and trends.* Rockville, MD: Author.

National Institute on Drug Abuse. (1994). *Current treatment client characteristics in the Washington, DC, metropolitan area: 1991* (Technical Report #5 under NIDA Contract No. 271-89-8340, Washington, DC, Metropolitan Area Drug Study, prepared by P. M. Flynn, J. W. Luckey, S. C. Wheeless, J. T. Lynch, L. A. Kroutil, & R. M. Bray, Research Triangle Institute). Rockville, MD: Author.

Newcomb, M. D., & Bentler, P. M. (1986). Frequency and sequence of drug use: A longitudinal study from early adolescence to young adulthood. *Journal of Drug Education, 16,* 101-120.

Office of Applied Studies. (1993). *1991 main findings report: National Drug and Alcoholism Treatment Unit Survey (NDATUS)* (DHHS Publication No. SMA 93-2007). Rockville, MD: Substance Abuse and Mental Health Services Administration.

Poole, W. K., Flynn, P. M., Rao, A. V., & Cooley, P. C. (1996). Estimating the prevalence of drug use from self-reports for which biologic data are available for a subsample. *American Journal of Epidemiology, 144,* 413-420.

Regier, D. A., Narrow, W. E., Rae, D. S., Manderscheid, R. W., Locke, B. Z., & Goodwin, F. K. (1993). The de facto US mental and addictive disorders service system: Epidemiologic Catchment Area prospective 1-year prevalence rates of disorders and services. *Archives of General Psychiatry, 50,* 85-94.

Rounsaville, B., & Carroll, K. (1991). Psychiatric disorders in treatment-entering cocaine abusers. In S. Schober & C. Schade (Eds.), *The epidemiology of cocaine use and abuse* (NIDA Research Monograph No. 110, DHHS Publication No. ADM 91-1787, pp. 227-251). Rockville, MD: National Institute on Drug Abuse.

Rounsaville, B. J., Weissman, M. M., Crits-Cristoph, K., Wilber, C. H., & Kleber, H. D. (1982). Diagnosis and symptoms of depression in opiate addicts. *Archives of General Psychiatry, 39,* 151-156.

Schlenger, W. E., Kroutil, L. A., Roland, E. J., & Dennis, M. L. (1992). *National evaluation of models for linking drug abuse treatment and primary care: Descriptive report of phase one findings* (Report prepared for the National Institute on Drug Abuse under Contract No. 283-90-0001). Research Triangle Park, NC: Research Triangle Institute.

Selwyn, P. A., Hartel, D., Lewis, V. A., Schoenbaum, E. E., Vermund, S. H., Klein, R. S., Walker, A. T., & Friedland, G. H. (1989). A prospective study of the risk of tuberculosis among intravenous drug users with human immunodeficiency virus infection. *New England Journal of Medicine, 320,* 545-550.

Simpson, D. D., & Sells, S. B. (1990). *Opioid addiction and treatment: A 12-year follow-up.* Malabar, FL: Krieger.

Substance Abuse and Mental Health Services Administration. (1993). *National Household Survey on Drug Abuse: Main findings 1991* (DHHS Publication No. SMA 93-1980). Rockville, MD: Author.

U.S. General Accounting Office. (1993). *Drug use measurement: Strengths, limitations, and recommendations for improvement* (GAO/PEMD-93-18). Washington, DC: Author.

Woody, G. E., McLellan, A. T., Luborsky, L., & O'Brien, C. P. (1985). Sociopathy and psychotherapy outcome. *Archives of General Psychiatry, 42,* 1081-1086.

8 Drug Use and Pregnancy

Wendy A. Visscher
Robert M. Bray
Larry A. Kroutil

The use of illicit drugs by women during pregnancy is an alarming aspect of the current epidemic of drug abuse in this country. This practice is exacting an increasingly heavy toll on infant health and medical resources, yet its magnitude is not well understood. The prevalence of drug use in a nationally representative sample of women giving birth in U.S. hospitals was assessed in the recently completed National Pregnancy and Health Survey (National Institute on Drug Abuse [NIDA], 1996). Estimates from that study suggest that 5.5% of women who gave birth during 1992 had used at least one illicit drug during pregnancy. Although useful, these data may not reflect the extent of the problem in metropolitan areas where drug use is more common and in which the need to combat the consequences of drug use during pregnancy is a priority for public health officials.

To address the need for local data, the DC*MADS Drug Use and Pregnancy Study was conducted (NIDA, 1995). Self-reported data about illicit drug, alcohol, and tobacco use during pregnancy were collected in 1992 from women who had just given birth in participating Washington, DC, hospitals. Urine samples were collected from an independent sample of delivering women to assess the validity of information on drug use. Data from DC*MADS suggest that the magnitude of drug use among pregnant women in this urban area is almost three times as high (14.7%) as that seen nationally.

Before describing the methods and findings of the Drug Use and Pregnancy Study in detail, the overall problem of drug use during pregnancy is discussed. Results of previous studies of prevalence, correlates, and outcomes are reviewed. Methodological limitations of these prior studies, and measurement problems inherent to the study of drug use in this population, also are discussed.

8.1 Studying Drug Use in Pregnancy

Estimating the magnitude of drug use by women during pregnancy is difficult. Measurement issues that researchers must address when designing studies to examine this problem include constructing representative samples of pregnant women and developing instruments or methods for obtaining valid information about women's use of drugs while pregnant. Hospital-based samples have been used for previous prevalence studies in selected hospitals and in different geographic areas. These samples represent most pregnant women in their target populations; however, a sample of *all* pregnant women would include not only women who deliver live infants in hospitals but also women who deliver at home or who have abortions or miscarriages. Another potential problem is that women who use drugs during pregnancy may not give honest information to researchers, fearing legal or social consequences. Thus, previous studies of drug use in pregnancy have used a variety of data sources to estimate prevalence or to identify risk factors for this practice. Some studies have used birth certificate data or urine test results to assess drug use by women during pregnancy, either alone or to supplement interview data obtained directly from pregnant women or new mothers.

8.1.1 Prevalence

Not surprisingly, estimates of the extent of the problem of drug use by pregnant women vary widely. The differences are partially the result of differences in methods of measuring drug use. A study at one municipal hospital in New York City estimated that 17% of women admitted for delivery used drugs, as determined either by urine test results or by self-reports (Feldman, Minkoff, McCalla, & Salwen, 1992). Chasnoff, Landress, and Barrett (1990) estimated a 14.8% prevalence of drug use by pregnant women based on urine test results for women attending prenatal clinics in Florida. A study by the Rhode Island Department of Health detected drugs in 7.5% of urine samples obtained from women admitted in active labor at area hospitals (Center for Disease Control and Prevention, 1990). A study of a probability sample of hospitals in California found evidence of drug use in 5.2% of urine samples obtained from women admitted for delivery (Vega, Kolody, Hwang, & Noble, 1993). As mentioned earlier, findings from the 1992 National Pregnancy and Health Survey found that 5.5% of women reported using at least one illicit drug during pregnancy (NIDA, 1996).

8.1.2 Correlates and Outcomes

In addition to prevalence studies, other studies have investigated demographic and other correlates of drug use by women during pregnancy. Comparisons of pregnant drug users and nonusers suggest that black women are more likely to have used cocaine during pregnancy, whereas white women more commonly use marijuana (Chasnoff et al., 1990; NIDA, 1996). Drug use during pregnancy is more prevalent in women who are not married, did not attend college, or are unemployed (NIDA, 1996). Women who receive little or no prenatal care also are more likely to have used drugs, especially cocaine (Cherukuri, Minkoff, Feldman, Parekh, & Glass, 1988; McCalla et al., 1991; Vega et al., 1993).

Other researchers have explored the relationships between substance use during pregnancy and adverse birth or developmental outcomes. Results of these studies suggest that cocaine users are more likely to have preterm or premature infants (Feldman et al., 1992; Little, Snell, Klein, & Gilstrap, 1989; MacGregor et al., 1987; Oro & Dixon, 1987). It is important to note that these apparent relationships may be confounded with other factors that are related to both drug use during pregnancy and adverse birth outcomes. As mentioned earlier, prior research indicates that black women and women who do not receive prenatal care have higher rates of cocaine use. Other studies have shown that prematurity is more common in black women and that lack of prenatal care is another risk factor for prematurity (Kempe et al., 1992; McCalla et al., 1991; Vega et al., 1993; World Health Organization [WHO], 1992). It is unclear, therefore, whether elevated rates of prematurity are related to cocaine use during pregnancy or to other factors related to both prematurity and cocaine (e.g., race/ethnicity or lack of prenatal care). More research is needed to describe more fully the complications that may arise from prenatal drug use, while controlling for the influence of potential confounding factors.

8.1.3 Measurement Issues

The studies described above illustrate some of the measurement issues inherent in the study of drug use during pregnancy. Much of the prior research in this area has had one or more of several methodological limitations: (a) data drawn from a single hospital (which limits the generalizability of the data, even within a city or metropolitan area), (b) data collection from women receiving prenatal care (which misses a subpopulation of drug-using women not receiving prenatal care), (c) prevalence estimation based on self-reports alone (which raises concerns about underreporting and associated validity), or (d) prevalence estimation based on urine test results alone (which limits detection to very recent drug use).

Prior studies have suggested apparent relationships between substance use during pregnancy and adverse infant outcomes. Some of these relationships, however, may be confounded by other factors that are related both to substance use during pregnancy and adverse birth outcomes, such as race or lack of prenatal care. Appropriate statistical methods are needed to separate the effects of possible confounding factors from any actual relationships that may exist between the drug use and an adverse infant outcome.

8.2 Overview of the Study

Building on the foundation of prior research, the DC MADS Drug Use and Pregnancy Study addressed a number of the methodological issues and limitations of earlier studies. The study findings have expanded the body of knowledge about the prevalence, correlates, and consequences of drug use during pregnancy among women in a large urban area.

8.2.1 Objectives

The Drug Use and Pregnancy Study presented several challenges, both from a data collection standpoint and from a political perspective. The study had four key objectives: (a) estimate the prevalence of use of illicit drugs, alcohol, and tobacco among women giving birth to live infants in DC hospitals; (b) compare rates of drug use among DC-resident women giving birth to infants of normal birthweight, intermediate low birthweight, and very low birthweight; (c) describe epidemiologic characteristics and health outcomes among drug-using and drug-free mothers and their newborn infants; and (d) serve as a methodological model for similar hospital-based, maternal drug use research in other metropolitan areas. The second objective was incorporated into the study design in response to the "DC Initiative," a joint effort between the Office for the Assistant Secretary for Health (OASH), the U.S. Department of Health and Human Services (DHHS), and the DC Commission of Public Health to address DC's unusually high rate of infant mortality and problems associated with infant drug exposure.

Findings from the study presented here are based on interviews conducted with 766 DC-resident women who gave birth to live infants in eight of nine DC hospitals participating in the study during the period from January through mid-December, 1992. Information was abstracted from the medical records for 527 of these women and 533 of their infants (including twins) to supplement the interview data. Nonresident women who gave birth in these hospitals also were included in the study sample; however, some hospitals denied the study access to a large proportion of their nonresident patients (those with private health insurance). The data collected from the nonresident women during the study therefore are not representative of all nonresident women giving birth in DC hospitals, and they are not included here. Details of the sampling and data collection methodologies used for the study are described in the final report for the study (NIDA, 1995) and in Appendix F (1998).

8.2.2 Unique Features

The Drug Use and Pregnancy Study made several important contributions. Unlike studies limited to a single hospital, this study used probability sampling methods to collect data from DC-resident women delivering livebirths in all DC civilian hospitals. Inferences therefore can be made about the broader *population* of DC-resident new mothers as a whole. In addition, inferences can be made about demographic correlates of drug use for this population of women.

Data on drug use during pregnancy and medical problems experienced by the mother and her newborn(s) were collected using a variety of methods, including interview data, record abstractions, and anonymous urine testing from a separate sample of women. Thus, this study drew on a broad spectrum of data to understand drug use issues and also provided important methodological information and recommendations for researchers interested in conducting a similar study in other cities or metropolitan areas.

Findings are presented relating alcohol, cigarette, and illicit drug use to low birthweight. These analyses control for the potential confounding effects of other risk factors such as race/ethnicity and receipt of prenatal care.

Finally, findings from the Drug Use and Pregnancy Study complement national-level data while allowing inferences to be made about a specific metropolitan population of interest. As such, the study provides useful information for planners, service providers, and policymakers, both within DC and more generally for other metropolitan areas or cities that have residents with characteristics similar to those in this study.

8.2.3 Characteristics of Women Delivering Livebirths

Information was collected from study participants about selected demographic and housing characteristics and about their use of prenatal care services during their most recent pregnancy. The findings indicate that the large majority of DC-resident women who delivered live infants in DC hospitals were black and unmarried at the time of delivery. Furthermore, the majority were Medicaid patients, and a sizable proportion lived in households that received at least some income from public sources, such as Supplemental Security Income (SSI) or Aid to Families With Dependent Children (AFDC).

Figure 8.1 shows the demographic characteristics and parity (i.e., number of previous livebirths) for DC-resident women delivering livebirths in eight participating DC hospitals. The 766 DC-resident women in the sample represented an estimated 9,332 DC-resident women who delivered livebirths in 1992. The population of mothers delivering babies had several characteristics. Nearly half (49.9%) of the DC-resident women delivering livebirths in DC hospitals were between the ages of 18 and 25. The large majority of these DC-resident women were black (83.9%). Nearly three fourths (73.7%) of the women were single at the time of delivery. The large majority of women aged 18 or older (72.3%) had at least a high school education; 27.7% had not completed high school. Roughly equal percentages of DC-resident women were in the different parity categories shown in Figure 8.1.

Most of the DC-resident women delivering livebirths in DC hospitals (72.0%) lived in households with two or more members under the age of 18, including their new babies. Nearly two thirds (63.8%) of the women lived in households with total annual incomes of $19,000 or below, and nearly one fifth (19.3%) lived in households with incomes of less than $5,000 annually. A large group of women (48.5%) came from households where members received at least some income from public sources, such as SSI or AFDC. For the large majority of the women, Medicaid was the expected main source of payment for the delivery and hospitalization (69.0%).

Prenatal care is an important predictor for pregnancy outcomes, so the women were asked whether they had obtained prenatal care during their current pregnancy, their main sources of prenatal care, and the pregnancy trimester in which they began prenatal care. Key findings related to prenatal care in the DC-resident women are presented in Figure 8.2. An estimated 5.3% of DC-resident women delivering livebirths in DC hospitals received *no* prenatal care prior to delivery. The main source of prenatal care for nearly half of the women (47.4%) was a hospital outpatient clinic. Fewer than one fourth of the women (23.3%) received their prenatal care mainly from a private physician or through

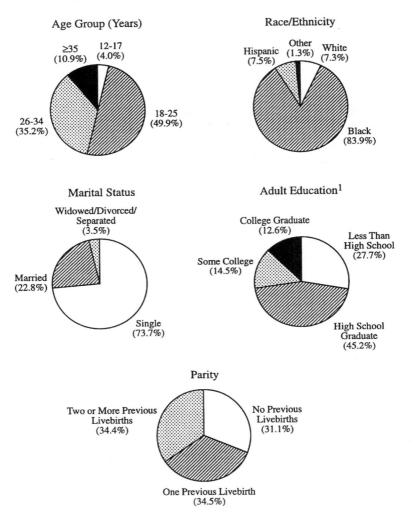

Figure 8.1. Demographic Characteristics and Parity Among DC Women Delivering Livebirths in DC Hospitals

SOURCE: Washington, DC, Metropolitan Area Drug Study (DC*MADS): 1989-1995.
NOTE: Total estimated number for DC-resident women delivering livebirths in DC hospitals in 1992 was 9,332.
1. Mothers aged 12 to 17 were excluded from estimates of adult education.

a health maintenance organization (HMO). Of those new mothers who had at least one prenatal care visit prior to delivery (94.7%), the majority

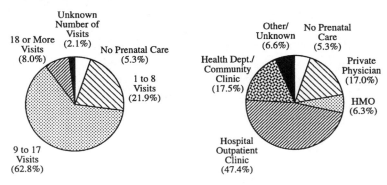

Frequency of Prenatal Visits　　　Type of Prenatal Providers

Trimester of First Prenatal Visit[1]

Figure 8.2. Frequency, Source, and Timing of Prenatal Care Services Received During Pregnancy Among DC Women Delivering Livebirths in DC Hospitals
SOURCE: Washington, DC, Metropolitan Area Drug Study (DC*MADS): 1989-1995.
NOTE: Some percentages do not add to 100.0% because of rounding.
1. Does not include women who received no prenatal care.

(59.0%) began prenatal care in the first trimester of their pregnancies. An estimated 7.6% of the new mothers who received any prenatal care did not begin receiving care until the third trimester.

Prior research has found drug use during pregnancy to be more prevalent among women who received little or no prenatal care (Cherukuri et al., 1988; McCalla et al., 1991; Vega et al., 1993). Thus, for the Drug Use and Pregnancy Study analyses, the women receiving prenatal care during their first or second trimesters of pregnancy were compared with the women who did not begin prenatal care until their third trimesters, or who received no prenatal care prior to delivery. Grouping together women who began prenatal care in the third trimester with those who received no prenatal care at all is consistent with prenatal care reporting procedures used in the National Vital Statistics System (National Center for Health Statistics [NCHS], 1994). Study findings indicate that most DC-resident women received at least some prenatal care during their first or second trimester of pregnancy. Younger mothers, single mothers, women with less education, mothers with two or more previous livebirths, and women on Medicaid appeared to be at increased risk for late (i.e., only during the third trimester) or no prenatal care.

8.3 Prevalence of Illicit Drug, Alcohol, and Tobacco Use Among Women Giving Birth

Cocaine was the drug of choice for DC-resident women who used drugs during pregnancy in this study. Almost 15% (14.7%) of the women in the study reported using an illicit drug during pregnancy; 10.5% reported using any cocaine during this period. Roughly equal percentages of women used any alcohol (21.1%) or smoked cigarettes (22.5%) at least once during their pregnancies. Estimates of the use of illicit drugs, alcohol, and cigarettes were developed for the past year and past month periods and during the current pregnancy.

Black women and women who had not completed high school were more likely to use drugs during pregnancy than women of other racial/ethnic or educational status groups. A trend toward increasing drug use with the age of the mother also was observed. Married women were less likely to use drugs during pregnancy than were women in other marital status groups.

8.3.1 Use During the Past Year, the Past Month, and Pregnancy

Figure 8.3 presents findings on the prevalence of illicit drug, alcohol, and cigarette use for DC-resident women during the past year, during the current pregnancy, and during the past month (supporting numbers appear in Table F.1, Appendix F [1998]). As shown, sizable percentages had used illicit drugs during the past year (15.5%). Most of these new

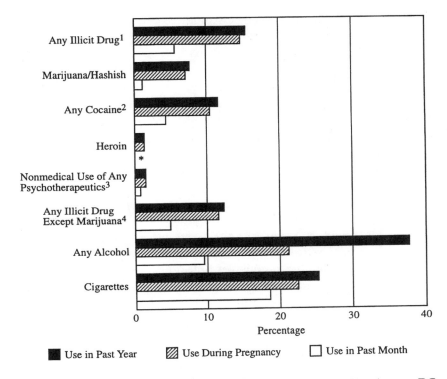

Figure 8.3. Prevalence of Illicit Drug, Alcohol, and Cigarette Use Among DC Women Delivering Livebirths in DC Hospitals

SOURCE: Washington, DC, Metropolitan Area Drug Study (DC*MADS): 1989-1995.
NOTE: See Table F.1 in Appendix F (1998) for the supporting data used to prepare this figure.
1. Use of marijuana or hashish, cocaine (including crack), heroin, or nonmedical use of psychotherapeutics at least once; does not include use of methamphetamine, inhalants, or hallucinogens (including phencyclidine or PCP).
2. Includes crack cocaine.
3. Nonmedical use of any prescription-type stimulants, sedatives, tranquilizers, or analgesics; does not include over-the-counter drugs.
4. Includes cocaine (including crack), inhalants, hallucinogens (including PCP), heroin, or psychotherapeutics for nonmedical reasons.
*Low precision.

mothers also used drugs at least once during their most recent pregnancies (14.7%).

Cocaine in any form (including crack cocaine) was the most commonly used illicit drug in the past year and during pregnancy. Some 11.5% of these new mothers used cocaine during the past year, and 10.5% used cocaine at least once during their pregnancies. These percentages translate to approximately 1,000 new mothers who used cocaine in any form during the past year and during their most recent pregnancies (1,063 and 973, respectively). An estimated 7.7% of the new mothers used marijuana/hashish during the past year, and a similar percentage (7.1%) used marijuana/hashish during their most recent pregnancies. Approximately 1.4% of the women used heroin during the past year, and the same percentage used heroin during their most recent pregnancies. An estimated 21.1% of the women used any alcohol during pregnancy, and 9.5% used alcohol at least once during the past month. Some 22.5% of the new mothers smoked cigarettes at least once during their pregnancies, and 18.6% of the women smoked during the past month.

As shown, sizable percentages of the new mothers indicated that they had used illicit drugs, alcohol, or cigarettes during their pregnancy. It should be noted, however, that the *during pregnancy* prevalence estimates reflect *any* use during the entire pregnancy, even if women used a substance only a limited number of times (e.g., once or twice). Some women may have used illicit drugs, alcohol, or cigarettes during pregnancy before they were aware that they were pregnant, even if they subsequently stopped once they knew they were pregnant. In contrast, the *past month* prevalence estimates represent women who used substances after they knew they were pregnant. Thus, these past month prevalence estimates are likely to be conservative estimates of the percentages of women who used (or continued to use) different substances after they knew they were pregnant. Recent research has emphasized the importance of the timing of exposures such as drug use in accurately assessing the consequences of an exposure on the newborn (Hertz-Picciotto, Pastore, & Beaumont, 1996).

8.3.2 Demographic Correlates of Use

Demographic correlates of illicit drug use, marijuana/hashish use, use of cocaine in any form (including crack cocaine), alcohol use, and cigarette use among DC-resident women delivering livebirths in DC hospitals are presented in Table 8.1. Prevalence estimates are presented for the past year and past month periods and during the most recent pregnancy. During all time periods, use of any illicit drug was more prevalent among women in the two oldest age groups (26 to 34 years, 35

Table 8.1 Prevalence of Any Illicit Drug Use, by Demographic Characteristics and Period of Use, for DC Women Delivering Livebirths in DC Hospitals

Characteristic	Past Year	During Pregnancy	Past Month
Total	15.5	14.7	5.6
Age group (years)			
12-17	7.9	7.9	**
18-25	11.9	11.0	4.2
26-34	20.5	19.3	8.0
≥ 35	18.3	18.3	5.3
Race/ethnicity[1]			
White	8.8	8.8	5.2
Black	17.4	16.4	5.8
Hispanic	3.4	3.4	3.4
Marital status			
Single	17.0	16.3	6.2
Married	8.8	7.7	1.8
Widowed/divorced/separated	23.0	19.1	*
Adult education[2]			
Less than high school	22.7	21.4	7.9
High school graduate	13.9	13.1	6.3
Some college	13.2	12.1	1.5
College graduate	10.4	10.3	3.8
Parity			
No previous livebirths	10.0	8.7	2.2
One previous livebirth	9.0	8.6	3.6
Two or more previous livebirths	27.3	26.4	10.5

SOURCE: Washington, DC, Metropolitan Area Drug Study (DC*MADS): 1989-1995.
NOTE: Data entries are percentages. Any illicit drug use is defined as any use of marijuana or hashish, cocaine (including crack), heroin, or nonmedical use of psychotherapeutics at least once; it does not include use of methamphetamine, inhalants, or hallucinogens (including phencyclidine or PCP).
1. The category "other" for race/ethnicity is not included.
2. Mothers aged 12 to 17 were excluded from estimates of adult education.
*Low precision.
**Estimate is less than 0.5%.

years or older) than among new mothers aged 12 to 17. Illicit drug use in the past year and during pregnancy was more prevalent among black women (17.4% and 16.4%, respectively) than among white women (8.8% for both time periods). Married women were less likely than women in the other marital status groups to have used illicit drugs in the past year or during pregnancy. Drug use in the past year or during pregnancy was most prevalent among women who had not completed high school (22.7% and 21.4%, respectively).

In each time period, drug use was most prevalent among women who had two or more previous livebirths. In particular, more than one fourth of the women who had two or more previous livebirths used drugs in the past year (27.3%) or during pregnancy (26.4%). This relationship between drug use and parity may be age-related; specifically, older women (who were more likely than younger women to have used drugs during all time periods) probably were more likely than younger women to have had previous livebirths.

The demographic correlates for marijuana, any form of cocaine, and cigarettes were similar to those for use of any illicit drug. The demographic correlates of alcohol use, however, varied somewhat from those observed for any illicit drug use, marijuana use, cocaine, and cigarette use. For example, alcohol use was more prevalent among women who were white; married women were more likely than were single women to use alcohol during pregnancy and in the past month; and alcohol use was most prevalent among women who had completed college compared with those having less education. These patterns were the reverse of those observed for the other substances.

In summary, nearly two thirds of DC-resident women who delivered liveborn infants in DC hospitals in 1992 abstained from alcohol, cigarettes, or illicit drugs during pregnancy; however, approximately one third did not. More specifically, approximately one in five new mothers used alcohol or smoked cigarettes during pregnancy, and about one in seven used illicit drugs. Cocaine was the illicit drug most often used by DC women who used drugs during pregnancy. In contrast, new mothers nationally were more likely to have used marijuana during pregnancy than any form of cocaine (NIDA, 1996).

8.4 Consequences and Correlates of Use

In addition to providing prevalence estimates, the DC*MADS Drug Use and Pregnancy Study was designed to identify factors that may be related to drug use during pregnancy and to describe the reproductive outcomes experienced by DC-resident women delivering livebirths in DC hospitals. Of particular interest was the relationship between infant birthweight and gestational age and a woman's use of drugs during pregnancy.

Logistic regression models were developed to estimate the relative odds of giving birth to a low birthweight infant rather than a normal birthweight infant for use versus no use of illicit drugs, alcohol, or cigarettes during pregnancy. Cigarette use during pregnancy was strongly related to giving birth to a low birthweight infant (under 2,500 grams), whereas illicit drug use was related only to giving birth to a *very* low birthweight infant (less than 1,500 grams). Alcohol use was not related to low birthweight in this study. Study findings confirmed previously identified demographic risk factors for prematurity and low birthweight. Lack of prenatal care was strongly related to both infant outcomes.

8.4.1 Low Birthweight and Preterm Births

Low birthweight infants and preterm infants are at higher risk for infant mortality and morbidity than infants of normal birthweight (Robertson et al., 1992). The relationship of these factors to the demographic characteristics, prenatal care, and drug use patterns of DC-resident mothers was examined in the Drug Use and Pregnancy Study. Three birthweight categories were used for study analyses: (a) normal birthweight = 2,500 grams or more (5 pounds, 8 ounces or more), (b) intermediate low birthweight = 1,500 to 2,499 grams (3 pounds, 5 ounces to 5 pounds, 7 ounces), and (c) very low birthweight = less than 1,500 grams (less than 3 pounds, 5 ounces). The second and third categories combined constitute the commonly used "low birthweight" category, defined as birthweight less than 2,500 grams (or less than 5 pounds, 8 ounces). Standard categories were used for gestational age. "Term" infants are those born at a gestational age of 37 weeks or more; "preterm" infants are those born at less than 37 weeks gestation.

Overall, most of the infants born to the DC-resident women were of normal birthweight (87.2%) and term gestation (87.2%). The prevalence of low birthweight and preterm births varied according to the demographic characteristics of the mothers, including age, race/ethnicity, educational level, and marital status. Infants born to women younger than 18 or 35 years or older were more than twice as likely to be low birthweight than were infants born to women of other ages. There were no significant differences among age groups for preterm births. Infants born to black women were much more likely to be either low birthweight or preterm than were infants born to either white or Hispanic women. Infants whose mothers were not married were more likely to be low birthweight or preterm than were infants born to married women. The likelihood of low birthweight and preterm infants generally decreased as the educational level of the mother increased. Infants born to women with one previous livebirth were less likely to be preterm than infants born either to women with no prior livebirths or to women with two or more previous livebirths.

These findings are consistent with previously identified demographic risk factors for low birthweight and preterm births (Adams, Sarno, Harlass, Rawlings, & Read, 1995; Feldman et al., 1992; Lieberman, Gremy, Lang, & Cohen, 1994). The study results also confirm that lack of prenatal care is strongly related to both infant birthweight and gestational age. Infants whose mothers had no prenatal care or late prenatal care (i.e., began during third trimester) were much more likely than infants whose mothers had at least one prenatal care visit during the first or second trimester of pregnancy to be either a low birthweight (22.7% vs. 11.5%) or preterm birth (18.6% vs. 12.0%).

8.4.2 Substance Use Exposure Categories

Many prior studies have focused on the prevalence of use of individual substances during pregnancy, independent of one another (Neerhof, MacGregor, Retzky, & Sullivan, 1989; Prager et al., 1983; Serdula, Williamson, Kendrick, Anda, & Byers, 1991). Such estimates do not indicate the percentages of women who used more than one substance, or those who used alcohol or cigarettes but not illicit drugs. The eight possible, mutually exclusive combinations of alcohol, tobacco, and illicit drug use were examined using the Drug Use and Pregnancy Study data. The sizes of these groups were too small to permit individual analyses, so the DC-resident women were grouped into three exposure categories for the study analyses: (a) nonusers of alcohol, cigarettes, *or* illicit drugs; (b) users of alcohol or cigarettes (or both), but not illicit drugs; and (c) users of illicit drugs, with or without alcohol or cigarettes.

The distributions of birthweight, gestational age, and prenatal care for the three exposure groups are presented in Table 8.2. For birthweight, gestational age, and a combined measure of birthweight and gestational age, women were classified according to their infants' birth outcomes.

Table 8.2 Drug Use Patterns During Pregnancy, by Infant Birthweight, Gestational Age, and Prenatal Care, for DC Women Delivering Livebirths in DC Hospitals

Characteristic	Nonuser	Alcohol/Cigarettes Only	Illicit Drugs[1]
Total	64.5	20.5	14.9
Birthweight[2]			
Normal	91.1	81.6	80.0
Intermediate low	8.1	15.8	13.9
Very low	0.8	2.6	6.2
Gestational age[3]			
Term	90.0	86.2	78.5
Preterm	10.0	13.8	21.5
Birthweight[4] and gestational age			
Normal birthweight and term	85.8	78.4	72.6
Normal birthweight and preterm	5.1	3.3	7.8
Low birthweight and term	4.1	7.7	5.9
Low birthweight and preterm	5.0	10.6	13.7
Prenatal care			
None or only in third trimester	8.3	12.0	24.6
Any in first or second trimester	91.7	88.0	75.4

SOURCE: Washington, DC, Metropolitan Area Drug Study (DC*MADS): 1989-1995.
NOTE: Data entries are percentages. Some columns do not add to 100% because of rounding. Births include 20 sets of twins; data for both twins were used to categorize the mother according to the birth outcomes of her twins.
1. Use of marijuana or hashish, cocaine (including crack), heroin, or nonmedical use of psychotherapeutics at least once; it does not include use of methamphetamine, inhalants, or hallucinogens (including phencyclidine or PCP). This group may include users of alcohol or cigarettes.
2. Specific birthweight categories are defined as follows: Normal = 2,500 grams or more (5 pounds, 8 ounces or more); Intermediate low = 1,500 to 2,499 grams (3 pounds, 5 ounces to 5 pounds, 7 ounces); Very low = under 1,500 grams (under 3 pounds, 5 ounces).
3. Gestational age categories are defined as follows: Term = 37 weeks or more; Preterm = fewer than 37 weeks.
4. Combined birthweight categories are defined as follows: Normal birthweight = 2,500 grams or more (5 pounds, 8 ounces or more); Low birthweight (very low or intermediate low) = under 2,500 grams (under 5 pounds, 8 ounces).

Women giving birth to twins were classified according to the highest risk category represented by their infants (e.g., a woman having both an intermediate low and a very low birthweight infant was classified as giving birth to a very low birthweight infant; note that only birthweight and not gestational age could vary for twins).

Several patterns are clear from Table 8.2. First, women who were users of alcohol/cigarettes (18.4%) or users of illicit drugs (20.1%) were more likely than nonusers (8.9%) to give birth to a low birthweight infant (i.e., intermediate low or very low). Second, users of illicit drugs (6.2%)

were somewhat more likely than users of alcohol/cigarettes only (2.6%) or nonusers (0.8%) to have an infant with very low birthweight. A similar pattern emerged for gestational age, with illicit drug users most likely to have a preterm infant (21.5%), followed by users of alcohol/cigarettes only (13.8%) and nonusers (10.0%).

As shown, mothers using illicit drugs during pregnancy were much less likely than either alcohol/cigarette users or nonusers to have received prenatal care services. Some 91.7% of the nonusing women had at least one prenatal visit during the first or second trimester, compared with only 75.4% of the women using illicit drugs. This finding is consistent with other research (e.g., Cherukuri et al., 1988; McCalla et al., 1991; Vega et al., 1993) showing that women who use illicit drugs during pregnancy are less likely to receive prenatal care.

These findings indicate that lack of prenatal care is related both to adverse infant outcomes of low birthweight and preterm birth and to the mother's use of drugs during pregnancy. Thus, lack of prenatal care is a clear confounder for analyses of drug use and infant birthweight and gestational age. Consequently, analyses examining relationships between drug use and adverse birth outcomes need to control for prenatal care. The methods used for adjusting for this variable and others in the calculation of odds ratios are described in the next section.

8.4.3 Substance Use and the Odds of Low Birthweight

To better understand the relationship between substance use during pregnancy and infant outcomes, logistic regression analyses were performed with low birthweight as the outcome variable. A separate logistic regression was conducted for each of the three birthweight categories (i.e., low, intermediate low, and very low). The referent group used in calculating the odds ratios for the three low birthweight groups was infants of normal birthweight (i.e., infants with birthweights of 2,500 grams or more). The referent group odds ratio was set to 1.0.

In all the logistic models, the odds ratios for illicit drug use, alcohol use, and cigarette use were adjusted for each other as well as for (a) demographic variables (mother's age, race/ethnicity, marital status, and educational level), (b) parity (zero, one, or two or more previous livebirths), and (c) prenatal care (any care during the first two trimesters

Table 8.3 Adjusted Odds Ratios of Infant Birthweight Categories for Substance Use During Pregnancy Among DC Women Delivering Livebirths in DC Hospitals

Substance/Birthweight[1]	Adjusted Odds Ratio[2]
Any illicit drug use	
Normal	1.00
Low	0.97
Intermediate low	0.79
Very low	2.46*
Any alcohol use	
Normal	1.00
Low	1.20
Intermediate low	1.25
Very low	0.98
Any cigarette use	
Normal	1.00
Low	3.31***
Intermediate low	3.22***
Very low	4.21**

SOURCE: Washington, DC, Metropolitan Drug Area Study (DC*MADS): 1989-1995.
NOTE: Births include 20 sets of twins. Data for both twins were used. Illicit drug use is defined as use of marijuana or hashish, cocaine (including crack), heroin, or nonmedical use of psychotherapeutics at least once during the pregnancy; it does not include use of methamphetamine, inhalants, or hallucinogens (including phencyclidine or PCP).
1. Birthweight categories are defined as follows: Normal = 2,500 grams or more (5 pounds, 8 ounces or more); Low = under 2,500 grams (under 5 pounds, 8 ounces); Intermediate low = 1,500 to 2,499 grams (3 pounds, 5 ounces to 5 pounds, 7 ounces); Very low = under 1,500 grams (under 3 pounds, 5 ounces).
2. Odds ratios have been adjusted for demographics, parity, prenatal care, and the other substances in the model (e.g., the odds ratio for cigarette smoking was also adjusted for illicit drug use and alcohol use).
*$p < .05$. **$p < .01$. ***$p < .001$.

versus no prenatal care or late prenatal care). Each of the three substance use variables (i.e., illicit drugs, alcohol, and cigarettes) was defined as a binary variable for which "1" indicated "any use during pregnancy" and "0" indicated "no use during pregnancy."

Main effects models were estimated to adjust the odds ratios for this study. This approach involved including all the variables listed above as explanatory variables in the logistic models, with no interaction terms. Variables with nonsignificant coefficients were not excluded from the models for these analyses.

Table 8.3 shows the adjusted odds ratios for illicit drug use, alcohol use, and cigarette use during pregnancy. The odds ratios indicate the relative odds of giving birth to a low birthweight infant rather than a normal birthweight infant, given the use of illicit drugs, alcohol, or cigarettes during pregnancy compared with no use of these substances during pregnancy.

The results indicate that illicit drug use during pregnancy is associated with *very low* birthweight infants. Specifically, the odds of having a very low birthweight infant versus a normal birthweight infant were nearly 2.5 times as high (odds ratio = 2.46) for women who used illicit drugs than for women who did not use drugs. This analysis adjusted for the mother's demographic characteristics, parity, prenatal care, alcohol use, and cigarette use. Thus, even after adjusting for the effects of other confounding variables, illicit drug use shows a strong relationship to very low birthweight. There was no significant association between illicit drug use and the probability of being in the intermediate low or overall low birthweight categories compared with the normal birthweight category.

In contrast to illicit drug use, alcohol use during pregnancy among DC-resident mothers was not associated with an increased risk of having an infant in any of the low birthweight categories. Women who used alcohol during pregnancy were no more likely than those who did not use alcohol to have a low birthweight infant. This finding should not be interpreted, however, to mean that alcohol use during pregnancy is a safe practice that is not related to adverse birth outcomes. Other research has shown clearly the adverse effects on infants that can result from the mother's alcohol use during pregnancy (e.g., Rossett & Weiner, 1984; Sokol, Ager, & Martier, 1986). The finding instead may suggest that women in this study did not use alcohol at levels that resulted in adverse outcomes.

The most striking association between substance use and low birthweight seen in the logistic regression analyses was for cigarette smoking. The odds of having an infant in *any* of the low birthweight categories relative to the normal birthweight category were significantly higher for smokers than for nonsmokers. The odds of low (overall), intermediate low, and very low birthweight relative to normal were 3.31, 3.22, and 4.21 times as high, respectively, for smokers than for nonsmokers. These results support findings of previous prenatal research, which has showed a strong association between smoking during pregnancy and the risk of a low birthweight infant (e.g., Finnegan, 1985; Kleinman & Madans, 1985; Prager et al., 1983). Lieberman and colleagues (1994) suggested that this increased risk of low birthweight for smokers stems primarily from smoking that occurs during the last trimester of pregnancy.

Overall, findings indicate that cigarette smoking by mothers during pregnancy was strongly related to both intermediate and very low birthweight of their infants and that illicit drug use during pregnancy was related to very low birthweight of infants. Alcohol use was not related to birthweight in this study.

8.4.4 Other Maternal and Infant Complications

In addition to assessing the adverse outcomes of low birthweight and preterm birth, the study gathered data about medical problems experienced by mothers and their infants. Medical records were used to supplement the information about complications provided by the women on their questionnaires. Thus, the results presented are based on data from the 766 questionnaire respondents as well as on abstraction data from 527 women who agreed to have their medical records, and those of their infants, reviewed. Comparison of medical records and questionnaire data suggest some underreporting of drug use during pregnancy. In contrast, the chart and interview data show similar estimates for insufficient prenatal care.

Study results related to maternal complications results revealed some interesting patterns. Women who used illicit drugs were more likely to have sexually transmitted diseases (STDs) reported on their medical records than were mothers who used alcohol/cigarettes only or who did not use drugs during pregnancy. Insufficient prenatal care was reported in the medical records for infants of 21.0% of illicit-drug-using mothers, 12.7% of cigarette or alcohol users, and 4.8% of nondrug-using women. This pattern is similar to that observed in Table 8.2 for self-reports of prenatal care. Women who used illicit drugs were more likely to be depressed or have another type of mental problem than were women who used alcohol/cigarettes only or who did not use drugs during pregnancy.

The study data offer conflicting information about the extent of illicit drug use by women during pregnancy. A larger proportion of questionnaire respondents reported using illicit drugs during pregnancy (14.7%) than was indicated in the medical records (6.5%). This is not surprising, however, because clinicians may be reluctant to document drug abuse in a woman's chart except in very severe cases when it might affect the treatment of the woman or her newborn. Thus, these results suggest that more than just women with severe cases of drug abuse reported their use of drugs on the questionnaire. An unexpected result was that drug abuse was noted not only on the charts of 33.9% of the women who reported using drugs during pregnancy, but also on the charts of 6.5% of the women who reported using only cigarettes or alcohol during pregnancy. This finding suggests that there may be underreporting of illicit drug use by some of the women who reported only cigarette and alcohol use.

The study also provided information on infant complications. The medical charts of 4.4% of the infants indicated that cocaine had affected the fetus. Although this estimate is much lower than the estimate from the questionnaire data that 10.5% of women used cocaine during pregnancy, it is identical to the questionnaire-derived estimate that 4.4% of women used cocaine in the past month. The proportion of infant charts indicating that cocaine had affected the fetus was highest among women who reported using drugs during pregnancy (20.9%), but this condition also was noted on 6.2% of the charts of infants born to mothers who reported using only alcohol or cigarettes during pregnancy. Drug withdrawal was noted on 9.5% of charts for infants of drug-using women, but also on 1.9% of charts for infants of cigarette or alcohol users.

These results, like those observed for maternal complications, suggest some underreporting of illicit drug use during pregnancy. It seems unlikely that mothers of infants whom clinicians judged to be affected by cocaine or suffering from drug withdrawal (and were certain enough of this diagnosis to write it in the infant's chart) would not be drug users. As noted above, however, 6.2% of infants of women who reported using only alcohol or cigarettes during pregnancy had a mention in their charts of cocaine affecting the fetus, and 1.9% of the charts of the infants of these women indicated drug withdrawal.

8.5 Discussion and Implications

The Drug Use and Pregnancy Study examined the prevalence, demographic and reproductive correlates, and medical problems associated with illicit drug, alcohol, and cigarette use during pregnancy. The study results suggest the need for future research and intervention efforts aimed at better understanding and preventing maternal drug use. For example, providing smoking cessation programs to pregnant women who use cigarettes, as well as providing accessible prenatal care to pregnant women who are not receiving care, would be expected to reduce the number of low birthweight infants born to these high-risk women.

8.5.1 Drug Use During Pregnancy

Results of the Drug Use and Pregnancy Study indicate that a sizable number of DC women smoked cigarettes during pregnancy and that such smoking was strongly associated with the delivery of low birthweight infants. Approximately one in five DC-resident women who delivered liveborn infants in DC hospitals smoked cigarettes during pregnancy. The odds of having a low birthweight baby relative to a normal birthweight baby were more than three times as high for smokers as for nonsmokers. These findings are consistent with prior research (e.g., Finnegan, 1985; Kleinman & Madans, 1985; Lieberman et al., 1994) indicating that cigarette smoking during pregnancy is strongly associated with delivering low birthweight infants.

Study findings also indicate that nearly one in seven new mothers in DC (14.7%) used illicit drugs at least once during pregnancy, with cocaine being their drug of choice. Approximately 1 in 10 new mothers (10.5%) used some form of cocaine during pregnancy, which translates to approximately 1,000 new mothers in DC. Illicit drug use by new mothers also was related to the delivery of very low birthweight babies. The odds of a very low birthweight infant relative to normal birthweight were nearly 2.5 times as great among women who used illicit drugs as among those who did not.

Taken together, these findings indicate that both cigarette-smoking and drug-using pregnant women are at risk for adverse infant outcomes, particularly low birthweight. Thus, both of these subgroups of women should be targeted for intervention efforts aimed at reducing infant morbidity.

8.5.2 Low Birthweight Issues

One of the objectives of the Drug Use and Pregnancy Study was to explore the relationship between low birthweight and drug use during pregnancy. Previously identified risk factors for low birthweight associated with age, race/ethnicity, and prenatal care were confirmed in this study. Low birthweight babies were more likely to be born to younger (age 17 or younger) or older (age 35 or older) women, to black women more often than to white or Hispanic women, and to women who lacked adequate prenatal care compared with women who received prenatal care in their first or second trimesters of pregnancy.

The finding that women over the age of 35 were at high risk for low birthweight babies is in agreement with other studies showing that women of older childbearing age are more likely to have poor pregnancy outcomes. This appears to be the case even after adjusting for a variety of confounding factors, including demographics, smoking, infertility, and selected diseases (e.g., Cnattingius, Forman, Berendes, & Isotalo, 1992).

The finding that African American women were more likely to have a low birthweight baby than white women also is well documented in the literature (e.g., Kempe et al., 1992; WHO, 1992). The underlying explanation for this finding is generally not well understood, although it is often attributed to lower socioeconomic status and poor access to and utilization of preventive health care among black women (e.g., Lieberman, Ryan, Monson, & Schoenbaum, 1987). Despite its intuitive appeal, this explanation is inadequate because the phenomenon still persists among black and white women of similar status who have comparable access to health care (Rawlings, Rawlings, & Read, 1995).

A more promising explanation may be associated with the interval between pregnancies. Rawlings and colleagues (1995) found that a short interval between pregnancies was a risk factor for low birthweight babies and that black women were more likely to have shorter interpregnancy intervals. Black women who waited at least 9 months between pregnancies reduced their risk level to normal levels, whereas white women needed to wait only 3 months for the same effect. A possible explanation for this finding is that of maternal depletion, in which the mother's body requires a period of time to restore essential nutrients to successfully nourish another baby. Apparently, black women need a longer period for this than do white women.

Logistic regression analyses assessing relationships between substance use and birthweight categories revealed that cigarette smoking was the strongest predictor of low birthweight and was related to both intermediate low and very low birthweight categories. The use of illicit drugs during pregnancy was related to very low birthweight but not to intermediate low birthweight. Alcohol use during pregnancy was not related to the low birthweight categories.

The study findings, while informative, suggest a number of areas for further research. Additional data are needed, for example, on the levels and patterns of substance use and their relationships to birthweight. The finding that cigarette smoking showed a stronger relationship to low birthweight than did illicit drug use or alcohol is likely to be a function of levels of use. In this study, a substantial group of women smoked at relatively high levels throughout their pregnancy compared with those who used drugs or alcohol. More data are needed from women who use cigarettes, drugs, and alcohol at similar levels to determine the relative effects of various substances on low birthweight.

More in-depth information also is needed about the effects of substance use and other variables on very low birthweight of infants. The sampling strategy used for this study selected DC-resident women with certainty if they had a low birthweight infant (i.e., under 2,500 grams) but did not control the number of very low birthweight infants (i.e., under 1,500 grams) selected into the sample. Comparisons of proportions of very low birthweight babies from the interview data with proportions reported by participating hospitals indicate that this group was underrepresented in the sample. It is not clear why this occurred, but it may have resulted from higher refusal rates among women with babies in this category. Consequently, the relatively small sample size for this group limits the type, number, and complexity of analyses that can be conducted in examining effects on very low birthweight infants. Future studies should take this problem into account and incorporate very low birthweight as a stratification variable to ensure that a larger number of respondents is in this group.

Researchers interested primarily in identifying and quantifying the effects of various risk factors on low birthweight, rather than in developing prevalence estimates, may wish to consider using a case-control design. This design will allow more in-depth exploration of each woman's behaviors during pregnancy because interviews would be required only for cases (women with low birthweight infants) and controls (a sample of women with normal birthweight infants).

8.5.3 Prenatal Care Services

Findings indicate that 12.2% of DC-resident women delivering live-births in DC hospitals received no prenatal care in the first or second trimesters of their pregnancies, and 5.3% received no prenatal care whatsoever prior to delivery. Of those women who received prenatal care, approximately one third (33.4%) delayed receiving care until the second trimester, and 7.6% did not receive care until the third trimester. In comparison, data from the National Center for Health Statistics (1994) indicate that 5.8% of *infants* in the United States in 1991 were born to women whose prenatal care began in the third trimester or who received no prenatal care. Thus, insufficient prenatal care appears to be a larger problem among DC women than among women nationally.

Data from the Drug Use and Pregnancy Study also document the benefits of prenatal care for DC women and their infants. Infants whose mothers had not received prenatal care (or only prenatal care in the third trimester) were about twice as likely to be low birthweight or preterm as infants whose mothers received prenatal care in the first or second trimesters of pregnancy. More specifically, approximately 1 in 5 infants born to women who received no prenatal care in their first or second trimesters were low birthweight or preterm, compared with about 1 in 10 born to mothers who had received prenatal care.

Approximately one fourth of the DC-resident women who used illicit drugs during pregnancy received no prenatal care in the first or second trimester. Robins and Mills (1993) cited four potential benefits for women who use drugs during pregnancy and for their infants if these women receive early and regular prenatal care: (a) women may be persuaded or receive support to reduce or stop their use of alcohol, cigarettes, or illicit drugs during pregnancy; (b) infections that often are associated with drug use (e.g., hepatitis B, STDs) can be detected and treated; (c) high blood pressure that may be associated with cocaine use can be detected and monitored; and (d) women can receive needed social services, including assistance with food costs. These data suggest the importance of continued outreach efforts and other initiatives to reach drug-using pregnant women in DC and provide them with prenatal care and other needed services. Furthermore, the association between illicit drug use during pregnancy and inadequate prenatal care may suggest the need for better linkage of prenatal care and drug treatment services.

8.5.4 Issues for Future Research

The results of the Drug Use and Pregnancy Study add to our understanding of the epidemic of drug use among pregnant women. Comparison of national prevalence estimates of drug use during pregnancy (NIDA, 1996) with the DC estimates obtained in this study suggest that this problem may be more acute in large metropolitan areas than in the country as a whole. Study findings related to illicit drug preferences, lack of or timing of prenatal care, and the relationship between substance use during pregnancy and low birthweight raise a number of issues that could be addressed by policymakers or pursued in future studies.

Cocaine was the drug of choice among DC-resident women who used illicit drugs during the past year and during pregnancy. In contrast, women of childbearing age in the overall DC metropolitan statistical area (MSA) household population in 1990 were more likely to have used marijuana in the past year than they were to have used cocaine (NIDA, 1992). Similarly, marijuana was the illicit drug used most commonly during pregnancy among women throughout the nation (NIDA, 1996). This raises questions about the underlying reasons that higher rates of cocaine use occurred in the present study. It is unclear whether the preference for cocaine found among DC-resident women was a function of attitudes, values, and norms specific to DC; whether it was a function of differing demographic characteristics, such as age and race/ethnicity among women in the various studies; or whether it was a phenomenon specific to urban areas.

Unfortunately, there are currently no definitive answers to these questions, although some data bear on these issues. A reanalysis of data from the 1988 National Household Survey on Drug Abuse (NHSDA) suggested that "neighborhood" risk factors, such as drug availability, should be considered as possible explanations for differences in cocaine use by different racial/ethnic groups (Lillie-Blanton, Anthony, & Schuster, 1993). The preference for cocaine seen for the women in the DC study may be related to neighborhood characteristics. If so, effective drug use intervention might focus on trying to change environmental factors in the neighborhoods in which the women live, rather than trying to change the behaviors of individual women.

Findings from the 1991 DC MSA oversample of the NHSDA (which includes data from DC as well as from the surrounding suburban and rural areas in Maryland and Virginia) indicated that past year use of crack cocaine was significantly more prevalent among the population in DC (2.9%) than in the Maryland counties of the MSA (0.3%) (NIDA, 1994). The Virginia counties showed a pattern of lower prevalence (0.7%) similar to Maryland's, although it was not different statistically from the estimate for DC. These data, however, included both men and women and were not adjusted for differing demographics of the DC, Maryland, and Virginia populations. Note that these overall rates were substantially lower than those reported by the DC-resident women in the hospital sample. This suggests that rates in the center city may differ from those in the suburbs of metropolitan areas.

Furthermore, findings from the 1991 NHSDA indicated that past year use of any form of cocaine and of crack cocaine tended to be more prevalent in large metropolitan areas (i.e., MSAs with a 1990 population of 1 million or more) than in nonmetropolitan areas (i.e., not part of an MSA as of 1990, and generally consisting of smaller communities, rural nonfarm areas, and farm areas) (Substance Abuse and Mental Health Services Administration, 1993). Additional research replicating the DC*MADS Drug Use and Pregnancy Study methodology in other large urban areas is needed to help clarify the underlying mechanisms for the higher rate of cocaine use during pregnancy and in the past year that was observed for DC-resident women. If cocaine is preferred by pregnant women in other metropolitan areas or by women with a demographic background similar to DC-resident women, prevention and drug treatment efforts should be focused on this drug and perhaps this specific subgroup of women.

A public health benefit of a study of drug use by women during pregnancy is to provide data that can be used by policymakers and health care providers. The Drug Use and Pregnancy Study provides information about prenatal care and low birthweight that may be used to identify high-risk women and develop effective policies for reducing infant morbidity and mortality. Approximately one fourth of the DC-resident women who used illicit drugs during pregnancy received no prenatal care in the first or second trimester. These women were about twice as likely to have low birthweight or preterm infants than were women who received prenatal care earlier in their pregnancies. These findings underscore the need for a better linkage between prenatal care and drug treatment services. This linkage would help social and health service providers identify drug-using pregnant women and provide them with both prenatal and drug treatment care.

Cigarette smoking during pregnancy was strongly related to low birthweight (less than 2,500 grams) in this study, even after controlling for the mother's demographic characteristics, parity, and prenatal care status. In contrast, illicit drug use during pregnancy was related only to very low birthweight (less than 1,500 grams), and alcohol use was not related to any low birthweight outcome. These findings suggest that smoking cessation programs may be the most critical need for pregnant women to reduce low birthweight births.

Finally, findings from the Drug Use and Pregnancy Study provide a baseline prevalence estimate of drug use during pregnancy from which to evaluate subsequent efforts in DC (and in other large cities or MSAs with similar demographic characteristics) to prevent or reduce the use of these substances among pregnant women. Similar studies in other metropolitan areas would provide baseline estimates of drug use by pregnant women, as well as correlates and consequences, to use to judge the effectiveness of drug use prevention programs in other communities.

References

Adams, M. M., Sarno, A. P., Harlass, F. E., Rawlings, J. S., & Read, J. A. (1995). Risk factors for preterm delivery in a healthy cohort. *Epidemiology, 6*, 525-532.

Appendix F: Drug Use and Pregnancy Study. (1998). (Available on the World Wide Web at http://www.sagepub.com/bray_druguse.htm)

Center for Disease Control. (1990). Statewide prevalence of illicit drug use by pregnant women—Rhode Island. *Morbidity and Mortality Weekly Report, 39*, 225-227.

Chasnoff, I. J., Landress, H. J., & Barrett, M. E. (1990). The prevalence of illicit drug or alcohol use during pregnancy and discrepancies in mandatory reporting in Pinellas County, Florida. *New England Journal of Medicine, 322*, 1202-1206.

Cherukuri, R., Minkoff, H., Feldman, J., Parekh, A., & Glass, L. (1988). A cohort study of alkaloidal cocaine ("crack") in pregnancy. *Obstetrics and Gynecology, 72*, 147-151.

Cnattingius, S., Forman, M. R., Berendes, H. W., & Isotalo, L. (1992). Delayed childbearing and risk of adverse perinatal outcome. *Journal of the American Medical Association, 268*, 886-890.

Feldman, J. G., Minkoff, H. L., McCalla, S., & Salwen, M. (1992). A cohort study of the impact of perinatal drug use on prematurity in an inner-city hospital. *American Journal of Public Health, 82*, 726-728.

Finnegan, L. P. (1985). Smoking and its effect on pregnancy and the newborn. In S. Harel & N. J. Anastasiow (Eds.), *The at-risk infant: Psycho/socio/medical aspects* (pp. 127-136). Baltimore: Paul H. Brookes.

Hertz-Picciotto, I., Pastore, L. M., & Beaumont, J. J. (1996). Timing and patterns of exposures during pregnancy and their implications for study methods. *American Journal of Epidemiology, 143*, 597-607.

Kempe, A., Wise, P. H., Barkan, S. E., Sappenfield, W. M., Sachs, B., Gortmaker, S. L., Sobol, A. M., First, L. R., Pursley, D., Rinehart, H., Kotelchuck, M., Cole, F. S., Gunter, N., & Stockbauer, J. W. (1992). Clinical determinants of the racial disparity in very low birth weight. *New England Journal of Medicine, 327*, 969-973.

Kleinman, J. C., & Madans, J. H. (1985). The effects of maternal smoking, physical stature, and educational attainment of the incidence of low birth weight. *American Journal of Epidemiology, 121*, 843-855.

Lieberman, E., Gremy, I., Lang, J. M., & Cohen, A. P. (1994). Low birthweight at term and the timing of fetal exposure to maternal smoking. *American Journal of Public Health, 84*, 1127-1131.

Lieberman, E., Ryan, K. J., Monson, R. R., & Schoenbaum, S. C. (1987). Risk factors accounting for racial differences in the rate of premature birth. *New England Journal of Medicine, 317*, 743-748.

Lillie-Blanton, M., Anthony, J. C., & Schuster, C. R. (1993). Probing the meaning of racial/ethnic group comparisons in crack cocaine smoking. *Journal of the American Medical Association, 269*, 993-997.

Little, B. B., Snell, L. M., Klein, V. R., & Gilstrap, L. C. (1989). Cocaine abuse during pregnancy: Maternal and fetal implications. *Obstetrics and Gynecology, 73*, 157-160.

MacGregor, S. N., Keith, L. G., Chasnoff, I. J., Rosner, M. A., Chisum, G. M., Shaw, P., & Minogue, J. P. (1987). Cocaine use during pregnancy: Adverse perinatal outcome. *American Journal of Obstetrics and Gynecology, 157*, 686-690.

McCalla, S., Minkoff, H. L., Feldman, J., Delke, I., Salwin, M., Valencia, G., & Glass, L. (1991). The biologic and social consequences of perinatal cocaine use in an inner-city population: Results of an anonymous cross-sectional study. *American Journal of Obstetrics and Gynecology, 164*, 625-630.

National Center for Health Statistics. (1994). *Health, United States, 1993* (DHHS Publication No. PHS 94-1232). Hyattsville, MD: U.S. Public Health Service.

National Institute on Drug Abuse. (1992). *Prevalence of drug use in the DC metropolitan area household population: 1990* (DHHS Publication No. ADM 92-1919). Rockville, MD: Author.

National Institute on Drug Abuse. (1994). *Prevalence of drug use in the DC metropolitan area household and nonhousehold populations: 1991* (Technical Report #8 under NIDA Contract No. 271-89-8340, Washington, DC, Metropolitan Area Drug Study, prepared by R. M. Bray, L. A. Kroutil, S. C. Wheeless, M. E. Marsden, & L. E. Packer, Research Triangle Institute). Rockville, MD: Author.

National Institute on Drug Abuse. (1995). *Prevalence of drug use among DC women delivering livebirths in DC hospitals: 1992* (Technical Report #7 under NIDA Contract No. 271-89-8340, Washington, DC, Metropolitan Area Drug Study, prepared by W. A. Visscher, R. M. Bray, L. A. Kroutil, D. A. Akin, M. A. Ardini, J. P. Thornberry, & M. McCall, Research Triangle Institute). Rockville, MD: Author.

National Institute on Drug Abuse. (1996). *National Pregnancy & Health Survey: Drug use among women delivering livebirths: 1992* (NIH Publication No. 96-3819). Rockville, MD: Author.

Neerhof, M. G., MacGregor, S. N., Retzky, S. S., & Sullivan, T. P. (1989). Cocaine abuse during pregnancy: Peripartum prevalence and perinatal outcome. *American Journal of Obstetrics and Gynecology, 161*, 633-638.

Oro, A. S., & Dixon, S. D. (1987). Perinatal cocaine and methamphetamine exposure: Maternal and neonatal correlates. *Journal of Pediatrics, 111*, 571-578.

Prager, K., Malin, H., Graves, C., Spiegler, D., Richards, L., & Placek, P. (1983). Maternal smoking and drinking before and during pregnancy. In *Health, United States: 1983* (DHHS Publication No. PHS 94-1232, pp. 19-24). Hyattsville, MD: National Center for Health Statistics.

Rawlings, J. S., Rawlings, V. B., & Read, J. A. (1995). Prevalence of low birth weight and preterm delivery in relation to the interval between pregnancies among white and black women. *New England Journal of Medicine, 332*, 69-74.

Robertson, P. A., Sniderman, S. H., Laros, R. K., Cowan, R., Heilbron, D., Goldenberg, R. L., Iams, J. D., & Creasy, R. K. I. (1992). Neonatal morbidity according to gestational age and birthweight from 5 tertiary care centers in the U.S. *American Journal of Obstetrics and Gynecology, 166*, 1629-1645.

Robins, L. N., & Mills, J. L. (1993). Effects of in utero exposure to street drugs. *American Journal of Public Health, 83*(Suppl.), 1-32.

Rossett, H. L., & Weiner, L. (1984). *Alcohol and the fetus: A clinical perspective.* New York: Oxford University Press.

Serdula, M., Williamson, D. F., Kendrick, J. S., Anda, R. F., & Byers, T. (1991). Trends in alcohol consumption by pregnant women. *Journal of the American Medical Association, 265*, 876-879.

Sokol, R. J., Ager, J., & Martier, S. (1986). Significant determinants of susceptibility to alcohol fratogenicity. *Annals of the New York Academy of Science, 477*, 87-102.

Substance Abuse and Mental Health Services Administration. (1993). *National Household Survey on Drug Abuse: Main findings 1991* (DHHS Publication No. SMA 93-1980). Rockville, MD: Author.

Vega, W. A., Kolody, B., Hwang, J., & Noble, A. (1993). Prevalence and magnitude of perinatal substance exposures in California. *New England Journal of Medicine, 329*, 850-854.

World Health Organization. (1992). *Low birth weight: A tabulation of available information* (Maternal Health and Safe Motherhood Programme, WHO/MCH/92.2). Geneva, Switzerland: Author.

9 Comparing and Integrating Findings Across Populations

Robert M. Bray
Larry A. Kroutil
Sara C. Wheeless

B efore we can effectively address the drug problem in metropolitan areas, we must have a clear understanding of its magnitude, dimensions, and complexity. Such information helps shape policies about the numbers and types of treatment and intervention services that are needed. Prior chapters in this book have examined the nature and extent of drug use and its related problems among selected populations. This chapter extends these analyses and contributes to our understanding of the drug problem by combining data from household and nonhousehold populations to yield estimates of the extent of the problem in the total civilian population. More specifically, this chapter, using data from the DC*MADS Household and Nonhousehold Populations Study, examines the need for total population estimates of drug use, describes our approach for combining data to develop broader population estimates, presents the resulting estimates from the household and composite populations, assesses the effects of combining data among three high-risk subgroups, and discusses the key findings and their implications.

9.1 Need for Total Civilian Population Estimates of Drug Use

Since 1971, the National Household Survey on Drug Abuse (NHSDA) series (see Chapters 2 and 3) has been the principal source of information for researchers and policymakers at the federal, state, and local levels about the extent of drug use and drug-related problems among people living in households in the United States (Substance Abuse and Mental Health Services Administration [SAMHSA], 1996). Despite the NHSDA's broad focus, it is limited in its ability to detect substance use among selected subgroups who may not reside in households or who are difficult to find and interview in households. Such groups have been categorized as "hidden populations" and are often referred to as the disadvantaged and disenfranchised—groups that include those who are homeless and transient, criminal and juvenile offenders, prostitutes, those who are chronically mentally ill, gang members, runaways, and institutionalized people (Lambert, 1990).

Indeed, some NHSDA estimates have been criticized because the survey series has excluded or been limited in its ability to cover adequately populations who potentially are at high risk for abusing alcohol or using illicit drugs, such as incarcerated or homeless people. For example, a report to the Senate Judiciary Committee suggested that the 1988 NHSDA underestimated the number of frequent, heavy cocaine users in the United States by a factor of more than 2.5 because the survey did not count drug users who were homeless, in prison, or in treatment (U.S. Senate, 1990). Similarly, a report by the U.S. General Accounting Office (US GAO, 1993) noted the potential in the NHSDA for noncoverage or undercoverage of groups at increased risk for using drugs.

Even though the NHSDA has been the standard for gauging drug use and related problems in the nation and in metropolitan areas, there have been few attempts to evaluate how well household data estimate use of alcohol and other drugs in the general population. Research by

Weisner and her colleagues (Weisner & Schmidt, 1995; Weisner, Schmidt, & Tam, 1995) bears on this issue. They produced prevalence estimates for problem drinkers and drug users in the household population and within alcohol treatment, drug treatment, mental health, criminal justice, and welfare agencies in a single county in northern California. Data were gathered in a series of coordinated surveys that were conducted from 1986 to 1989 using probability samples. Data from the agency studies were merged, and a subset of respondents was classified as a nonhousehold subsample. Although Weisner and colleagues did not merge data from the household and nonhousehold samples, comparisons of the two groups showed substantially higher rates of problem drinking (48% vs. 11%) and weekly drug use (47% vs. 6%) among the nonhousehold population. Data presented earlier in this book for household, homeless, and institutionalized populations (see Chapters 3, 4, and 5) show similar findings, which suggests that estimates based on household samples alone are likely to underrepresent the numbers and proportions of drug users in the general population.

Another study bearing on this issue examined the effects of school dropout rates on overall estimates of adolescent substance use (Swaim, Beauvais, Chavez, & Oetting, 1997). The problem of excluding dropouts, who are likely to have higher rates of substance use (e.g., Chavez, Edwards, & Oetting, 1989; Mensch & Kandel, 1988), has been recognized as a general limitation of school-based studies, such as the Monitoring the Future survey (Johnston, O'Malley, & Bachman, 1997a), which annually provides national estimates of substance use rates among high school seniors (US GAO, 1993). Swaim et al. (1997) obtained data from students and dropouts in four different racial/ethnic groups (Mexican American, white, non-Hispanic, and Native American), then used a weighting correction to adjust overall estimates to take account of the higher observed rates among dropouts. Their findings indicated that overall rates of substance use by adolescents were significantly higher when dropouts were included in the estimates. They also showed that the rates varied by drug and ethnic group and were related to, but not necessarily proportional to, the size of the dropout population. For example, although the dropout rate was 50% for Native Americans and 46% for Mexican Americans, the average increase in substance use rates after including dropouts in the estimates was 8.4% for Native Americans and 11.4% for Mexican Americans. These data again point out that when important subgroups of the population are omitted from studies, overall population estimates will underrepresent the magnitude of the total problem when the omitted subgroups have high prevalence rates.

The impact of school absentees and dropouts on overall substance use rates of adolescents also has been examined by Johnston and colleagues for the Monitoring the Future survey (Johnston & O'Malley, 1985; Johnston et al., 1997a). To assess the effect of absenteeism, the investigators classified students into groups based on answers they gave about how often students were absent from school. Students absent half the time were placed in one group, those absent a third of the time in another group, and so on. Next, they weighted students in the various groups to represent themselves plus absentees like them who were missing that day (e.g., students absent half the time received a weight of two; those absent two thirds of the time received a weight of three). Analyses found that absentees had substantially higher rates of substance use than did other students. A combined estimate also was computed by weighting the information from absentees and other students proportional to their representation in the population. These adjustments for the 1983 data showed that omitting absentees suppressed overall rates of substance use up to 2.7 percentage points depending on the drug examined.

For dropouts, Johnston et al. (1997a) used census data to estimate the rate of dropping out (about 15%), then used two methods for estimating substance use rates among dropouts using the 1983 data: (a) extrapolating from absentees and assuming that substance use rates of dropouts were the same as those for absentees, 1.5 times as high, or twice as high; and (b) extrapolating from the NHSDA (i.e., comparing data from dropouts with data from those who remained in school). By definition, the former method resulted in higher rates of substance use among dropouts compared with students; the largest correction ranged from 5.0% to 7.5% in annual prevalence of marijuana depending on the correction factor used. The rates using the NHSDA approximated those from the middle group of the first method (i.e., assuming rates 1.5 times as high). An update of these analyses conducted using 1991 data from Monitoring the Future and from the NHSDA also showed that rates of use from dropouts were notably higher than rates from school students, and combined estimates also were higher (Johnston et al., 1997a). The method of adjusting the data for the combined estimate consisted of weighting the estimates from the students and dropouts proportional to their representation in the population.

Ongoing research sponsored by the Center for Substance Abuse Treatment (CSAT) is supporting state offices that provide drug and alcohol treatment services to estimate their state's need for substance abuse treatment and intervention services. For that effort, states are conducting a family of studies from a variety of populations (e.g., households, arrestees) that include a telephone survey of the household population as the foundation study (e.g., Bray et al., 1997). States will be attempting to integrate data from these various studies to obtain a composite estimate of the need for substance abuse treatment. A matrix approach has been proposed by the National Technical Center from Harvard University as the method for combining the data (Geller, 1996). This approach obtains data from the family of studies and other available information from the literature or related studies to estimate the size of the various populations throughout the state who are in need of treatment. These estimates are then summed across subpopulations to arrive at an overall estimate of the treatment need for the state.

Taken together, these several studies indicate the need for total population estimates of substance abuse rates and suggest that information based just on the household population is likely to miss important subgroups who may be at high risk for use. Prior efforts to address this problem have relied mainly on weighting approaches to adjust data. Little work has been done on combining data across populations to provide composite information and to examine the contribution of nonhousehold populations to the total population estimates. The Household and Nonhousehold Populations Study described in this chapter provides an important step in addressing this gap.

9.2 Overview of the Study

This chapter builds on work from prior research as applicable and examines and quantifies the contribution of nonhousehold data to estimates of drug use and problems in the general population for the Household and Nonhousehold Populations Study. It first describes our approach to combining data among members of household, institutionalized, and homeless or transient populations aged 12 or older into a "composite" population. These three populations were selected because, conceptually, they represent the full range of independent living situations that cover all persons in the civilian population. Even though in principle the frame conceptually includes the total civilian population, for practical considerations the Institutionalized Study (see Chapter 5) omitted some institutions from the study and thus did not have full coverage. Of course, subsets of the three populations may be of interest in their own right (e.g., new mothers, criminal offenders, treatment clients), and some of them have been described in earlier chapters in this book. From a population standpoint, however, they are represented in one of the three nonoverlapping frames of the household, institutionalized, or homeless and transient populations.

Findings about drug use prevalence (percentages and numbers of users) are next presented for household, nonhousehold, and composite populations. These results show the relative size of the drug use problem in one metropolitan area and the effect that adding data from nonhousehold populations has on estimates based on the household data alone.

This is followed by an examination of the drug use prevalence of three high-risk drug-abusing subgroups in the composite population: crack cocaine users, heroin users, and needle users. The implications of our findings are considered for future studies that attempt to estimate prevalence rates and treatment needs.

9.3 Combining Data to Develop Broader Population Estimates

The estimates presented in this chapter comprise the Household and Nonhousehold Populations Study and are based on data from three separate sample surveys conducted in the Washington, DC, metropolitan statistical area (DC MSA) during 1991: the NHSDA's DC MSA household population, the DC*MADS Homeless and Transient Population Study, and the DC*MADS Institutionalized Study. As was noted in Chapter 2, these three populations conceptually define the total population of the MSA and together encompass the full range of individuals' possible living situations in that all persons can be characterized as belonging to one of them. Thus, construction of the composite population was limited to combining data from these three populations rather than attempting to combine data from all the studies in the DC*MADS project.

Data from the individual studies were described in detail earlier in Chapters 3 through 5, respectively. Data are combined from these three surveys to form a composite population. As noted above, the composite population does not fully represent the total population because some eligible groups were not included in the Institutionalized Study. In addition, active-duty military personnel living in the DC MSA were not included in the sample frames for any of these three studies, even if they were living off-base in civilian housing. These omitted groups were small relative to the overall size of the metropolitan area, and, practically speaking, the composite population very closely approximates the over-all general population. Some of these groups are covered by other population surveys. For example, the Worldwide Surveys of Substance Abuse and Health Behaviors Among U.S. Military Personnel (e.g., Bray et al., 1992; Bray et al., 1995) have provided information since 1980 on trends in alcohol, tobacco, and other drug use among active-duty military personnel.

The subpopulations surveyed in these separate studies generally were defined in terms of where respondents were residing at the time of data collection. The NHSDA surveyed the civilian, noninstitutional population, including civilians living on military bases and persons living in noninstitutional group quarters (e.g., rooming houses, dormitories, shelters for homeless people, and group homes). There were 32,594 respondents in the overall 1991 NHSDA and 2,547 respondents in the DC MSA household portion of the study (SAMHSA, 1993b). For 4 years, from 1990 to 1993, the NHSDA oversampled the DC MSA as part of an effort to obtain expanded estimates for selected metropolitan areas of the nation (Washington, DC, from 1990 to 1993; Chicago, Denver, Los Angeles, Miami, and New York from 1991 to 1993).

The DC*MADS Homeless and Transient Population Study surveyed persons who were either literally homeless or at imminent risk of becoming homeless, including persons who spent the previous night in an emergency shelter or in a nondomicile (i.e., vacant building, public or commercial facility, city park, car, or the street) or who were using soup kitchens or emergency food banks for homeless people. There were 908 respondents in this study (National Institute on Drug Abuse [NIDA], 1993).

The DC*MADS Institutionalized Study surveyed persons in institutional and noninstitutional group quarters. Institutional group quarters included correctional facilities, mental or psychiatric hospitals, and other institutions, such as noncorrectional facilities for juveniles. Noninstitutional group quarters included group homes for people who were mentally retarded, homes for people with physical disabilities, and transitional homes for people leaving treatment for alcohol or other drug abuse. Nursing homes and hospitals or wards providing treatment for alcohol or other drug abuse were excluded. There were 1,203 respondents from 42 institutions in this study (NIDA, 1994b).

A number of steps were taken while planning the Homeless and Transient Population Study and the Institutionalized Population Study to permit the data to be integrated with the NHSDA data. These included coordinating the timing of data collection, defining the subpopulations, ensuring similar structure and content of questionnaires, and following similar estimation procedures. Although the populations surveyed by the three studies generally were defined by place of residence, the target populations overlapped slightly. The NHSDA and the Institutionalized Study included some portions of the noninstitutionalized group quarters population. The NHSDA and the Homeless and Transient Population Study included persons living in homeless shelters and persons who, although not literally homeless, may have been at risk of homelessness, as evidenced by their use of soup kitchens or food banks.

Figure 9.1 shows graphically the potential overlap in the target population for the three surveys. Of the 4,658 persons interviewed, 637 potentially could have participated in more than one of the studies. In terms of the total *number* of persons represented, however, the overlap was very small; less than 0.5% of the total combined population potentially was represented by more than one of the surveys. To address these potential overlaps, it was necessary to make adjustments to avoid multiple counting of the subpopulations when producing composite estimates. Respondents were first classified according to the number of overlapping surveys for which they could have been selected. At most, the overlap occurred only in two of the three surveys (i.e., household and homeless, household and institutionalized, or homeless and institutionalized). It was not known whether persons interviewed for the NHSDA may have been at risk of homelessness, as evidenced by their use of soup kitchens. Although it was not possible to adjust completely for this

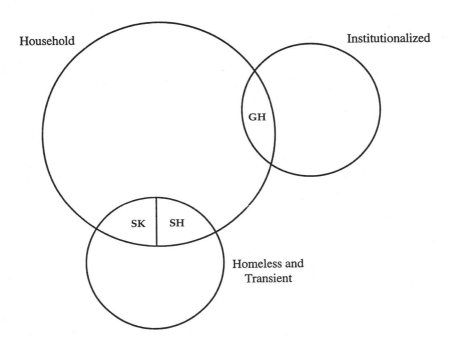

Figure 9.1. Overlap of Sampling Frames for the DC MSA Household, Homeless and Transient, and Institutionalized Populations
SOURCE: Washington, DC, Metropolitan Area Drug Study (DC*MADS): 1989-1995.
NOTE: Populations not drawn to scale.
GH = noninstitutionalized group homes; SK = not literally homeless who used soup kitchens; SH = homeless shelters.

potential multiplicity, it was assumed that only a small proportion of persons who were linked to the area frame used for the NHSDA were also linked to the soup kitchen frame.

Analysis weights were adjusted for persons who could have been selected for two surveys by multiplying them by 0.5. These adjusted weights were then summed with the final analysis weights for other individuals in the three surveys to form multiplicity-adjusted weights for the composite population. The combined data set provides unbiased estimates of the prevalence of illicit drug, alcohol, and cigarette use among the composite population in the DC MSA. The procedures used

Table 9.1　Percentages and Estimated Numbers of People in the DC MSA Composite Population

Subpopulation	Percentage	Number
Total	100.0	3,198,698
Household	99.2	3,171,915
Homeless	0.2	7,388[1]
Institutionalized[2]	0.6	19,395

SOURCE: Household data are from the 1991 National Household Survey on Drug Abuse: DC MSA. Homeless data are from the 1991 DC*MADS Homeless and Transient Population Study. Data on institutionalized persons are from the 1991 DC*MADS Institutionalized Study.
NOTE: Estimates have been adjusted for potential multiplicity in the sample frames. The DC MSA is defined in Chapter 2.
1. Estimate differs slightly from that given in Chapter 4 because of multiplicity adjustments (e.g., shelter residents who could have been sampled for both the NHSDA and DC*MADS).
2. Does not include nursing homes, residential schools for hearing-impaired people, homes for developmentally disabled individuals, or religious group quarters.

to adjust for multiplicity are discussed in more detail in the final technical report for the Household and Nonhousehold Populations Study (NIDA, 1994a) and in Appendix G (1998).

Table 9.1 shows the percentages of the DC MSA composite population and estimated numbers of people from the household, institutionalized, and homeless populations. As shown in this table, the household population constituted more than 99% of the composite population. If nursing home residents and other excluded institutionalized subpopulations had been sampled for the Institutionalized Study, the percentage of the composite population living in institutions would be greater than the 0.6% shown in Table 9.1; however, inclusion of these other institutionalized subpopulations would not change the conclusion that the overwhelming majority of the DC MSA composite population consists of people living in households.

9.4 Drug Use Among the Composite Population and Subpopulations

Figure 9.2 shows 1991 rates of illicit drug use in the DC MSA composite population consisting of people aged 12 or older in household and nonhousehold populations in the metropolitan area (see supporting data in Table G.3 in Appendix G [1998]). Nearly one in eight people aged 12

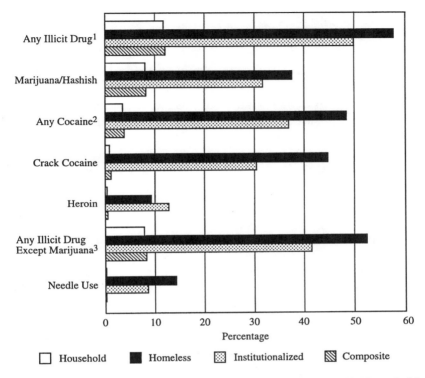

Figure 9.2. Prevalence of Past Year Illicit Drug Use in the DC MSA Household, Homeless and Transient, Institutionalized, and Composite Populations

SOURCE: Household data are from the 1991 National Household Survey on Drug Abuse: DC MSA. Homeless data are from the 1991 DC*MADS Homeless and Transient Population Study. Data on institutionalized persons are from the 1991 DC*MADS Institutionalized Study.

NOTE: Composite population includes the combined household, homeless and transient, and institutionalized populations. See Table G.3 in Appendix G (1998) for the supplementary data used to prepare this figure.

1. Use of marijuana or hashish, cocaine (including crack), inhalants, hallucinogens (including phencyclidine or PCP), heroin, or nonmedical use of psychotherapeutics at least once.

2. Includes crack cocaine.

3. Includes cocaine (including crack), inhalants, hallucinogens (including PCP), heroin, or psychotherapeutics for nonmedical reasons.

or older in the "composite" population (12.0%) used one or more illicit drugs in the past year, and 8.3% used marijuana/hashish. Overall, 8.1% of the composite population used one or more illicit drugs besides marijuana. Considerably smaller segments of the composite population used cocaine in any form (3.9%), crack cocaine (1.2%), heroin (0.5%), or needles to inject drugs (0.3%).

9.4.1 Comparative Rates of Use

Figure 9.2 also shows rates of illicit drug use for the DC MSA household population, homeless and transient population, and "high-risk" people in institutions. As shown in this figure, the rates of illicit drug use were considerably higher in the two nonhousehold populations than they were in the household population. In particular, more than half of the homeless people (57.7%) and almost half of the "high-risk" people in institutions (49.9%) used one or more illicit drugs in the past year. In comparison, fewer than one in eight people in the household population (11.7%) were past year users of illicit drugs.

The higher rates of substance use in the nonhousehold populations could result, in part, from a greater representation of demographic subgroups who are more likely to be heavy alcohol or illicit drug users. As was shown earlier in Table 2.2, there were notable differences in demographic characteristics between the household and nonhousehold populations. In particular, these nonhousehold populations in the DC MSA had higher percentages of males (75.9% of the homeless population and 90.7% of the institutionalized population covered vs. 47.7% of the household population) and blacks (75.8% and 69.3% of the homeless and institutionalized populations, respectively, vs. 27.2% of the household population). Both the homeless and institutionalized populations showed higher rates of use than their counterparts. Analyses that partially controlled for these demographic differences examined rates of illicit drug use within demographic subgroups and found that nonhousehold populations still reported rates of use that were significantly and notably higher, often by several orders of magnitude, than those indicated by members of the household population. For example, the age-specific rates of past year use of any illicit drug among persons 12 to 25 years of age were 45.3% for the homeless population and 17.5% in the household population; among persons 26 to 34 years old, the rates were 69.8% and 19.6%, respectively, in the two populations; and for those 35 years of age and older, the rates were 52.3% and 5.7%, respectively (NIDA, 1993). Thus, differences in the distribution of demographic characteristics among household and nonhousehold populations were not sufficient to account for the differences in rates of use.

Figure 9.2 also shows that combining data from nonhousehold populations with household population data to produce "composite" population estimates had relatively little effect on estimates of the percentages of people who used illicit drugs, compared with the percentages based on household data alone. For example, adding data from nonhousehold populations to the household data raised the prevalence estimate of any illicit drug use only slightly, from 11.7% in the household population to 12.0% in the composite population. Conversely, however, these data suggest that household population data would miss some seriously high rates of use among nonhousehold populations because of the small proportion of nonhousehold populations in the overall general population. This is consistent with findings noted earlier by Weisner and colleagues (1995).

In addition, the household and nonhousehold populations in the DC MSA differed in terms of the most commonly used drugs in the past year. For the household and composite populations, marijuana/hashish was the most commonly used illicit drug. Approximately 8% of people in these populations used marijuana/hashish in the past year, compared with less than 4% who used cocaine in any form and less than 1% who used crack cocaine or heroin.

Among the two nonhousehold populations, however, people were more likely to have used cocaine in the past year than they were to have used marijuana/hashish. Among the homeless and transient population, for example, nearly half (48.4%) used cocaine in any form and approximately 45% used crack cocaine in the past year, compared with 38% who used marijuana/hashish. Similarly, approximately 37% of high-risk people in institutions used some form of cocaine in the past year, compared with approximately 32% who used marijuana/hashish.

Rates of heroin use and injection drug use also were considerably higher in the two nonhousehold populations. Approximately 1 in 10 people in the two nonhousehold populations used heroin in the past year. In comparison, only about 1 in 200 people in the household and composite populations were past year heroin users.

9.4.2 Contribution of Nonhousehold Populations to the Numbers of Composite Population Drug Users

Estimating the numbers of illicit drug users in a population is also important for assessing the magnitude of a metropolitan area's drug use problem. Such estimates provide a picture of the total size of the drug-using population in an area as well as the total size of specific drug-using subpopulations, such as marijuana/hashish users, cocaine users, or heroin users. Moreover, estimates of the numbers of people who used different drugs provide some indication of the number of people in a metropolitan area who might be in need of intervention or treatment related to their substance use.

As stated previously, the nonhousehold populations in the DC MSA contributed relatively little to estimates of the percentages of the composite population who used illicit drugs. Given the high rates of drug use in these nonhousehold populations, however, data from these populations could aid considerably in estimating the number of drug users in a metropolitan area, compared with estimates based on household data alone. In particular, users of such drugs as heroin are relatively rare in the household population, both in the DC MSA (0.4% who used in the past year, Figure 9.2) and in the broader household population nationally (SAMHSA, 1996). Consequently, data from nonhousehold populations could improve the ability to estimate the size of some drug-using subgroups who are less likely to be represented in the household population.

Figure 9.3 compares estimates of the *numbers* of drug users in the DC MSA for the household population alone and for the composite population comprising both the household and nonhousehold populations (see supporting data in Table G.3 in Appendix G [1998]). The size of the household population who used any illicit drugs in the past year was estimated to be about 370,500 people. Adding data from nonhousehold populations raised the composite population estimate to approximately 384,700 people, an increase of about 14,200 people. The large majority of illicit drug users came from the household population, but roughly 4% of illicit drug users would be missed by relying on the household estimate alone.

Similarly, estimates of the number of past year marijuana/hashish users increased from approximately 257,000 in the household population to approximately 266,000 in the composite population, a difference of about 4%. The estimated number of past year users of any form of cocaine was approximately 115,000 in the household population and 126,000 in the composite population, an increase of about 10%. The

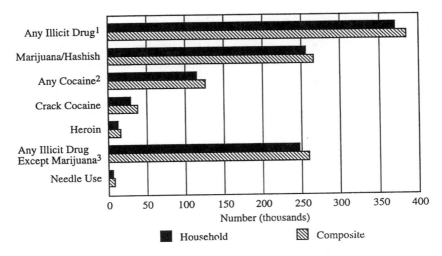

Figure 9.3. Number of Past Year Illicit Drug and Needle Users in the DC MSA Household and Composite Populations

SOURCE: Household data are from the 1991 National Household Survey on Drug Abuse: DC MSA. Homeless data are from the 1991 DC*MADS Homeless and Transient Population Study. Data on institutionalized persons are from the 1991 DC*MADS Institutionalized Study.

NOTE: Composite population includes the combined household, homeless and transient, and institutionalized populations. See Table G.3 in Appendix G (1998) for the supplementary data used to prepare this figure.

1. Use of marijuana or hashish, cocaine (including crack), inhalants, hallucinogens (including phencyclidine or PCP), heroin, or nonmedical use of psychotherapeutics at least once.

2. Includes crack cocaine.

3. Includes cocaine (including crack), inhalants, hallucinogens (including PCP), heroin, or psychotherapeutics for nonmedical reasons.

number of users of any drug except marijuana increased from about 248,000 to over 260,000, a change of about 5%.

In all these estimates, the household population accounted for the large majority of illicit drug users in the composite population. This finding should not be surprising considering its large size relative to the size of the nonhousehold populations. The more important point, however, is to recognize the number of users who would likely have been missed (from 9,000 to 14,000 depending on the drug examined) if estimates relied only on drug use among household residents.

Further examination also indicates additional and notable variation for other classes of users. For example, substantial proportions of crack cocaine, heroin, and needle users would be missed if estimates of the number of people who engaged in these behaviors were based on household data alone. Specifically, although household data would have accounted for approximately three fourths of the past year crack users in the composite population (i.e., approximately 29,000 users in the household population vs. approximately 38,400 in the composite population), about one in four would be missed if estimates did not include data from nonhousehold populations. Statistical tests that took into account the relationship between the household and composite estimates indicated that the number of crack cocaine users in the composite population was significantly greater than the number based on household data alone.

Similarly, of the estimated 15,500 past year heroin users in the DC MSA composite population, household data accounted for about 12,300, or about four fifths of the composite estimate. Although one fifth would be missed by relying solely on the household data, the composite estimate was not significantly different from the household estimate for heroin.

About two thirds of the past year needle users for injection drugs estimated to be in the composite population (8,740) were accounted for in the household population (5,987). Thus, approximately one third of the past year needle users in the DC MSA composite population were likely to be found outside the household population. Statistical tests showed that the composite estimate of the number of past year needle users was significantly greater than the household estimate.

These findings for crack cocaine, heroin, and needle use are even more striking when one considers the small size of the nonhousehold populations relative to the household population (Table 9.1). Specifically, members of the two nonhousehold populations account for less than 1% of the people in the composite population, but they account for about one fourth of the crack cocaine users, about one fifth of the heroin users, and about one third of the needle users in the past year in the composite population.

Although the number of past year needle users was small compared with users of any illicit drugs or of marijuana/hashish, the ability to obtain more comprehensive estimates of the number of injection drug users in a metropolitan area is very important from a public health standpoint. The increased risk of human immunodeficiency virus (HIV) infection or transmission associated with injection drug use is well established (Association of State and Territorial Health Officials [AS-THO], 1988; Brown & Beschner, 1993; Centers for Disease Control, 1989; Centers for Disease Control and Prevention, 1992a, 1992b; Des Jarlais et al., 1989; Turner, Miller, & Moses, 1989). In addition to risk for HIV infection, injection drug users are at increased risk for a variety of other infectious diseases, including hepatitis B, tuberculosis (including multidrug-resistant strains), endocarditis, and skin and soft tissue infections (Frieden et al., 1993; Haverkos & Lange, 1990; Selwyn et al., 1989). Consequently, data from nonhousehold populations fill an important gap in estimating the size of the injection drug-using population in a metropolitan area.

9.4.3 Differences in Drug Use Among Demographic Subgroups

Table 9.2 shows estimates of any illicit drug use in the past 12 months for selected demographic subgroups within the DC MSA household, homeless, institutionalized, and composite populations. As was the case in Figure 9.2, large and notable differences can be observed in the rates of drug use among the household and nonhousehold populations, both overall and within demographic subgroups. The nonhousehold populations show much higher rates of use than the household population. Similarly, for the composite population estimates of any illicit drug use, adding data from the nonhousehold populations had only a small effect on estimates of drug use within demographic subgroups relative to the household population estimates. For the household and composite populations, illicit drug use was more prevalent among men than among women, among people aged 18 to 34 compared with people in other age groups, and among people who were single (i.e., never married). In these two populations, rates of drug use in the past year were comparable for whites and blacks.

Table 9.2 Prevalence of Any Illicit Drug Use in the Past Year for Household, Homeless, Institutionalized, and Composite Populations, by Demographic Characteristics

Demographic Characteristic	Household (n = 2,547)	Homeless (n = 908)	Institutionalized (n = 1,203)	Composite (n = 4,658)
Total	11.7	57.7	49.9	12.0
Sex				
Male	15.0	63.4	50.5	15.6
Female	8.6	39.6	43.4*	8.7
Age (years)				
12-17	8.7	—	37.4	8.9
18-25	23.1	45.3[1]	55.2	23.5
26-34	19.6	69.8	54.5	20.1
35 or older	5.7	52.3	41.2	5.9
Race/ethnicity[2]				
White	12.7	42.3	55.1	12.9
Black	11.3	64.2	49.2	11.9
Hispanic	8.1	27.3*	54.0*	8.5
Marital status				
Single	20.3	59.2	51.7	20.8
Married	6.0	52.3*	42.2	6.1
Widowed/divorced/separated	11.5	56.5	49.1	12.1

SOURCE: Household data are from the 1991 National Household Survey on Drug Abuse: DC MSA. Homeless data are from the 1991 DC*MADS Homeless and Transient Population Study. Data on institutionalized persons are from the 1991 DC*MADS Institutionalized Study.
NOTE: Data entries are percentages.
1. Estimate for homeless population is for 12- to 25-year-olds but is based primarily on persons aged 18 to 25.
2. The category "other" for race/ethnicity is not included in estimates.
*Low precision.

9.5 High-Risk Drug-Abusing Subgroups

In addition to examining the effects on prevalence estimates of combining data from household, homeless, and institutionalized populations, we also assessed these effects among three high-risk drug-abusing subgroups: crack cocaine users, heroin users, and needle users. In this section, we discuss the importance of studying these subgroups and examine overlaps among them.

9.5.1 Significance of High-Risk Groups

The nature and size of the drug-abusing population in any community affects the magnitude of the burden placed on law enforcement, schools, families, and other societal institutions. NHSDA data show that use of most illicit drugs has been decreasing since about 1979 among members of the civilian, noninstitutionalized (and predominantly household) population (SAMHSA, 1996). Notwithstanding this general trend of decreasing use, there have been increases for some drugs and for some subgroups. For example, crack cocaine use increased dramatically during the mid- to late 1980s during the "cocaine epidemic." Similarly, after more than a decade of decreases in drug use among adolescents, recent years have shown increases in use among youth aged 12 to 17 in the NHSDA data (SAMHSA, 1996), findings that have been corroborated among high school seniors in the High School Senior Survey (Bachman, Wadsworth, O'Malley, Johnston, & Schulenberg, 1997; Johnston et al., 1997a; Johnston, O'Malley, & Bachman, 1997b).

Despite the value of such broad-based data collected by the NHSDA, a potential limitation of these data is that frequent, chronic users of cocaine and heroin might be disproportionately found in subpopulations who are either unrepresented (e.g., people in institutions) or underrepresented (e.g., homeless people) in the survey (US GAO, 1993). Consequently, the NHSDA is likely to yield conservative estimates or to be unable to make reliable estimates for drugs that have a low prevalence of use among the household population, such as crack cocaine or heroin (SAMHSA, 1993b). In addition, analyses of the prevalence of crack cocaine use in areas of low socioeconomic status (SES) and other SES areas within the DC MSA showed that past month crack cocaine use was significantly more prevalent in low SES areas (NIDA, 1994a). If frequent, heavy users of such drugs as crack cocaine and heroin tend to be disproportionately located in more urbanized areas, already overburdened law enforcement and other societal institutions delivering services to residents of such areas may be further strained.

Although the drug-abusing population may be variously defined—in terms of specific drugs of abuse, frequency of use, or route of administration—our focus here is on three potentially overlapping high-risk subpopulations: crack cocaine users, heroin users, and needle users. Crack cocaine and heroin users are of interest because use of these drugs often is associated with crime and other adverse effects, such as emergency room visits and deaths from overdose and drug interactions (Chaiken & Chaiken, 1990; Hunt, 1990; Johnson, Williams, Dei, & Sanabria, 1990; NIDA, 1992; SAMHSA, 1993a). In addition, as noted earlier (see Section 9.4.2), crack cocaine or heroin users who engage in prostitution to obtain money to buy drugs or who exchange sex for drugs can place themselves or their partners at increased risk for HIV infection, infection with other sexually transmitted diseases (STDs) (Centers for Disease Control, 1987; Chitwood, 1993), and other infectious diseases (e.g., hepatitis B, tuberculosis).

The presentation of findings for both the household and composite populations is useful for examining the effect that data from nonhousehold populations has on prevalence estimates of drug use and the estimated numbers of drug users. In addition, crack cocaine use, heroin use, and needle use are not necessarily mutually exclusive behaviors, as noted above. Because of the low prevalence of these behaviors in the household population (SAMHSA, 1996), however, analysis of the overlap among these different subpopulations has not been possible from household data alone.

9.5.2 Comparative Rates of Crack Cocaine, Heroin, and Needle Use

Figure 9.4 graphically represents the estimated numbers of crack cocaine, heroin, and needle users in the past year in the DC MSA composite population. These behaviors are not mutually exclusive, because these high-risk individuals could have engaged in more than one of them (e.g., past year crack cocaine users could also have used heroin or needles in the past year). Also shown in the right-hand bar of Figure 9.4 is the estimated number of people who engaged in any of these three behaviors in the past year. This latter estimate is smaller than the sum of the three individual behaviors because it has been adjusted for overlaps among the three drug-using subgroups.

Findings shown in Figure 9.4 indicate that a substantial number of high-risk drug abusers were in the DC MSA composite population in 1991. In the past year, an estimated 53,241 persons in the DC MSA used crack cocaine, heroin, or needles. Crack cocaine users were the most common of the three specific subgroups. Some 38,433 members of the DC MSA composite population had used crack cocaine at least once in the past year. The estimated number of past year heroin users in the DC MSA composite population was 15,549, and the estimated number of past year needle users was 8,740.

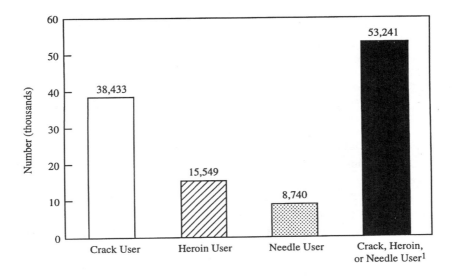

Figure 9.4. Estimated Numbers of Past Year Crack Cocaine, Heroin, and Needle Users in the DC MSA Composite Population

SOURCE: Household data are from the 1991 National Household Survey on Drug Abuse: DC MSA. Homeless data are from the 1991 DC*MADS Homeless and Transient Population Study. Data on institutionalized persons are from the 1991 DC*MADS Institutionalized Study.
NOTE: Composite population includes the combined household, homeless and transient, and institutionalized populations.
1. Crack, heroin, or needle use group has been adjusted for overlaps (e.g., crack users who also used heroin or needles).

These findings clearly show that a substantial number of persons have engaged in high-risk drug use behaviors that are widely held to show need for drug treatment and/or intervention and provide a basis in the DC MSA for making estimates about the kinds of resources needed to address these needs. They also show crack cocaine to be the most common of the three behaviors, a finding that is not surprising in view of the relative ease with which crack cocaine can be obtained and its cheaper price than heroin. Finally, the finding of a larger estimated number of past year heroin users than needle users suggests that a sizable number of heroin users did not use needles in the past year. Noninjection heroin users may take heroin intranasally (e.g., "snort" heroin) or they may smoke it as routes of administration. This latter finding is somewhat surprising because of the knowledge that injection drug use is fairly common among heroin users, or is even the preferred route of administration. Additional research is needed to examine changes in the relative frequency and preferences of various routes of administration among heroin users.

. 9.5.3 Lifetime Needle Sharing

In addition to obtaining data about needle use, we also asked respondents whether they shared needles with others. Because any needle sharing since the mid-1970s puts a person at high risk for HIV infection or transmission (Friedman, Des Jarlais, & Ward, 1993), we examined data on the prevalence of needle sharing in the lifetime rather than for a more recent time period. Figure 9.5 presents rates of needle sharing in the lifetime separately for the DC MSA household, institutionalized, homeless, and composite populations. Consistent with data about needle use shown previously in Figure 9.2, rates of needle sharing were dramatically higher in the nonhousehold populations of institutionalized and homeless people than in the household population. An estimated 12.5% of the institutionalized population and 15.3% of the homeless and transient population had ever engaged in needle sharing, compared with 1.0% of the household population. However, because the institutionalized and homeless populations constitute such small proportions of the composite population (0.6% and 0.2%, respectively), their higher rates of needle sharing did not substantially raise the composite rate compared with the household rate (1.1% vs. 1.0%, respectively).

9.6 Discussion and Implications

An important underlying assumption for this study was that people in a metropolitan area can be found in one of the following living situations: (a) in households, (b) in homeless shelters or as homeless people living in nondomiciles, or (c) in institutions or group quarters (other than homeless shelters). Although the Institutionalized Study did not completely represent people in institutions (see Chapter 5), combining data from these nonhousehold populations with data from a household population provides nearly complete coverage of the overall population,

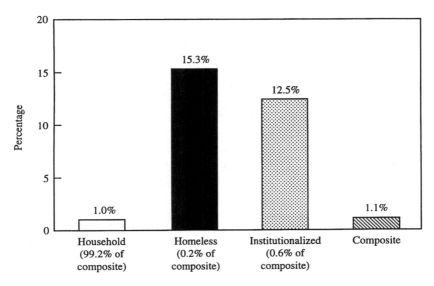

Figure 9.5. Prevalence of Lifetime Needle Sharing in the DC MSA Household, Homeless and Transient, Institutionalized, and Composite Populations

SOURCE: Household data are from the 1991 National Household Survey on Drug Abuse: DC MSA. Homeless data are from the 1991 DC*MADS Homeless and Transient Population Study. Data on institutionalized persons are from the 1991 DC*MADS Institutionalized Study.

NOTE: Composite population includes the combined household, homeless and transient, and institutionalized populations.

and especially of those population subgroups that might be more likely to use drugs.

9.6.1 Prevalence Estimates

Combining data from household and nonhousehold populations resulted in prevalence estimates (i.e., percentages) that were only slightly higher than the estimates that were obtained from household data alone, even though these nonhousehold populations had relatively high rates of drug use. Adding data from nonhousehold populations also had relatively little effect on prevalence estimates within demographic subgroups for any illicit drug use, any alcohol use, and heavy alcohol use. These findings are not surprising considering the small size of the nonhousehold populations relative to the household population. Indeed, the impact of subpopulations on a combined population varies directly with the size of the subpopulations (see Swaim et al., 1997).

A different picture emerges, however, when examining *numbers* of users. Specifically, the composite population data yielded estimates of approximately 14,000 more illicit drug users, 9,000 more marijuana/hashish users, 11,000 more users of any form of cocaine, 9,000 more crack cocaine users, 3,000 more heroin users in the past year, and about 3,000 more needle users compared with the corresponding estimates for the household population. In addition, comparisons of the numbers of past year crack cocaine users and heroin users indicate that estimates based on household data alone would fail to capture about 25% of the past year crack cocaine users and 20% of the past year heroin users in the composite population. These findings suggest that data from the household population alone may yield somewhat conservative estimates of the *numbers* of users of illicit drugs, including marijuana/hashish, cocaine in any form, crack cocaine, and heroin in the past year.

9.6.2 Treatment and Other Service Needs

The higher estimates of the numbers of past year crack cocaine and heroin users based on composite data may be of particular interest because of the low rates of use of these substances in the household population. Furthermore, data from nonhousehold populations may be important to researchers and policymakers concerned about total counts rather than percentages, such as treatment providers trying to estimate the need or demand for services.

Even though rates of past year and past month drug use were relatively low among the household and composite populations, findings indicated considerably higher rates of use among people in selected institutions and among homeless people. Given the low percentage of the composite population coming from these two nonhousehold populations, the high rates of use among these two populations might be overlooked if data were reported only at a household or composite level. Furthermore, as noted in Chapters 4 and 5, in addition to high rates of drug use, members of the homeless and institutionalized populations reported numerous other medical, mental health, and social service needs (see also NIDA, 1993, 1994b). Thus, studies of these two nonhousehold populations are useful in their own right to identify problems and service needs among these special populations, even though these populations constitute a very small percentage of the composite population.

Examination of high-risk drug-using subgroups found that more than 50,000 people in the composite population used crack cocaine, heroin, or needles in the past year. To the extent that these drug-abusing subgroups are at increased risk for a variety of legal, medical, mental health, and other problems, these composite population data suggest that there is a fairly large high-risk subpopulation that may be in need of a variety of services. It further suggests that the size of this subpopulation is substantially larger than what would be estimated based on household data alone. Moreover, the finding that nonhousehold populations, who account for less than 1% of the composite population, account for one fifth to one third of the past year crack cocaine, heroin, and needle users confirms that these drug-using subgroups are disproportionately found in nonhousehold populations.

Findings from this study underscore a potential limitation in reporting overall "macrolevel" estimates for a large population. Such general estimates can obscure high rates of drug use or related problems among subgroups who constitute only a small percentage of the overall population. If these problems go undetected, policymakers and service providers may fail to develop appropriate strategies to address them. Because these findings were observed in the DC MSA, strictly speaking, they cannot be generalized immediately to other metropolitan areas or to national estimates of drug use. As we observed in Chapter 3, however, the DC MSA appears typical of other large metropolitan areas. Thus, although the specific prevalence estimates vary somewhat across metropolitan areas, the general patterns of findings observed in the DC MSA are indicative of those likely to be observed in other metropolitan areas.

9.6.3 Research Implications

Assuming that similar findings were observed in other metropolitan areas, decisions about the importance of including nonhousehold populations in future epidemiological surveys of drug use depend on the aims of the studies. If the study's aim is strictly to estimate percentages of persons who have used various drugs during different time periods, then the findings here suggest that coverage of the household population may be sufficient. The additional time, effort, and resources necessary to obtain permission to interview nonhousehold respondents, and to collect and analyze the data, are likely to yield little improvement over the household population prevalence estimates. If, however, the aims include estimating the size of the drug-abusing population or conducting more detailed examination of high-risk behaviors, such as crack cocaine, heroin, or needle use, important subgroups of drug abusers are likely to be missed without the inclusion of nonhousehold populations. In particular, efforts to assess the need for substance abuse treatment or other services would underestimate the extent of need if relevant information is not gathered from these nonhousehold populations.

Overall, this study demonstrates the feasibility of combining data from coordinated surveys of drug use among household and nonhousehold populations in a metropolitan area to produce prevalence estimates that cover a broader population. Combining data from household, institutionalized, and homeless and transient populations offers key insights about the strengths and limitations of the coverage from the household population on prevalence rates of drug use, estimated numbers of drug users, and drug use behaviors.

References

Appendix G: Combining Household, Homeless, and Institutionalized Data. (1998). (Available on the World Wide Web at http://www.sagepub.com/bray_druguse.htm)

Association of State and Territorial Health Officials. (1988). *Intravenous drug use and HIV transmission: Recommendations by the ASTHO committee on HIV*. Washington, DC: Author.

Bachman, J. G., Wadsworth, K. N., O'Malley, P. M., Johnston, L. D., & Schulenberg, J. E. (1997). *Smoking, drinking, and drug use in young adulthood: The impacts of new freedoms and new responsibilities*. Mahwah, NJ: Lawrence Erlbaum.

Bray, R. M., Camlin, C. S., Kroutil, L. A., Rounds-Bryant, J. L., Bonito, A. J., & Apao, W. (1997). *Use of alcohol and illicit drugs and need for treatment among the Vermont household population: 1995* (technical report prepared by Research Triangle Institute and Vermont Office of Alcohol and Drug Abuse Programs). Rockville, MD: Center for Substance Abuse Treatment.

Bray, R. M., Kroutil, L. A., Luckey, J. W., Wheeless, S. C., Iannacchione, V. G., Anderson, D. W., Marsden, M. E., & Dunteman, G. H. (1992). *1992 Worldwide Survey of Substance Abuse and Health Behaviors Among Military Personnel*. Research Triangle Park, NC: Research Triangle Institute.

Bray, R. M., Kroutil, L. A., Wheeless, S. C., Marsden, M. E., Bailey, S. L., Fairbank, J. A., & Harford, T. C. (1995). *1995 Department of Defense Survey of Health Related Behaviors*

Among Military Personnel (RTI/6019-6). Research Triangle Park, NC: Research Triangle Institute.

Brown, B. S., & Beschner, G. M. (Eds.). (1993). *Handbook on risk of AIDS: Injection drug users and sexual partners.* Westport, CT: Greenwood.

Centers for Disease Control. (1987, March 17). Antibody to human deficiency virus in female prostitutes. *Morbidity and Mortality Weekly Report*, pp. 157-161.

Centers for Disease Control. (1989, March 17). Update: Acquired immunodeficiency syndrome associated with intravenous-drug use—United States, 1988. *Morbidity and Mortality Weekly Report*, pp. 165-170.

Centers for Disease Control and Prevention. (1992a, August 28). Condom use among male injecting-drug users-New York City, 1987-1990. *Morbidity and Mortality Weekly Report*, pp. 617-620.

Centers for Disease Control and Prevention. (1992b, January). *HIV/AIDS surveillance report.* Atlanta: U.S. Department of Health and Human Services, Public Health Service.

Chaiken, J. M., & Chaiken, M. R. (1990). Drugs and predatory crime. In M. Tonry & J. Q. Wilson (Eds.), *Drugs and crime* (pp. 203-239). Chicago: University of Chicago Press.

Chavez, E. L., Edwards, R. W., & Oetting E. R. (1989). Mexican American and White American school dropouts' drug use, health status, and involvement in violence. *Public Health Reports, 104*, 595-604.

Chitwood, D. D. (1993). Epidemiology of crack use among injection drug users and sex partners of injection drug users. In B. S. Brown & G. M. Beschner (Eds.), *Handbook on risk of AIDS: Injection drug users and sexual partners* (pp. 155-169). Westport, CT: Greenwood.

Des Jarlais, D. C., Friedman, S. R., Novick, D. M., Sotheran, J. L., Thomas, P., Yancovitz, S. R., Mildvan, D., Weber, J., Kreek, M. J., Maslansky, R., Bartelme, S., Spira, T., & Marmor, M. (1989). HIV-1 infection among intravenous drug users in Manhattan, New York City, from 1977 through 1987. *Journal of the American Medical Association, 261*, 1008-1012.

Frieden, T. R., Sterling, T., Pablos-Mendez, A., Kilburn, J. O., Cauthen, G. M., & Dooley, S. W. (1993). The emergence of drug-resistant tuberculosis in New York City. *New England Journal of Medicine, 328*, 521-526.

Friedman, S. R., Des Jarlais, D. C., & Ward, T. P. (1993). Overview of the history of the HIV epidemic among drug injectors. In B. S. Brown & G. M. Beschner (Eds.), *Handbook on risk of AIDS: Injection drug users and sexual partners* (pp. 3-15). Westport, CT: Greenwood.

Geller, S. (1996, November). *Integrating results from the family of studies.* Paper presented at the State Needs Assessment & Resource Allocation Workshop, Washington, DC.

Haverkos, H. W., & Lange, W. R. (1990). Serious infections other than human immunodeficiency virus among intravenous drug abusers. *Journal of Infectious Diseases, 161*, 894-902.

Hunt, D. E. (1990). Drugs and consensual crimes: Drug dealing and prostitution. In M. Tonry & J. Q. Wilson (Eds.), *Drugs and crime* (pp. 159-202). Chicago: University of Chicago Press.

Johnson, B. D., Williams, T., Dei, K. A., & Sanabria, H. (1990). Drug abuse in the inner city: Impact on hard-drug users and the community. In M. Tonry & J. Q. Wilson (Eds.), *Drugs and crime* (pp. 9-67). Chicago: University of Chicago Press.

Johnston, L. D., & O'Malley, P. M. (1985). Issues of validity and population coverage in student surveys of drug use. In B. A. Rouse, N. J. Casual, & L. G. Richards (Eds.), *Self-report methods of estimating drug use: Meeting current challenges to validity* (NIDA

Research Monograph No. 57, ADM 85-1402, pp. 13-54). Rockville, MD: National Institute on Drug Abuse.

Johnston, L. D., O'Malley, P. M., & Bachman, J. G. (1997a). *Drug use among American high school seniors, college students and young adults, 1975-1995: Vol. 1. Secondary school students* (DHHS Publication No. NIH 97-4139). Rockville, MD: National Institute on Drug Abuse.

Johnston, L. D., O'Malley, P. M., & Bachman, J. G. (1997b). *Drug use among American high school seniors, college students and young adults, 1975-1995: Vol. 2. College students and young adults* (DHHS Publication No. NIH 97-4140). Rockville, MD: National Institute on Drug Abuse.

Lambert, E. Y. (Ed.). (1990). *The collection and interpretation of data from hidden populations* (NIDA Research Monograph 98). Rockville, MD: National Institute on Drug Abuse.

Mensch, B. S., & Kandel, D. B. (1988). Dropping out of high school and drug involvement. *Sociology of Education, 61*, 95-113.

National Institute on Drug Abuse. (1992). *Annual emergency room data: 1991: Data from the Drug Abuse Warning Network* (Statistical Series, Series I, No. 11-A, DHHS Publication No. ADM 92-1955). Rockville, MD: Author.

National Institute on Drug Abuse. (1993). *Prevalence of drug use in the Washington, DC, metropolitan area homeless and transient population: 1991* (Technical Report #2 under NIDA Contract No. 271-89-8340, Washington, DC, Metropolitan Area Drug Study, prepared by M. L. Dennis, R. Iachan, J. P. Thornberry, R. M. Bray, L. E. Packer, & G. S. Bieler, Research Triangle Institute). Rockville, MD: Author.

National Institute on Drug Abuse. (1994a). *Prevalence of drug use in the Washington, DC, metropolitan area household and nonhousehold populations: 1991* (Technical Report #8 under NIDA Contract No. 271-89-8340, Washington, DC, Metropolitan Area Drug Study, prepared by R. M. Bray, L. A. Kroutil, S. C. Wheeless, M. E. Marsden, & L. E. Packer, Research Triangle Institute). Rockville, MD: Author.

National Institute on Drug Abuse. (1994b). *Prevalence of drug use in the Washington, DC, metropolitan area institutionalized population: 1991* (Technical Report #4 under NIDA Contract No. 271-89-8340, Washington, DC, Metropolitan Area Drug Study, prepared by D. Cantor, G. H. Gaertner, & L. Keil, Westat, Inc., & R. M. Bray, Research Triangle Institute). Rockville, MD: Author.

Selwyn, P. A., Hartel, D., Lewis, V. A., Schoenbaum, E. E., Vermund, S. H., Klein, R. S., Walker, A. T., & Friedland, G. H. (1989). A prospective study of the risk of tuberculosis among intravenous drug users with human immunodeficiency virus infection. *New England Journal of Medicine, 320*, 545-550.

Substance Abuse and Mental Health Services Administration. (1993a). *Estimates from the Drug Abuse Warning Network: 1992 estimates of drug-related emergency room episodes* (Advance Report No. 4). Rockville, MD: Author.

Substance Abuse and Mental Health Services Administration. (1993b). *National Household Survey on Drug Abuse: Main findings 1991* (DHHS Publication No. SMA 93-1980). Rockville, MD: Author.

Substance Abuse and Mental Health Services Administration. (1996). *National Household Survey on Drug Abuse: Main findings 1994* (DHHS Publication No. SMA 96-3085). Rockville, MD: Author.

Swaim, R. C., Beauvais, F., Chavez, E. L., & Oetting, E. R. (1997). The effect of school dropout rates on estimates of adolescent substance use among three racial/ethnic groups. *American Journal of Public Health, 87*, 51-55.

Turner, C. F., Miller, H. G., & Moses, L. E. (Eds.). (1989). *AIDS: Sexual behavior and intravenous drug abuse*. Washington, DC: National Academy Press.

U.S. General Accounting Office. (1993). *Drug use measurement: Strengths, limitations, and recommendations for improvement* (Report prepared for the Chairman, Committee on Government Operations, U.S. House of Representatives, GAO/PEMD-93-18). Washington, DC: Author.

U.S. Senate. (1990). *Hard-core cocaine addicts: Measuring and fighting the epidemic* (S. Rep. No. 6, 101st Cong., May 10, Committee on Judiciary). Washington, DC: Government Printing Office.

Weisner, C., & Schmidt, L. (1995). The community epidemiology laboratory: Studying alcohol problems in community and agency-based populations. *Addiction, 90*, 329-341.

Weisner, C., Schmidt, L., & Tam, T. (1995). Assessing bias in community-based prevalence estimates: Towards an unduplicated count of problem drinkers and drug users. *Addiction, 90*, 391-405.

10 Implications of Findings for Policy and Research

Robert M. Bray
Mary Ellen Marsden

This book has documented the prevalence, correlates, and consequences of alcohol and other drug use among household and
nonhousehold populations in the DC metropolitan statistical area (MSA).
The Washington, DC, Metropolitan Area Drug Study (DC*MADS),
described in these chapters, has been the first to examine all types of
people in a metropolitan area with the goal of assessing the full extent
of the drug abuse problem. The study included people who resided in
households and institutions, those who were homeless and transient,
adult and juvenile offenders, drug treatment clients, and new mothers
who had just given birth to live infants. The inclusion of hard-to-reach
and less frequently studied populations (homeless and transient persons, institutionalized persons), along with more frequently studied
populations (household residents), under the umbrella of a single integrated study is one of the major contributions of DC*MADS. Much

information about drug use prevalence and patterns is drawn from studies of household populations, but that information is incomplete.

This chapter summarizes key findings from the six population studies included in DC*MADS, identifies major themes emerging from the findings, discusses policy and program implications of the findings, and considers issues needing further research.

10.1 Summary of Findings and the Issue of Generalizability

DC*MADS findings from the collection of studies on household and nonhousehold populations in the DC MSA offer insights into the nature of the multifaceted drug problem confronting metropolitan areas. Selected key findings are noted briefly below, but readers are urged to examine the earlier chapters in this book for a more complete discussion and understanding of the findings for each of the subpopulations examined. The question of generalizability also is addressed.

10.1.1 Key Findings

The DC oversample of the National Household Survey on Drug Abuse (NHSDA) in 1991 provides the context to examine research findings from the other subpopulations included in the DC MSA. Findings are summarized in Chapters 3 and 9 of this book and are fully described in two DC*MADS reports for the National Institute on Drug Abuse (NIDA, 1992, 1994b). The findings indicated that many members of the DC household population had used illicit drugs: about 40% in their lifetimes, 12% in the past year, and nearly 6% in the past month. About three fourths had consumed alcohol in the past year and more than half in the past month. These rates of use of illicit drugs and alcohol were similar to those in other large metropolitan areas in the United States, as shown in Chapter 3 (see also Substance Abuse and Mental Health Services Administration [SAMHSA], 1996). Although there was a pattern for both past year and past month rates of use for most drugs to be somewhat higher in DC than in the Maryland or Virginia parts of the DC MSA, most of the differences were not statistically significant. Use of any illicit drug, marijuana/hashish, and crack cocaine tended to be higher in low socioeconomic status (SES) areas than in other SES areas in the urbanized area of the DC MSA, but these differences generally were not significant. Although rates of illicit drug use were not negligible in the household population, they were considerably higher in each of the subpopulations considered in the DC*MADS project, as discussed below. Together, these findings reveal the divergence of rates of illicit drug use among the various population segments and also suggest that household data, if used alone, are likely to underestimate the number of users in the general population.

The Homeless and Transient Population Study offers insights about the methodological challenges of studying the homeless population, the characteristics of homeless people, the prevalence and correlates of substance abuse, and the co-occurring problems and service utilization of this small but vulnerable population. Findings from this study are summarized in Chapters 4 and 9 of this book and are fully described in two DC*MADS reports for NIDA (NIDA, 1993, 1994b). The findings indicated that estimates of the population size vary considerably because of differences in definitions, methodology, and the unit of measurement (e.g., unique people or person-service contacts). This study estimated that about 10,000 homeless and transient people were in the DC MSA based on samples from shelters, streets, encampments, and soup kitchens. Homeless and transient people showed high rates of drug use, alcohol use, needle use, and symptoms of dependence. Substance use generally was lowest in shelters (the focus of much research on homelessness) and highest in soup kitchens; substance use also was higher among people who were intermittently homeless and at risk of homelessness than among those newly or chronically homeless. Indeed, as discussed in Chapter 4, drug use has been identified as one of the antecedents of homelessness. More than half (58%) of the homeless people were past year users of illicit drugs, more than one fourth were heavy drinkers, one in seven were injection drug users, more than half were dependent on illicit drugs, and more than three fourths were dependent on alcohol. In this homeless population, current drug users were more likely than past drug users and nonusers to report drug- and alcohol-related problems, mental health problems, drug-related illnesses (human immunodeficiency virus [HIV], acquired immune deficiency syndrome [AIDS], sexually transmitted diseases [STDs], hepatitis), and illegal activity and illegal income/expenses. They also were more likely to have used soup kitchens, to have been in substance abuse or mental health treatment, and to have relied on emergency medical services. Although homeless people constituted only a small fraction of the general DC population and of people who used drugs, they represented a significant segment of hard-core drug users both in and out of treatment. Finally, homeless people often were underserved and, based on their self-reports of substance use, treatment history, and treatment need, may require a service system that allows for considerable variation in the types and duration of required services.

The Institutionalized Study provides the most comprehensive picture to date of substance use, related problems, and service utilization among institutionalized persons, including residents of correctional facilities, psychiatric facilities, and homes for dependent and neglected children and adolescents. Findings from this study are summarized in Chapters 5 and 9 of this book and are fully described in two DC*MADS reports (NIDA, 1994b, 1994c). The findings showed that use of drugs and alcohol was common among the institutionalized population prior to institutionalization. About half (49.9%) had used drugs during the past year (when a substantial portion of time was outside an institution), and two out of three had consumed alcohol during this same period. A particularly important finding was that drug use continued after admission to an institution for nearly 1 in 10 residents and can be viewed as a factor contributing to institutionalization. Indeed, many members of the institutionalized population were incarcerated or committed because of their drug use. The institutionalized population had high rates of problems associated with the use of illicit drugs and alcohol, and these problems were more serious among the groups using drugs more heavily. Many residents were in need of substance abuse treatment both while institutionalized and prior to institutionalization, when their rates of drug and alcohol use were notably higher, but they often were unable to pay for it and consequently were less likely to receive it. A substance use typology indicated that because both alcohol and drugs were used substantially, a combined drug *and* alcohol treatment regimen was likely to be required. Most residents of institutions reported that they eventually returned to the household population, but that they have substantial service needs prior to and during institutionalization.

Data from the Adult Criminal Offenders Study and Juvenile Offenders Study help elucidate our understanding of the relationship between drug use and offending behavior for offenders who have been convicted and subsequently incarcerated. Findings from these studies are summarized in Chapter 6 of this book and are described in detail in a DC*MADS report (NIDA, 1995b). The findings showed that convicted offenders were heavy drug users. About 54% of adult offenders and 50% of juvenile offenders had used illicit drugs in the past year. Drugs played a significant role in the commission of property and violent crimes; for adult offenders, nearly 4 in 10 committed their last property and violent crimes for some type of drug-related reason, whereas for juvenile offenders about 1 in 5 committed a violent crime and 1 in 10 a property crime for a drug-related reason. More than 40% of violent crimes and 50% of the property crimes committed by adults were preceded by use of a drug (alcohol being used most commonly and crack cocaine making up a substantial portion of the illicit drug use). Half of the adult drug users reported that they would not have committed the crime if they had not taken the drug (i.e., approximately 20% of the convicted incarcerated population). Although drugs were associated with predatory crime, the majority of these crimes were *not* linked to involvement with drugs, which suggests that it will require more than reducing drug use to reduce significantly the high levels of crime in the United States.

The Current Treatment Client Characteristics Study provides important information about the prevalence of drug abuse and its consequences and co-occurring problems among a population of known drug abusers: drug abuse treatment clients. Findings from this study are summarized in Chapter 7 of this book and are described in detail in a DC*MADS report (NIDA, 1994a). The findings showed that those entering drug treatment used many types of drugs and typically had a long history of use that varied by treatment modality. Virtually all had used illicit drugs during the past year, and alcohol use also was nearly universal. Patterns of abuse changed in the decade prior to DC*MADS, and cocaine (including crack) had replaced heroin as the most widely used drug among newly admitted treatment clients in the DC MSA. Studying a treatment population permitted examination of issues related to heroin and heavy cocaine use, which are both relatively uncommon behaviors in the household population, and provided an opportunity to improve understanding of the characteristics of these users, patterns and context of drug use, consequences, and comorbid conditions. Not surprisingly, drug treatment clients had a wide range of health and human service needs along with problems of drug abuse. To address these needs, effective treatment programs may need to provide psychological, vocational, educational, medical, and social services or effective linkages with other multifaceted programs in addition to treating substance use problems.

The Drug Use and Pregnancy Study examined the prevalence, demographic and reproductive correlates, and medical problems associated with illicit drug, alcohol, and cigarette use during pregnancy. Findings from this study are summarized in Chapter 8 of this book and are described in detail in a DC*MADS report (NIDA, 1995a). The findings indicated that during the past year, more than 15% of DC-resident women who delivered liveborn infants in DC hospitals used illicit drugs. Approximately one in seven new mothers used illicit drugs during pregnancy, with crack cocaine being their drug of choice, and about one in five new mothers used alcohol or smoked cigarettes during pregnancy. The odds of having a low birthweight baby (fewer than 2,500 grams or 5 pounds, 8 ounces) relative to a normal birthweight baby were more than three times as high for smokers as for nonsmokers. The odds of a *very* low birthweight infant (fewer than 1,500 grams or 3 pounds, 5 ounces) relative to having a normal birthweight infant were nearly 2.5 times as high among women who used illicit drugs than among those who did not. Infants whose mothers had not received prenatal care (or only prenatal care in the third trimester) were about twice as likely to be low birthweight or preterm as were infants whose mothers received prenatal care in the first or second trimesters of pregnancy.

The Household and Nonhousehold Populations Study contributes to our understanding of the drug problem by combining data from household, homeless and transient, and institutionalized populations to yield estimates of the extent of the problem in the total civilian population. Findings from this study, as mentioned earlier, are given in Chapter 9 of this book and in NIDA (1994b). The findings showed that data from studies can be readily and meaningfully combined if the studies are designed to include comparable measures and if field periods occur in close proximity. Estimates of the prevalence of past year illicit drug use in the composite population (12.0%) were only slightly higher than estimates based on household data alone (11.7%), a finding attributable to the small size of the nonhousehold populations relative to the household population. Estimates of the *numbers* of users, however, were significantly larger in the composite population, accounting for more than 14,000 more people than in the household population. This finding suggests (as discussed in more detail below) that data from the household population alone will yield conservative estimates of the *numbers* of illicit drug users.

10.1.2 Generalizability of Findings

Although the DC*MADS findings are of considerable interest in their own right, the question arises about the extent to which these findings are applicable to other large metropolitan areas. An underlying assumption of this book (see Chapter 2) has been that many (although clearly not all) findings observed in the DC MSA as part of the DC*MADS project are likely to be observed in most other large metropolitan areas throughout the country. The key issue underlying this assertion is whether the studies in the project have high external validity (see Cook & Campbell, 1979; Runkel & McGrath, 1972), such that findings are generalizable beyond the specific conditions observed in the DC MSA to other metropolitan areas of the country.

Two key features of the studies described in earlier chapters of this book suggest that, indeed, many findings can be generalized to other metropolitan areas. First, all the studies in the DC*MADS project included rigorous study designs that used probabilistic sampling procedures, a set of comparable measures across instruments, and sensitive and effective interviewing techniques that included assurances of confidentiality. Data were collected in field settings among the populations of interest, and the studies had reasonably high response rates. Second, there are numerous commonalities between the DC MSA and other large metropolitan areas in the types of people and problems they encounter, including substance use, homelessness, institutionalization, crime, and unemployment. This should not be interpreted to mean that we expect to see no differences between findings from studies fielded in DC*MADS and findings from similar studies conducted in other metropolitan areas. It is almost certain that there will be some variation in substance use rates for specific subpopulations because of both sampling variation and variation resulting from unique features of metropolitan areas. The important point, however, is that the basic patterns of results observed in DC*MADS—including the overall type and range of problems—are typical of those likely to be observed in other metropolitan areas.

To illustrate, rates of substance abuse in the household population are expected to be highly similar across metropolitan areas (see Chapter 3). For the homeless and transient population, relatively high rates of drug use are expected, along with a wide range of problems that include a variety of physical, mental, financial, and legal difficulties. For the institutionalized population, relatively high rates of substance use are expected while residents are outside institutions, with much less use while they are in institutions, although more use still is expected than among persons in the household population. Similar to homeless and transient people, institutionalized persons also are expected to experience substantial behavioral, health, and psychological problems requiring treatment, but they are unlikely to have such resources as insurance to get the care they would need outside an institution.

10.2 Emerging Themes

In reviewing the prior chapters and distilling findings across the subpopulation studies, three themes emerge. First, drug use affects all segments of the population. It is not only inner-city residents and youth who use drugs. Second, household estimates do not provide a total picture of the drug problem. Although household data are the basis for most of our prevalence estimates of drug use, prevalence is substantially higher in nonhousehold populations. Finally, drug use exerts a profound burden on our service delivery system. Drug users are a multiple-problem population and are high users of health care, drug treatment, social services, and other types of services.

10.2.1 Drug Use Affects All Segments of the Population

The first theme emerging from the DC*MADS findings is that all segments of the population—in both household and nonhousehold settings—show some degree of involvement in drug use. Of course, to combat and deal with the drug problem, service providers and policymakers must first be aware of its magnitude and the extent to which different segments are affected. Findings briefly noted above and re-ported in earlier chapters show that drug use and related problems among household and nonhousehold populations differed both quanti-tatively and qualitatively. Rates of drug use among persons in house-holds were substantially lower (although not negligible) than those among nonhousehold populations. Rates of any illicit drug use in the past year were 12% for the household population, compared with 58% for the homeless and transient population, 50% for the institutionalized population, 54% for adult offenders, and 50% for juvenile offenders.

These large differences in rates among household and nonhouse-hold populations appear to reflect different patterns of use, different drug preferences, and perhaps different types of drug users. Among the household population, marijuana/hashish was the drug of choice, whereas among nonhousehold populations, cocaine (primarily crack cocaine) was the drug used most commonly. Members of the household population also were much less likely than those in nonhousehold populations to use hallucinogens, heroin, and psychotherapeutics for nonmedical purposes. Rates of any alcohol use across household and nonhousehold populations tended to be fairly comparable, but heavy alcohol use was more common among nonhousehold populations. For example, approximately 4% of household members drank heavily in the past month, compared with about 28% of homeless and transient people.

Not only were persons in the household population less likely to use drugs, but they also used fewer drugs and experienced fewer prob-lems from use than did those in nonhousehold populations. These data are consistent with a characterization of the household population as recreational or occasional users (see discussion by Bachman, Wadsworth, O'Malley, Johnston, & Schulenberg, 1997, pp. 153-154). Of course, al-though this characterization may be accurate in general among house-hold residents, it should not be interpreted to mean that all drug users in households were casual or recreational users. Indeed, as was shown in Chapter 1, examination of trends in crack cocaine use from the NHSDA identified both occasional and weekly users and showed that occasional use was declining, but weekly use generally was flat and nonfluctuating. It is important to recognize, however, that despite the overall picture of declining crack cocaine use among the household population, the number of occasional users is much larger than the number of weekly users (see also Gfroerer & Brodsky, 1993). In contrast to the preponderance of occasional users residing in households, persons in nonhousehold populations studied here were more likely to be regular or chronic users, to report use of (and possibly have addictions to) hard-core drugs such as heroin, and to experience a wide range of financial, emotional, and physical problems associated with their use. Many committed crimes to help support their drug habits.

One possible explanation for the differences in substance use rates among nonhousehold and household populations may be the variation in their demographic characteristics. Nonhousehold populations comprised demographic subgroups who were at higher risk of use (i.e., persons who were likely to be younger, single, and male, and to have less education). Nonhousehold populations tended to be aged 26 or older, black, male, and single, and to have a high school education or less, whereas the household population tended to be aged 35 or older, white, and equally likely to be female or male, and to have some college experience. Despite the plausibility of demographic differences as a possible explanation for varying rates of use, exploratory analyses indicated that this was not a sufficient explanation. Indeed, comparisons of rates of illicit drug use *within* demographic subgroups (i.e., analyses that partially controlled for demographic variation) for household and homeless and transient populations (NIDA, 1993) still showed that rates of illicit drug use were consistently much higher among nonhousehold populations, often by several orders of magnitude. For example, the age-specific rates of past month use of any illicit drug among persons 12 to 25 years old were 21% in the homeless population and 10% in the household population; among persons 26 to 34 years old, the rates were 44% and 9%, respectively, and for those 35 years of age or older, the rates were 31% and 3%, respectively.

The precise factors accounting for differences in substance use between household and nonhousehold populations are not known but plausibly may be associated with a broad array of variables. These variables include differences in perceptions of the risks of drug use, attitudes about drug use, and perceived norms about the acceptability of drug use. The variables also include a range of personal problems, including mental and physical health problems, unemployment and income problems, poor self-concept, and a fatalistic outlook engendered by lack of opportunities.

Research from the Monitoring the Future Survey found that trends in use among high school seniors over a 20-year period were closely associated with perceptions that drug use was risky and norms indicating disapproval of illicit drug use (Bachman, Johnston, & O'Malley, 1990; Bachman et al., 1997). These findings also are consistent with a large body of literature showing that behavior is strongly influenced by attitudinal and normative factors (e.g., Ajzen & Fishbein, 1980; Cook, Lounsbury, & Fontenelle, 1980; Fishbein & Ajzen, 1975). Substance use itself may help perpetuate a vicious cycle that compounds other problems and contributes to people living in settings outside households. Indeed, substance use may be the key reason that many are living outside household settings. Homelessness, for example, may occur because the substance user has lost his or her job and had serious problems with family relationships. Other substance users may have been incarcerated for crimes they committed under the influence of or associated with drug use.

Persistent differences in perceptions, attitudes, norms, and personal problems can result in notably different experiences and perhaps, at the extreme, even different cultures associated with drug use. Indeed, the dramatic differences in rates of drug use between household and nonhousehold populations are consistent with a vivid description and characterization by Gerstein and Green (1993) of two different worlds of drug use:

> In one world, that of relatively low-intensity consumption (drug *use*) among individuals who can be found in schools and households, drug experience is self-reported more frequently by the wealthy than the less wealthy and by whites than Hispanics or blacks. In this world, there have been steady and cumulatively very marked declines in the prevalence of marijuana use since the late 1970s and of cocaine since the middle 1980s, and heroin use is so rare as to be barely measurable. In another world, that of emergency rooms, morgues, drug clinics, juvenile detention centers, jails, and prisons, in which indicators of intensive drug consumption (*abuse* and *dependence*) are collected, the poor predominate, blacks and Hispanics appearing in numbers much higher than their household or school proportions; marijuana and heroin use are common (though less so in some areas than in the 1970s); and cocaine use increased explosively throughout the 1980s and simply leveled off at high levels in the 1990s. (p. 2)

To a large extent, these two different types of users are captured by people from household and nonhousehold populations, respectively. It also appears that substance use and housing settings tend to perpetuate a vicious cycle. On one hand, drug and alcohol use contributes to living outside households, whereas on the other hand, living outside households also perpetuates drug and alcohol use.

10.2.2 Household Estimates
Do Not Provide a Total Picture

A second key theme that emerges from DC*MADS is that nonhousehold populations make an important contribution to an overall understanding of substance use behavior in the general population beyond what can be learned from household data. A basic assumption underlying the DC*MADS research is that the general civilian population in a metropolitan area (or any geographical area, including the nation as a whole) comprises the household population, the homeless and transient population, and the institutionalized population. All other populations are subsets of one of these foundation populations. For example, the new mothers studied here are largely household residents, and the offenders are part of the institutionalized population. Thus, combining data from these three foundation populations provides a reasonable picture of the general civilian population to the extent that there is good coverage of the foundation populations. Overall, DC*MADS provided broad coverage of the foundation populations with regard to drug use despite the omission of some groups from the Institutionalized Study; omitted institutions, such as nursing homes, were relatively unimportant with regard to substance use behaviors (see Chapter 5 and NIDA, 1994c).

Without question, the household population is by far the largest component of the general population and dwarfs the nonhousehold components by its sheer size. Consequently, studies attempting to examine the drug problem regularly gather and use household data as the primary barometer of substance use and related problems. Although most would not fault this approach, findings from DC*MADS clearly point out that household data considered alone may lead researchers to different conclusions than would be reached using data from a more inclusive population. Even though household data closely approximate *percentage* estimates of substance use prevalence in the composite population, they can significantly underestimate the *numbers* of substance users in the composite population. Specifically, for the DC MSA, the composite population data yielded estimates of approximately 14,000 more illicit drug users and about 3,000 more needle users compared with the corresponding estimates for the household population. In addition, analyses indicated that estimates based on household data alone would fail to capture about 25% of the past year crack cocaine users and 20% of the past year heroin users in the composite population.

Not only were members of nonhousehold populations more likely than those in the household population to show substantially higher rates of substance use, but they also were much more likely to experience drug-related problems (see Chapters 3 through 5). Additionally, members of the homeless and institutionalized populations reported numerous other medical, mental health, and social service needs (see also NIDA, 1993, 1994c). Information about the most accurate number of users and the type and range of problems is particularly important to researchers and policymakers, such as treatment providers, who are trying to estimate the need or demand for services. Even relatively small differences in percentages or counts can translate into substantial additional costs for governmental agencies and service providers.

Analyses of high-risk drug-using subgroups showed further evidence of the relative importance of nonhousehold populations. More than 50,000 people in the composite population used crack cocaine, heroin, or needles in the past year, and even though nonhousehold populations constituted less than 1% of the total, they accounted for between one fifth and one third of the past year crack cocaine, heroin, and needle users. Thus, these high-risk drug-using subgroups were disproportionately found in nonhousehold populations and were substantially larger than what would be estimated based on household data alone. Additionally, these subgroups are likely to be at increased risk for a variety of legal, medical, mental health, and other problems that require a range of services.

10.2.3 Drug Use Exerts a Burden on the Service Delivery System

The third emerging theme from DC*MADS concerns the burden and demands that drug users impose on the service delivery system. One of the important clear messages is that many users, especially those in the nonhousehold populations (homeless and transient, institutionalized, treatment clients), have multiple problems that co-occur with drug use and require attention, some of it immediate, if they are to make a successful transition back into mainstream society.

Findings showed that the homeless and transient population (see Chapter 4) had multiple needs for treatment and other services that add to the load on the service system. Homelessness appears to be related to a constellation of problems that create stress on health care, social service, and other resources and suggests that a wide range of services are needed for agencies serving this population. The somewhat elusive nature of the homeless population, however—as well as the fact that there are multiple pathways both into and out of homelessness and the cyclical pattern of shifting between homeless and household populations—complicates the delivery of services. It also helps to define the type of service system that may be needed to address problems of homeless people and points to some of the concerns of policymakers as they grapple with how to provide the services. For example, the broad range of problems and the variation in the types and duration of required services suggest that a flexible service system that offers different sets of services at different points in time may be needed to provide optimal assistance to homeless people. The issues become complicated, however, by policymakers' concerns about trade-offs between breadth and depth of services and the potential for clients to become dependent on the emergency system.

The finding that most homeless people move into and out of homelessness relatively quickly with minimal assistance and never return suggests that there is a need for a short-term (e.g., 1- to 7-day) emergency service with minimal requirements. By the time people have been homeless 30 days, there are likely to be individual or situational factors complicating their return to independence. This suggests that programs should begin the process of assessment and referral to other appropriate services somewhere between 7 and 30 days (or where the need is self-evident). When a person is chronically mentally ill, disabled, or elderly, a case manager or more extensive assistance program likely will be required. Substance abusers are at high risk of relapse to homelessness, but ironically, current policies often shun such people from shelters. This suggests a need for specialized services to handle homeless and transient substance abusers and for programs that also can handle comorbid mental and physical health problems, as well as families, children, and pregnant women. Additionally, both chronically and intermittently homeless people are likely to require assistance in obtaining long-term (preferably drug- and alcohol-free) housing for recovery.

The institutionalized population (see Chapter 5) also is a multiple-problem, high-service-using population. Even though most residents of institutions eventually return to the household population, they have substantial service needs prior to and during institutionalization. Similarly, by extension, incarcerated offenders (Chapter 6), who compose a substantial proportion of the institutionalized population, also have high service needs. Some of the needs of institutionalized residents are related to drug and alcohol use, but like homeless people, they also experience a variety of other health, financial, and emotional problems. Improved prevention and treatment programs may help decrease the numbers of people in institutions because drug and alcohol abuse contribute to people becoming institutionalized.

Institutions have a goal of *no* illicit drug or alcohol use while residents are under their care and custody. An equally important goal should be to provide services that give residents the tools and opportunities to curtail their use in noninstitutional settings because that is where most of their time is spent and where most use occurs. Giving institutionalized residents the tools to cope with drug and alcohol abuse outside the institution ultimately may make their return to institutionalization less likely because many residents are committed to institutions for crimes related to substance use or for substance abuse treatment.

Like homeless and institutionalized persons, drug treatment clients (see Chapter 7) have, in addition to problems of drug abuse, a wide range of health and human service needs. Drug abuse does not occur in isolation and is associated with a wide range of other problems that need attention but often fall outside the purview of services provided for drug treatment. This points to the need for broad-based treatment that addresses not only the individual's addiction but also the problems commonly co-occurring with abuse. Addressing these problems requires either treatment programs that provide psychological, vocational, educational, medical, and social services or effective linkages with other multifaceted programs.

Findings from the Drug Use and Pregnancy Study (see Chapter 8) document the benefits of prenatal care for women and their infants.

Infants whose mothers had not received prenatal care (or prenatal care only in the third trimester) were about twice as likely to be low birth-weight or preterm as infants whose mothers received prenatal care in the first or second trimesters of pregnancy. Findings also showed a connection between drug use and lack of prenatal care. Approximately one fourth of the DC-resident women who used illicit drugs during pregnancy received no prenatal care in the first or second trimester of their pregnancies. These data suggest the importance of continued outreach efforts and other initiatives to reach drug-using pregnant women in DC and provide them with prenatal care and other needed services. Furthermore, the association between illicit drug use during pregnancy and inadequate prenatal care may suggest the need for better linkage of prenatal care and drug treatment services.

Thus, it seems clear that alcohol and drug use is associated with a range of problems that have a strong impact on the social service system in metropolitan cities and communities and add to the burden of services that these systems provide. Because nonhousehold populations experience a wide range of problems, some of which are connected to or exacerbated by drug use, it seems likely that these populations will continue to place heavy demands on the service system. Finding ways to help prevent or reduce drug use among these populations not only will benefit the individuals but also holds promise for providing a measure of relief to the service system.

10.3 Implications for Policymakers and Service Providers

Information about the prevalence, correlates, and consequences of illicit drug use and alcohol use among segments of a population in one metropolitan area or in the United States as a whole can provide the basis for decisions about resource allocation among policy alternatives or about the types of services needed by segments of that population. Epidemiological data on drug and alcohol use and related problems of the nature reported in this book can be used to monitor overall trends in use, changes in the use of specific drugs, and the distribution of use and nature of use in specific populations in a geographic area. These types of data can be used to guide policy decisions about an array of questions concerning the magnitude of needed resources and the most effective allocation of those resources. What is the size of the substance-abusing population, what treatment capacity is needed, and which segments of the population are heavy drug users and most in need of treatment? Are alcohol and drug treatment services needed in the same programs? What other types of services are needed in substance abuse treatment programs (e.g., health care, psychological counseling, employment counseling and assistance)? What services are needed for street populations or for those who are institutionalized? To which groups in which areas should services be targeted?

The set of studies in the DC*MADS project has documented the fact that illicit drug use and heavy alcohol use are problems in all segments of the population, although they are much more pervasive in nonhousehold populations than in the household population. Drug and alcohol abusers place a serious burden on the health care, social service, and criminal justice systems, and drug or alcohol use often is a contributing factor to becoming homeless or institutionalized. These findings suggest the need for a host of different types of programs directed at all segments of the population: prevention programs to delay or forestall use, intervention programs to help contain experimental or nonproblematic use from escalating, and intervention and treatment programs for those for whom drug abuse or alcohol use has become a significant problem that interferes with day-to-day functioning.

Expenditures for substance abuse prevention and treatment programs have grown rapidly in the past decade in response to an increasing recognition of the need to take action and because of growing public intolerance with substance abuse and its consequences. Huber, Pope, and Dayhoff (1994), for example, documented the more than doubling of national spending for alcoholism treatment between 1979 and 1989, from $1.6 billion to $3.8 billion. McCarty, Capitman, Hallfors, and Skwara (1997) cited total federal expenditures for alcohol and drug prevention and treatment of $8.4 billion, along with $548 million for research, in fiscal year 1998. State expenditures for prevention and treatment totaled about $1.8 billion in fiscal year 1995, and private foundation expenditures were about $39 million in fiscal year 1993.

Despite these substantial expenditures, drug and alcohol abuse continues to burden our nation and continues to require concerted action. Although drug and alcohol use have declined overall since the late 1970s, heavy alcohol and drug use have remained more stable and are threatening our cities. Use of heroin and methamphetamines, which results in increases in criminal activity, is increasing according to reports of medical examiners, emergency rooms, and drug treatment facilities (SAMHSA, 1997, pp. 30-31). These findings and those reported in this book indicate the need for continued high levels of public expenditures to combat drug and alcohol abuse and for more effective targeting of populations who are at high risk of developing problems related to drug and alcohol abuse.

Findings reported in this book demonstrate that nonhousehold populations are high users of health care, social service agencies, and the criminal justice system and yet have a great remaining unmet need for services. Drug and alcohol abuse carry with them multiple problems, ranging from medical problems to psychological problems, to problems getting and keeping employment. Several studies have documented the increasing intensity of psychological problems among drug abuse treatment clients that interfere with recovery (McLellan, Luborsky, O'Brien, Barr, & Evans, 1986; Rounsaville, Dolinsky, Babor, & Meyer, 1987). Information on service needs and service utilization presented here illuminate the types of services that are needed for specific subpopulations at particular points in time. For example, the nature of homelessness suggests the need for short-term emergency services for intermittently homeless persons as well as longer-term services for chronically homeless people. Substance abuse treatment may be provided effectively on an outreach basis for homeless and transient persons or within jails and prisons or other institutions with high proportions of substance abusers. The fact that about one fourth of DC-resident women who used illicit drugs during pregnancy received no prenatal care in the first or second trimester and were about twice as likely to have low birthweight or preterm infants as women who received prenatal care earlier in their pregnancies underscores the need to provide better linkage between prenatal care and drug treatment services. This linkage would help social and health service providers identify drug-using pregnant women and provide them with both prenatal and drug treatment care.

Similarly, improved linkages between health care and social service agencies and drug treatment providers can help to identify persons at high risk of becoming drug or alcohol dependent and provide needed services for the substance-abusing population once involved. Weisner and Schmidt (1993) showed that many types of health and social service agencies had a high proportion of alcohol and drug users and argued that this presents opportunities for identifying and referring substance abusers to treatment. DC*MADS researchers also found a high prevalence of drug and alcohol use in nontreatment populations, suggesting the need for more effective referral to treatment.

Once a substance user is in treatment, a broad variety of different types of services is needed to support his or her recovery. This includes services that focus specifically on the addiction, as well as services targeted toward related problems. The latter might include psychological counseling, medical examinations and other health services, employment counseling and services, and legal services to help foster recovery and a return to a productive life. "Wraparound" services, such as child care or assistance with transportation that enable participation in treatment, also may foster recovery by lengthening stays in treatment. Although the population of drug and alcohol abusers in treatment is in need of multiple types of services to support recovery, Etheridge, Craddock, Dunteman, and Hubbard (1995) found a marked decrease in the past decade in the number of services provided in treatment and a related increase in unmet service needs. This decrease in services is likely related to increasing pressures toward cost containment exerted by payors for substance abuse treatment, including managed care organizations (Marsden, 1996).

Drug and alcohol abuse continue to burden our nation's cities, as well as their health, social service, and criminal justice systems. Continued high levels of public expenditures are needed to combat the problems associated with substance abuse. Findings reported here suggest ways in which these expenditures can be more effectively targeted toward interventions that deliver needed services at critical times or toward delivering a wide range of services in treatment programs.

10.4 Implications for Future Studies

The DC*MADS project provides a broad-based picture of the prevalence, correlates, and consequences of illicit drug use and alcohol use within a large metropolitan area. Despite the depth of the project's contribution to our understanding of substance use, it raises a number of implications for new investigations. These include implications about populations and information that should be included in studies of drug use prevalence, about the utility of DC*MADS as a methodological model for new studies, and about issues in need of further study.

10.4.1 Implications for Prevalence Studies

A key question for future studies of drug use prevalence is whether the sample needs to include the homeless and transient and institutionalized populations in addition to the household population (i.e., the three foundation populations). The answer largely depends on the aims of the study (although it often may be dictated by practical considerations of study resources). If the primary aim is strictly to estimate percentages of persons who have used illicit drugs, then focusing on the household population may be sufficient. As noted in Chapter 9, adding nonhousehold populations to the household population resulted in only small increases in the percentage estimates (thought to be more accurate estimates) for the composite population compared with those obtained from the household population. For percentage estimates, this small increase in accuracy may not be worth the additional time, effort, and resources necessary to obtain the data from nonhousehold populations. If, however, the aims include estimating the size of the drug-abusing population or conducting more detailed examination of subsets of the composite population or of high-risk behaviors such as use of crack cocaine, heroin, or needles for drug injections, it is extremely important to include the nonhousehold populations. Important subgroups of drug abusers will be missed if nonhousehold populations are omitted. These can become very important to policymakers and program planners as the focus shifts from rates of any use to more recent use, use of needles, use of hard drugs, and dependence criteria.

The fact that estimates of service needs are based on *numbers* of people, not on *percentages*, clearly suggests the importance of including nonhousehold populations in prevalence studies of metropolitan areas. It also suggests that the major studies that serve as surveillance systems should be broadened to include these populations in sufficient numbers that separate estimates can be made for them. The NHSDA is probably the most prominent surveillance study used to track substance use in the United States. Beginning in the mid-1990s, its sampling approach was expanded to include homeless and transient people, but the survey still makes no attempt to include members of the institutionalized population. Despite including homeless people in the sampling frame, the selection procedures minimize the presence of people who are homeless and/or in nontraditional or unstable housing situations; thus, data are not available from the NHSDA to make independent estimates of rates of substance use among homeless and transient persons. It would be relatively easy, however, to modify the selection criteria to oversample this important population segment, at least those residing in emergency shelters and using soup kitchens.

Another implication for future prevalence studies concerns the relative breadth and depth of information that is collected. Typically, increasing breadth by exploring a larger number of issues is at odds with assessing fewer issues in more depth and detail because interviews generally need to be conducted within a relatively fixed amount of time to avoid problems of respondent fatigue and/or unwillingness to cooperate. Knowing estimates of drug prevalence is useful, but understanding the reasons for drug use or the conditions and other risk factors associated with use would provide insights needed to better address the problem. The studies conducted in DC*MADS tried to strike a balance between breadth and depth but, like many other studies, tended to give greater emphasis to breadth. Consequently, DC*MADS questionnaires did not include sufficient in-depth items to explain many observed phenomena. Thus, where possible, it would be beneficial for future studies to examine drug use issues in greater depth. For example, more information is needed on the frequency of drug use, patterns and context of use for both illicit drugs and alcohol, dependence, treatment history and effects, mental health needs and treatment, service utilization patterns, and conditions with unmet need.

10.4.2 DC*MADS as a Prototype

A basic objective of DC*MADS was to serve as a methodological prototype that researchers in other metropolitan areas could use in designing similar studies. To facilitate that use, the methods of the studies fielded in DC*MADS, including an assessment of their strengths and limitations, were described in detail, and the questionnaires were provided in the final technical reports for each of the studies. Even though study methods and questionnaires from DC*MADS are readily available to other researchers, the feasibility and advisability of conducting some or all of the studies in other metropolitan areas will depend on a number of factors. These include such considerations as the need for data that are specific to a given metropolitan area; findings that are available from other local, regional, or national studies; the scope of data that are needed; and the resources that are available to support the conduct of the research.

When new data are needed for other metropolitan areas, the most cost-effective method is to rely on findings from existing studies or, when feasible, to adjust the weights of the DC*MADS data or other data from studies at the national or state level to reflect local demographic characteristics. In addition to DC*MADS data that could be used, household data on substance use are available in each state from recent telephone surveys of the household population (e.g., Bray et al., 1997; Kroutil, Bray, Camlin, & Rounds-Bryant, 1997; Kroutil, Ducharme, et al., 1997; Kroutil, Federman, Akin, Rounds-Bryant, & Rachal, 1997). These telephone surveys were conducted as part of a large-scale effort sponsored by the Center for Substance Abuse Treatment (CSAT) to assess the need for treatment for alcohol and other drugs. Similarly, household data collected annually as part of the NHSDA may be able to be adapted for regional or metropolitan use. SAMHSA, the sponsoring agency, is giving consideration to expanding the NHSDA to provide state-level estimates. If done, this may provide even more useful prevalence data for the states than the CSAT-sponsored telephone surveys because it will mean broader coverage of all households in a state, not just those with telephones.

Despite the potential for adapting data from other sources to local conditions, this strategy may not be adequate for local needs, and primary data collection may be needed. When this is the case, DC*MADS may serve as a prototype for such studies and provide useful guidance on methodological and substantive issues. Even if there is sufficient interest, institutional support, and adequate resources to conduct new studies within a metropolitan area, it may not be feasible or necessary to replicate all the studies fielded in DC*MADS. One of the lessons learned from DC*MADS is that the critical substance use information about the population can be gleaned from data about the three foundation populations—household, homeless and transient, and institutionalized—without including all the other populations. Because household data are likely to be available from other sources, it may be possible to focus just on obtaining new data from homeless and transient populations and institutionalized populations. Even though this greatly simplifies the research task, there still will be substantial challenges in obtaining quality data from these latter two populations. These include acquiring sufficient backing from local policymakers to ensure that critical gatekeepers support the studies and facilitate access to the populations as well as taking steps to ensure the safety and well-being of interviewers. Thus, it is probably more realistic to think of DC*MADS as a prototype of selected studies that may be done elsewhere, but not as a prototype for the entire set of studies.

10.4.3 Issues for Further Research

Besides providing useful and informative data, the DC*MADS project also has raised many issues and questions in need of further study. These range from issues concerning specific population segments to broader questions spanning the entire population.

As discussed above, there were substantial numbers of drug users in both nonhousehold and household populations, although rates of use were much higher in nonhousehold populations. The findings in this book represent important first steps in furthering knowledge of such use by nonhousehold and composite populations; however, additional research is needed to expand our understanding of the characteristics of these users in both household and nonhousehold populations and the patterns, context, and consequences of their use. More in-depth assessment is needed of drug abusers who are not currently in treatment because treatment clients may represent a special group of users (Regier et al., 1993; Rounsaville & Carroll, 1991) and may offer a very different perspective about use patterns and prognosis for recovery than typical household members (e.g., Robins, Helzer, & Davis, 1975; Robins & Regier, 1991). Validation studies also are needed to assess the magnitude and possible effects of underreporting of highly sensitive behaviors, such as heroin use and needle use, particularly among the household population.

Many persons in the nonhousehold populations were using multiple substances and had co-occurring alcohol problems, mental health problems, and physical health problems that were also related to patterns of illegal activity, unemployment, income, and service utilization. More research is needed to understand relationships among these problems, to identify characteristics of persons most likely to display some or all of these problems and other outcomes, to begin to tease out the causal sequences among the problems and other outcomes, and to assess the effectiveness of prevention initiatives and treatment programs in addressing this array of issues.

More complete information is needed on housing characteristics and movement patterns of household and nonhousehold populations. Such studies can help identify the antecedents and structural issues related to the onset of homelessness and institutionalization and to address why some people have a single and fairly brief period of homelessness or institutionalization, whereas others remain in these settings for longer periods or experience multiple intermittent episodes. Such research also could have methodological implications for improving coverage of specific drug-abusing subgroups in household and/or nonhousehold populations.

In addition, related issues are in need of examination that were not studied in DC*MADS. These include issues ranging from effective prevention approaches for youth and young adults in household and nonhousehold populations to acquiring a better understanding of the workings of the drug economy and the dynamics of the drug trade among drug dealers. Newly emerging issues also need research, such as effects of tighter budgets and likely cutbacks in state funding on services to homeless and institutionalized persons. This is an issue of considerable importance in the wake of recently enacted welfare reform (see discussion in Chapter 4). Similarly, more study is needed of the effects of shifts to managed care on the availability of and access to services.

Of course, to address these research questions effectively, rigorous scientific studies of household, nonhousehold, and—where possible—composite populations will be needed. Such studies will require adequate resources and ample planning to carry them out and to develop useful population estimates.

10.5 Concluding Comments

Findings from each of the subpopulation studies in DC*MADS contribute to our understanding of the extent of illicit drug use and alcohol use in the total civilian population of a metropolitan area and its distribution among segments of that population. Although household surveys provide our basic information about illicit drug use, the magnitude of rates of use in nonhousehold populations reveals that household data alone are likely to be underestimates of the number of users. Furthermore, drug and alcohol use have contributed to the current status of many persons not residing in household settings (i.e., homeless and transient people and institutionalized persons). Although for most persons in those situations, the status is temporary and they return to a household residence, drug use often is implicated in becoming homeless or institutionalized. Indeed, drug use continues for many during the time that they are homeless or institutionalized. Thus, studies of segments of the population not typically covered in epidemiological surveys of drug use round out the view provided by household surveys alone. Because of continual changes in drug use habits and patterns of users, there is an ongoing need for high-quality data to monitor use and its impacts and to direct services toward the problem. The studies fielded during DC*MADS provide a useful prototype for future studies.

References

Ajzen, I., & Fishbein, M. (1980). *Understanding attitudes and predicting social behavior.* Englewood Cliffs, NJ: Prentice Hall.

Bachman, J. G., Johnston, L. D., & O'Malley, P. M. (1990). Explaining the recent decline in cocaine use among young adults: Further evidence that perceived risks and disapproval lead to reduced drug use. *Journal of Health and Social Behavior, 3,* 173-184.

Bachman, J. G., Wadsworth, K. N., O'Malley, P. M., Johnston, L. D., & Schulenberg, J. E. (1997). *Smoking, drinking, and drug use in young adulthood: The impacts of new freedoms and new responsibilities.* Mahwah, NJ: Lawrence Erlbaum.

Bray, R. M., Camlin, C. S., Kroutil, L. A., Rounds-Bryant, J. L., Bonito, A. J., & Apao, W. (1997). *Use of alcohol and illicit drugs and need for treatment among the Vermont household population: 1995* (prepared for Vermont Office of Alcohol and Drug Abuse Programs under Contract No. CSAT 270-94-0022). Rockville, MD: Center for Substance Abuse Treatment.

Cook, M. P., Lounsbury, J. W., & Fontenelle, G. A. (1980). An application of Fishbein and Ajzen's attitudes-subjective norms model to the study of drug use. *Journal of Social Psychology, 110*, 193-201.

Cook, T. D., & Campbell, D. T. (1979). *Quasi-experimentation: Design and analysis issues for field settings.* Chicago: Rand McNally.

Etheridge, R. M., Craddock, S. G., Dunteman, G. H., & Hubbard, R. L. (1995). Treatment services in two national studies of community-based drug abuse treatment programs. *Journal of Substance Abuse, 7*, 9-26.

Fishbein, M., & Ajzen, I. (1975). *Belief, attitude, intention, and behavior: An introduction to theory and research.* Reading, MA: Addison-Wesley.

Gerstein, D. R., & Green, L. W. (Eds.). (1993). *Preventing drug abuse: What do we know?* (Committee on Drug Abuse Prevention Research, Commission on Behavioral and Social Sciences and Education, National Research Council). Washington, DC: National Academy Press.

Gfroerer, J. C., & Brodsky, M. D. (1993). Frequent cocaine users and their use of treatment. *American Journal of Public Health, 83*, 1149-1154.

Huber, J. H., Pope, G. C., & Dayhoff, D. A. (1994). National and state spending on specialty alcoholism treatment: 1979 and 1989. *American Journal of Public Health, 84*, 1662-1666.

Kroutil, L. A., Bray, R. M., Camlin, C. S., & Rounds-Bryant, J. L. (1997). *Substance use and need for comprehensive treatment and services in North Carolina's adult household population: 1995* (final report prepared for the North Carolina Division of Mental Health, Developmental Disabilities and Substance Abuse Services under Contract No. CSAT 270-93-0005). Rockville, MD: Center for Substance Abuse Treatment.

Kroutil, L. A., Ducharme, L. J., Bonito, A. J., Vincus, A. A., Bray, R. M., Akin, D. R., & Walker, J. A. (1997). *Substance use and need for treatment: Findings from the 1996 South Dakota Household Telephone Survey* (prepared for the South Dakota Department of Human Services, Division of Alcohol and Drug Abuse, under Contract No. CSAT 270-95-0028; RTI/6528-10). Rockville, MD: Center for Substance Abuse Treatment.

Kroutil, L. A., Federman, E. B., Akin, D. R., Rounds-Bryant, J. L., & Rachal, J. V. (1997). *Use of alcohol and illicit drugs and need for treatment among Louisiana adult household residents: 1996* (prepared for the Louisiana Department of Health and Hospitals, Office of Alcohol and Drug Abuse, under Contract No. CSAT 94-0022/RTI/6142-01). Rockville, MD: Center for Substance Abuse Treatment.

Marsden, M. E. (1996). *A provider-level view of the delivery of alcohol treatment and prevention services: Final report. Panel on financing and organization.* Rockville, MD: National Institute on Alcohol Abuse and Alcoholism, National Advisory Council on Alcohol Abuse and Alcoholism.

McCarty, D., Capitman, J., Hallfors, D., & Skwara, K. C. (1997). *Who is doing what for the treatment and prevention of alcohol, tobacco, and other drug use, abuse, and dependence?* Princeton, NJ: Robert Wood Johnson Foundation.

McLellan, A. T., Luborsky, L., O'Brien, C. P., Barr, H. L., & Evans, F. (1986). Alcohol and drug abuse treatment in three different populations: Is there improvement and is it predictable? *American Journal of Drug and Alcohol Abuse, 12*, 101-120.

National Institute on Drug Abuse. (1992). *Prevalence of drug use in the DC metropolitan area household population: 1990* (Technical Report #1 under NIDA Contract No. 271-89-8340, Washington, DC, Metropolitan Area Drug Study, DHHS Publication No. ADM 92-1919, prepared by M. E. Marsden, R. M. Bray, A. C. Theisen, L. E. Packer, & J. M. Greene, Research Triangle Institute). Rockville, MD: Author.

National Institute on Drug Abuse. (1993). *Prevalence of drug use in the Washington, DC, metropolitan area homeless and transient population: 1991* (Technical Report #2 under NIDA Contract No. 271-89-8340, Washington, DC, Metropolitan Area Drug Study, prepared by M. L. Dennis, R. Iachan, J. P. Thornberry, R. M. Bray, L. E. Packer, & G. S. Bieler, Research Triangle Institute). Rockville, MD: Author.

National Institute on Drug Abuse. (1994a). *Current treatment client characteristics in the Washington, DC, metropolitan area: 1991* (Technical Report #5 under NIDA Contract No. 271-89-8340, Washington, DC, Metropolitan Area Drug Study, prepared by P. M. Flynn, J. W. Luckey, S. C. Wheeless, J. T. Lynch, L. A. Kroutil, & R. M. Bray, Research Triangle Institute). Rockville, MD: Author.

National Institute on Drug Abuse. (1994b). *Prevalence of drug use in the DC metropolitan area household and nonhousehold populations: 1991* (Technical Report #8 under NIDA Contract No. 271-89-8340, Washington, DC, Metropolitan Area Drug Study, prepared by R. M. Bray, L. A. Kroutil, S. C. Wheeless, M. E. Marsden, & L. E. Packer, Research Triangle Institute). Rockville, MD: Author.

National Institute on Drug Abuse. (1994c). *Prevalence of drug use in the DC metropolitan area institutionalized population: 1991* (Technical Report #4 under NIDA Contract No. 271-89-8340, Washington, DC, Metropolitan Area Drug Study, prepared by D. Cantor, G. H. Gaertner, & L. Keil, Westat, Inc., & R. M. Bray, Research Triangle Institute). Rockville, MD: Author.

National Institute on Drug Abuse. (1995a). *Prevalence of drug use among DC women delivering livebirths in DC hospitals: 1992* (Technical Report #7 under NIDA Contract No. 271-89-8340, Washington, DC, Metropolitan Area Drug Study, prepared by W. A. Visscher, R. M. Bray, L. A. Kroutil, D. A. Akin, M. A. Ardini, & J. P. Thornberry, Research Triangle Institute, & M. McCall, Westat, Inc.). Rockville, MD: Author.

National Institute on Drug Abuse. (1995b). *Prevalence of drug use in the DC metropolitan area adult and juvenile offender populations: 1991* (Technical Report #6 under NIDA Contract No. 271-89-8340, Washington, DC, Metropolitan Area Drug Study, prepared by D. Cantor, Westat, Inc.). Rockville, MD: Author.

Regier, D. A., Narrow, W. E., Rae, D. S., Manderscheid, R. W., Locke, B. Z., & Goodwin, F. K. (1993). The de facto US mental and addictive disorders service system: Epidemiologic Catchment Area prospective 1-year prevalence rates of disorders and services. *Archives of General Psychiatry, 50,* 85-94.

Robins, L. N., Helzer, J. E., & Davis, D. H. (1975). Narcotic use in southeast Asia and afterward. *Archives of General Psychiatry, 32,* 955-961.

Robins, L. N., & Regier, D. A. (1991). *Psychiatric disorders in America.* New York: Macmillan.

Rounsaville, B., & Carroll, K. (1991). Psychiatric disorders in treatment-entering cocaine abusers. In S. Schober & C. Schade (Eds.), *The epidemiology of cocaine use and abuse* (NIDA Research Monograph No. 110, DHHS Publication No. ADM 91-1787, pp. 227-251). Rockville, MD: National Institute on Drug Abuse.

Rounsaville, B. J., Dolinsky, Z. S., Babor, T. F., & Meyer, R. E. (1987). Psychopathology as a predictor of treatment outcome in alcoholics. *Archives of General Psychiatry, 44,* 505-513.

Runkel, P. J., & McGrath, J. E. (1972). *Research on human behavior.* New York: Holt, Rinehart, and Winston.

Substance Abuse and Mental Health Services Administration. (1996). *Substance abuse in states and metropolitan areas: Model based estimates from the 1991-1993 National Household Surveys on Drug Abuse. Summary report* (DHHS Publication No. SMA 96-3095). Rockville, MD: Author.

Substance Abuse and Mental Health Services Administration. (1997). *Preliminary results from the 1996 National Household Survey on Drug Abuse* (DHHS Publication No. SMA 97-3149). Rockville, MD: Author.

Weisner, C., & Schmidt, L. (1993). Alcohol and drug problems among diverse health and social service populations. *American Journal of Public Health, 83,* 824-829.

Index

About the Authors

Robert M. Bray, Ph.D., a senior research psychologist, is a principal investigator and project director at Research Triangle Institute with nearly 20 years of experience directing and analyzing complex surveys. His recent work has focused on the epidemiology of substance use and other health behaviors in civilian and military populations. For DC*MADS, he was overall project director, study leader for the Household and Nonhousehold Populations Study (see Chapters 3 and 9 of this book), and co-study leader for the Drug Use and Pregnancy Study (see Chapter 8). He also directed the 1982, 1985, 1988, 1992, and 1995 Worldwide Surveys of Substance Use and Health Behaviors Among U.S. Military Personnel; was coordinator of analytic reports for the 1988 and 1990 National Household Surveys on Drug Abuse; and conducted comparative analyses of military and civilian rates of substance use. He is currently directing a series of studies of various populations in several states assessing the need for substance abuse treatment services, including studies of household populations, homeless people, adolescents, students attending school, arrestees, and Native Americans. He also is principal investigator of two studies examining the health status, behaviors, and performance of military women and men. He has coauthored several chapters for other books, has published articles in a variety of journals, and is coeditor of *The Psychology of the Courtroom*. Dr. Bray is an ad hoc journal and grant reviewer and served on the Committee on Drug Use in the Workplace for the National Research

Council, Institute of Medicine. He received his doctorate in social psychology from the University of Illinois, Urbana-Champaign.

David Cantor, Ph.D., is a senior research associate with Westat, Inc., in Rockville, Maryland. He is currently conducting research on violence in schools, assisting in the design of a household survey to monitor the impact of recent changes in federal law to reform welfare (as well as other government programs), and designing a survey to measure the impact of federal medical savings accounts. For DC*MADS, he was study leader for the Adult Criminal Offenders Study and for the Juvenile Offenders Study (see Chapter 6 of this book). He also was a principal analyst and author for the Institutionalized Study. His research interests include the causes and consequences of predatory victimization, the relationship between drugs and crime, and methodological issues related to monitoring social issues and problems. He has a master's degree in applied and mathematical statistics and a doctorate in sociology from the University of Illinois, Urbana-Champaign.

Michael L. Dennis, Ph.D., is a senior research psychologist at Chestnut Health Systems and director of its Drug Outcome Monitoring System. His recent work has focused on developing a biopsychosocial model of outcome monitoring for people with chronic substance use disorders, a group that moves in and out of the treatment system and has a variety of problems. During the past 10 years, he has worked as a principal investigator, evaluator, and methodologist for more than a dozen studies. These have addressed a variety of substantive issues (e.g., homelessness, vocational/ancillary services, case management, counselor training) and methodological challenges (e.g., randomized field experiments, time series, scale development, outcome monitoring). For DC*MADS, Dr. Dennis was the study leader for the Homeless and Transient Population Study (see Chapter 4 of this book). At the time of the study, he was at Research Triangle Institute. He also has served as an evaluator, consultant, and/or reviewer on work related to homelessness that has been done by the (former) Alcohol, Drug Abuse, and Mental Health Administration; Bureau of Health Care Delivery Assistance; Fannie Mae (Federal National Mortgage Association); Interagency Council on Homelessness; U.S. Department of Housing and Urban Development; National Institute on Alcohol Abuse and Alcoholism; National Institute on Drug Abuse; National Institute of Mental Health; North Carolina Interagency Council on Homeless Assistance Programs; and the Urban Institute. He has completed more than 75 major publications or technical reports and averaged four to six professional presentations per year. He received his psychology doctorate at Northwestern University, where he specialized in methodology and evaluation research.

Patrick M. Flynn, Ph.D., a senior research psychologist, is currently a principal investigator and project director with the National Development and Research Institutes, Inc. He was the project director for the National Institute on Drug Abuse's (NIDA's) Cocaine Treatment Outcome Study, project codirector of the Drug Abuse Treatment Outcome Study, and project leader and task leader on a half dozen other important NIDA-funded research projects. For DC*MADS, he was study leader for the Current Treatment Client Characteristics Study (described in Chapter 7 of this book). He is currently the coprincipal investigator of NIDA's Cooperative Drug Abuse Treatment Outcome Study Coordinating Center. Early in his career, he was a counselor in a therapeutic community for drug abusers and was a program researcher on NIDA's Treatment Outcome Prospective Study (TOPS). He also has served in upper-level management positions in higher education and has held several academic positions, including tenured associate professor, college vice president, and dean of academic affairs. His research interests, in addition to substance abuse issues, include comorbid disorders, particularly personality disorders, psychological testing, and treatment improvement. He has authored or coauthored several book chapters and numerous journal publications, including those appearing in the *American Journal of Drug and Alcohol Abuse, American Journal of Epidemiology, Journal of Addictive Diseases, Journal of Clinical Psychology, Journal of Personality Assessment, Journal of Personality Disorders*, and *Journal of Substance Abuse Treatment*. He received his Ph.D. from the University of Miami, Coral Gables, Florida.

Gregory H. Gaertner, Ph.D., is a vice president and managing director at the Gallup Organization's Government and Education Division. At the time that the DC*MADS research was conducted, he was employed at Westat, Inc. He oversaw Westat's participation in DC*MADS, which included studies of drug use among the institutionalized population, adult criminal offenders, juvenile offenders, school dropouts, elementary and secondary school students, and college-age young adults. Dr. Gaertner directed the Institutionalized Study described in Chapter 5 of this book. He is currently involved in multiple state-based assessments of the need for drug treatment funded by the Center for Substance Abuse Treatment. These assessments include studies of the incidence and prevalence of drug use and the need for treatment in household populations, and among homeless people, pregnant women, adolescents, criminal offenders, and Native Americans. He has taught research methods on the faculties of Case Western Reserve University and Bucknell University. He has written extensively on organizational change in the *Academy of Management Review*, *Decision Sciences*, the *Academy of Management Journal*, *Public Administration Review*, *Human Relations*, and other journals, as well as in various book chapters. He received his doctorate from the University of Chicago.

Ronaldo Iachan, Ph.D., is a statistical consultant and serves as a statistical editor for the *Journal of the American Medical Association* with expertise in sample survey design and analysis. He was a research statistician with the Research Triangle Institute from 1985 to 1996, providing statistical task leadership for a variety of health, social, environmental, and economic studies. These included a national study of runaway and homeless youth and studies of HIV risk among the same population, state needs assessments of substance abuse treatment and prevention, living standards studies in several Central Asian republics, and evaluations of several educational programs. For DC*MADS, he led sampling and weighting activities for the Homeless and Transient Population Study and assisted with data analysis for the Adverse Effects of Drug Abuse Study. Dr. Iachan was an assistant professor at Iowa State University from 1981 to 1985, teaching graduate courses in sampling theory. He also taught statistics at the University of Wisconsin-Madison and at Duke University. His research also has extended to other areas of social statistics, including measures of agreement, spatial statistics, and robust statistics. He has published articles in a variety of peer-reviewed journals, including the *Journal of the American Statistical Association*, *Biometrics*, *International Statistical Review*, *Psychometrics*, *Educational and Psychological Measurement*, *Journal of Official Statistics*, and *Survey Methodology*. He received his doctorate and his master's degree in statistics from the University of California, Berkeley and his B.S. degrees in mathematics and systems engineering from PUC, Rio de Janeiro.

Linda J. Keil, Ph.D., is a social psychologist employed by the Gallup Organization as a vice president and senior study director in the Government and Education Division. Over the past 12 years, her research has focused on hard-to-reach populations, including those described in Chapter 5 of this book. Other studies she has directed include a study of drug use among school dropouts, an evaluation of intervention programs for high-risk youth, an evaluation of the Job Corps' HIV policy, and a study of probation experiences among convicted drug felons. She received her graduate training at the University of California, Santa Barbara.

Larry A. Kroutil, M.P.H., is a research analyst at Research Triangle Institute. His current research interests and activities involve estimating the prevalence and correlates of substance use among a variety of populations, assessing problems associated with substance use, and assessing the need for substance abuse treatment services among various populations. For the DC*MADS project, he worked primarily on the Household and Nonhousehold Populations Study (see Chapters 3 and 9), the Current Treatment Client Characteristics Study (see Chapter 7), and the Drug Use and Pregnancy Study (see Chapter 8). He recently has been lead author or coauthor of a series of papers and technical reports assessing the prevalence and trends in substance use among military and civilian populations. He received a Master of Public Health degree in health education in 1987 from the University of North Carolina at Chapel Hill.

James W. Luckey, Ph.D., is a senior research psychologist at Research Triangle Institute. During the past decade, he has led or played a major role in more than a dozen substance abuse projects funded by the National Institute on Drug Abuse, the National Institute on Alcohol Abuse and Alcoholism, and the Center for Substance Abuse Treatment. Current projects he is leading include assessing the viability and value of an outcomes monitoring system for narcotic addiction treatment programs, studying alcohol treatment outcomes under managed care, and examining treatment needs for North Carolina. He is interested in research that can be applied directly to improving substance abuse treatment systems and enjoys studies that involve collaboration among providers, policymakers, and researchers. For DC*MADS, he was analytic leader for the Current Treatment Client Characteristics Study described in Chapter 7 of this book. Prior to coming to RTI, Dr. Luckey was on the faculty at the School of Public Health, University of North Carolina, for 10 years, and he is currently an adjunct associate professor there. He has served as a reviewer for several journals and on NIH grant review panels. He has authored and coauthored several book chapters and numerous journal publications, including articles for the *Journal of Substance Abuse Treatment*, *American Journal of Drug and Alcohol Abuse*, *Journal of Addictive Diseases*, *Journal of Maintenance in the Addictions*, *American Journal of Public Health*,

International Journal of the Addictions, Evaluation and Program Planning, and *Journal of Personality Disorders.* He received his doctorate from the University of Nebraska–Lincoln.

Mary Ellen Marsden, Ph.D., is Associate Research Professor at the Institute for Health Policy at Brandeis University and was formerly a senior research sociologist with Research Triangle Institute. Her research has focused on the study of substance use epidemiology, treatment effectiveness, and policy issues. For DC*MADS, she was costudy leader for the Household and Nonhousehold Populations Study (see Chapter 3 of this book). Dr. Marsden is currently study director for the treatment outcomes component of the Alcohol and Drug Services Study and coordinator of substance abuse sites for the Coordinating Center for Managed Care and Vulnerable Populations. She is principal investigator for a study to improve outcomes monitoring for the Massachusetts substance abuse treatment system and coprincipal investigator for a study of the health and performance of military women and a study of the effectiveness of prison-based substance abuse treatment. She was a lead author of *Drug Abuse Treatment: A National Study of Effectiveness,* the book summarizing the results of the Treatment Outcome Prospective Study, and author of several reports from the National Household Survey on Drug Abuse. She received her doctorate in sociology from the University of Chicago.

Jutta Thornberry is a senior survey specialist for the Research Triangle Institute. She has 28 years of experience in developing data collection methodologies and in supervising data collection activities for various research projects. Prior to joining RTI in 1986, she was the head of field operations for the Survey Research Laboratory at the University of Illinois. Currently, she is project director for the Sources of Mediators of Alzheimer's Caregiver Stress study, which is being conducted for the University of Maryland. She also is coprincipal investigator for the NIH-DC Initiative to Reduce Infant Mortality in the District of Columbia and serves as the project director for one of the six DC Initiative protocols, titled Lack of Age-Appropriate Immunization Among Infants and Children Born in DC. Ms. Thornberry specializes in designing methodologies and managing studies utilizing computer-assisted interviewing, especially on studies involving sensitive topics and behaviors, and with nontraditional populations. She served as the Washington, DC, area coordinator for DC*MADS and helped provide comparability for the core modules for the study questionnaires. She functioned as the data collection manager for the Homeless and Transient Population Study (see Chapter 4 of this book), the Drug Use and Pregnancy Study (see Chapter 8), the Current Treatment Client Characteristics Study (see Chapter 7), and the Young Adults Study. She received a B.A. in sociology from the University of Illinois at Urbana.

Amy A. Vincus, M.P.H., is a research analyst at Research Triangle Institute. Her current research interests and activities include developing instruments to assess the relationships between psychosocial constructs and substance abuse, studying military women's health, and evaluating the effects of community-level substance abuse prevention. She recently coauthored a methodological paper on implementing a lay health adviser program. For DC*MADS, she served as this book's manuscript coordinator. She received a Master of Public Health degree in health behavior and health education in 1995 from the University of North Carolina at Chapel Hill.

Wendy A. Visscher, M.P.H., Ph.D., is a senior research epidemiologist and the director of the Epidemiology and Medical Studies Program at the Research Triangle Institute. She has a broad range of research experience and is expert in the design and conduct of epidemiologic surveys, case-control studies, and cohort studies. She is experienced with all modes of data collection, including record abstraction, mail surveys, household screening and interviewing, telephone interviewing, biological specimen collection, and clinical interviews and exams. She currently leads several research studies and chairs one of RTI's human subjects committees. For DC*MADS, she was costudy leader for the Drug Use and Pregnancy Study described in Chapter 8 of this book. She has contributed to a variety of health-related studies at RTI. She currently serves as project director for Project DIRECT (Diabetes Intervention Reaching and Educating Communities Together), a community intervention study designed to reduce the risk of diabetes and its complications in African Americans. She also directs the Plastic Surgery Outcomes Study, a patient outcomes study designed to determine psychological and quality of life measures associated with the removal of silicone and saline breast implants. Her other research areas include reproductive outcomes, radiation, cancer, drug abuse, mental health, and HIV/AIDS. She has presented research findings at professional conferences and has been published in the *American Journal of Public Health*, the *Journal of the National Cancer Institute*, and *Spine*. She received her graduate training at the University of Minnesota.

Sara C. Wheeless, Ph.D., is a senior research statistician at the Research Triangle Institute with more than 17 years of experience in the analysis of data from complex sample surveys. She also has expertise in the design and selection of probability samples and in using Kuhn-Tucker theory for optimum sample allocation and sample size determination. She has directed the statistical analysis on numerous projects involving item imputations using weighted and unweighted hot deck techniques, weight construction using multiplicity and poststratification adjustments, and specification of variable recodes and analysis file construction. She has used or directed the use of SUDAAN, RTI's software for the analysis of data from complex sample surveys, on numerous large data sets for producing descriptive analysis, multivariate modeling using linear and logistic regression, and standardized comparisons. For DC*MADS, Dr. Wheeless was responsible for sample design, weight construction, and analysis for the Current Treatment Client Characteristics Study (see Chapter 7) and was the statistical analyst for the Drug Use and Pregnancy Study (see Chapter 8). In addition, she constructed the weights for combining data from the household, institutionalized, and homeless populations (see Chapter 9) and provided consultation on analyses and codebook development for several other studies within the DC*MADS project. She received her doctorate in statistics from North Carolina State University.